# THORNTON WILDER

BOOKS EDITED BY RICHARD H. GOLDSTONE

*Contexts of the Drama* (1968)

*Masterworks of Modern Drama* (1969)

*The Mentor Book of Short Plays* (with Abraham Lass) (1969)

Saturday Review Press | E. P. Dutton & Co., Inc.

New York

# THORNTON WILDER

## An
## Intimate
## Portrait

Richard H. Goldstone

*cop. b*

*0906*

Grateful acknowledgment is made to the following for permission to reprint published materials:

Mr. Robert Ardrey and Atheneum Publishers for excerpt from *Plays of Three Decades;*
Harper & Row for excerpts from Mr. Wilder's plays and novels;
*The Nation* for a quotation from an essay by Edmund Wilson;
The President of Oberlin College and the editor of the *Oberlin Alumni Magazine;*
Calman A. Levin and Dr. Donald Gallup for an excerpt from a letter by Gertrude Stein;
The Viking Press and *The Atlantic* for an excerpt from an essay by Alexander Woollcott;
Yale University Library for photographs from its collections;
The New York Public Library for photographs from its collections;
Permission has been granted by the Evelyn Singer Agency to quote from Michael Gold's essay on Wilder, copyright 1930 *New Republic;* and by *The New York Times* to quote from a review by John Chamberlain, copyright 1935 The New York Times Company.

*Library of Congress Cataloging in Publication Data*

*Goldstone, Richard Henry.*
*Thornton Wilder, an intimate portrait.*

*Includes bibliographical references.*
*1. Wilder, Thornton Niven, 1897–      I. Title.*
*PS3545.I345Z664      813'.5'2 [B]      75-12990*

*Published simultaneously in Canada by Clarke, Irwin & Company Limited,*
*Toronto and Vancouver*
*ISBN: 0-8415-0392-3*
*Designed by The Etheredges*

TO THE ENGLISH FACULTY

*Past and Present—*

*of*

THE COLLEGE OF THE CITY OF NEW YORK

\*

I dedicate this book

to a department from which so many books

of great excellence have come.

My dear colleagues,

your assistance and encouragement provided

both the means and the example.

RHG

# Contents

**ix**

# Foreword

"If Elizabeth, Frederick or Dr. Johnson were to read their biographies, they would exclaim, 'Ah, my secret is still safe!' But if Natasha Rostova were to read *War and Peace,* she would cry out as she covered her face with her hands: 'How did he know! How did he know!' "

This book had its inception in conversations I had with Isabel Wilder; we agreed that before time exacted further tolls, the documents and recollections relating to the life of her brother Thornton should be assembled and organized. The task was assigned to me partly because I had already published a number of pieces on Wilder; partly because I had the conventional academic credentials; but mainly, I suppose, because I had known Wilder since 1942 when we began our officer training in the United States Army Air Force. Accordingly, I started collecting data in the late sixties. But the book that both of us had envisaged emerged greatly changed both in form and content. I had intended to write a critical study with extensive biographical background. As I began to write, however, I discovered that given the materials at hand, I was composing what has turned out to be a detailed portrait, derived to some extent from Wilder's novels and plays, but based principally upon a great many other sources. So great was the change of the book's direction that an arrangement I had effected with Wilder's publisher, Harper & Row, ended amicably when it became apparent to both Cass Canfield, Sr., and me that it would be inappropriate for his firm to publish my manuscript.

Thornton Wilder is one of the last survivors of the group of American writers who flourished in the first half of the twentieth century. Gathering the materials for this portrait has been a fascinating and altogether gratifying experience. My research took me to many places distant from my New York–Long Island home base: Rome, Italy; Berkeley, California; Berkshire, England; southern Illinois; rural Maine; Princeton; Cambridge; Chicago and—New Haven. I attended a performance of *Our Town* in Dublin and one of *The Skin of Our Teeth* in Chichester; I lodged at the Hotel Buckingham in Paris where Wilder had put up in the thirties; I visited woodlands in southern California which more than a half century earlier Wilder had explored on horseback.

Research led me not only to a number of faraway places, but to a great number of interesting men and women. Some of them have since died and I am privileged in having known them; others have become friends and I am thankful for their friendship. I received assistance by letter from utter strangers who learned of my interest in Wilder's life and wrote me of moments when his life touched theirs. The casual thoughtfulness that I have been the beneficiary of reinforces my conviction that Americans' generosity to those involved in scholarly pursuits is one of the most agreeable aspects of our national character.

At the very outset of this undertaking, Glenway Wescott provided me with recollections of his long association with Wilder and copied for me letters and other materials from his files going back forty years. Mr. Wescott's conscientious and boundless generosity provided me with the momentum to move ahead. At the same time, Isabel Wilder showed me her voluminous scrapbooks of clippings, answered my many questions, particularly about the Wilder family, and introduced me to Donald Gallup, Curator of the Yale Collection of American Literature. There are few scholars working in American literature who are not indebted to Dr. Gallup in one way or another; my debt to him is of such proportions that it would be mawkish to detail its complexity. I shall content myself with saying my labors would have been deprived of vital detail, especially in respect to the relationship between Wilder and Gertrude Stein, had it not been for Donald Gallup's sage, generous counsel and assistance.

Several friends, associates, and former students of Wilder have been correspondingly helpful; Albert Boni, John Vincent Healy, Harry T. Moore, Robert W. Stallman, and the late Amy Wertheimer all shared with me reminiscences, letters and memorabilia, and extended to me the hospitality of their homes. I held lengthy conversations with Robert

Ardrey, the late Tallulah Bankhead, Jed Harris, Robert Maynard Hutchins, the late Henry Luce, and Gene Tunney, each of whom provided me
with a fresh perspective on the many facets of Thornton Wilder. Others
who made available to me either documentary information or recollections about Wilder and his career include Edward Albee, Mrs. Amyas
Ames, Miss Gladys Campbell, Miss Janet Cohn, Professor F. W. Dupee,
Wendell Frederici, Thomas Hatcher, Walter Hochschild, Miss Catharine
Huntington, my colleague and friend Professor Edgar Johnson, faculty
and alumni of the Lawrenceville School, Attorney General Edward Levi,
Dwight Macdonald, Alan Schneider, Professor Warren Taylor (of Ober-
lin), Anson Thacher, Napier Wilt, Clinton Wilder, the late Edmund
Wilson, Thew Wright and Ms. Marguerite Young and Sir John Gielgud.

Of those, whom through my forgetfulness I have failed to list, I ask
pardon.

So as not to place an additional burden upon him, I refrained from
showing my manuscript to my friend Leon Edel. But I greatly benefited
from the many long talks we have had on the subject of biographical
problems. Moreover anyone acquainted with Professor Edel's *Henry
James* will recognize its influence on the writing of this book.

Editorial suggestions have come from a number of friends and colleagues, including Philip Roddman, Arthur Laurents, and Samuel
Ziskind. Various chapters have received comments from Sidney Feshbach,
Arthur Waldhorn, Robert Halsband, Mrs. Gilbert Chapman, Lillian
Feder, Robert W. Gutman, and Leo Hamalian. In the summer of 1974,
directly after teaching a rigorous summer program, my colleague Arthur
Zeiger spent the major part of his visit to the Hamptons reading and
correcting working copy before it went to the typist. The number of
published manuscripts upon which Dr. Zeiger has exercised his editorial
acumen can no longer be reckoned. . . .

The closest reading my manuscript received was from Carlos Baker,
whom I have never met. Commissioned to evaluate this work, he accepted
the assignment as a routine and official academic obligation and, in an
act of extraordinary generosity, devoted a substantial part of *his* 1974
vacation to emendations of the final typescript. Earlier, Professor Baker
had counseled me by letter in the matter of the Wilder-Hemingway
friendship, so that I am doubly in his debt. Another Princetonian, editor
Thomas J. Davis, of Saturday Review Press, applied his professional zeal
to eliminating whatever stylistic quirks my academic colleagues had
charitably overlooked.

In addition to the materials in the Beinecke Library at Yale, I
consulted letters in the custody of the Houghton Library at Harvard, the
Princeton Library, the manuscript collection of the University of Chi-

cago, and through the good offices of James Wells, the Newberry Library in Chicago. I made good use of the New York Public Library and the Library of Hampton Bays. As every scholar knows, the gates of heaven must open most widely and readily to the American librarians whose efficiency, zeal, and helpfulness make possible the writing of books.

Wilder's school and college records, together with data relating to his teaching were made available by their custodians at Thacher School (Ojai, California), Berkeley (California) High School, Yale, Princeton, and the University of Chicago.

My greatest debt, of course, is to Thornton Wilder. A substantial part of this portrait is based on conversations and correspondence between him and me over three decades, principally before work on this book began. Occasionally, Wilder's memory played tricks on him and there were a few instances when he misunderstood some of my questions. Yet Wilder is one of the most forthright and sincere men I have ever known. In my research, nothing emerged of any consequence that did not square with what Wilder had told me at one time or another. Free of deceit, he does not indulge in self-deception.

In the text of this book I have directly or obliquely cited critiques and assessments of Wilder's work by critics such as R. P. Blackmur, Malcolm Cowley, Benjamin De Mott, Edmund Fuller, Michael Gold, Granville Hicks, Mary McCarthy, and Edmund Wilson. In addition, I am acquainted with a number of critical studies of Wilder including those by Francis Fergusson, Malcolm Goldstein, Bernard Grebanier, and Helmut Papajewski but I do not believe I incorporated their critical evaluations into this book.

I also made use of factual material contained in John Mason Brown's uncompleted biography of Robert Sherwood; the John Malcolm Brinnin, James Mellow, and W. G. Rogers studies of Gertrude Stein; Arthur Mizener's and Andrew Turnbull's biographies of Scott Fitzgerald; Joseph Blotner's biography of William Faulkner; and Carlos Baker's *Ernest Hemingway*.

I cannot forebear mention of the Siamese four, Guy, Germaine, Giselle, and Gabrielle, whose advent into my household coincided with the preparation and writing of this study. Writing is a lonely endeavor and their quiet and undemanding companionship was a boon.

As the title indicates, this work is not a formal biography. It is a portrait—an *intimate* portrait because it presents impressions of its subject by a number of persons who have stood close to Thornton Wilder. To a considerable extent, we have Wilder's self-portrait within these pages, since much that is revealed is derived from his writings, letters, and conversations. The "secret" of Wilder, whatever it may be, is not to be found in this book. For as Wilder wisely observed (in the epigraph to this foreword), no biographer ever penetrates the secret of his subject. Nor have I made any great effort to speculate on why and how Wilder composed his novels and plays. As Browning wrote, and as we are cautioned by both Yeats and Wilder:

> *Where the apple reddens*
> *Never pry—*
> *Lest we lose our Edens*
> *Eve and I.*

What is to follow, I dearly hope, is a good likeness, a revealing likeness, an honest likeness of an extraordinary and fascinating subject.

# THORNTON WILDER

### JED HARRIS
presents

# OUR TOWN

### A PLAY BY
## THORNTON WILDER

with

## MR. WILDER
*during Frank Craven's brief absence*

*Production by Mr. Harris*
*Technical Direction by Raymond Sovey*
*Costumes Designed by Helene Pons*

## THE CAST
*[ In the order of their appearance ]*

| | |
|---|---|
| Stage Manager | Thornton Wilder |
| Dr. Gibbs | Jay Fassett |
| Joe Crowell | Raymond Roe |
| Howie Newsome | Tom Fadden |
| Mrs. Gibbs | Evelyn Varden |

**FIRE NOTICE:** The exit, indicated by a red light and sign, nearest to the seat you occupy, is the shortest route to the street.
In the event of fire or other emergency please do not run—WALK TO THAT EXIT.
**JOHN J. McELLIGOTT, Fire Chief and Commissioner**

Wilder, together with Mae West, George M. Cohan and Noel Coward, was one of the few playwrights to star on Broadway.

# Nineteen Twenty-Seven

*"Perhaps an Accident"*—THE BRIDGE OF SAN LUIS REY

On Sunday, November 20, 1927, the *New York Herald Tribune,* the most respected newspaper of the Eastern establishment, published a review of a new novel by an obscure schoolmaster, thereby launching a literary career with a suddenness virtually unparalleled in American letters.

Every week of every year, scores of aspiring young writers (and writers no longer young) hoped that the Sunday book supplements of New York's great newspapers would discover their artistic genius and report it to a waiting world. But such discoveries were infrequent, so that when young Thornton N. Wilder, who had, it seems, just emerged from the valley of the shadow of death, read on that November Sunday in the book section of the *Herald Tribune* that he was "a distinguished artist" taking his place "among the ranks of American writers," he could only ask himself: Why me? Why me?

From the perspective of a half century later, we can also ask how it was that so modest and unspectacular a work as *The Bridge of San Luis Rey* should have propelled its earnest and bespectacled young author into almost instant national celebrity, with the result that his leisure activities would be chronicled on the front page of the *New York Times*

1

and his views on music, literature, philosophy, and religion would be recorded in both literary and mass-circulation magazines. The circumstances of Wilder's sudden rise to fame become intelligible if we pause to recall a few aspects of the cultural ambience of America during the postwar years of the jazz decade.

Ever since the end of World War I, when Americans suddenly understood themselves to be the predominant world power, the process of hero making, hero worship, and iconoclasm had become a national pastime. It was as though America were impelled to create a series of supermen to reinforce and reassure herself about the validity of the national image. Our standing in the world—we felt—was based on our capacity for breeding the best athletes, aviators, soldiers, politicos, explorers, scientists, inventors, industrialists, film stars, and—God save the mark!—gunmen . . . not necessarily in that order of importance.

Of all the years of the postwar decade (1919–29), 1927, on second look, shows up as the year that best reinforced America's sense of itself, the time when everyone tried his hardest, sometimes with memorable results. In 1927, Babe Ruth, for example, established a new record for home runs. Bobby Jones regained his amateur golf championship. Lou Gehrig batted in the all-time record number of runs. Though Red Grange had retired from college playing, his team, Illinois, won the national football championship. Gene Tunney successfully defended his title of heavyweight boxing champion of the world. Helen Wills regained the Women's Singles Championship (though Big Bill Tilden was not to recapture the men's from France for another two years.) Douglas Fairbanks and Mary Pickford reigned supreme in Hollywood and at Pickfair, while one million people in New York City flocked to the showrooms for a glimpse of Henry Ford's new Model A. The American vocabulary was enriched in 1927 by a new-minted word, *racketeer,* coinciding with Al Capone's gang's amassing a record, illegal $105 million. In August of 1927, Calvin Coolidge startled his countrymen with the laconic announcement that he "did not choose to run for President in 1928." And Arthur Compton won the Nobel Prize for physics.

If American world superiority was making itself felt on the playing fields, in the boxing ring, the movies, industrial complexes, laboratories, and even in its gigantic illicit gangster-run enterprises, in the mercurial field of the arts our claim to world leadership was less than assured. All the really expensive paintings seemed to originate in Paris. Our symphony conductors were imported Slavs, Germans, or Italians. Some ridiculously small area in Russia-Poland was providing us with all our violinists (*pace* Albert Spaulding) and with an astonishing number of pianists as well.

The Metropolitan Opera Company, to be sure, had in 1927 two authentic American singing stars: Lawrence Tibbett and Rosa Ponselle. Sensing perhaps the imbalance of native talent, the Metropolitan management under Giulio Gatti-Casazza had made strenuous efforts the year before to launch a new coloratura from the cornfields of Missouri. But Marion Talley's debut was not successful, and Amelita Galli-Curci remained queen of the high C until ultimately she was replaced by Lily Pons from the south of France. Meanwhile, our leading American composer, Deems Taylor, aided by a libretto from the hand of Edna St. Vincent Millay, completed his opera, *The King's Henchman* for a February premiere; like all previous American operas, it failed to establish itself in the Metropolitan repertory, or in any other repertory. Except for the fact that we paid our visiting artists the highest fees, musically we were still, it seemed, colonial dependents upon central and eastern Europe.

Our literary situation was not quite so bleak. Over the years we had, after all, exported at least five distinguished writers to Europe where they had taken root and flowered, even if relatively few Americans knew or cared about their work. In 1927, Henry James had been dead eleven years and his reputation was in a temporary decline; Gertrude Stein, whatever influence she wielded in those years, was busy wielding it in Paris. To the extent that she was known in her native country at all, she was considered an unintelligible eccentric. T. S. Eliot, Ezra Pound, and Ernest Hemingway were known, of course, to readers of the *Dial* and *Poetry* and the *New Republic,* but they had not yet become household words, even in the households of Cambridge, Massachusetts, or Princeton, New Jersey.

The luminaries in American letters in 1927 were Louis Bromfield, Willa Cather, Theodore Dreiser, Robert Frost, Sinclair Lewis, Upton Sinclair, Eugene O'Neill, and Edwin Arlington Robinson—all inheritors of a realist-naturalist tradition that had already passed its crest in Europe . . . as only Willa Cather seemed to have noticed. Yet, however distinguished our native literary talent, it was somehow overshadowed by productions imported from abroad. In 1927, the final volume of Proust's *Remembrance of Things Past* was published in the United States. Knopf was circulating Thomas Mann's *The Magic Mountain.* And copies of James Joyce's *Ulysses* were slipping through customs at a fast clip. At the same time, Sinclair Lewis's *Elmer Gantry* and Willa Cather's *Death Comes for the Archbishop* were enjoying a moderate success, but many readers felt that Lewis lacked either the chic of satirist Aldous Huxley or the solid balance of Arnold Bennett. And Willa Cather seemed slightly provincial and dowdy in comparison with the late Katherine Mansfield,

Virginia Woolf, V. Sackville West, and Rosamond Lehmann. (Edith Wharton, alas, had also published a novel that year whose very title, *Twilight Sleep*, was a measure of the decline of her talent and status.)

Highly respected, though not very exciting, were the regional novelists Ellen Glasgow and Ole Rölvaag whose humorless and earnest realism serious readers welcomed as an antidote to the zany fantasies of James Branch Cabell or to the indignant exposés of Upton Sinclair.

Such was the landscape of the literary scene on November 20, 1927, when the *Herald Tribune*'s Isabel Patterson described *The Bridge of San Luis Rey* as a "little masterpiece," "a contribution to literature [whose] narrative and fine textured prose are but a means to an end, like the bridge itself." Words like these in the respected, conservative journal of the Eastern seaboard upper middle class were not likely to be ignored either by the reading public or by the literary fraternity whose enormous popular influence spread out in waves from the Round Table of the Hotel Algonquin. A new reputation was ready to be launched; and only four days later Thornton Wilder's arrival became a certainty.

By a stroke of good fortune, the panjandrum of English letters—Mr. Arnold Bennett, no less—stumbled upon the newly published *Bridge* and wrote of it in his weekly column in London's *Evening Standard* that he was "dazzled by its accomplishment" and that its writing had not been "surpassed in the present epoch." Bennett's enormous prestige at that time, particularly in the United States, derived not only from the solid worth of his three or four masterworks, but from his reputation as a hardheaded, no-nonsense reviewer of other men's books. The praise that Bennett lavished upon *The Bridge* was nothing short of extraordinary, and so was its effect.

In retrospect, one might deduce that Bennett had shrewdly calculated the effect of his words and that for months and years he had been waiting for a book to which he could give unstinting praise. In this book by an unknown *American*—all the better for his purposes—he found what he had been waiting for: the perfect instrument for a long-awaited response.

Behind Bennett's sponsoring *The Bridge* lay a skein of friendships and resentments in literary London. The Bloomsbury group, in general, and Virginia Woolf, in particular, had privately and publicly displayed their aristocratic-aesthetic contempt for the work of Bennett and for that of his coevals, H. G. Wells and John Galsworthy. The focus of this attack was Mrs. Woolf's 1924 essay, "Mr. Bennett and Mrs. Brown," in which she dismissed the best work of Arnold Bennett as something less than literature or art. In 1927, Mrs. Woolf published her newest novel, *To the Lighthouse,* whose reception was modest—deservedly so, Bennett might have thought. But when Bennett came upon *The Bridge of San Luis*

*Rey,* which he perceived as classic in tone, unconventional in technique, and simple but elegant in style, he saw the book as the kind of writing that challenged the standards of the Bloomsbury group. By conferring praise on an obscure American writer with *style,* Bennett was responding to Mrs. Woolf, Lytton Strachey, and E. M. Forster.

On the heels of Bennett's extraordinary review came another extravagant tribute, this one from Yale professor William Lyon Phelps, the "beau ideal" of the women's clubs of America, who hailed *The Bridge* as a "work of genius" and Wilder as "having already attained to the front rank of living novelists." The importance of such a judgment—Phelps was probably the best-known academic belletrist in America—can hardly be underestimated. Phelps kept in close touch with the English literary situation, and he knew Arnold Bennett's dictum on *The Bridge* as well as the generally favorable reviews in the *Observer* of London, the *Manchester Guardian,* and the *New Statesman.* Nothing could have pleased Professor Phelps more than that the English—to whose taste he deferred in such matters—should be dazzled by the work of young Thornton Wilder who, as it happened, was both a former student and a family friend.

Despite a few ineffectual dissents from Cyril Connolly and Clifton Fadiman, the most influential reviewers on both sides of the ocean had no difficulty in descrying a new star in the literary firmament. Within six weeks of the publication of *The Bridge,* its publisher, A. & C. Boni displayed in the Sunday *New York Times Book Review* a full page advertisement of its "Philosophical Novel Which Has Become A Best Seller." At the top center of the page was a 3-by-4½-inch likeness of Wilder looking exactly the way the distinguished author of "a classic" (Burton Rascoe) of "so much wisdom" (Harry Hansen) is supposed to look. To the left of the photograph were displayed, in addition to the comments of Rascoe and Hansen, those of Professor Phelps, Arnold Bennett, and, of course, the *Herald Tribune*'s Isabel Patterson who could, with some justice, claim to have been the first on the critical bandwagon.

*The Bridge*'s extraordinary success puzzled the book-publishing world—not because the book was a poor one but because, on the contrary, it was excellent. Truly "literary" novels seldom achieved such popularity. Puzzling too, was Wilder's emergence as a bona fide celebrity, even though he did not project a public personality. Actually, the picture in the *Times* advertisement had considerable influence in establishing Wilder's public persona. It was the portrait of a handsome, scholarly, and serious man—silent, sad, spiritual, and ascetic. His book and his portrait were enough to establish him as America's newest culture-hero: the hero as literary artist . . . entirely worthy of standing side by side, figuratively speaking, with another hero of 1927—Charles A. Lindbergh, a young man who had also built a bridge.

But neither encomiums, nor shrewd promotion, nor Thornton Wilder's handsome portrait could account entirely for the fantastic sales of *The Bridge of San Luis Rey,* which exceeded a quarter of a million in the first year alone and in fact, have continued at a high level throughout the fifty years since the book's publication. *The Bridge* had little in common with the fiction of Fannie Hurst, Edna Ferber, or Kathleen Norris; yet, it entered the same households as the novels of those indefatigable ladies. At the same time, it engaged the absorbed attention of R. P. Blackmur, Edmund Wilson, F. Scott Fitzgerald, and Ernest Hemingway. *The Bridge of San Luis Rey* seemed to have something for everybody: Even today it still has.

Book watchers of the time, accounting for *The Bridge*'s phenomenal critical and popular success, attributed it to Wilder's exquisite and pellucid style; to his rejection of the realistic-naturalistic mode of Dreiser-Lewis–Upton Sinclair; to the American public's desire to escape from the ugliness and crassness of the contemporary scene; to the spiritual-theological questions the novel raises. (Was Wilder's position essentially Roman Catholic? Calvinist? Agnostic? Atheist?) *The Bridge* combines a sound narrative technique with a Puritan perspective, a combination that evoked a profound response from an America whose popular national leader was Calvin Coolidge, who, like William Lyon Phelps, had been a Sunday School teacher.

Puritanism, the denial of nature in general and the appetites of human nature in particular, opposes the consummation of sexual drives that do not have procreation as their aim; it detests sloth, vanity, gluttony, and outward shows of affection. Puritanism embodied in a work of literature generally appears unpleasant. Wilder achieved what no twentieth century writer had succeeded in doing. Placing his novel in an exotic setting, giving his characters Spanish names, he endowed Puritanism with a kind of surface beauty. In such surroundings the reader could accept situations in which an Abbess could expel a loving novice; a courtesan-actress could reject both the man to whom she owed everything and her little son for whom she was the center of the universe; a young man could abandon his hopelessly dependent twin brother first by a single-minded pursuit of the actress and then by dying for love of her; a beautiful daughter could coldly separate herself from and then ignore her foolishly devoted mother. Five victims, suffering the pangs of disprized love, are killed when the bridge of San Luis Rey breaks, plunging them to their deaths. Very sad, but somehow right. Since it was unthinkable, if not impossible, that any of the five should consummate their love in whatever way their love *could* be consummated, it was just as well that they die. And the Abbess reflects that at least they will be remembered, for "there is the land of the living, and the land of the dead and the bridge is love."

Now Edmund Wilson quite promptly and perceptively identified Marcel Proust as Wilder's chief model and influence. One of Proust's major themes, in Wilson's words, "the abject and agonizing love on the part of a superior for an inferior person, or, at least, on the part of a gentle person for a person who behaves toward him with cruelty," is the central theme of *The Bridge*. But Edmund Wilson chose not to show how the theme is transformed in its journey from a ripely civilized France to a Puritan United States. In Proust's novel, abject and agonizing love is the source of both pain *and* pleasure, agony *and* ecstasy; in Wilder's, the sufferer finds release only, as a good Christian should, in death . . . "for there is the land of the living and the land of the dead and the bridge is love, the only survival, the only meaning."

So it was that *The Bridge* enjoyed success in all the Puritan countries: The United States, Great Britain, Australia, Germany, Austria, and Scandinavia. (The Italians liked it also, but, perhaps, for the reason that Italians admire any work where men and women die for love.) The French, of course, except for André Gide, rejected it utterly, despite the novel's several and considerable debts to the literature of France.

Calvin Coolidge, Charles Lindbergh, Gene Tunney, and Thornton Wilder were America's chief heroes of 1927, good Puritans all. Of solid and indisputable accomplishment, each in his own way set the right moral tone. One fundamental difference set Wilder off from the other three. Coolidge, Tunney, and Lindbergh had, by 1927, essentially fulfilled their destinies. Wilder, whose growth and development were, through his capacity for self-renewal, to continue, had reached only the beginning of his fulfillment.

But Wilder's struggles—which had already been considerable—had only just begun. His new fame found him perplexed, uncertain, and astonished. And even more astonished was a stern and upright New England resident of New Haven, Connecticut, a man who a few years before had voiced serious misgivings about Thornton Wilder's capacity to earn a living for himself, Wilder's father, Amos.

# II

## Carving Olive Pits

"Your stern and rockbound conscience . . ."
—ERNEST HEMINGWAY TO THORNTON WILDER, JUNE 1929

For Amos Parker Wilder, the seventeenth of April 1897, was a day of rejoicing and a day of mourning. His wife, Isabella, in her second accouchement, had given birth to twins. After a few hours, one died; the other, to be christened Thornton Niven, clung to life.

Amos Wilder, given his particular qualities of mind and character, had he been an Englishman would most certainly have been a clergyman. He was robust, handsome, articulate, well-educated, and even devout, a perfect specimen of a British divine. But because he was an American, of stout New England puritan ancestry, and coming of age at a time when the clergy had begun to lose its force, he entered upon a vocation only one step removed from the pulpit: journalism. Or to be more precise, newspaper editing. America in the 1890s could provide no better outlet for a man whose ability was matched only by his self-assurance, a quality firmly expressed in his views on politics, morals, and religion.

Born in 1862, a native of Calais, Maine, Amos was graduated in 1884 from Yale where he was a member of the most prestigious secret student society, Skull and Bones. For the next eight years after his graduation, he remained mainly in New Haven where he worked as a journalist and pursued graduate study. In 1892, he became one of the first recipients in the United States of the doctor of philosophy degree in political science. After working as a journalist in New York for two years, Amos married and moved to Madison, Wisconsin, where he began his tenure as editor of the *Wisconsin State Journal*. Within a year, a hardy male child, Amos Niven, was born in September 1895, a year and a half before the birth of the frail survivor, Thornton, whose first year, his mother said, was spent on a pillow that she carried about the house with her.

Two more children were born to Amos and Isabella during the Madison years, both girls—Charlotte (1898) and Isabel (1900). Another daughter, Janet, was born some years later. The Wilders lived earnestly and modestly in a house not far from the university, in the tranquillity and beauty of a city whose principal industries were education and government. The four children thrived and began, one by one, attending school, and church on Sunday. During the long Sunday sermon Father Amos, to prevent Thornton from becoming restless, allowed the small boy to draw pictures on his father's proper starched Sunday cuffs. Madison was a safe, secure environment for small growing children. As for their transplanted Eastern parents, if they had to live in the Midwest, Madison—surrounded by its lakes—was as cultivated a city as one could hope to find in this section of the country; it was, indeed, an oasis of culture surrounded by dairy farms and sausage factories.

Unfortunately, Amos Wilder had chosen for himself the wrong state in which to launch his career. A forthright, uncompromising man, intoxicated by the vigor of his ideas, he found himself in opposition to a man equally forthright, equally uncompromising, equally vigorous—and substantially more powerful: Senator Robert M. La Follette. The temper of Wisconsin was not in tune with an exponent of traditional Republicanism; Amos Wilder had chosen, perhaps, the state whose politics he least understood and from whom recognition of the viability of his ideas was least likely to come.

By 1906, Amos Wilder was inclined to leave Wisconsin. And somehow it was arranged that he be offered the appointment of consul general in Hong Kong, almost as far away from the *Wisconsin State Journal* as man could get. Wilder accepted the appointment, but he did not technically terminate his connection with the newspaper for another five years. The removal, of course, involved uprooting his family. For Isabella, who had already left her Dobbs Ferry, New York home, and moved to Wisconsin, this next journey lay within her considerable capacities. But for the children, their universe was turned upside down. It was not so shocking for the lively young Amos—going on twelve—nor for Isabel, who was, at six, still hardly more than a baby; but for the introspective

Thornton and Charlotte, aged nine and eight respectively, the change was most affecting.

As it turned out, the mother and children remained in Hong Kong for only half a year. Appalled by the inadequacy of available educational facilities and the high cost of living, and disturbed by the children's disorientation, Amos and Isabella agreed to a temporary separation. Together with her children, Isabella left the Orient and took up residence in Berkeley, California.

Isabella Niven Wilder, daughter of a minister (who did not believe in the education of females) and a great granddaughter of the New England abolitionist and philanthropist, Arthur Tappan, was a woman of considerable intelligence, character, independence, and maternal ferocity. Also she was an autodidact. Most other American women in her situation would have remained (and many did remain) in China with their husbands—their children, to be adequately educated, were sent away to boarding schools. The reasons Isabella gave for returning to the United States are persuasive and valid; but there is no avoiding what is more than a possibility that, in 1906, she effected the separation of her children from her husband because she had already observed that his influence was unwholesome and psychologically damaging. Not only did Amos's stern Calvinism hang like a cloud over the young children, but he imposed on them his iron will, his lofty standards of conduct, achievement, and principle, and his sense of himself—law-giver and dispenser of absolute justice.

Maintaining a fatherless household was to be a struggle—financial and physical—for Isabella. For the next four years, her life in Berkeley crept along the periphery of genteel poverty, a state of existence that was to provide material for Isabel Wilder's autobiographically revealing novel, *Mother and Four* (1933) and much later for Thornton's *The Eighth Day* (1967). But whatever the physical handicaps she encountered in making do with the meager allowance remitted by her husband, Isabella was enabled to remedy—if remedy she could—the psychologically crippling influence that her husband exerted upon their children.

Two questions arise: Why should the American consul general in Hong Kong be so hard pressed for money? And, under such conditions, why did Amos Wilder remain in the consular service for eight years?

American consuls in remote parts of the world—where their chief function was to facilitate trade relations—were paid an absurdly small salary: about two thousand dollars a year. The reason that the United States government could staff these outposts with competent and trained men (if indeed it did) —and in today's context the explanation seems incredible—was that "it was understood" that the American consul would supplement his income by performing services for the business enterprises whose papers passed across the consular desk. Such gratuities and commissions substantially augmented the inadequate income allotted by the United States government, and the practice of accepting them—while never officially countenanced—was never explicitly proscribed. But no such understanding was reached by Amos Wilder, a man of unimpeachable rectitude. He would see his wife and children starve before he would pocket a penny from the hands of men whose interests he was obligated to serve disinterestedly.

Virtue has its own rewards, but there were no others for Amos Wilder. Not only did he refuse emoluments from grateful American and Chinese interests, but he interposed his personal convictions upon the flow of normal and conventional trade relationships. For example, an American brewer who communicated with Wilder about an arrangement by which he could sell beer to the Chinese was brusquely refused the opportunity to do so. When the State Department reprimanded its consul general on the matter, it received the following response:

> . . . While recognizing the force of the Department's argument as a working rule of administration, as regards myself it is more important that I be true to the light I have on this question than that I should fall in with the conventions of government. The conventions of government always lag behind the convictions of the few; and if the few who think they have new light accepted as unchanging the policies of the day, civilization would have no advances to record.
> My resignation . . . is at the disposal of the Government.

But Amos Wilder did not resign and we may wonder why he did not seek out a more congenial and remunerative means of livelihood. He was, of course, a man who found in the exercise of power a means of self-fulfillment. Steeped in the Calvinist tradition, he may even have felt that God had marked him for His purposes and that the post in China would lead to other official positions carrying greater responsibility and prestige.

It is unlikely that Amos Wilder ever grasped the extent of the privations his family suffered. His own tastes were Spartan, and except for a month in their company spent once every two years, an ocean separated them during the most difficult times. Not only did he subject them to financial hardship, but he intensified their difficulties with an unremitting stream of letters chiding, counseling, and exhorting both wife and children. He demanded that he be kept informed about the smallest details of life in Berkeley, and he immediately responded with the details of his reactions and the expressions of his will. The scholastic achievements of the children, while they were not discreditable, were not always spectacular; whenever the children failed to excel, they could count on a forceful admonishment administered from across the sea. In the minds of these young children, the accounting for laxity of effort or, heaven forfend, impropriety of conduct (such as jaywalking) was a clear manifestation of the Divine interest in the affairs of men. Their absent and invisible father was somehow connected with the omnipresent spirit of an interested God.

Among the four children, Amos and Charlotte exerted the greatest effort to appease their father. Isabel, because she was the youngest, seemed least affected by him. And Thornton, though not indifferent to his father's wishes, seemed willfully to retreat into a world of his own. His school grades were not much better than average; he showed interest neither in athletics nor in developing his physique; except within the limits of his immediate family, he appeared withdrawn and isolated; his only interests were reading, music, and playacting, the latter activity in collaboration with his sisters. By the time he was ten, Thornton was a model chorister in Berkeley's St. Mark's Episcopal Church—a circumstance which Amos viewed with mixed feeling.

In 1909, the incorruptible Consul Wilder was transferred from Hong Kong to Shanghai and, in the following year, arrangements were made for his family to join him there. After their arrival, Thornton, almost fourteen years old, was sent first to a German school in Shanghai and then to the China Inland Mission School at Chefoo, a school staffed by English masters and run along the lines of the English public schools— complete with such time-honored practices as caning and fagging. Of the 150 students, about half were the sons of American missionaries, the remainder, boys of the British Commonwealth. One of the American missionaries' sons was Henry Luce; the two boys did not at that time become friends though for the remainder of Luce's life their paths were to cross again and again—in New Haven, in Rome, and in New York. Young "Harry" regarded Thornton at that time as eccentric, solitary, and withdrawn; worst of all, he was bookish without being bright. Half a century later, Luce recalled, that although Wilder was usually to be seen carrying a copy of Ovid (presumably in translation or a "trot"), he performed badly in Latin class, because of his difficulty with conjugations and declensions.*

The discipline at Chefoo was severe. Caning was the punishment for a certain number of poor recitations, and the boys habitually brutalized each other. Boys' schools, Thornton quickly realized, were not to his

* Luce failed to take into account the considerable difference in the Latin preparation he had had at Chefoo and the preparation Wilder would have received in the Berkeley grade schools. A further curiosity about Luce's report on Wilder's inadequate Latin stems from his account of a meeting with Wilder in Rome, Christmas week 1920, when Wilder took him on a tour and "translated for me all the Latin inscriptions on all those hundreds of monuments." That is to say, Wilder seems to have learned a great deal of Latin and Luce seems to have forgotten all of his.

liking; the China Inland Mission School, in fact, left him with a lifelong prejudice against the English public school and its products. After a year at Chefoo, however, Amos withdrew him and enrolled him at the Thacher School at Ojai, California, where he joined his older brother.

Sherman Thacher, headmaster and founder of the Thacher School, had been a friend of Amos Wilder in their days at Yale. Whatever financial arrangement was effected between the two old friends, there is no question that Thornton's enrollment at Thacher placed a further strain on the family finances, a strain that could have been eased had Thornton remained with his mother and attended a public high school. But that was precisely what Amos did not want; Thornton, now in his sixteenth year had become a source of serious concern to his father: having outgrown the sickliness of his infancy, he had—the father felt— accumulated a residue of spiritual frailty. This inadequacy of spirit revealed itself to Amos in several ways: the boy performed poorly in history, geography, and mathematics; he lacked "the power of concentration and the ability to do uncongenial things"; he had "nerves," was "silent, sensitive," and slept badly; he could swim, but beyond that had no interest in sports; his interests, rather, were directed toward "music, art, drama and literature"; he was "not a good mixer," but was sensitive and self-conscious, though "radiantly happy when with those who like and understand him." Amos added, in relaying these unfortunate characteristics to Headmaster Thacher, that "he may develope (sic) 'moods'."
While it is most unlikely that Thornton ever had occasion to come upon the evaluation that Amos communicated to Thacher, he was aware of his father's disappointed judgment of his character and capacities. Years later at a party that Albert Boni gave for Thornton, Art Young, the artist, compared Wilder to an ironwood tree. Wilder's impulsive response was, "Oh, I wish my father were here to hear you say that! He's always considered me a weeping willow."
So Thornton went from Chefoo to Ojai with only a transpacific voyage as respite. Thacher, then as now, looked more like a summer camp than a school. The new institution had three primary aims:

> toward health and happiness, toward unselfish manly character, and toward accurate, thorough, and self-reliant habits of thought and study. An object constantly in view is to help a boy toward the simplest way of living a happy, useful life . . . with other people."

To achieve these aims, the school provided academic instruction (more like interludes between explorations on horseback of the wooded trails through the mountains that separated Thacher from Santa Barbara and the sea, thirty miles distant) along with opportunities for camping and out-of-doors living. In addition, there were the conventional sports; and, of course, considerable attention was given to character and spiritual development which Sherman Thacher regarded, like Dr. Arnold of Rugby, as the natural concomitant of competitive exercises.

Thornton's lowly status at the school was exacerbated by the circumstance that his brother Amos was California Interscholastic Tennis Champion, an excellent baseball player, and a good general athlete. Frank Peavey Heffelfinger, who was Thornton's precise contemporary at Thacher and later on at Yale, and who subsequently became sincerely proud of the accomplishments of his twofold classmate, was not, in 1968, able to recall anything about Thornton at Thacher, though he could remember him at Yale. But Heffelfinger remembered Amos Wilder at Thacher quite vividly.

At the Thacher School, Thornton was almost as estranged as he had been at Chefoo, in one sense even more so. At Chefoo, he could justify his isolation because he was in a strange country where at least half of his classmates were of a nationality different from his own. But at Thacher he was back in his own country, surrounded by boys who were his countrymen. So despite the assurance provided by the proximity of his older brother and of a headmaster who was his father's friend, Thornton felt isolated and friendless. On one occasion, one of the masters espied Thornton in the middle of a field adjacent to the school grounds and called out: "Wilder, what in heaven's name are you doing out there?" The boy's earnest response was: "Sir, I'm looking for an asphodel."

The incident symbolizes the vanity of Amos Wilder's hope that Thacher would transform his younger son into a scholar-athlete-marksman-horseman. What Amos did not know was that Thornton's eyesight was defective, that his vision required corrective lenses (which had not yet been prescribed for him), and that under the circumstances shooting and playing ball were both difficult and distasteful. He did succeed in improving his horsemanship to the extent that he rode comfortably, a minor feat for a myopic boy; he was to recollect, decades later, that his happiest hours at Thacher were those when he could take solitary rides into the surrounding woods where there was quiet and where he could think his thoughts.

Headmaster Thacher was, by all reports, a kind and conscientious man. Aware of Thornton's failure to integrate in the life of the school, he invited Thornton to his study in an attempt to correct some of the boy's deficiencies and to build up his self-confidence. While in general his efforts met with no success (he did attempt to correct Thornton's overprecise and bookish speech), he made a friend of his old friend's younger son, and exchanged letters with him for some years after Thornton left the school, in 1913, after only one year. Indeed, fifteen years later, when Wilder had become Thacher's most celebrated alumnus, he befriended Sherman Thacher's son, Anson, when they accidentally encountered one another in New York. Subsequently, he visited the school on the occasion of Anson's succeeding to the headmastership. In his visits and communications to the school, Wilder never alluded to his own stay at Thacher as anything less than idyllic; he remains, to this day, one of the school heroes.

Neither Thacher School nor Thornton was to blame for the unhappy year ending in his withdrawal. The fault lay partly in the constitution of the younger Wilder and partly in his father's literal mindedness and conventional attitude about what a male adolescent should be. The father's lack of imagination rendered him incapable of understanding the nature of his younger son; he could describe the boy as possessed of "a delicate fine nature" who found "rough boys not congenial," but he chose to regard such a nature as alterable in an environment where rough, competitive behavior was the desirable norm. Fortunately, he did not insist on Thornton's being subjected to any more of Thacher than he had already. With some reluctance, perhaps, he acceded to the idea of Thornton's rejoining his mother and sisters, who, by this time, had again taken up residence in Berkeley.

Thornton's final two years of college preparation were thus spent at Berkeley High School. Yale was his goal; it was, in fact—unaccountably—his dream.

He enrolled at Berkeley, along with his sister Charlotte who transferred from Claremont High School in Southern California, as a member of the junior class, and followed a program of studies consisting of English, mathematics, German, and Latin. In his first term he received the highest grades awarded in Latin and mathematics and good grades in English and German. During the second term his mathematics dropped a grade, but his English went up, so that his grade average for the year was a creditable B+. In his second and final year, his grades deteriorated.

Quite clearly Thornton was not giving most of his attention to his school work. On what then was he expending his energies? For one thing, after two and a half years in China and Ojai, California, he was frequenting—the way an alcoholic released from confinement seeks out the saloon—the Liberty Theater in Oakland and its repertory of melodramas and farces. The impact of this encounter was to have astonishing results for the American theater.

But his passion for theater could not be satisfied through mere vicarious enjoyment; his school provided another outlet. In the spring term of each year, the Berkeley high school students composed a vaudeville, which consisted, among other things, of original sketches and playlets by the students. Thornton, in collaboration with Violette Stitt Wilson, composed a short play (reflecting the Liberty Theater repertory), in which Miss Wilson played the heroine with "the sure touch of real talent"; Thornton, in a minor role, "carried his part with ease." In Thornton's first term, that is to say, the fall of 1913, the school staged Shakespeare's *As You Like It*. Perhaps because he was a new boy, Thornton was cast in the small role of M. Le Beau.

Actually, neither Thornton nor Charlotte ever penetrated the inner reaches of student life at Berkeley High, perhaps because the Wilder family had not embroidered itself into the social fabric of the community; they had no roots there, and the personality of neither of the two children was strong enough to make itself felt. Moreover, they had entered the school midway in the four-year sequence, long after cliques had formed and alliances had crystallized. A prominent member of Thornton's and Charlotte's Berkeley High School class (1915), Katherine Towle—who later became a dean at The University of California— in 1966, possessed virtually no recollections of either Wilder: "Thornton was a pleasant young man, somewhat reserved, though always friendly and engaging. He left Berkeley High School very soon, I seem to remember, to attend the Thacher School in Ojai." Dean Towle's confusions about Thornton's years at Berkeley reflects her remoteness from both Wilders. "I scarcely knew Thornton's family. His sister Charlotte was not much more than a name to me. Wasn't there a younger sister too?"

Some years later, in October 1926, Katherine encountered Thornton aboard the S. S. *Lancastria*, a meeting she recalled in vivid detail; by then, he had become the author of a published novel, a copy of which he inscribed: "For Kate Towle with the best wishes of her friend Thornton Wilder." Although Wilder was not yet a celebrity, he was nevertheless a man who had developed a personality and a presence; he obviously stood in sharp contrast with the ghost of a boy whom Katherine Towle dimly remembered from a dozen years before.

The Berkeley High School Yearbook of 1915, *Olla Podrida*, gives further evidence of the class's indifference to the one who was to become its most prominent member: the listing misspells Wilder's name in two places—Thorton Neven Wilder. And while the yearbook takes note of his participation in the spring vaudeville of 1914 and in the *As You Like It* production of the fall of 1913, there is no mention of his involvement in any class activities during his senior year. Moreover, of the eight courses he completed in his senior year, that is to say two semesters each of English, history, German, and science, in five he received the grade of C;

only in the English courses did he earn "A's." The picture in the yearbook is that of a somber, sad-eyed adolescent from whose expression one might predict a bleak future.

And indeed, the year of Thornton's graduation from Berkeley High School was not the best of times for him. On July 28, 1915, he left California to join his father in New Haven, since Amos had taken up residence there to head the Yale-in-China program. Although Amos was already a member of Thornton's favorite university and despite Thornton's assiduous participation at the Yale entrance examinations, Amos had already enrolled his son at Oberlin College in Ohio for the coming fall. Amos felt that the intense religious atmosphere at Oberlin might have the salubrious effect of counteracting the worldly ambience of Yale, an atmosphere which the elder Wilder devoted untold hours to improving, with his lay sermons to undergraduate groups.

Thornton was dismayed at the prospect of Oberlin. "I have his promise in writing for one year only," he wrote Sherman Thacher. Somehow the promise wasn't kept; his tenure at Oberlin was two years. But for the summer at least, he could stay in the East. After the reunion with his father—who would by then have seen the disappointing final grades amassed by his younger son, an "A" and three "C's"—Thornton was scheduled along with brother Amos to work on a Vermont farm or else rusticate at Miss Baron's Summer Camp in New Hampshire, or both. (The younger Amos had just completed *his* two-year term at Oberlin, before being permitted to transfer to Yale.)

There exist no written reports of a confrontation between Amos and his son over Thornton's most disappointing final term's achievement. If, indeed, Amos did demand an explanation, it seems unlikely that Thornton would have produced one—at the time. Ultimately, though, he did throw light on his failure to distinguish himself at Berkeley High, in his foreword to *The Angel That Troubled the Waters* (1928). There, he said that authors of fifteen and sixteen spend their time drawing up title pages and adjusting table of contents of works they have neither the perseverance nor the ability to execute; in addition, he had found lately one of his early table of contents for it, written in the flyleaves of a first-year algebra. Two of the plays in *The Angel That Troubled the Waters, Brother Fire* and *Proserpina and the Devil* are the work of a high school senior; the sombre, sad-eyed photograph in the high school yearbook was, in fact, a portrait of the artist as a young man.

Anyone with a feeling for literature who had come upon the short plays and short stories of eighteen-year-old Thornton Wilder in 1915 would instantly have become aware of an important, if unfulfilled, talent, one that required careful nurture and affectionate appreciation.

Mrs. Isabella Wilder was fortunately the first to read her son's early writings; she made manifest her pride in them and bestowed upon them her judicious praise. But when they were called to the attention of Amos Parker Wilder, almost angrily he brushed them aside, saying of them that his poor, unpromising, pathetic younger son was "Carving olive pits! Carving olive pits!"

# III

## The College Years

*"One might have imagined him a porcelain figurine of a witty French abbé of the Enlightenment come to life . . . and no one could have guessed his age, for, if he was not old in appearance, certainly neither was he exactly youthful looking."*
—"A FEW MEMORIES" BY FREDERICK B. ARTZ

Amos Wilder's choice of Oberlin College for Thornton was determined principally by the college's evangelical character. The founders, two Congregational ministers, established the institution in 1833 in order to "train teachers and other Christian leaders" who might then go West and promulgate learning and Christian ideals. By 1915, the college was open to students of all religious faiths; but Chapel remained nevertheless, a fixed part of the daily ritual and a considerable number of Oberlin graduates still departed for missionary work, mostly to Asia. The Department of Religion was the college's most prestigious, and Oberlin's Memorial Arch honored the martyred Christian missionaries who in 1900, had been killed during the Boxer Rebellion.

Oberlin is in Ohio, not too far from Cleveland; in 1916, the community consisted of little more than the college buildings, the residences of the faculty, and a few stores. If Amos Wilder feared that Yale was too worldly for his sons, Oberlin offered no worldly temptations at all.

19

Whatever his reasons were for sending Thornton to Oberlin, his choice, as it turned out, was a good one: Oberlin provided the first really fertile ground for Thornton's artistic development.*

When Amos rejected worldly Yale for his two sons, he may have had matters other than sin and temptations of the flesh in mind. Yale attracted, in those decades at least, a disproportionate number of students from wealthy families; Amos may have felt that Thornton at eighteen was not yet ready to become involved with the arrogant and callous sons of the rich and that he had better begin his college years associating with Oberlin students who originated in the earnest middle class of midwestern towns and rural areas. But if the student body was solidly middle class and predominantly midwestern, Oberlin was by no means either a Bible institute or a cow college; the Oberlin community, on the contrary, was one of several which regarded itself—with some justice—as an oasis of culture in a somewhat bleak landscape.

Of vital importance was that Oberlin received young Thornton, aged eighteen and a half, with a certain interest and respect. Frederick Artz, an Oberlin senior at the time and later to be chairman of its department of history, was a participant in rehearsals of Bernard Shaw's *Candida* when Thornton—a newly arrived freshman—came around.

> What a fantastic freshman he was. He spoke in an excited and exotic manner, highly punctuated with epigrams. Everything about him— appearance, dress, speech and manner—was precise, even precious. One might have imagined him a porcelain figurine of a witty French abbé of the Enlightenment come to life. There was something of the "gamin" the mischievous boy, about him, too. And no one could have guessed his age, for, if he was not old in appearance, certainly neither was he exactly youthful looking . . . I am reminded of Wilde's comment on Max Beerbohm. "Max was born with the gift of eternal old age."

Not only did Oberlin provide Thornton with an outlet for his passionate interest in theater—before his departure, he played the poet in Lord Dunsany's *The Lost Silk Hat*—but with a music department of some distinction Oberlin also was able to gratify his well-developed musical tastes and interests. In addition, the wife of one of the professors, a Mrs. Martin, "a gifted and handsome woman who knew the world as few others in our strangely unworldly village"—as she was recalled by Frederick Artz—entertained a circle of students on Sunday afternoons, the first of several "salons" that Thornton frequented during much of his life. Mrs. Martin's Sunday afternoons were of considerable importance to the young man's development of poise and self-assurance; there he could

* Coincidentally, thirteen years before Thornton's arrival at Oberlin, young Harry Sinclair Lewis spent a year preparing at Oberlin Academy for his entrance to Yale.

talk about theater, about new writers—George Moore was one of his enthusiasms—and he was respectfully listened to.

Thornton became quickly and totally immersed in the cultural life of the college. He got to know the best musicians and wheedled them into playing and singing music of the baroque era as a relief and a diversion from the nineteenth-century romantic music that constituted the taste of the period. He wrote short plays, at least one of which he performed in the parlor of the Men's Building. This piece concerns an artist at an exhibition of his own paintings, where he hears his work discussed by the visitors, most of whom make the most hilariously fatuous remarks. Thornton played all the parts—in the manner of Ruth Draper.

The central influence upon Thornton at Oberlin was the chairman of the English Department, Professor Charles H. A. Wager. Wager's big course dealt with the great classics of literature read in translation: Homer, the Greek tragic playwrights, Vergil, and Dante. A quarter of a century later, Thornton himself offered essentially the same course at the University of Chicago. While he was home in New Haven, Thornton had taken short courses in literature with Yale professors Charles Gayley and William Lyon Phelps; nevertheless, he described Wager as "the greatest class lecturer I have ever heard." Wager recognized Thornton's exceptional qualities, invited him to his home, and encouraged him to read aloud the stories and plays which, a year or so before, he could show only to his mother.

Wilder's characterization of Professor Wager was reinforced over forty years later by another of Wager's students, Professor Henry Sams, who later became English head at Penn State. Dr. Sams has described Charles Wager as a man of "firm New England dignity who did not invite relaxation or camaraderie. No one ever told him jokes or touched him physically, or slouched in the chair of his study . . . or handed him scamped and unfinished work. He was a formidable man, despite his warmth and wit. . . ."

Obviously he was, at that moment, a good teacher for Wilder and the younger man's response was immediate. Wilder contributed to the *Oberlin Literary Magazine* a sonnet which the holograph identifies as its subject: C.H.A.W.

TO A TEACHER

*Oh, let me listen on that saving word*
*That brings to leaf the branches of the mind,—*
*As Saul leaned to Gamaliel, strangely stirred*
*Urgent for God and that dim work assigned;*
*As Plato turned his streaming eyes away*
*When paused the patient sitting Socrates,*
*Or those rapt students on a later day*

*Gazed in the echoing loft of Saint-Sulpice;—*
*So may I listen, bear away the Spark,*
*So may I raise it up for others living,*
*Praying for fruitage, but content to hark*
*Knowing myself enriched though poor in giving,*
*Enriched and freed from fear, thy face toward mine—*
*As Vergil led the hooded Florentine.*

Another of Thornton's haunts in Oberlin was the home of Professor and Mrs. William Hutchins. Hutchins, a professor of religion, was favorably impressed by young Thornton's sincere interest in religious ideas and regarded him as a suitable friend for his son Robert, a classmate of Thornton's and something of a skeptic. What the two young men had principally in common was their lack of rapport with their respective fathers. Writing to Sherman Thacher, Thornton observed that Professor Hutchins's son, who was the president of the class and the most promising boy on campus, had said that his father didn't care to listen to any opinion he might wish to express, adding that it was this way all the time.

Apart from their common dissatisfactions, the two hadn't much to build a friendship upon. Physically, they were an incongruous pair: Thornton—nervous, slight, and bespectacled—was dwarfed by the tall, relaxed, and incredibly handsome Bob Hutchins. Wilder's interests were focused on the arts and belles lettres, while Hutchins was a political-philosophical animal, already easily accustomed to the hero worship he received from scores of Oberlin freshmen. Indeed, he received it from Thornton Wilder, who recognized in Hutchins the type of young man Amos Wilder would have preferred his second son to be. Had the two young men not fortuitously been reunited in 1919, it is unlikely, once they left Oberlin, that they would have kept in touch with each other.

Hutchins demanded of anyone who came into his orbit that that person provide some kind of solid intellectual stimulus; Thornton, unfortunately, was all response. Hutchins, the rationalist-ironist, demanded of people that they feed his intellect, provide fuel for his inquiring mind; Wilder asked only that people reveal themselves—their anxieties, their aspirations, their perplexities. In their Oberlin days, Wilder's ideas were of no great interest to Hutchins and Hutchins had little inclination to make Wilder his confidant. Years later, when they had developed a kind of symbiotic relationship, Hutchins asked Wilder why he tolerated the company of the many inconsequential people who clustered about him. "Why, Bob," Wilder explained, "every pair of eyes is a new book." Hutchins, in recalling Wilder's response, seems to have misunderstood Wilder's meaning: if each person represented a new book for Wilder, it was not a book that he might write, but rather a book that he could read.

Professor Wager's impact on Wilder went beyond that of lecturer and reader. Wager was interested in the traditionalist Oxford revival and medieval mysticism, in Saint Teresa and Cardinal Newman; these interests struck a responsive chord in Thornton who was at that time, and for many years after, profoundly religious or, at least, aesthetically drawn to spiritual matters. The kind of spiritual world that Wager revealed to Thornton was a feast for the young man's senses, after the lean years of the New England Congregationalism of his parents' house. If Wager was playing Vergil to a young Dante, he was a Vergil respectably garbed in New England Puritan attire, who opened doors upon the rich, colorful world of Catholicism, but took care that his charge—while he filled his eyes with the gorgeous spectacle—never entered the room, nor participated in the forbidden rituals.

The June 1917 issue of the *Oberlin Literary Magazine* published Wilder's last contribution before leaving the college:

### THE MARRIAGE OF ZABETT
#### *Thornton N. Wilder,* '19.

In the days when Martinus Scheihoffen was pursuing the Devil with forty armed men about the yellow lakes, there lived in the village of Kaage a woman named Zabett der Derken. Her father, Peder, the merchant, was a rich man, and it was on his gold pieces that the family enjoyed a merry life made up of guests and drinking. On the feast days, Zabett loved to go to church and muse with closed eyes on the sufferings of the saints. At such times she regretted her idle life, but when she left the church and stopped in the sunlight, laughing and mocking with the women, she wondered if anything were ever better than gossiping on the church porch. Zabett was past the age when most girls marry, and, although she was beautiful and sought-after and enjoyed most the laughter and talk with the men, she remembered how when a man tried to catch hold of her hands, the touch set her a-trembling, and thereafter she lays (sic) shuddering the whole night through. This she could not explain, and it made her afraid.

One day her father gave her a string of pearls—pear-shaped—of which every alternate pearl was rose-colored; this, he said, was sent to her from his new partner in Lubeck. Her father said nothing more about it until, a month later, he gave her a *stuckle* for her dress, of cloth-of-gold, with the three towers of Lubeck embroidered on it in black thread; this, he said, was sent her by Jans Ketterlingen, his new partner in Lubeck. From then on, Zabett thought often of the stranger, whose portrait, dark-smiling, and holding in his hand astronomical instruments, hung in her father's counting-house. At last the day came when her father stopped her, lifting her hands from the organum on which she was playing, and told her that his partner at

Lubeck, one Jans Ketterlingen, had heard often of her beauty and high spirits and would come in a month to Kaage to ask for her in marriage. This intention he must declare to her before his visit, since his stay in the village must not exceed two or three days. Zabett smiled shyly up at her father as he put into her hands an inlaid box from the Turks, a gift from Mynheer Ketterlingen of Lubeck, and she forgot, foolish girl, how when some man stole a kiss from her in the dance, she turned pale and sickened and shuddered.

After that when she went to church and pondered upon the exhaustion and sufferings of the holy men and women who had hungered and gone naked and bled and died for the love of God, she mentioned in her prayers to them a new name, and in her mind were the delicate hands and black beard of Ketterlingen, her betrothed. The thought of him induced a new mood in her, and after the congregation had left the church and the old stableman was blowing out the lamps, she went up to the altar and wonderingly put her hands upon the wounded feet of the statue, and looked musingly into the suffering eyes, remembering the whole of His story. And the time drew on when Mynheer was daily expected.

On the very afternoon of Jan's arrival, the two walked through the fields together, and he spoke to her of the cause of his coming and the brevity of his visit; then he fell silent, waiting for her to speak. Zabett suddenly felt the grain quiver, and terror of the man slid into her heart as water rushes into the lungs of a drowning man. But she could not answer him, no, for about her neck rested the pearls of two colors; on her shoulders floated his scarf and at home her mother was kneading the wedding breads. Moreover, that evening she did not cry out when, seated by the fire, he took her in his arms and kissed her, albeit she suffered the fire of fires, such as burns for heretics.

That night the wretched woman left the house, ran through the cold, wet streets, and kneeling in the church porch, cast herself with a sudden surrender into the wisdom of God. Then was the whole porch illuminated with a pulsing light, and the door of the church was opened by a hand unseen. She went in, and flinging herself upon the pavement, rehearsed before a great and mystical company the history of her stony heart; how that a lifelong blindness had prevented her seeing that the warning of her body was a result of the jealous care of her heavenly husband, to whom she had been betrothed since the hills were made. And a voice answered her: "Go back, Zabett, delay thy marriage with the merchant of Lubeck. Live a little longer as a child of the world, until the sign of thy release be shown in a sudden hour. Let no one mark a change in thee." And Zabett arose and returned home.

Oh, to tell of the torments of a life unaltered about an altered spirit. What groanings she suppressed as she went about her daily life, laughing and chattering in the church porch with the women of Kaage. She persuaded Jans to put off the date of the marriage, but his caresses she could not put off, and often she would hide from him, trembling, behind doors and hangings. She talked long to her father and mother, but in her heart she strained away from the increasing discussion of gold and wedding-feasts and respectable guests, to listen to the attributes of God and the lengths to which a soul may approach unto them. So she waited for the miraculous intimation of her release.

But none came. At last she could delay the wedding no longer, nor did it seem that she could any longer feign merriment and gaiety; the strange struggle had left strange wounds. Ah, Zabett, distracted wert thou on the eve of thy wedding; thou lookedst for signs on earth and in the sky and in the flights of birds. No archangel burned against the sunset; no virgin mother smiled from among the first stars; the moon arose not out of due season; no trees were visited by unconsuming flame; no visitor with unmistakable eyes knocked at thy door. Nay, saintly lady, but in thy last and frantic hour, as thou satst yearning at the window, three white and delicate feathers floated against thy face and cooled thy eyelids and thy wan brow. And a voice distant and tremulous said: "Take nothing with thee. Go. Found for me an order of women, bound by vows to expect my return daily." Then Zabett arose with a glad heart, and taking in her hand a penny for bread in the morning, she stole forth into the dusk. But as she ran, she lost her way thrice, and thrice came into a street that ended in a stone wall, where a voice said: "Trust in God." The third time she understood, and threw away the penny which she carried; straightway the stone wall disappeared, and she went on rejoicing.

This was the St. Zabett of Kaage who founded the great convent wherein I write these words; me and many another she spared from that exile of a woman's soul from Heaven, the marriage of the body. She is our intervention; without her we should be dead, slain by the caresses of our husbands.

In "The Marriage of Zabett," we can easily recognize the style of the Wilder who composed his first three novels. From the very first sentence, we derive the sense of security provided by the work of a genuine writer. And if the first sentence assures us that we have come upon the work of a talented writer, the phrase, "about the yellow lakes," is the touch of an artist. The story's slightly archaic tone, so appropriate to the subject and the setting, with its echoes of the Jacobean Bible, emerges without strain, with no sense of labored mannerism.

The subject of the story is unusual for a very young man, and ordinarily we would not expect such a writer to deal so easily and disinterestedly with the twin mysteries of sex and religion. But Wilder's adolescence was spent mainly in a household of respectable, genteel females of New England background whose chastity was perhaps their only passion. And the heroine of his story, driven by the watchword, *Noli me Tangere* and zealously guarding her inviolability, was to reappear again and again in each of Wilder's novels, from early to late, in a remarkable series of transformations: *The Cabala*'s James Blair, *The Bridge of San Luis Rey*'s Abbess . . . to *The Eighth Day*'s John Ashley. Even the protagonist of Wilder's first Broadway play was a woman who, for centuries, had been the very prototype of chastity, the legendary matron of Rome, Lucrèce.

Just below the surface of "The Marriage of Zabett" is the idea of devoting one's life to the service of those in need of help. The lives of Saint Clare and Saint Francis had impinged on Thornton's sensibilities; Francis had already served as the subject of one of the three-minute plays (and years later would serve again for one of the *Plays for Bleecker Street*). The idea of service, however, was more than a source of literary inspiration. Writing to Sherman Thacher in March 1917, Thornton wondered whether it would be good for him to serve as an assistant in a hospital for wounded veterans in northern Italy—to carry swill for the trained nurses, to read aloud the *Nuova Testamenta,* to harden himself to frightful sights and sounds. The experience would not be pretty, but if the hospital were beautifully situated—on Assisi hill, perhaps. . . . But there might be war tomorrow and then St. Francis of Assisi would be the last person in their minds.

A month later, war, in fact, did come to the United States; but Thornton's aspirations to serve were—for the time being—frustrated by his nearsightedness. Instead, in September 1917, he became a member of the class of 1920 of Yale University.

Thornton's transfer from Oberlin to Yale, in retrospect, could be called a mixed blessing. The reasons for the change are clear enough: the family, now established in New Haven, wanted to end the long series of separations that circumstances had thrust upon them; undoubtedly money could be saved (Amos, now executive secretary of Yale-in-China, was far from affluent); finally, from the point of view of Thornton's future as a teacher, a degree from Yale was more prestigious than one from Oberlin.

But there were reasons, also, for his remaining at Oberlin. Even though he had been passionately eager to attend Yale while he was still a high school student, Thornton—to quote his own words—had become "completely devoted to Oberlin and deeply resented [his] father's moving [him] to the East." The kind of intimate and careful teaching and counsel that he received from the Oberlin faculty he would not receive at Yale. The vistas opened to him by Charles Wager would not be appreciably extended by William Lyon Phelps, who was renowned for his ability to "sell" Browning, Tennyson, and a sampling of continental novelists to Yale undergraduates who would otherwise remain indifferent to anything more complex than *Lorna Doone* or *A Tale of Two Cities.* The quality of undergraduate education that Wilder received at Yale was later characterized as puerile and contemptible by no less an authority than Robert Maynard Hutchins (who as president of the University of Chicago would enroll Wilder in the drive to provide the undergraduates with an education specifically designated as being better than they could get at Yale).

Thornton was leaving behind at Oberlin an old-fashioned American egalitarianism for the structured undergraduate society at Yale. It is impossible to measure precisely how the shift from one kind of campus atmosphere to another affected Wilder's artistic development and maturation; but certainly, in exchanging the West for the East, Thornton's view of the world necessarily changed. Equally important, so did his audience. He had written first, principally, for his mother's eyes, then for Wager's; in going to Yale, he began writing for his classmates—whose friendship he cultivated and whose approval he sought.

The class of 1920 was a typical Yale class of its era. It was clearly stratified: Occupying positions of unchallenged social superiority were the son of a Morgan partner, Harry Pomeroy Davison, Jr.; a nephew of a former president of the United States, David Ingalls; a Schermerhorn; an Auchincloss; an Adams; a du Pont; and the young Mr. Phelps Phelps (*geb.* von Rottenberg), son of one of Bismarck's chief secretaries, who enlisted in the Canadian Air Force in 1917 and did not return to Yale.

The next level consisted of men intimately connected with some of the great American industries: Frank Heffelfinger (grain); John Weyerhaeuser (timber); Ralph Hanes (woolens); Morehead Patterson (machinery). A larger segment of the class was drawn from the upper middle class, sons of prosperous physicians, merchants, ministers, lawyers, architects. Prominent among this group were De Forest Van Slyck, Briton Hadden, William Dwight Whitney, Benjamin Jennings, and Stuart Heminway. Another portion of the student body was drawn from genteel Protestant families of moderate financial means, who were determined to provide their sons with what they regarded as the best available college education. Among these were Walter Millis, who achieved fame as a popular historian; William Clyde De Vane, who became a Yale professor of English and dean of the college; Joseph Francis Jackson, who became head of the Department of Romance Languages at the University of Illinois; Henry Robinson Luce; and Thornton Wilder.

In addition to all these groups, who constituted the bulk of the class, there were the miscellaneous pariahs, sons of immigrants—Irish janitors and Jewish grocers—who were single mindedly concerned with getting the education that would enable them to study medicine or law. These were silent, poorly dressed young men who did not participate in campus activities, who were never considered for membership in the fraternities, clubs, and secret societies, who generally lived at home, or if they occupied quarters in one of the residence colleges they shared their rooms with other untouchables.

Coming upon so elaborately structured a society, Thornton understood that he had a problem to face and a puzzle to solve. He arrived at Yale a full year after alignments had been formed and groups had coalesced. Once again he was cast in the role of an outsider, a newcomer at a great ball where all the tables seem occupied and everyone has already chosen his partner. But with the memories of his previous failures and of his father's despair over these failures, he determined that at Yale, his father's own college, he would succeed, and particularly on the level where success really counted: he would become a bona-fide Yaleman!

But before he could integrate himself into the Yale complex, he had first to puzzle out how all the pieces fitted together. These questions concerning the Yale way of life he was reluctant to put before either his father or his brother Amos—now preparing for the ministry: Instead he went to "Harry" Luce, a classmate during the year at Chefoo. Even as early as 1917, Luce was already one of the prominent members of the class and Thornton went to him, not with the idea of drawing upon Luce's influence, but rather with the hope of benefiting from Luce's highly developed powers of exposition and explanation. Once Luce revealed the secret of how it all worked at Yale, Thornton felt he could sensibly make his way.

A half century later, shortly before his sudden and untimely death, Henry Luce recalled without difficulty his reunion at Yale with Thornton Wilder:

> Thornton approached me at Yale, not only on the basis that we had attended school together at Chefoo—where I hardly knew him—but with the assumption that there existed between us a common religious bond. Very naively he asked me to explain what would now be called the power structure—a term the Negro militants have taken over from the Communists; he didn't, of course, use that phrase—at Yale. But the truth is that although Thornton made friends with everyone he could, including the football players, he was always on the outside looking in. He got to know and was even known by the 400 but he was not accepted by the elite.

Luce, of course, *was*. His account implies a harsh, slightly malicious picture of Wilder at twenty. One gets a sense of Wilder as an American Rastignac arriving at New Haven, determined to conquer Yale. Luce went on with his reminiscence, recalling his membership in the secret society, Skull and Bones.

> Wilder wasn't eligible for Skull and Bones, even though his father was a member. But he'd never have been considered if he *had* been eligible . . . (*Luce paused at this point savouring a recollection*). Now Robert Maynard Hutchins, on the other hand, *was*

eligible. He would have been tapped for Bones, but I was—fortunately
—able to blackball him. . . .

Luce's estimate of Wilder's position at Yale is deadly accurate but,
paradoxically, it is also misleading. From Luce's point of view and for
others in the inner circle of Skull and Bones or Scroll and Key, Wilder
never made it at Yale; but this is hardly to say that he was consigned to
outer darkness. Luce himself not only wished to wield power, which he
could do as managing editor of the *Yale Daily News,* and as a member of
Bones, but he also sought honors and achieved them as a member of Phi
Beta Kappa and with citations for proficiency in Greek and in public
speaking. But there was something more that Luce wanted: recognition
as a litterateur. For this aim, he had to accept membership in the
Elizabethan Club and serve on the editorial board of the *Yale Literary
Magazine.* Thus, in addition to his association with the most important
men on campus, Luce found himself in contact with the literary group.
And the bookish circle at Yale had a prestige of its own, numbering
among its members Walter Millis, Philip Barry, Stephen Vincent Benet
. . . and Thornton Wilder.

For Wilder, despite Luce's casual dismissal of him as "a literary
type . . . an eccentric," did make a place for himself at Yale. In the
senior class vote, a number of Wilder's classmates voted for him as most
scholarly, most original, most brilliant, and most entertaining. If Luce
was accorded by his classmates their earnest respect, Wilder made the
greater impact both as a writer and as a personality. And while the
majority of the class chose *Lorna Doone* as its favorite novel and "Crossing the Bar" its favorite poem, there was a smaller contingent who
preferred *Tom Jones* and *Pickwick Papers,* "Lycidas" and "Prospice." To
this small and serious group, Wilder meant something. His leadership
among the writers led to his election to Pundits, a group which included
members of Luce's "elite," Morehead Patterson and David Ingalls, but
not Luce himself. Nor was Luce among the senior class officers who
included Morehead Patterson, Harry P. Davison, Stuart Heminway,
and—as composer of the Ivy Ode—Thornton Wilder. Considering that
Thornton lacked three or four of the major attributes for collegiate
success—money, social position, athleticism, or impressive masculine good
looks—he had traveled a long way from the undistinguished and joyless
school years in China and California. Since Berkeley High School, there
had clearly been a transformation; where Thornton had been among the
most forgettable members of his high school class, he now enjoyed the
respect and admiration of many of his college classmates, few of whom
were likely to forget him.

As Thornton became a little more the kind of young man Amos

wanted him to be, and as his life at Yale brought him satisfactions he had not before sought—most notably, popularity—the quality of his writing deteriorated. In "The Marriage of Zabett," one could see an undeniable artistry and great promise—in the theme, in the style, in the subject. He went on writing at Yale, and the June 1920 issue of the *Yale Literary Magazine* contains a Wilder story. It is, simply, not very good. Entitled "Eddy Greater," a more ambitious and even pretentious effort than "The Marriage of Zabett," the story deals with a biographer of a literary figure whose diaries and poems are now in the possession of the man's old mistress. The story bears an embarrassing resemblance to Henry James's *The Aspern Papers,* though it is not a very persuasive imitation of James. It is, rather, the work of a bookish undergraduate who had read widely in James, Stevenson, and miscellaneous minor Edwardians and Georgians and who produced an undistinguished version of a kind of short story that had gone out of fashion ten years before. One of the most damaging comments that can be made about Wilder's story (and about Yale) is that it might have been written by any one of a dozen of Wilder's classmates—even, perhaps, by Harry Luce.

Wilder had become too conscious of his audience's expectations—of the mores of an audience of young men from good homes, together with their gentlemanly, well-bred, and wholly cultivated teachers. His work at Yale was drawn less from the depths of his private experiences and feelings than it was from what he and his literary-minded classmates were reading; composition had become for him a virtuoso performance, demonstrating the development of one's writing skill. And unhappily, there was no one at Yale, either among his peers or in the faculty, who could deflect or even modify the direction Wilder's writing was taking him. Puritan notions about writing, such as the idea that it was primarily an intellectual and moralistic enterprise, prevailed at Yale, and, for the time being, took hold of Wilder.

If Yale did not contribute much to his development as an artist, the university did provide Thornton with some of the self-confidence he desperately needed and with the welcome respect of other worthy young men. Had he received the total rejection which the Yale undergraduates had administered a dozen years before to Sinclair Lewis, the experience might have changed the course of his artistic development. Or it might, on the other hand, have destroyed it.

It is worth pointing out that in the decade ending in 1920, Harvard produced a group of new writers that included E. E. Cummings, T. S. Eliot, and John Dos Passos, while from Princeton erupted—prematurely, it is true—Eugene O'Neill and, in due course, Scott Fitzgerald. The roustabout life or newspaper reporting or magazine editing had already accounted for Dreiser and Willa Cather and would produce Faulkner and Hemingway and Kay Boyle. Among Wilder's generation of writers, a great many would "go to Paris," some to starve, others to thrive, and all to participate in the changes and irruptions stirred up by Pound and Joyce and Gertrude Stein.

But the so-called Yale literary renaissance, if we except the blighted and emotionally crippled Sinclair Lewis, consisted principally of writers who remained, at least for a time—until Yale wore off—in a more comfortable tradition: Archibald MacLeish, Stephen Vincent Benét, Philip Barry, and Thornton Wilder. The influence of Yale and the specter of Professor William Lyon Phelps, together with the admirable and gentlemanly Yale classmates who thought well of Wilder, hung heavily over the composition of his first three novels. It is suggestive that while he later traveled to remote parts of the earth to write his stories and then his plays, Wilder invariably read his galley proofs at home— home, from 1915 on, never being more than a few minutes' distance from the Yale campus.

For Fitzgerald, Cummings, Dos Passos, and Hemingway, the first World War was a liberating influence providing the psychological breakthrough that enabled them to find their highly distinctive voices. Wilder, as we know, was eager to become a part of the armed services. And although the war had transformed Yale from an academy into a vast reserve officers training school, with the majority of Wilder's classmates in one kind of unit or another, it was not until September 18, 1918, that Thornton was finally accepted into the Coast Artillery Corps which dispatched him to Fort Adams, Newport, Rhode Island. As a member of Company I, he rose to the rank of corporal and after little more than three months' service was discharged on December 31, in time to resume studies at Yale in January 1919.

Among those who entered Yale after the war's interruption was Robert Hutchins, who would normally have begun his studies at New Haven in 1917 had he not volunteered to serve overseas with the Ambulance Corps. Upon enrolling at Yale, Hutchins found himself in a situation different from the Oberlin milieu, where he had effortlessly become the dominant figure in his class. In 1919, Yale was overrun with tall, good-looking young men—war heroes all—ready to resume their interrupted studies. And they were already established Yalemen. Hutchins, arriving as a total stranger, had difficulty in making his presence felt until his former Oberlin classmate, Thornton Wilder, joyously welcomed him and, in short order, made known to everyone of consequence that his old friend, Bob Hutchins, class president at Oberlin, was—with his impressive mien—gracing the class of 1921. It was Henry Luce's contention that Wilder single-handedly launched Hutchins at Yale, an accomplishment

that Luce deplored but that proved to have far-reaching effects on both
Wilder's and Hutchins's future.

At Oberlin, Wilder had been merely one of Hutchins's myrmidons,
but at Yale he served Hutchins as sponsor. Their reunion marked the
beginning of a friendship based on equality, one of the few sustained
relationships in Thornton Wilder's lifetime. Yet, their life-long association had little real basis in feeling; it was less a friendship than an
alliance, covered over, to be sure, by a patina of wan New England
affection. In their seventies, each would still declare the other his best
friend, though neither had made the slightest move to see the other for
almost a decade. Their actual collaboration—their real relationship—
lasted a little more than twenty years; when it ended, in the early
1940s—with the two men parting philosophic company over the question
of America's involvement in World War II—there was little between
them, either of feeling or of mutual understanding. On the other hand,
there was no residue of bitterness or animosity; but that observation
again underscores the essential bloodlessness of their long-time association.

There were two other students at Yale who were ultimately to affect
prodigiously the course of Wilder's life. The first was a casual acquaintance of Wilder; the second, he did not know at all at the time, not even
of his existence. The students were Lewis Baer and Jacob Horowitz; both
were Jews.

Jewish students constituted a small percentage of the class of 1920,
slightly less than 7 percent of about 25 out of a total enrollment of 375.
Like the class as a whole, the Jews made up a miniature spectrum,
ranging from the sons of German international banking families and
department store magnates to the offspring of New Haven grocers and
plumbers. To different degrees, the Jewish student experienced discrimi-
nation, but the form of anti-Semitism existing at Yale in those years
cannot be easily described. The wealthy German Jews who have remained loyal to Yale come near to denying that it existed. And they have
plenty of evidence that they were accepted. Richard Gimbel, for example, was a popular member of his class and voted "most original" over
Wilder, Stuart Heminway, and William Clyde De Vane; Walter Hochschild, the son of a prominent industrialist and connected with the well-
known German banking family from Frankfurt, was taken into the Psi
Upsilon fraternity. But no Jew was considered for membership in either
the secret societies or in most of the clubs. Nor were Jews likely to be
invited to the homes of classmates as casually and easily as others. One
Jewish member of the class stated that he was friendly both at Yale and
for the next forty years with the men that Luce called the elite. "Those
men were cordial to me when I was an undergraduate; later, Brit Had-

den came to me for money when he and Harry Luce were starting *Time;* and I had many lunches with Harry Davison. But, of course, I never got to know any of those fellows socially." He added this forthrightly, *senza rancore,* as befitted the head of a $900-million industry. Lewis Baer, son of a German-Jewish Saint Louis family, had literary aspirations and cultural interests. Though he was not a member of the Elizabethan Club he came to know Wilder. The association was warm and amiable, and five years later, when Baer became affiliated with a publishing firm, he remembered the gifted Thornton Wilder who, Baer felt certain, was capable of producing a publishable novel.

The Jews at Yale of middle- and lower-middle class origins, particularly those whose parents had migrated to the United States from Eastern Europe, had a more difficult task in adjusting to a campus life that began and ended for them in the classroom. Faced by indifference at best and a barely concealed hostility at worst, a great many of these exotics withdrew from Yale after a year or two, to no one's regret.

Among the Jews who left Yale after a year was Jacob Horowitz of Newark, New Jersey. Shyly interested in theater and in writing, Horowitz lived in the same residence college as Wilder, whom he silently admired from a distance. Horowitz and Wilder never met during the former's short tenure at Yale, though once, as they passed on the narrow winding stone stairs of the residence college, Wilder's elbow accidentally touched Horowitz, as the shy Jewish boy made room for Wilder and his companion. Ten years passed before the two strangers met again—on a train going from Florida to New York. By that time, Wilder was celebrated as the author of a best selling novel; but the poor boy from Newark had metamorphosed also, into the most celebrated theatrical producer in America of his day. His life was to become deeply involved with Wilder's.

That Wilder remained immune to the virus of anti-Semitism at an age when young men are most susceptible is one of the more cheering aspects of his life at Yale. Unfortunately, his encounters with Yale's Jewish students were insufficiently meaningful to break the spell that genteel Christian attitudes and values had cast upon him. The beautiful people in Wilder's Yale experience, both among the faculty and the student body were, for the most part, the well-to-do, of Anglo-Saxon background, brought up in the Protestant church. Flattered and gratified by their qualified acceptance of him, Wilder experienced an infatuation with the Yale–New Haven community, of which he never quite divested himself and which, to some degree and for a certain time, retarded his development as a novelist.

# IV

## The Graduate

*"I guess I was the only writer of my generation who didn't 'go to Paris.'"*
—THORNTON WILDER

By the time Thornton Wilder received his diploma from Yale in June 1920, he had a very clear idea of how he wanted to earn a living. Father Amos was equally clear about Thornton's professional future. Unfortunately, their respective views on the matter did not coincide. Thornton, quite simply, wanted to write for a living. In the Yale yearbook, he listed his intended profession as journalist.

Amos, however, had worked out his own plan for Thornton. Now fifty-six years old, his earning potential limited by age and dwindling opportunities, Amos, the head of a household consisting of four females and an elder son about to enter the ministry, saw in Thornton the only bulwark—and an insubstantial one at that—against poverty and disgrace should he, Amos, be stricken and incapacitated. Not for a moment did Amos entertain the thought that Thornton could, through writing, maintain even himself ("Carving olive pits!" "Carving olive pits!"). Viewing his second son as basically ineffectual, somewhat indolent, and not overly intelligent, Amos reached the conclusion that Thornton could

34

eke out a living in the only way open to failures and incompetents: as a schoolmaster. Having arrived at that decision through his own inexorable logic, Amos communicated it to Thornton who, faced with the vision of his mother and sisters facing starvation, bowed to Necessity and accepted his Lot.

It was also decided that Thornton would spend a year abroad, not on a traditional grand tour, which would have been prohibitively expensive, but as a resident visitor at the American Academy in Rome, an establishment principally concerned with archaeology and classical languages. It was Amos's expectation that in a year at the academy Thornton would learn Italian, improve his Latin, and by wielding a pickax and participating in the archaeological digging, reinforce his understanding and appreciation of Rome's ancient past. In addition to these educational advantages, there was also the indisputable cachet of a year's study abroad, important to an aspirant for a position in a quality preparatory school.

Wilder was to say in later years, "I guess I was the only one of my generation of writers who did not 'go to Paris.'" His statement comes close to being literally true: During the 1920s, following the lead of the century's most celebrated expatriates—Henry James, Edith Wharton, Gertrude Stein, Ezra Pound, T. S. Eliot, and symbolically the archetype expatriate, James Joyce—virtually every American writer of consequence begged or borrowed his boat passage to Paris. Americans living in Paris between the end of World War I and 1925 included Margaret Anderson, Sherwood Anderson, Djuna Barnes, Kay Boyle, Louis Bromfield, Morley Callaghan, Robert Coates, Malcolm Cowley, John Dos Passos, William Faulkner, Scott Fitzgerald, Janet Flanner, Ernest Hemingway, Eugene Jolas, Robert McAlmon, Gertrude Stein, Alice Toklas, Glenway Wescott, and William Carlos Williams. The Paris experience was, to be sure, of greater importance for some than it was for others, but Paris made its impact upon all—if least upon Faulkner then most upon Hemingway. The city and its galaxies of writers, painters, critics, and aficionados left a mark upon American literature of the 1920s that is unique in the annals of cultural history. Wilder was not ultimately to escape the impact of Paris, but the effect was indirect, and it came long after he had passed through the initial stage of his development.

The exact nature of the Paris impact would be difficult to characterize and it is hard to define precisely what the American artists were seeking in an alien civilization. But, very broadly, we can recognize that Paris provided the Americans with raw experience that they could transmute into some form of expression and also with the courage and insights that made possible new and original forms of art. The Americans in Paris had the feeling, as Robert McAlmon described it, of "being geniuses together;" these men and women were impelled to exert their greatest efforts because of the immediate response they provided one another and because they were aware of what other workers were doing. At the very time that Sinclair Lewis had emerged in America and England as the foremost luminary in fiction, someone shouted him down in a Paris cafe (where he was drunkenly asserting his superiority to Flaubert) with the cry: "Sit down, you're just another best seller."

Even Faulkner, still unknown and very much out of things during the months that he was unsuccessfully trying to write in Paris, took heart from being able to observe (from a distance) James Joyce and his circle of friends refreshing themselves at the Trianon.

Rome in 1920 offered no such intellectual ferment; American intellectuals who could afford the trip made pilgrimages to view Rome's ruins and Renaissance palazzi; but these visitors did not form clusters or colonies of writers and painters. So provincial was Rome in 1920–21 that Wilder, attending a gathering at the home of Adolpho de Bosis, was not told that one of the guests with whom he spoke was in fact a well-known poet and man of letters. Twenty-eight years later, Wilder visited Ezra Pound at St. Elizabeth's Hospital for the Insane in Washington, Wilder assuming he was meeting the poet for the first time; but Pound reminded him of their previous meeting in Rome, in 1921.

The American Academy, which provided both housing and class-rooms for its fellows and resident visitors, was situated across the Tiber in what, in those days, was considered the country. Wilder attended classes and accompanied academy fellows on their archaeological explorations in the area. He learned Italian and, what was even more important, developed his lifelong infatuation for Vergil, classical Rome, and the ancient world. The Italians fascinated him, warmed his soul, and quickened his spirit. Like every Anglo-Saxon before him pursuing his Wanderjahre, he found his congealed reserve and stiff restraint melting in Roman surroundings.

His friends were, for the most part, the bright and eager young American men and women who were fellows at the academy. But he did become acquainted with a number of Europeans, among them Prince Dimitri Mirsky, nephew of the academy's assistant librarian, Colonel de Daehn. Prince Mirsky was a figure out of Tolstoi; Wilder was to describe him as "self-effacing, very correct and sartorially elegant." Later on, Mirsky achieved an international reputation for his *History of Russian Literature*.

Another interesting young man whom Wilder first met at that time was Lauro de Bosis, the son of Adolpho, an Italian married to an American whose salon Wilder frequented. The young de Bosis was a poet and a translator of Sophocles; he greatly impressed Wilder, not only with his poetic gifts which were of a certain magnitude, but with his fierce and intense spirit. De Bosis was awarded, in due course, the rights to translate *The Bridge of San Luis Rey*, and his later life has been memorialized by Glenway Wescott in *Images of Truth*. De Bosis came to the United States, became sympathetically associated with Ruth Draper, was encouraged by Bernard Shaw to fight against the Fascist regime, and died a hero's death. Over a quarter of a century after their first meeting in Rome, Wilder dedicated *The Ides of March* (1948) to Edward Sheldon and de Bosis:

> Roman poet, who lost his life marshalling a resistance against the absolute power of Mussolini: his aircraft pursued by those of the Duce plunged into the Tyrrhenian Sea . . .

During Christmas week of 1920, Wilder had an adventitious encounter with Henry Luce and William Dwight Whitney at the Hotel Excelsior, where the two, because of the cold at their pension, had taken refuge. At the time, Whitney and Luce were on vacation from their year at Oxford and welcomed Wilder's cordial invitation to be shown Rome's monuments and treasures. More important, from Luce's point of view, Wilder invited them to a New Year's Eve dance at the academy. There Luce met his future bride, Lila Hotz, a student at a nearby finishing school; the two married in 1923.

But the real importance of Rome lay not in the friendships he formed at the academy, nor in the encounters with visitors from home. The Rome experience provided him with much of the raw material out of which slowly and painstakingly he began his *Memoirs of a Roman Student*. In 1920, Rome was artistically considerably more than the thousand actual miles from Paris; and where Paris might have stifled or overwhelmed the twenty-three-year-old Wilder, Rome seems to have provided him with the ideal soil for his subsequent development.

For one thing, this was Pirandello's city and Wilder was on hand for the premiere of *Sei Personaggi in Cerca d'Autore*. Now Wilder, in addition to his three-minute plays (which were essentially literary exercises) during his undergraduate years, had written a full-scale play in four acts: *The Trumpet Shall Sound*. Published one act at a time in the October, November, December, and January issues of the *Yale Literary Magazine*, 1919–20, the play displays few of the characteristics that, even ten years later, would become associated with Wilder, the experimental playwright. But while it was not avant-garde, the play did represent a reaction against two religious melodramas popular during Wilder's adolescence, Jerome K. Jerome's *The Passing of the Third Floor Back* and Charles Rann Kennedy's *A Servant in the House*. In *The Trumpet Shall*

*Sound,* Wilder comments on what to him were the earlier plays' simple-minded blasphemy in both form and content (Jesus appeared as a character in both). Considering that Thornton composed his play while still an undergraduate in between geology laboratory reports and assignments in intermediate French composition, *The Trumpet Shall Sound* is a remarkable achievement. Much of the dialogue has a fresh authentic ring (which Eugene O'Neill in the very same year was not able to achieve in his Pulitzer prize winner, *Beyond the Horizon*). The strong central situation, involving an illiterate young woman of intelligence and passion who hopelessly and fatally involves herself with an unworthy man, was both so persuasively credible and so unhackneyed that Boleslavsky could produce the play in New York at a time when Wilder was still an obscure writer.

But *The Trumpet Shall Sound* was constructed along conventional lines, and it was conventional structure that Wilder came to recognize as a block to his fulfillment as a dramatist. And so it was Rome that in bringing him face to face with Pirandello's masterwork, *Six Characters in Search of an Author,* provided the key enabling Wilder to escape the conventions that would otherwise have confined his great gifts as a dramatist.

Rome's impact, however, was to be seen more immediately in Wilder's fiction than in his dramatic composition. The difference between New Haven and Rome, between high-minded Puritanism and worldly Catholicism, between New England manners and Italian ritual, between common sense practicality and emotional prodigality—all these differences fascinated and absorbed Wilder as he sought to get them down on paper. Like Henry James a half century earlier, Wilder was overjoyed to discover a society, which despite revolutions and political upheavals, continued to indulge itself in an aristocracy—a thin stratum of the population who still took seriously their feelings, their sensibilities, and their pleasures.

For Rome was a city where the past, like a vaporous mist, hung heavily over everything. Wilder, at this stage of his life, had no great desire to confront the present or the future. For the time being, the past suited him. From it, for the next ten years, he would choose colors and textures and weave them into his slightly bizarre, ironical tapestries.

The present, however, hurled itself upon Wilder's Roman consciousness when on a late spring day he received a cable from home: HAVE JOB FOR YOU TEACHING AT LAWRENCEVILLE LEARN FRENCH LOVE PAPA

Lawrenceville, a select boarding school near Princeton, New Jersey, had been in a decline until several months before, when it had installed a new headmaster, Mather Abbott. If anyone was the prototype for the concept of muscular Christianity, Abbott was such a man. A Canadian with an Oxford degree in classics, "The Bott"—as he is still apprehensively referred to in the Lawrenceville compound, though he has been long dead—was maniacally committed to athletics and high scholarship. Before his appointment to the headmastership in 1919, he had taught at Groton and served as Yale's coach of crew and as professor of Latin.

Abbott had agreed to accept Wilder on his faculty at Amos's behest. The senior Wilder and Abbott held a common vision of life. The two men agreed that Thornton would make an effective teacher, even though he was lacking in athletic proficiency and was coming to the school with a minimal preparation in French; certainly he was committed to both Christian ideals and the liberal and associated arts. If Abbott remembered Thornton at Yale as one of the literary-arty set who inevitably establish themselves at even the best universities, he may have calculated that Lawrenceville might be a better school for the kind of polish and cultivation that young Wilder displayed. At least the parents would think so.

Upon receiving the news of his appointment, Thornton sped to Paris, not to join the growing band of expatriates in the Montparnasse district, but to acquire as quickly as possible whatever fluency in French he could achieve in the few months before he returned to America. He took a room at the Hôtel d'Orléans in the Rue Jacob where another American student residing there remembered him years later as

> a charming slender lithe youth darting about seemingly on the points of his toes . . . I still have a copy of "Ma Mere l'Oie" which he gave me. We must have been playing it at the piano. He pointed to the first two measures and said, "that is what is the matter with the French". . . . One of our friends said, he's like a little bird.

Thus, Thornton did not favorably impress Headmaster Abbott when he reported for duty in September 1921. Still, he remained at Lawrenceville for seven years, with interruptions, and rose to the position of Master of Davis House in the process.

At the center of the Lawrenceville campus are several red buildings arranged around an oval. Davis House, however, to which Wilder was assigned as assistant master, was a frame building half a mile away from the main campus. Housing second through fourth form boys, that is to say boys ranging in age from thirteen to seventeen, Davis was the only residence building not close to the center of things. Socially, as well as geographically, Wilder was outside the mainstream of Lawrenceville life. Abbott rode the young man hard; he was held accountable if the boys' grades lagged behind those in other houses, or if there were infractions of discipline. Nor did Wilder conceal, at least from his few intimates, his intense dislike of Abbott whom he regarded as "brutal and impetuous." Years later, Wilder revenged himself on the headmaster, characterizing Abbott in the novel *The Eighth Day*.

To Amos's pleased astonishment and to Abbott's, Wilder showed an unexpected vein of iron in dealing with his charges and in maintaining good classroom discipline. Despite apprehensions in certain quarters, he also displayed all the requisite competence for teaching French. He had a natural aptitude for languages; that, combined with his summer in Paris and a flair for mimicry, provided him with a good accent and a capacity to produce results in the classroom. Moreover, now that he was earning a livelihood from the French language, his interest in the literature of France quickened and intensified. His growing acquaintance with Mme. de Sévigné, Saint-Simon, Merimée, and Proust, among others, were to have profound effects upon his subsequent achievements.

He grew accustomed to life at a boarding school. Teaching elementary French to young adolescents, while it was not exhilarating, was not as irksome as teaching English composition. The boys at Davis House were restless but not unmanageable. Only occasionally did they succeed in upsetting the amiable Mr. Wilder; once, for example, one or two of the boys conspired to subscribe to the mildly risqué *Police Gazette;* addressed to a nonexistent resident of Davis House, the journal began making a regular appearance. Wilder called the boys together to express his horrified displeasure.

Social life at the school was limited. Many of the faculty were married; others who were bachelors—bachelors who conformed to Abbott's standards—maintained a certain reserve toward Wilder; that he spoke rapidly, compulsively so, in a voice that was high pitched, rather than booming and deliberate, somewhat estranged them. But Wilder, who was indefatigably congenial, maintained pleasant relations with everyone. If he was not greatly admired by the faculty, nor even drawn deeply into the life of the school, neither did he make enemies, and no one worked against him. Eventually, he acquired a friend or two.

Five days and three evenings of his week were taken up with school duties, in the classroom or at Davis House. But there were always the few hours every day just before and after midnight when the last French exercise, having been indignantly marked up with red crayon, was read, and Wilder could turn to his own notebooks. Sometimes he composed another of the three-minute plays he had first begun writing in Berkeley; other times he worked on his *Memoirs of a Roman Student*.

Busy as he was teaching, Wilder wrote comparatively little. Still, he was not entirely unpublished during his Lawrenceville years. The September 1922 issue of a little magazine called *The Double Dealer* is a collector's item. Its contributors included the Black writer Jean Toomer;

the poet Oscar Williams; the novelist Margaret Widdemar; an emerging critic, Edmund Wilson; and Wilder. The Wilder piece, a single-page excerpt from his *Memoirs of a Roman Student*, was his first published work since he had left Yale and the *Yale Literary Magazine*.* A year and a half later, a short story of Wilder's came out in the February 1924 issue of the magazine *S4N*. Entitled "A Diary: First and Last Entry," it is the last short story Wilder ever submitted for publication in a commercial periodical.

In 1924, through the intercession of drama critic Stark Young (whom Wilder met on shipboard during one of the summers that he escorted one young student or another to Europe, this being his only means of getting to Europe in those years), Wilder was invited to call upon Edith Isaacs, editor of *Theater Arts Monthly*. He brought with him his schoolboy notebooks containing the *Memoirs of a Roman Student*, from which he read aloud, acting out all the characters of the narrative. Greatly impressed, Mrs. Isaacs became helpful to Wilder in several ways: she recommended him for a scholarship at the MacDowell Colony where, in 1924, he spent the first of several summers; in addition, since the *Theater Arts* drama critic, John Mason Brown, was to be in Europe during the first several weeks after the new year of 1925, Mrs. Isaacs commissioned Wilder to review the fifteen or so plays opening in New York after Christmas. As a consequence, the March 1925 issue of *Theater Arts Monthly* has, for its lead article, "The Turn of the Year," a professional, authoritative, witty, hard-headed, and perceptive account of new plays by the unknown French master of Lawrenceville. While we cannot know for certain what Headmaster Abbott's reaction was to Wilder's appearance in a periodical of international réclame, there is reason to believe he would have preferred that the assistant master of Davis House spend fewer nights in New York—time that could be more profitably given over to the service of the academy.

At about the same time that Wilder appeared in *Theater Arts*, his classmate from Yale, Lewis Baer, who had left the publishing firm of Alfred Knopf to become a partner of the newly formed A. & C. Boni, wrote to ask if Wilder did not perhaps have a publishable book in progress. Wilder submitted some portions of *Memoirs of a Roman Student* to Baer who, in turn, showed them to his senior partner, Albert Boni.

In 1925, Boni was still in his early thirties and already had an extraordinary record of achievement behind him. As owner of the Washington Square Book Shop which he had opened with his brother Charles in 1913, he was one of the founders of The Theater Guild; known then

---

* *The Double Dealer* was also the first magazine to publish writings by William Faulkner (1922). Also in 1922, it published Hemingway's first poem.

as the Washington Square Players, the group was begun in 1914 by some
members of the Liberal Club that occupied quarters in a MacDougall
Street brownstone in Greenwich Village next to Boni's store. The first
production, an impromptu performance of Lord Dunsany's *The Glittering Gate*—selected because there were several copies of the play on Boni's
shelves—was given in Boni's bookstore. Later, Boni sold the bookstore,
and went into partnership with Horace Liveright, an itinerant business-
man. Liveright was intrigued by Boni's idea of publishing inexpensive
reprint editions in a series to be called the Modern Library. But in
addition to launching this series of classics, Boni and Liveright sought
newer writers and the firm turned out to be one of the most spectacular
publishing houses of the post–World War I decade. Authors on the list
included Dreiser, E. E. Cummings, James Joyce, T. S. Eliot, and Leon
Trotski; in addition, the firm launched the first books of Eugene O'Neill,
Ernest Hemingway, and William Faulkner.

Very soon, Boni found Liveright impossible to work with, and he
dissolved the partnership, again joining forces with his brother Charles to
establish the firm of A. & C. Boni in 1923. Their most notable authors
included Proust (whom Boni acquired through his uncle, Thomas
Seltzer), D. H. Lawrence, and Colette.

Boni, obviously, was an unusual figure in the publishing world; he
was the head of a book company with a feeling for good writing, and,
although the concern was not destined to become a financial success, it
left its mark upon American literary history. In the completed parts of
*Memoirs of a Roman Student,* Boni recognized the work of a new talent,
with style, authority, and tone. It was the kind of work that Boni liked to
gamble on, a *cosmopolitan* work. He instructed Wilder to continue
writing and assured him that a contract would be forthcoming.

Boni's unequivocal encouragement brought Wilder face to face with
a dilemma. If he remained at Lawrenceville during the academic year
1925–26, his energies would be mainly given over to the school and his
progress on *Memoirs* would drag along as it had for over four years. He
made inquiries of one of his colleagues who had enrolled for graduate
study at Princeton and thereby discovered that the solution to his problem lay in his becoming a graduate student. By enrolling for a master of
arts degree in French at Princeton, an enterprise that required no great
expenditure of effort, he could appease both his father and Abbott, and
he would have won the freedom to bring the *Memoirs* to a conclusion
and possibly start something new.

Wilder's stratagem almost didn't work: Upon receiving Wilder's
undergraduate transcript from Yale and discovering that he was offering
nothing more than second year college French, the chairman of the
Princeton French department approved the application only with reluc-

tance. Had he had any inkling that Wilder was more interested in finding time for writing—and in English!—than he was in studying French, his misgivings would surely have been transformed into a rejection.

In the summer of 1925, to earn money against the parlous year ahead, Wilder took employment at Ira Williams's tutoring camp at Lake Sunapee, New Hampshire, an establishment principally serving Lawrenceville boys who were prepping for their college boards. Not far from the camp, living in a large house on the lake, was a young Jewish matron from Cedarhurst, Long Island. Amy (Weil) Wertheimer, the wife of a Wall Street broker and the mother of two small girls, was a tall, striking, dark-haired woman, some five or six years older than Wilder. When Wilder met Amy he found reflected in her dark eyes interest, sympathy, understanding, and intelligence. He recognized that despite her cultivation and sound education there was nothing of the bluestocking about her, that her response to him was that of warmth and spontaneous admiration, qualities wholly lacking in the self-conscious, prim decorousness that he associated with the Gentile ladies of New Haven.

In the relationship that grew out of their first meeting, one would like to conjure up echoes of Young Werther and Lotte; but while there were some surface similarities, the two couples provide no real basis for comparison. For, if Wilder harbored adulterous thoughts (which is doubtful), he expressed none. He found in Amy a confidante-friend, a correspondent, a responsive listener to his work in progress.

What is noteworthy and relevant about Wilder's friendship with Amy Wertheimer, coming as it did in his twenty-ninth year and on the eve, so to speak, of his rise to fame, is that such a friendship was necessary and important to him. Despite the surface amiability which his years at college and at Lawrenceville had enabled him to polish to a fine sheen, Wilder's sense of isolation and detachment from the life around him had persisted. He could articulate his deeper feelings only in conversations with and letters to the deeply concerned woman who was profoundly stirred by the younger man's need.

This is not to say that Wilder used Mrs Wertheimer as a repository for all the gloom and melancholy of his nature; on the contrary, his letters to her almost boyishly catalogued his enthusiasm, his private games, his writing projects, his day-to-day routines, and his hour-by-hour schedules. But he was not constrained from revealing his self-doubts, his melancholy, his uncertainties. Soul-baring did not come easily for Wilder and his disclosures to Amy Wertheimer, while they were neither scandalous nor unconventional, represented a breach in the tight-lipped reserve of New England, where to confess a headache was bad manners. Wilder's outpouring of feeling to Amy coincided with the last stage of his not very youthful youth. When he ceased making her his confidante—less than two years after their first meeting—he had left his youth behind him and, instead, had abruptly become a personage.

In the fall of 1925, Wilder began his graduate work at Princeton. The experience was a blessed relief after four years of teaching French to adolescents. He enjoyed being in the company of men instead of boys, of being a student instead of a teacher. He practiced swimming and took up boxing and handball. He received visitors at Princeton, took them on tours of the campus, and gave them afternoon tea. He entered into a correspondence with a subdeb, Rosemary Ames, who invited him to a dance at the Vanderbilt Hotel in New York. (Debutante dances had not been a part of his undergraduate life at Yale.) In addition, again thanks to the helpful Mrs. Isaacs, he was in touch with Richard Boleslavsky, director of the American Laboratory Theater, who accepted a play of Wilder's entitled *Geraldine de Gray,* but, a year later, produced instead *The Trumpet Shall Sound.*

That fall also, Albert Boni came to Princeton; *Memoirs of a Roman Student,* which in a few months would be published as *The Cabala,* was, by November, close to completion and Boni tendered Wilder a firm contract. The royalty terms were standard: ten and twelve and a half percent on the first and second 5,000 copies sold, fifteen percent thereafter; but Wilder, wholly inexperienced in such matters, privately felt that the terms were less generous than they in fact were. Boni was a man brusque of manner; he had no intimations that Wilder required reassurance that he was being treated like most authors. Not only did Boni fail to explain to Wilder that he would be receiving standard royalties, but Wilder's reservations about his fairness were further aggravated when someone in the firm offered to increase the advertising allotment for *The Cabala* if Wilder would give up a matching amount in royalties—a proposal that Wilder rejected.*

But other clouds formed in Wilder's consciousness. He found himself experiencing difficulties in bringing the work to a conclusion. One section of the novel had to do with the faith of a fanatically religious, aristocratic French spinster in confrontation with the steel-like intelligence of a disillusioned and world-weary prince of the church; and Wilder experienced difficulty with it, particularly since he was now working against a deadline. He was dismayed to discover that he lacked the discipline of the professional writer who routinely covered a certain number of pages a day. The experience was Wilder's first acute case of writer's block, a malady which for the next forty years would intermittently recur.

* Albert Boni, forty years later, denied that he had authorized anyone to make such an offer. But, obviously, someone did, planting in Wilder a potent seed of resentment.

Even as the writing of the novel drew to a conclusion, Wilder fell into a deeper depression. He had just nursed another graduate-student friend through a nervous breakdown, and other pressures—preparation for classroom recitations, anxiety about the reception of the novel, the sustaining of his genial persona, and a complex of social commitments—all combined to upset him to the extent that he became obsessed with the notion of simply running away from Princeton. The small space at home that enclosed his cot loomed large in his thinking as a refuge and retreat.

But by Christmas, 1925, he had finished the novel and things in general were looking up. Boleslavsky had accepted a second play and Wilder was hoping that sales from the publication of *The Cabala* would make possible a second year away from Lawrenceville and the writing of another novel. *The Cabala* appeared promptly in April; and on May first, the reviews began to come out.

*The Cabala* was accorded a generally favorable reception. In New York, London, and Australia, the reviewers were uniformly impressed by the prose style. The reviewer in the *New York Times Book Review* stated that the work marked "the debut of a new American stylist . . . a significant literary event because Mr. Wilder is the first of the post-war crop of American writers to consider prose as something more than a medium of expression." But having praised the style and summarized the content, the reviewers were at something of a loss as to what else to say. The characters were well drawn, the episodes were interesting, and yet . . . and yet. . . . There was a vague, unformulated dissatisfaction in their reactions to the book which the reviewers could not wholly conceal.

The problem lay in a certain doubt on the author's part about the nature of the book. Certainly, *The Cabala* had the look of a novel and what appeared to be the standard ingredients—a young man from America arriving for the first time in one of Europe's great capitals, undergoing a series of adventures, and finally leaving, having matured through the experience—in other words, a *Bildungsroman*. Yet, despite these novelistic elements, the book was not, properly speaking, a novel at all.

We recall that Wilder's working title for his work-in-progress was *Memoirs of a Roman Student*—fictional memoirs, to be sure, and memoirs intended to serve as a framework for a series of stories having as their common background Rome and its environs. Wilder had begun the work long before Boni offered to publish it; it was the prospect of publication, presumably, that decided Wilder on recasting the work into the form of a novel. Thus, the simple change of title from *Memoirs of a Roman*

*Student* to *The Cabala* signals a change of emphasis which was to be of near fatal consequence to the book.

The work is in five parts. Part I, called "First Encounters," begins with a train ride from Naples to Rome in which the Narrator, accompanied by another American—a handsome, but bookish, young archaeologist named James Blair—arrives in Rome to begin a year of study. Blair introduces him into the society of several powerful Roman residents—except for an old Cardinal, they are all older women—known in Rome as the Cabala. "They've each got one thing, some great gift, and that binds them together." The nature of their gift is not always clear—apart from their money and position. The leading members of the Cabala are a wealthy American spinster, Miss Grier, a devotée of baroque music; Alix, Princess d'Espoli, a charming and attractive young matron, unhappily married; Mlle. de Morfontaine, a very rich and devout Catholic spinster; Mme. Bernstein, heir to a German banking fortune; the Duchess d'Aquilanera, matriarch of a distinguished Italian family and mother of sixteen-year-old Marcantonio, spoiled and reckless; and the old and wise Cardinal Vaini. The first book ends, after the narrator's first meeting with the Cabala, with a visit he and Blair pay to a dying poet in an apartment looking on the Spanish Steps. The episode—which the reader recognizes as a re-creation of the last days of John Keats—is not integrated into the remainder of *The Cabala*.

Book II, "Marcantonio," finds the narrator, named Samuele by the Cabala, commissioned by the various members of the group to befriend and reform the errant Marcantonio—lest his impending marriage be threatened by scandal arising from his sexual exploits. At first, reluctant to attempt the boy's reform, Samuele is persuaded by the irresistible Alix. After spending some days at the country villa of the Aquilanera household, Samuele's New England eloquence and Puritan passion help him convince the boy of his sinful follies. Overcome by this sense of sin, Marcantonio accepts the older man's judgment; but tempted by his older half sister, the boy commits incest and then kills himself. The section essentially deals with a collision of two cultures. In the most memorable sentence in the book, Samuele reflects upon the Cardinal's observation: *"We are in the world,"* thinking to himself, "How clear that makes all Italy, all Europe. Never try to do anything against the bent of human nature. I came from a colony guided by exactly the opposite principle. . . ."

If Samuele has any haunting sense of failure, of guilt or responsibility for the boy's death, he never says so. The next part, Book III, "Alix,"—the most fully realized episode of the entire work—is an account of the hopeless infatuation of the Princess d'Espoli for James Blair. Samuele's role becomes that of observer and confidant of the mismatched

pair. The pervasive ironic detachment of the first two books is diminished; the narrator (and therefore the reader) becomes more involved in
the Proustian narrative of a boorish young Adonis unworthy of the love
offered by a woman whose charm, beauty, and wit have earned her the
adoration of everyone except the object of her heart's desire.

Book IV, entitled "Astrée-Luce and the Cardinal" was the section
Wilder found most difficult to write, and it shows. Marie Astrée-Luce de
Morfontaine is a simple-minded single woman of great wealth, with an
idée fixe: to restore the Bourbons to the throne and to establish the
principle of the Divine Right of Kings as Church dogma. Wilder attempts a comic irony that cannot be sustained. Eventually Astrée-Luce,
in a conversation with the Cardinal, has intimations that she is a foolish
woman, and hysterically (and ineptly) she attempts to shoot the old
man. Filled with consternation and regret, the Cardinal decides to return
to China, the scene of his great triumphs; but he dies at sea en route.

In the final book called "Dusk of the Gods," Samuele returns to the
center of the stage. He discovers that he is the historian of gods who are
dying, that he is Mercury, and that his destiny lies—as he is informed by
the shade of Vergil—in the new world and in a new city. ("Seek out some
city that is young. The secret is to make a city, not to rest in it.") And
aware of the sad Vergilian music that sings of the *lacrimae rerum,*
Samuele sails away from Italy bound for his destiny in the New World.

What Wilder produced was a work in which the parts were generally
superior to the whole. The work's principal failure lies in the narrator,
Samuele. It is he, rather than the Cabala, who gives the work its unity—
as the original title made clear. In the opening pages, he is an observant
young man, of good family, with well-developed taste for music and the
arts, who can appreciate good brocade and antique furniture, and can be
admitted into the charmed circle of rich and influential Roman ladies
whose concerns are not the concerns of the Italy of 1920. But Samuele
does not emerge as the protagonist of the work; he turns out, rather, to be
an ineffectual, sentimental blundering prig, adored by all of the Cabala
because, despite his New World origins, his sensibilities—like Miss
Grier's—match the Cabala's in their exquisiteness. Even though Vergil
pronounces his blessings upon Samuele, the reader cannot.

Like Lambert Strether in Henry James's novel *The Ambassadors,*
Samuele functions as the work's focus of consciousness, but unlike
Strether, it is impossible to care about him. Since Wilder deals with
Samuele neither ironically nor sympathetically, in the end, we don't care
what becomes of him. A number of people reading *The Cabala* took for
granted that Wilder was giving an account of his life in Rome, that the
work was an autobiographical novel. Wilder himself has pointed out that
he did not frequent such rarefied company during his year at the acad-

emy and the Cabala, as such, were the construction of his imaginative faculties.

But Wilder knew—as how could he not—that such groups of women exist in every city, even in New Haven. They scheme, they make arrangements, they use their power to advance X or Y at the same time that they frustrate the ambitions of A or B. As Ruth Draper's Mrs. Hubert Clancy in "The Italian Lesson" says in her bloodthirsty, cultivated voice: "How did she get on the committee anyway! Well, we'll simply have to get rid of her. We'll have to devise a plan. Yes. . . ."

Wilder also knew about the Marcantonios of the world. He had been given charge of more than one adolescent, taken him off to Europe, with the parents' fervent hope that somehow the ascetic and high-minded Thornton Wilder would change the boy's bad habits to others, less repulsive and distressing.

The sad infatuation of Alix for James Blair correlates with an event in Wilder's year in Rome. According to his own testimony, he did undergo an emotional *crise* of a certain magnitude. And although he only once or twice confided the explicit details of his unhappy experience in Rome, he has more than once alluded to its existence and even that it had been transmuted into a section of *The Cabala*. If an event in Wilder's personal life is, indeed, the genesis of the unhappy love affair between Alix and James Blair, it is the last time that Wilder gave direct literary expression to a profound and personal hurt.

Whatever may be the weaknesses of *The Cabala* in its construction, it is a work, nonetheless, of consequence and durability. Today, even more than in its own time, its style is an oasis in a desert of bad writing. Ernest Hemingway was one of the early readers of *The Cabala,* and when he met Wilder, before either of them had achieved reputations, he was generous in revealing his admiration and respect. For *The Cabala* is not an example of "fine" writing with a liberal sprinkling of ornate comparisons and sententious observations. As in his earliest student writing, Wilder achieved a clarity which manifested urbanity, irony, and wit; he was always gracious, almost flattering, but never patronizing toward his reader. He treats his audience, not as though they were members of the Cabala, but as persons who would know how to behave in the Cabala's presence.

His first novel, then, was a blueprint of his early strengths and weaknesses. Intelligence and an extraordinary command of the language combined with certain inadequacies: a failure, for example, to come to terms in his writing with mature, male sexuality; an acceptance of the mystique that surrounds persons of great wealth and distinguished lineage; a preoccupation with the irrelevancies (for postwar America, at any rate) of Christian faith and morals, matters on which Wilder was at that time of his life tremulously uncertain. Moreover, though he wrote surpassingly well, the style was not of its time; it looked back to George Moore. Nor had he found his setting; the milieu of *The Cabala* is reminiscent of the world of Henry James and Edith Wharton. Wilder had not, indeed, gone to Paris. His not having gone there brought him early success; but his missing the connections and stimulus of Paris ultimately brought about a critical reaction which was to take him to the very threshold of oblivion as a writer.

# V

## The Bridge to Fame
and Fortune

*". . . for months I had no time to think solidly and happily."*
—WILDER

It was while he was still attending graduate school at Princeton and while *The Cabala* was being set in type that Wilder began the composition of *The Bridge of San Luis Rey,* in the winter 1925–26. How he happened to choose eighteenth-century Peru as the setting for his second novel—a time and place in which he had neither a particular interest nor an academic competence—was largely a fortunate accident. Wilder was to say, some thirty years later, that the idea for the novel came to him as he walked across the Princeton campus, a recollection that provides a minor, but relevant, clue. Wilder was studying French literature; in the course of his reading, he encountered a short play by Prosper Merimée, "Le Carosse du Saint Sacrement." The play, which Wilder had seen during its revival in New York by Jacques Copeau's company in 1919 (later transformed into a film by Jean Renoir in the 1950s), focuses upon the tempestuous love affair between Don Andres de Ribera, viceroy of Peru, and La Perichole, a low-born actress. What caught Wilder's attention was the circumstance that the leading character was an actress of such genius that her fame had survived the passage of two centuries.

Wilder's obsession with ladies of the stage had its roots in his adolescence. He himself had played the role of Miss Prism in *The Importance of Being Earnest* while he was a schoolboy. ("The evils of typecasting!" Alexander Woollcott exclaimed when Wilder confided this choice tidbit of autobiography.) As more conventional boys idolized baseball players, the young Wilder worshiped leading ladies, and the fascination persisted throughout his life. Over the years, he formed friendships or associations (or crushes) with Mary Pickford, Katharine Cornell, Lynn Fontanne, Helen Hayes, Vivien Leigh, and Irene Worth. His relationship with Ruth Gordon, in whom he thought there was a great potential—but whom he was finally to describe as "all mannerisms"—endured, despite several mutual disservices, for over forty years.

In the novel, the bridge called San Luis Rey collapses, causing the death of five innocent persons, an old woman, a middle-aged man, a youth, a teenage girl, and a child. Wilder pietistically attributed this framework to the New Testament (Luke 13:4):

> Or those eighteen, upon whom the tower in Siloam fell and slew them, think ye that they were sinners above all men that dwelt in Jerusalem?

But it is safe to assume that Voltaire's observations on the earthquake in Lisbon also provided Wilder with a philosophical basis for *The Bridge,* just as Mme. de Sévigné, whose ghost haunted the pages of the emerging Marcel Proust, provided the model for *The Bridge*'s Marquesa de Montemayor.

While these complicated narrative threads of the new novel were forming patterns in Wilder's mind, he succeeded in finishing up his master of arts degree at Princeton in June 1926. Although he was the author of a novel that a few weeks before, had been favorably reviewed in the *New York Times,* he left Princeton virtually penniless, uncertain how he would find the means of writing *The Bridge.* After another session at the MacDowell Colony, working in isolation, he succeeded in completing a sizable portion of the first draft of *The Bridge.* But the MacDowell Colony, though it provided food and quarters, awarded no cash; by August, Wilder was back at the Lake Sunapee Camp tutoring Lawrenceville boys. After accompanying his mother for a week in Atlantic City, he sailed for Europe in September—his expenses paid by the parents of Andy Townsend, a teenage boy who was in Wilder's charge for the next four months.

Once in Paris, Wilder did not, despite the publication of *The Cabala,* penetrate the American enclave, few of whose members had ever heard of him. However, he *did* make the acquaintance of Sylvia Beach, the proprietress of the famous bookstore Shakespeare & Co. and publisher of Joyce's *Ulysses*. One of Miss Beach's patrons was Ernest Hemingway, a familiar figure in Paris, but little known in the United States. Wilder met Hemingway after the completion, but before the publication, of *The Sun Also Rises* which was being set in type by Scribner's. Both men, in other words, had published, but neither had *arrived*.

Their meeting came about just at the time when Hemingway's relationship with Gertrude Stein had deteriorated. These two had first become acquainted in 1922, when Hemingway had only recently been married. Aged twenty-three, he was at his physical peak, while the forty-eight-year-old woman was shapeless, short, and unadorned. A sexual liaison between the two, considering the physical contrast, would seem not only improbable but, to anyone contemplating the possibility, grotesque. Notwithstanding, the long and intimate conversations between them stimulated Hemingway, not only intellectually but affectionally. In a letter to W. G. Rogers, he reiterates that he loved her and, as he characteristically phrased it, asserts that he wanted to fuck her, that she was aware of his desire, and (he implies) that only the omnipresent Alice blocked the consummation of their desire for one another.

Even allowing for Hemingway's tendency toward overstatement in such matters, it seems entirely likely that his sexual response to Gertrude Stein was a powerful one. In the first three years of their friendship, that is between 1922 and 1925, she was hospitable, informative, intensely interested in his thinking, his writing, his personal welfare, and his education. The sound of her voice was a caress and the quality of her mind embraced him. Hemingway must have felt that by achieving sexual union with her he could somehow incorporate into himself her wisdom, her power, her self-assurance, and the magic that bound the lost generation to her. Then, in 1925, their friendship underwent a modification for reasons that no one can agree upon. And although the association continued for several years thereafter, the intimacy and the warmth appreciably diminished. Thus, by the time that Wilder and Hemingway met in Paris in 1926, there was a kind of void in Hemingway's life. For a time at least, it appeared that Hemingway looked to Wilder as the figure who could play the role which, a few months before, Gertrude Stein had abandoned.

The relationship that developed between the two aspirants was amicable and respectful, though anyone knowing the two would have expected them to have been antagonistic, or at least indifferent to each other. Except that they were both writers, they seemed to have little in common. (And Hemingway didn't necessarily like writers; he and Glenway Wescott, for example, despised one another.) The physical discrepancy between Wilder and Hemingway symbolized their personality differences: Hemingway towered over Wilder's spare five-foot-eight-inch frame, the bigger man's masculine good looks contrasting with Wilder's bespectacled, ascetic, schoolmaster's features. Hemingway's manner was relaxed and confident, where Wilder's was tense, hurried, and nervous. Hemingway's familiarity with guns, and boxing gloves, and fishing rods could be inferred from the languorous grace of his carriage, while Wilder's emphatic gestures, graceless and theatrical, were those of a man who could not manipulate anything more complicated than a piece of chalk. Both men were, of course, stylists, the two most accomplished of their generation—a fact that each understood about the other. But the big man had developed in the autodidact tradition of Mark Twain and Stephen Crane, the other in the academic belletristic tradition of George Moore and a host of French models. Capable of appreciating the other's kind of art, both were securely confident that there was no possibility of influence, no basis for comparison. Their position as artists aside, Wilder respected Hemingway's athleticism, his bravado, his openness, his professionalism; and Hemingway, in turn, admired Wilder's cultivation, his taste, his wit, and his detachment. It was as though the two men were wholly complementary: One was born to confide, the other to be a confidant.

What neither understood at the outset of their friendship was that they were both actors, role players. Both had learned to conceal the unamiable and unappealing elements of their natures: abnormal vulnerability to slights; deep-seated fears about their masculinity; perverse commitments to the irrational values of their genteel, Puritan parents. Conscious of their differences, but unconsciously aware of their similarities, the two young men wanted somehow to establish an intimate friendship. But intimacy is built upon truth, and neither had the courage to strip himself naked before the other. Hemingway tried; like a big friendly dog radiating nothing but good will, he was toward Wilder affectionate, respectful, and open. He confessed, if confessed is the word, the details of his uncontrollable libido: That copulation with his wife in the morning and at night was not enough to satisfy him; that deprived of her company in the afternoon, he was forced to relieve himself in solitary fashion. Whether Hemingway expected to elicit comparable details from Wilder—as he did from the unfortunate Scott Fitzgerald, whose secret fears about the size of his penis Hemingway wrote down and ultimately incorporated into a manuscript published as *A Moveable Feast*—can only be guessed. But Wilder, whose years as a master at Lawrenceville accustomed him to receiving unsought confidences and confessions though he made none, maintained a certain reserve; he was, after all, more than two years Hemingway's senior. His restraint seemed somehow justified by his fuller maturity, his familiarity with worlds to which Hemingway was a stranger. Both men were at home in their respective roles of confessor and confesser, both men felt that somehow they had something to give one another; but just what it was they never really found out. For the next several years, Hemingway would importune Wilder to join him on fishing trips or camping expeditions where, away from everything and everyone, they could talk, talk, talk. These invitations Wilder ignored. He would find a retreat, a quiet village, and urge Hemingway to join him there for work, work, work. These invitations Hemingway ignored. Drawn as the two were to one another, the truth served as a threat to each other's awareness, and no real friendship ever developed. But neither did enmity. Wilder never received the tip of the lash in anything that Hemingway ever published; and Wilder never spoke or wrote disparagingly of Hemingway.

Only once did their association transcend that of two hearty brothers-in-arms: in 1929, Wilder, confronted by the necessity of bringing to a successful conclusion his third novel, fell into a suicidal depression, not unlike the one which he had undergone during his year at Princeton. Confiding his dark melancholy to Hemingway, Wilder quickly regretted his lapse and followed up the first letter with a second in which he described his suicidal fantasies as a passing dramatization of a mood.

Wilder was touring Europe during the fall of 1926 in the company of Andy Townsend, a bored adolescent whose indifference to Wilder and the glories of Europe's treasures was matched by Wilder's exasperation and contempt. But curiously enough, Wilder's annoyance with Andy served to stimulate his creative faculties so that he was continually pouring into his notebook ideas, anecdotes, and developments for *The Bridge*. Relieved in midwinter of his responsibility for Andy, Wilder visited Hemingway in Paris before settling down for several weeks at Juan-les-Pins on the Riviera in a pension inhabited by a brood of Rhodes scholars on vacation from Oxford. The company of these energetic and conscientious scholar-athletes was a source of pleasure to Wilder; but they were also a poignant reminder to him that these young men represented what his father would have liked him to become. Fascinated as he was by the Côte d'Azur, once the Rhodes scholars left Wilder decided to return home. Aided by royalties and small advances from Albert Boni, Wilder spent the later winter and spring of 1927 first in New Haven and then at Briarcliff Lodge, near New York City. That summer he was back at the MacDowell Colony and was able to submit the completed manuscript to Boni by July; thereupon he once again took up his tutoring chores at Lake Sunapee, a depressing preparation for the resumption of his teaching duties.

Returning to Lawrenceville in the fall term of 1927, Wilder was confronted by the sudden death of the master of Davis House, and Headmaster Abbott decided to place Wilder the prodigal in charge. Despite the additional responsibilities and duties of the post, Wilder accepted; his achieving the position of housemaster at the age of thirty, in his father's eyes and in the eyes of most of his colleagues, represented a greater accomplishment than his being the author of a novel called *The Cabala*. More important, the post at Lawrenceville was Wilder's only assurance of a regular and dependable income. His application for a Guggenheim Fellowship had been rejected; income from writing was negligible. Even if the new novel were received as favorably as the first, the combined royalties, he felt, could not sustain him. (Boni, too, worried about the new book, adding illustrations in order to justify the price of two and a half dollars for so slender—195 pages—a volume.) So, despite his promotion—after a two-year reprieve and two novels completed—Wilder found himself back where he had started; he resumed his teaching duties with a heavy heart, feeling sickish and headachy. His indefatigable good health and generally high spirits quite deserted him. After Paris, the miracles of the European cities, and the beautiful people of the French Riviera, this sudden resumption of drill in the irregular verbs of French, this life engulfed by ingenuous adolescents, this chitchat with Lawrenceville faculty (and their wives) all brought to Wilder a sickness nigh unto death. Literally.

His physical condition worsened. His energy, his intensity, and his ebullience deserted him. His predecessor in the master's job had died quite suddenly and Wilder, too, in the first few weeks of the term, seemed to be wasting away. By October, a diagnosis was made: appendicitis. In 1927, abdominal surgery was still a grave matter. But the operation was performed and it was a success. By mid-November the convalescent was back at Davis House. And quietly published in England and the United States was the convalescent's second novel, celebrating, it would seem, his escape from the grave.

The review in the Sunday book section of the *New York Herald Tribune* on November 20, 1927, was Wilder's first intimation that his fragile bark, after plowing for ten years through shoals and shallows and depressing estuaries was finally emerging into open waters—that he might, indeed, attain the status of (professional) writer. For the *Herald Tribune* critic, the highly respected Isabel Patterson, called *The Bridge of San Luis Rey* a little masterpiece, deemed its ironies worthy of Anatole France, and welcomed Wilder as a distinguished author joining the ranks of American writers. Moreover, the news of Arnold Bennett's London encomium of November 24 reached New York before the month's end, and a brisk demand for the book began building up.

Wilder decided that he could afford to conclude his convalescence—

during the Christmas recess—at Miami Beach, Florida, where, as it turned out, America's most influential litterateur, William Lyon Phelps, family friend, neighbor, and former teacher, was also taking *his* Christmas break.

Wilder's visit to Miami Beach, fortuitously coinciding with Professor Phelps's, provided the former student and teacher with the opportunity for discussing *The Bridge of San Luis Rey* at length and in depth. Wilder disclosed to the devoutly Presbyterian Mr. Phelps the connection between the collapse of the bridge of San Luis Rey and the fall of the tower of Siloam; it is doubtful that Wilder suggested parallels between the collapse of the bridge and the Lisbon earthquake. The atheist Voltaire was not one of Mr. Phelps's enthusiasms.

During this visit to Miami Beach, there began one of those zany episodes for which the 1920s is famous; this episode was ultimately to land Wilder on the front page of the *New York Times,* for several days running. Wilder, several years before, had consciously and deliberately overcome his adolescent shyness and diffidence. Having built up his self-confidence, he would habitually seek people out, introduce himself, and win them over. Meeting strangers was usually no more than a game he played to satisfy his curiosity or to prove to himself, again and again, the power of his capably developed geniality. During this Christmas season of 1927 Miami Beach's most illustrious visitor was none other than the heavyweight boxing champion of the world, James Joseph (Gene) Tunney. Having twice defeated Jack Dempsey and having conducted himself with extraordinary decorum, modesty, and civility, the personable Gene Tunney had achieved an eminence that no other living athlete enjoyed. In dethroning Dempsey—"the savage ruthless Manassa Mauler"—Tunney had shocked and antagonized the professional sports world; but Tunney's modest good looks, his creditable manners, his devotion to the eternal verities, and his shy admission that he was addicted to the practice of serious reading, all combined to endear him to the general American public.

The magnitude of Tunney's celebrity can best be grasped by noting that George Bernard Shaw, whose capacity for self-exploitation easily exceeded that of any other writer before or since his time, established with Tunney a friendship so cordial that it produced an extensive correspondence between them, letters now housed in the Cornell University library. The only other Americans, in fact, who were as well known as Tunney in 1927—though slightly less accessible—were President Calvin Coolidge and Charles Lindbergh.

Wilder, whose own celebrity had barely begun, paid his respects to the world's outstanding athlete by sending a note to Tunney's hotel.

After consulting with Billy Powell, a public relations man, Tunney responded to Wilder's note with an invitation to breakfast. Learning that Wilder was interested in serious music, Tunney arranged that the waiter serving breakfast be a singer, so that midway through their scrambled eggs Wilder's ears were assailed by a rendition of the toreador song. But Tunney was genuinely charmed by Wilder who, unlike other men of letters in Tunney's acquaintance, was still a young man—about the same age as Tunney, in fact. Having discovered a good companion, Tunney invited Wilder to play some golf, an invitation Wilder had to decline, never having held a club in his hands. But he suggested Professor Phelps as a golfing partner for Tunney, an arrangement that was entirely agreeable both to the boxer and to Yale's distinguished man of letters. After a lunch Wilder arranged for Tunney and Phelps, the two golfers adjourned to the golf links, with Wilder accompanying them on their rounds. One consequence of the meeting was that Phelps invited Tunney to address his Yale students on the subject of Shakespeare, an author for whom Tunney had already publicly expressed considerable admiration.

But Tunney's invitation to lecture at Yale was not the only consequence of Wilder's impulsive note; this unlikely pair became friends, and their friendship was celebrated by columnists, cartoonists, chroniclers, and editorial writers in the months ahead.

An even more fateful encounter that week still lay ahead for Wilder. On the train returning north, he was joined by a darkly handsome young man of dynamic presence who introduced himself as a former classmate at Yale. This was Jacob Horowitz, the shy adolescent from Newark, who at the university had admired and envied Wilder from afar. Young Horowitz had metamorphosed into Jed Harris, New York's leading producer-director, reputed to have earned five million dollars in his brief career on Broadway. Although both men had resided in the same residence-college at Yale, Wilder had no recollection of ever having set eyes on Harris before, though he was very much aware of the living legend that Harris had already become. For the remainder of the journey, the two men fascinated one another; before they separated Wilder promised Harris that he would have first refusal whenever Wilder completed a play which he considered worthy of Harris's talents. Ten years later, Wilder kept his word.

Nineteen twenty-eight was perhaps the happiest year of Wilder's life; certainly it was his most bewildering and exhilarating time. On January 8, A. & C. Boni's half-page advertisement of *The Bridge*, featuring Wilder's handsome portrait, appeared in the Sunday book sections. The quoted tributes from William Lyon Phelps, Arnold Bennett, Henry

Seidel Canby, Burton Rascoe, and Harry Hansen emphasized the magnitude of the book's success. Within days of his return from Florida, Wilder began feeling the consequences and responsibilities of celebrity. At Davis House—in addition to his chores as housemaster and classroom teacher—he found himself devoting hours each day to correspondence. Letters from relatives, family friends, classmates, his own intimates and acquaintances, and from complete strangers and well-wishers piled up; to each correspondent Wilder wrote a courteous and thoughtful reply. A man from Brooklyn had gone through *The Bridge* correcting Wilder's diction and usage; Wilder conscientiously answered each quibble with patience and tact. A woman from Pennsylvania received, in answer to her inquiry, a detailed summary of the origins and sources of *The Bridge:* not only did Wilder discuss the Siloam tower in the New Testament, Madame de Sévigné as prototype of the Marquesa, and Merimée's play, but he volunteered the information that he had himself been born a twin and that his aunt, who was chairman of the International Committee of the Y.M.C.A. had inspired his concept of the Abbess.

He began leaving the Lawrenceville enclave with greater frequency. One evening his Yale classmate Lewis Baer, on behalf of A. & C. Boni, tendered him a cocktail party at an apartment on lower Fifth Avenue. The guests included novelist Manuel Komroff and his wife; public relations specialist Edward Bernays—a nephew of Sigmund Freud; the Brooks Atkinsons; and the left-wing artist and caricaturist Art Young. It was on this occasion, when Young was associating the guests with various trees, that he compared Wilder to an ironwood tree, which evoked from Wilder the response: "I wish my father could hear you say that; he'd identify me with the weeping willow."

Also, early in 1928, Wilder attended a weekend party at the Scott Fitzgeralds' in Wilmington, Delaware. The guests included the book editor of the *New Republic* Edmund Wilson, who was favorably impressed by Wilder. Expecting the author of *The Bridge of San Luis Rey* to be a languorous aesthete, Wilson was delighted with Wilder's hearty, boisterous manner which, combined with a basic seriousness and common sense, rendered him excellent company. The two men began a correspondence that was to continue for nearly thirty years, its high point being the series of letters they exchanged about their respective close readings of Joyce's *Finnegans Wake*.

Wilder's invitation to Wilmington was the outcome of a congratulatory letter that Fitzgerald sent shortly after the new year. Though only a year older than Wilder, Fitzgerald had been an established writer for nearly a decade and had already published his masterpiece, *The Great Gatsby*. In his January 12 response to Fitzgerald's letter, Wilder mentioned knowing Hemingway and implied that he knew Glenway Wescott.* These four writers were born in the five-year period between 1896 and 1901 (Fitzgerald, at thirty-one, being the senior). Wilder characterized them in his letter as protesting against the whole cardboard generation that preceded them, from Wharton through Cabell and Anderson to Sinclair Lewis.

This was only the first of a number of lengthy letters that Wilder wrote to the Fitzgeralds. His visit seems to have overwhelmed him; his extravagant praise of Fitzgerald's wife and daughter was almost fulsome, not at all typical of most of Wilder's correspondence which has been, with a few notable exceptions, controlled, discreet, and classically severe. But apart from the overzealous tributes to Zelda's and Scottie's beauty, Wilder's comments were witty and delightfully malicious. He described the tantrums of Elinor Wylie, whose fury stemmed from the reviewers who found her latest novel merely "great and beautiful." According to Wilder, she resented the laurels of the dead. Wilder added that he himself found a number of living persons overrated; among them he listed John Barrymore, Utrillo, James Branch Cabell, and Stravinsky.

At about the time that he met the Fitzgeralds, Wilder renewed and reinforced a casual acquaintance with another practicing critic whom he had met a year before at one of Mrs. Timmy Coward's Sunday breakfasts. This was Alexander Woollcott, whose influence in the literary marketplace was monumentally out of proportion to his talents, either as a critic or as an essayist. Lacking the profound insights of Samuel Johnson, but possessing something of Johnson's worldliness, as well as the Doctor's ready wit and authoritative bulk, Woollcott occupied a firm place in the center of kitsch for over a decade. He was the pivot of the Hotel Algonquin's celebrated Round Table, along with George S. Kaufman, Dorothy Parker, and Franklin Pierce Adams. His views on books and related topics were broadcast weekly on a cross-country radio network. His articles and critical pieces appeared in the *New York Times,* the *New Yorker,* and the *Atlantic,* as well as in less prestigious, but more widely circulated, periodicals. Though he was testy and obstreperous (a side of him portrayed by George Kaufman in *The Man Who Came to Dinner*), his personality captivated the literate, if not the literary, segment of the American public. He was, in time, to become sufficiently friendly with Franklin and Eleanor Roosevelt to be their houseguest for days on end at the White House. Of all the new alliances Wilder formed at this time, only the friendship with Woollcott (and shortly thereafter his association

---

* There is some mystery here. Wescott, in his memoir of Wilder, included in *Images of Truth,* states that he met Wilder during the winter of 1928–29, an assertion Wescott held to in a conversation with this writer. A letter written by Wilder to Wescott which, unfortunately is not dated, tends to support Mr. Wescott's memory of their first meeting; but it is not impossible for them to have met in the winter of 1927–28 since Wilder was staying at Juan-les-Pins—no great distance from Wescott's residence in Villefranche.

with the actress Ruth Gordon) flourished and endured. While the demands which the two men of letters imposed upon one another were inconsiderable, the benefits accruing from their mutuality were far from negligible. In the beginning, however, each was mainly aware of no more than the other's celebrity.

Wilder's celebrity grew apace. The May issue of *McCall's*, in the column "Book of the Month" written by Laurence Stallings, coauthor of *What Price Glory?*, favorably compared Wilder to Anatole France and James Branch Cabell and described *The Bridge* as "the philosophical novel brought to perfection." Accompanying the panegyric was a dashing drawing of Wilder labeling him "the most talked-of young writer in America." Another periodical with a vast nationwide circulation, *The Literary Digest*, devoted two pages of its April 21 issue to excerpts from English and American critiques of *The Bridge* and to an analysis of Wilder's rise to fame. This is to say that after having comprehensively reviewed *The Bridge*, the magazines and newspapers were now reviewing its author and his phenomenal success.

By late spring, Wilder had made a number of decisions. Most important, he had decided to resign from Lawrenceville, although he was reluctant to say so publicly; in interviews given to the press as late as June he said he would return to Lawrenceville after a year's leave. Wilder was always reluctant to burn his bridges behind him; supporting Thornton's basic caution, his father, back in New Haven, regarded the success of *The Bridge* as a temporary aberration on the part of the critics and the public. Amos apparently could not believe that Thornton was anything more than an ineffectual amateur momentarily enjoying a stroke of good fortune. Wilder, obviously, was not entirely convinced that the situation was otherwise; all the same, his hopes for the future were high. Wilder planned to spend the summer of 1928 in an English country house with his mother and his sisters Isabel and Janet as his companions. He wrote Woollcott that he was trying to rent Henry James's house at Rye and invited Woollcott to join this ménage, an opportunity that Woollcott chose to let slip through his fingers. And, as it turned out, fortunately for the modest and unpretentious image that Wilder presented to the world, he did not get the James house and settled for a place in Surrey, with no ghosts of former tenants whose literary gifts might be invidiously compared to those of its summer occupant.

His uncertainty that he could indefinitely support himself and, when the time came, his parents also, influenced Wilder to accept a cross-country lecture tour (to begin a year hence, in the spring of 1929) —although his commitment was not to lecturing. With the image of his father's forensic gifts, Wilder could offer nothing beyond readings of his three-minute plays. The time would come, however, when he would attempt something beyond that. But at thirty-one, a public audience terrorized him.

The last major decision Wilder reached in the glorious springtime of his career concerned the composition of his next novel; having correctly gauged the taste of his reading public, Wilder chose to construct a work of fiction on a play by the Roman Dramatist Publius Terentius Afer (185–159 B.C.), who was admired for his subtle delineation of character and elegance of style. The play was Terence's *Andria* (the woman of Andros), a picture of life on an Aegean island, which Wilder was planning to transform into a study of "the pagan world shot through with intimations of Christianity." The project was one that Wilder could happily confide to Professor Phelps, whose benediction on so wholesome and Christian a theme was a foregone conclusion. Wilder appeared to cling to his Christian faith despite his exposure to the paganism attending his Roman sojourn and the more recent liberating ambience of Paris and the French Riviera—and this is not entirely surprising. Thornton's home officially and in fact, was with his parents, in a household where the Christian ideal remained all-pervasive and where the younger son was not permitted, when the ground was damp, to leave the house without wearing his rubbers. Writing to Henry B. Fuller, an elderly Chicago novelist, Wilder described the germinating *Woman of Andros* as "full of inner hopes and dejections and finally a religious book. I can do no other." What Wilder did not and could not know was that the book he was planning would nearly ruin his career as a man of letters and alter his image as a serious American artist.

But in the spring of 1928—aside from a contemptuous review of *The Bridge* in the March issue of *transition* (mercifully published and circulated only in Paris)—there was nothing to becloud the golden skies of Wilder's existence. At Lawrenceville, the students stood in awe of him; those on the faculty who were well disposed toward him congratulated him while the few who disliked him took little pains to disguise their astonished envy. His royalty checks from Boni were now for thousands of dollars; by July he had received—in the years of low income taxes— $47,000. He was meeting all kinds of distinguished people. Woollcott presented him to that queen of sophisticates, Dorothy Parker, who later allowed that she liked him—a morsel of intelligence which Wilder wrote Woollcott struck him dumb, presumably with joy. News clippings drifting in from as far afield as Perth, Australia, and Uganda, East Africa, confirmed, that he had conquered not only America, but the British Empire as well.

In addition, Wilder had become a bona fide celebrity; that is to say, he was becoming known to people who had neither read his books, nor the reviews of his books. His name was appearing not only in intellectual and genteel magazines and in the book columns and feature sections of newspapers, but by late spring and early summer he was turning up on the sports pages and finally on the front pages of, among other journals, the *New York Times*. The modest and unworldly schoolmaster, had, it appeared, stumbled into a situation which no press agent, however ingenious, could have deliberately planned and executed. The situation was this: Wilder, though he had in the months since his trip to Miami Beach established a number of new relationships, such as those with Fitzgerald, Edmund Wilson, and Woollcott, also continued to maintain contact with Gene Tunney. It is doubtful that his motives were self-serving; he was, after all, a writer and he was fascinated by Tunney, the foremost athlete in the world, the fighter who, from the most vicious and most vulgar commercial sports enterprise the country had thus far devised, had emerged physically, morally, and psychologically clean, modest, gentle, and attractive. In his first novel, Wilder had written about the ancient gods living in contemporary Rome; he was understandably curious to observe, at close hand, the man whom a combination of native ability, circumstance, and the world press had fashioned into a contemporary god. His initial impulse in sending the note to Tunney's hotel in Miami Beach may have had its origin in little more than the desire to have a story to fascinate his young charges in Davis House, when the Christmas vacation ended. But the whole matter was not to end that simply.

Tunney, like many men inadequately educated because of poverty and other circumstances having nothing to do with their native intelligence, responded with immediacy to imaginative literature and to the men who produced it. He was greatly impressed by Maugham's *Of Human Bondage*, which he finished reading on the eve of his second bout with Dempsey. He had established a friendship with Shaw; now he found the bouncy, ebullient Thornton Wilder eminently good company; moreover, Wilder was a professional teacher and Tunney, already planning his retirement from the ring, felt that Wilder could further his instruction in the civilized arts. Indeed, in contrast to the coarse men who necessarily formed a part of a prizefighter's entourage and offended Tunney's sensibilities, Wilder's companionship was a draught of fresh air. By June of 1928, Wilder's casual encounter with Tunney had developed into a friendship. The two met in New Haven, in New York, and in the Adirondack mountains where Tunney was training for his final prizefight—against the New Zealand heavyweight, Tom Heeney.

Maintaining simultaneous ties with Woollcott and Tunney required of Wilder considerable delicacy. Woollcott and his Round Table companions regarded Tunney's intellectual pretensions as absurd and they would bait Wilder into reconstructing his conversations with Tunney. After a session at the Algonquin, Wilder would be uneasy for days on end, fearful that his reports to Woollcott would be leaked to the gossip columns. Meetings with the Woollcott set were something of a trial for Wilder; he found himself weighing his words, unable to compete in the tone of measured malice that dominated conversational exchanges on Forty-fourth Street. His interludes with Tunney were less demanding; Tunney offered his friendship—unlike the athletes of Wilder's undergraduate years at Yale—without patronizing reservations. Thus, despite Woollcott's jibes and the newspaper columnists' sneers (a number of sports writers preferred Dempsey's savage arrogance to Tunney's earnest gentility), Wilder developed the association with Tunney to a degree of intimacy that enabled them to plan a trip through Europe after the Heeney bout and prior to Tunney's wedding in Rome.

News of their projected "walking tour" of Europe achieved for Wilder a kind of exposure that not even *The Bridge* could achieve for him. The prizefighter's announcement of his plans to tour Europe with the young novelist had the same kind of impact that President Coolidge might have achieved if he had announced that after *his* retirement he was joining Helen Keller to open a gift shop in Albuquerque. The *New York Times* and newspapers all over America displayed considerable breathlessness over the Tunney-Wilder tour, and British papers such as the *London Daily Chronicle* and the *London Daily Mail* heralded the imminent arrival of the two celebrities with uncontained excitement. The *Daily Mail*'s account, inaccurate and garbled, contains some typical hyperbole.

> Not since Sinclair Lewis, has an American author captured English attention as Thornton Wilder, author of *The Cabala* and *The Bridge of San Luis Rey*. Moreover he is soon to visit London . . . a very retiring young man and is still professor of French at . . . Lawrenceville . . . a close friend of champion Gene Tunney who may come to Europe as Wilder's travelling companion. It was the idea of the writer and the pugilist to settle down for a quiet English summer at Rye. They have been trying to lease the house there which the late Henry James occupied for many years. . . .

In actuality, Wilder, together with his mother and sisters Isabel and Janet, sailed for England on July 7, 1928, and upon arrival settled down in a house in Surrey. Tunney defeated Heeney on July 26 and forthwith retired from the ring and sailed for Ireland on August 16. About ten days later, Tunney and Wilder met and proceeded to make final plans for their tour of the continent; whenever the two men emerged out of doors, English villagers and members of the working press followed them. Wilder had already established that he was the source of good copy; before Tunney's arrival he gave the following account to a representative of the *Yorkshire Evening Press:*

> I first met Tunney in Florida and we soon became fast friends. . . .
> Not long ago I was in a canoe with him on a lake in the Adirondacks
> and our craft overturned. Tunney had a copy of Hazlitt's essays. It
> went down with him but when he came up again that book was
> between his teeth. . . . Tunney is a modest retiring fellow who
> prefers to be left alone with his reading, which is his great passion in
> life. . . .

Tunney arranged for Wilder to call upon Mr. and Mrs. Bernard
Shaw; at his behest Mrs. Shaw arranged a lunch. The meeting between
Shaw and Wilder was not a success; the two men disliked each other on
sight. A few months later while visiting Glenway Wescott in the south of
France, Wilder told his American contemporary that Shaw seemed "smug
and affected in his patriarchal role," a judgment identical with that
reached by Leon Edel a few years later. (Much later, in his 1956 *Paris
Review* interview, Wilder disparaged Shaw's whole approach to literature.) Subsequent to the unfortunate lunch, when Tunney revisited the
Shaws, he learned that while Mrs. Shaw loved *The Bridge,* Shaw did not.
And when Tunney realized that Shaw did not like Wilder personally, he
said that Shaw had not really got to know him well enough. Shaw's
response was, "I think we understood him very well indeed."

At the end of August, Wilder and Tunney agreed that after Wilder
had made appropriate travel arrangements for his mother's and Janet's
return to the United States, the two men would meet in Paris, the
starting point of their journey. So their redoubtable adventure began, in
actuality, in the French capital. On the third of September, Tunney and
his entourage checked into the newly opened Hotel George V—along
with such distinguished fellow guests as Zelda and Scott Fitzgerald.
Wilder arrived shortly afterward, but characteristically headed for a
more modest hostelry on the left bank. For Tunney, a highlight of the
Paris visit was a gathering Wilder arranged with a number of his friends.
Converging at the Ritz Bar were Wilder and Tunney; three friends of
Tunney's (Leonard Hanna, Billy Powell, and Bill McGeehan) ; Robert
Maynard Hutchins, then dean of the Yale Law School, and his wife
Maude; and Scott Fitzgerald. Maude Hutchins, a young, strikingly attractive brunette, was not then (and as it turned out subsequently never
was) content to be a mere adjunct to her handsome, brilliant husband.
Intelligent, perceptive, and gifted, she wanted more than anything to be
taken very seriously. Scott Fitzgerald, who, ironically, was married to a
woman of similar disposition, utterly failed to assess Mrs. Hutchins
properly. Not entirely sober, Fitzgerald was able to see in her only a good-
looking young bride; to his eyes, her attractive femininity was all that
distinguished her in this gathering of successful and celebrated men. He
chose to flatter, fulsomely and patronizingly, this very self-contained

woman, and after a few minutes, she proceeded to lay him out with a number of well-chosen phrases. Tunney was so shocked at the spectacle that he left, together with his friends, Hanna and Powell, in a taxi; Hutchins, wholly composed, calmly gathered up his wife and serenely departed. Wilder, in a state of excruciating embarrassment, disappeared while Fitzgerald, unnerved and bewildered, remained at the bar comforted only by sports writer Bill McGeehan.*

A day or two after the unfortuntae incident at the Ritz Bar, on September 12, Wilder sent a note over to the Hotel George V bidding Fitzgerald goodbye, adding reassuringly, "You made a great hit with Gene."† But the budding friendship between Wilder and Fitzgerald did not really survive the unhappy encounter between Fitzgerald and Maude Hutchins. Given the tragic circumstances of Fitzgerald's life, his drinking problem, his wife's breakdown, the imminent drying up of his creative powers, along with Wilder's incapacity to involve himself with troublesome or unconventional situations, there was really no possible future in the relationship between the two writers. Although they were almost the same age, in 1928 Fitzgerald and Wilder were very nearly at opposite ends of their artistic odysseys.

On September 12, Tunney and Wilder left Paris in a comfortable big car provided by Mr. Raymond Graham, of the Graham-Paige Automobile Company, who had arranged that the vehicle be delivered in Paris for Tunney's use. Their first stop was the villa of a wealthy American, Mr. Carruthers Ewing, general counsel of the A & P. Thence they proceeded to Chamounix, the village at the foot of Mont Blanc; ascending by lifts to the snow-filled ledges, the two travelers, in conventional business suits, were photographed with Wilder holding an alpenstock presumably supplied by the photographer. From Chamounix, they proceeded to Arles where Wilder pointed out scenes painted by van Gogh; in nearby Nîmes they attended the bullfights presented in the ancient Roman amphitheater, a dramatic reminder that Provence was once a thriving Roman colony. Arriving in Marseilles, they were sought out by the American consul general who invited them to lunch. Tunney, however, was more interested in seeking out the Italian consul general who could provide him with practical advice and otherwise facilitate his impending wedding in Rome.

---

* This account accords with Tunney's recollection. Maude Hutchins recalls that Fitzgerald left the café, commandeered a taxi, and pursued her through the Paris streets and avenues vainly attempting to placate her whenever his vehicle approached hers.

† A year later, in Paris, Wilder introduced Tunney to Ernest Hemingway. Nearly forty years later, Tunney was to say, with deep feeling, that he was obliged to Wilder for a number of kindnesses, but, above everything else, he "was most appreciative of Wilder's having brought me together with Ernest who became my dear and life-long friend."

Driving on to Naples via Nice, Genoa, and Rome, Tunney was on hand to meet the ship transporting his bride-to-be, Miss Polly Lauder, and her large entourage. The details surrounding the marriage at the Hotel di Russe were reported as exhaustively as though they involved a wedding between crowned heads of state. Several days before the ceremony, Tunney asked Wilder to serve as best man; characteristically, Wilder declined, explaining that someone who had known Tunney longer would be more worthy of the honor. So the best man was Dr. C. S. Weeks, and John McCormack and the Reverend Francis Spellman were among the honored guests at the ceremony. Curiously enough, though he refused at the time to be designated as Tunney's best man, Wilder—having been given the option—restrospectively felt that he had actually served in that capacity. During World War II, he pointed out to a fellow officer the site "where I stood up for Gene Tunney when he was married there."

The "walking tour" of Europe, which was not actually a tour undertaken on foot, but rather a leisurely motorcar journey from Paris to Rome, established Wilder as a full-fledged celebrity. He and Tunney were cartooned and caricatured; the newspapers devoted yards of front-page coverage to the journey; Robert Benchley, the most genial and widely read American satirist, composed a piece called "The Bridge of Don Gene's Nose," which was an imaginary reconstruction of the conversations between Wilder and Tunney on their hike through Europe. Asked nearly forty years later his impression of the trip with Wilder, Tunney responded earnestly that it had been a satisfying experience: "I had a charming companion and saw a part of life with an intelligent teacher." But unlike his warm feeling about Hemingway, Tunney's sense of Wilder—of whom he saw little after the wedding—was that his friend, in having withdrawn, had somehow let him down: their meetings afterward were usually accidental, and Wilder generally failed to answer letters.

One part of Wilder's nature was irrepressibly gregarious and avidly curious. While a graduate student at Princeton he was consistently ignored by a fellow graduate student, a teacher of mathematics named Church who, like himself, was on leave from Lawrenceville. His mind filled with formulas and equations, Church was hardly aware of Wilder, even though they dined in the same hall every day; but Wilder, having decided to gain Church's attention and good will, succeeded. And having done so, Wilder realized—finally—that he and Church had nothing of any importance in common beyond Lawrenceville, that they had little to communicate to one another. The budding friendship quickly withered. Presumably, neither Wilder nor Church (who was to become chairman of the Department of Mathematics at Princeton) ever thought very much about their abortive friendship. But a third graduate student—also from Lawrenceville—remembered for the remainder of his life Wilder's inexplicable demarche.

Not long after Tunney's marriage, Wilder returned to France, visiting Villefranche and calling upon Glenway Wescott whose novel, *The Grandmothers,* had won the Harper Prize. Wescott recorded in his memoir of Wilder that within minutes of this meeting Wilder was sharing with him confidences and literary insights that one would expect only from a long-standing friend. And when Wilder left, he dispatched a note so cordial and intimate as to suggest to Wescott that a profound literary friendship—like that between Galsworthy and Conrad—had begun. It hadn't. In their relationship, there would come hiatuses of three or four or five years. Wescott never succeeded in nurturing and strengthening the friendship. Finally, in 1962, when Wescott published his recollection of Wilder, an account that was honest, open, and full of respectful praise, Wilder never acknowledged seeing the piece in Wescott's *Images of Truth*; in fact, Wescott seldom heard from Wilder after 1962.

Gene Tunney and Glenway Wescott were notable among the interminable procession of persons in and out of Wilder's life, a great many of whom, like Banquo's ghost, unexpectedly made reappearances. Wilder was acutely aware when a relationship had reached its limit—and it might reach its limit in an hour, a day, a week, or a year. But he was capable of giving more in a few hours to a new-found friend—more interest, more solicitude, and more intimate and privileged information—than one ordinarily receives in a decade. By the late 1920s, he had developed a remarkable capacity, a kind of genius, for inspiring friendships; but he remained, for the most part, characteristically incapable of sustaining them.

After the Tunney-Lauder nuptials in Rome on October 3, 1928, Wilder found himself footloose in Europe with money in his pocket and five months of leisure in his schedule. All was well. *The Bridge,* having received the Pulitzer Prize in May, was being brought out in a deluxe, signed, limited edition, illustrated by Rockwell Kent. Wilder read in the August 8 issue of the *New Republic,* a respectful essay by Edmund Wilson discussing the impact of Proust on Wilder's fiction. Since Boni turned them down, Coward McCann was bringing out an edition of Wilder's three-minute plays, the dramatic exercises he had begun when he was a high school student and had continued to compose for a decade. Entitled *The Angel that Troubled the Waters,* the volume was politely reviewed upon its publication in November. Nothing was troubling Wilder's waters at this point, however, except those two nagging inner voices, one of which was bidding him to get on with *The Woman of*

*Andros* and the other which warned him that it might not be good enough.

He resolved the matter of working on the new novel (after the sojourn in the south of France) by taking his sister Isabel on a trip through central Europe. Visiting the playhouses and opera houses of Berlin and Vienna, they collaborated on an account of what they saw in an article entitled "Playgoing Nights," which was published by Mrs. Isaac's *Theater Arts Monthly* in June 1929.

Wilder's decision to travel with Isabel pointed up the closer link between these two than that which existed among the other Wilder children. Brother Amos, off toiling in the vineyards of theology, was ultimately to marry and raise his own family. Janet, in 1928 still a schoolgirl, was also destined for marriage and a life of her own. Charlotte, who taught at Vassar, became a struggling writer and resident of New York's Greenwich Village; by 1928 she had already firmly separated herself from her parents' home. But Isabel and Thornton continued to make their home with their parents. Wilder made this a de facto situation the following spring when he bought land outside New Haven for a house for his parents, Isabel, Janet, and himself—once and for all. The European tour of Wilder and Isabel, then, symbolized an alliance between them which neither one of them—as it turned out—could ever break. In time, both would complain to friends and relatives about their difficulties. During the thirties, Isabel turned to writing (and published three novels), to thoughts of marriage, and to acquiring some kind of professional or occupational competence—all in vain. Her destiny was to become guardian of the house, first for her parents and finally for Thornton. And she served—with increasing autonomy—as Wilder's secretary and representative during those extended periods when he was away from home. Before she was fifty, Isabel was to develop a partially disabling form of arthritis and various nervous symptoms which she attributed to her onerous position as household organizer-secretary-buffer. And Wilder was to feel alternately guilty and trapped in having permitted his sister's life to become an appendage, a hollow echo, of his own. The last thing in the world he wanted from his sister was her "sacrifice"; but, in time, he realized that an alternative didn't exist. Ultimately, he could express gratitude to Isabel for what she had given up, but he was not gratified by it. Their 1928–29 winter pilgrimage to the playhouses of Berlin and Vienna was a fateful move for both of them; it initiated a collaboration and an association which was to prove for both of them a burden and a relief.

# VI

## Reversal of Fortune

*"I'm sorry I've ever said anything bad about anyone. Now I know how it feels."*—THORNTON WILDER TO STUDENT FRIENDS, 1930.

Wilder and his sister Isabel returned to the United States in February 1929. Sales of *The Bridge* were now close to 300,000 copies, so that Wilder presumably had earned over $100,000; moreover, Albert Boni had sold the motion picture rights for $30,000, half of which was paid to Wilder. Wilder felt that the time had come when he could give his mother something she had never possessed in all her married life; her own home. For several years the Wilders had been renting a frame house at 75 Mansfield Street in New Haven. Now, going north on Whitney Avenue toward the village of Hamden, a New Haven suburb, they found just off Whitney, on a curving road rising into a hilly wooded area and appropriately named Deepwood Drive, a plot of land large enough to provide for a garden, a terrace, and enough privacy so that no adjoining house would look into a house built on the site.

The house they had designed was simple, practical, and unpretentious: a rectangular brown, wooden, shingled structure placed at right angles to the road. On the first floor, at the far end and occupying roughly half of the entire rectangle, was a commodious living room; in addition there was an entrance hall, a dining room, a kitchen, and a small utility room. Beyond the kitchen was a two-car garage. There were a number of cell-like bedrooms on the second floor along with the master chamber which looked out over Deepwood Drive and was to serve as a study and workroom for Wilder. Having selected the site for the house, Wilder turned to his next commitment.

Sixteen states, two provinces of Canada, thirty-six appearances in two months' time—all distances covered by railroad . . . that was the lecture schedule confronting Wilder in March 1929. He traveled as far north as Toronto, as far south as Texas, and as far west as Kansas City. While this was not the same as returning to Lawrenceville, the lecture circuit was certainly as punishing a regimen as teaching. The advantage was that it lasted only two months and that the pay for two months was greater than for a year in the classroom. Wilder's fondness for culture-hungry matrons was put under a strain by the great numbers of them he encountered and by the excessive attention they lavished upon him as members of welcoming committees. When he could finally get away from them and sneak off to the movies, he invoked Mme. de Sévigné's comment: *"Enfin, j'ai vu qu'elles me préparaient les délices d'un adieu."* (At last I perceived that they were readying for me the rites of a grateful farewell.)

Wilder returned from the tour in early May, and he was in New Haven when his friend Robert Hutchins received a telephone call from the University of Chicago offering him the presidency. According to Hutchins's account, Wilder was having dinner with him at the Yale Graduates Club when Hutchins took the call. Hutchins interrupted it to exact from Wilder a promise that he would go to Chicago with Hutchins as the condition of his accepting the offer. Wilder impulsively and enthusiastically agreed, giving his life a new direction and postponing his commitment to the lonely life of a professional writer. When arrangements were completed, it was decided that Wilder would take up his teaching duties in the spring of 1930, that his rank would be visiting lecturer, and that he would offer two courses, one of them a seminar in creative writing.

Why, at this point in his career, free at last from his onerous duties at Lawrenceville, did Wilder undertake a series of lecture tours and, in addition, accept a quarter schedule of teaching at the University of Chicago? With the success of *The Bridge* to his credit, why did he not follow the examples of Hemingway, Faulkner, and Fitzgerald and devote himself exclusively to writing? The answer is somewhat complicated. For one thing, Fitzgerald, Hemingway, and Faulkner were not only novelists, but also established and practiced short-story writers. Short stories, particularly those which could be sold to mass circulation publications, such as the *Saturday Evening Post, Cosmopolitan,* and *Red Book,* were a novelist's bread and butter. And Wilder was not a short-story writer. After 1924, he published only a single short story, which he contributed gratis to a commemorative issue of the *Yale Literary Magazine.* Rightly or wrongly, he felt the form was not suited to his capacities. Another reason Wilder sought regular employment and a salary was the family obligation that pressed hard upon him. He had often been reminded by his father that Amos's choice of the ministry as a profession left Thornton as the family's chief support. And Thornton's new prosperity seemed somehow to have coincided with his father's failure in business. The senior Wilder had given up his position as secretary to Yale-in-China and had assumed an interest in a New Haven newspaper. The paper was the victim of a strike, and it suffered financial stresses that broke Amos Wilder both physically and financially. Thus, Thornton became the sole supporter of his parents and his sisters Isabel and Janet. Janet's education expenses, in 1929, still lay ahead. But regardless of the financial pressures on him, Wilder did not even attempt to meet his obligations through writing. Was this a failure of nerve? To a considerable extent it was. Or to put it another way: Wilder was more prudent than venturesome. Circumstances made him the head of a family and he would never ask anyone else to share the responsibility with him. Moreover, he was the kind of writer—and he was to say this many times, even when his royalties made it no longer relevant—who, if he had to earn money from his pen, couldn't. He knew that for him writing would never be easy, that though sometimes the words flowed, more often they did not.

But still another reason for Wilder's accepting lecture tours and his post at Chicago was the powerful impulse that had revealed itself in him from the time of his adolescence: to mount a platform and *perform.* Performing with the French language, before Lawrenceville students who were not, for the most part, greatly involved with the subject matter, had not been gratifying. But appearing before audiences who voluntarily enrolled or paid admission—that was something else again. Wilder's love of performing was to lead him to many platforms and many stages; it would also lead him to acting in a New York theater, the undisputed leading player of a successful Broadway play. For the next twenty-five years, his public appearances were many and varied. He never became as effective on the platform as his father, of course, but he achieved a wider repertoire and commanded larger audiences. With the advent of television, he could playact before a national audience. And do so very well.

In common with his father, Wilder felt it his duty to instruct, to share his moral vision with the young and unenlightened; he also enjoyed communicating his aesthetic perceptions, his intellectual discoveries, and his whole sense of life. During the next eight months of 1929, Wilder lived the peripatetic existence that characterized his life style for the next forty years.

During the lecture tour, in May, he received a letter from Paris that had the effect of helping him get back to work on *The Woman of Andros.*

Hemingway wrote in effect that it was good to hear from Thornton and that he was pleased to see that as a move toward higher things *Scribner's* illustrated the personal piece about "old Hem" with a photo of Wilder and the late William Lyon Phelps. [Phelps was, of course, very much alive.] He was awfully glad if Thornton liked the book but hated to have him read it in chunks and possibly bowdlerized. . . . [*A Farewell to Arms* was being serialized in *Scribner's* magazine.] He felt the best part wasn't for about two or three more installments and he wanted to know how Wilder liked the Italians in it. He hoped the hell Wilder would really like it. Hemingway and his wife would be back in the fall probably not in New York. . . . Maybe they could get together somewhere. Christ, Hemingway explained, he couldn't write a letter but he wished they could talk. They should see each other somewhere inside of the next six months. . . . All of "us guys" shouldn't be so far apart that they never meet. Hemingway added, he only got rid of shit by talking it.

Hemingway referred to a former student of Wilder's and added that Wilder could send along any ex-pupils he wanted. That he was always at Wilder's service and that he wouldn't send Wilder any former pupils on account of having none, but that he would take it out in telling people that he was a great friend of Wilder's, which had won him the respect of many a citizen. During the fourteen months that they were in America, he observed, he at no time encountered anyone who had read anything of his, but by judicious use of Wilder's name he acquired quite a reputation as a literary gent.

Speaking of *A Farewell to Arms,* he said that he worked like a convict on it for a year—wrote it everywhere—Paris, Key West, Arkansas, K.C., Wyoming—back in Key West, that he drove 17,000 miles in a new Ford and then laid off and fished and shot with Pauline and Dos Passos and old Waldo Pierce. Now he couldn't write a damned thing. To Hemingway it always seemed like that—either working and not speaking to anyone and afraid each day that he'd get out of it and living like a damned monk for it—then a fine time after it's done then hellish depression until he got into it again. Hemingway continued that his father had gone in for shooting himself and leaving a family on his hands to support, adding that with this serialize they'll support for quite a while. He cautioned that if ever Wilder heard that he was dead that Wilder was not to believe a word of it as he would be turning up in black face having changed his name or something to get rid of economic pressure . . . Paris, he added is going to pot with more traffic than New York and with everybody having too much money and its being expensive as hell. He complained that after where they'd been and what they'd seen there was no fun in drinking in a cafe with a lot of hard-faced lesbians and all the little fairies, that when you'd been out day after day on the Caribbean in a small boat with people you like and were black from the sun and never wore shoes or underwear and had champagne in the water butt covered over with a chunk of ice and a wet sack—when you'd dove for the champagne out on the reef where a rum boat had gone aground— where there were flying fish instead of fairies—when with only so long to live why, he asked, come back to cafes and all the little sniveling shit of literary politics.

He asked what the hell does success get you. Money, but he didn't always get that. Success results, he said, in people treating you snottily because they think you must have a swelled head. He might quit the whole business and buy a boat with what dough he could get together and shove off. Then he would have a book every five or ten years or whenever he *had* one and that he wouldn't have to write because someone brought some bloody pressure on him.

On the other hand, he reflected, pressure might be good but he doubted it. He always had plenty of pressure to write without it having to be economic.

He asked Wilder how he was and urged him to write how everything was going. Hemingway added that he wasn't as gloomy as he sounded, that in reality he was damned fit—only in the wrong place—that he would like to be off the coast of Mexico opposite Lower California someplace—Would Wilder like to go on a tough trip sometime before the two of them were both too old, that he had a couple of fine ones figured out.

Hemingway ended by saying that Wilder was a hell of a good writer—better even than they think and urged Wilder not to let "Them" Hurry Him.

This extraordinary letter struck a number of chords in Wilder and reflected many of the thoughts that had been assailing him. Family responsibilities, the not always sweet smell of success, the joy and anguish of writing, the impulse to run away from familiar people and familiar places, economic pressures, critics, and literary politics. And finally there was Hemingway's praise—praise from a fellow writer whom Wilder respected and admired.

During the summer of 1929, Wilder worked hard on *The Woman of Andros* at the MacDowell Colony and at Lake Sunapee Summer School. Then, late in the summer, he fell into a depression which he communicated to Hemingway before sailing for Europe—Thornton was treating his mother to another trip, more extensive than the previous summer's sojourn in England. He saw Hemingway in Paris, bringing Gene Tunney up to Hemingway's apartment on the Left Bank. Seeing friends in England and France lifted Wilder's spirits, though he had a temporary setback in London on October 29, when he saw the Metro-Goldwyn-Mayer production of *The Bridge of San Luis Rey,* an undistinguished and disappointing filming in which Lily Damita starred in the role of La Perichole. He resolved not to sell the motion picture rights of *The Woman of Andros,* now virtually finished—a resolve that he ignored four years later when a successive novel was completed. Back in New Haven in November, he read proof of the portion of *The Woman of Andros* that was already set in type and completed the manuscript before Christmas. After less than two months in New Haven, he set out for California in December via the southern route, stopping off at El Paso and crossing the border into Juarez around New Year's. Arriving in California early in January 1930, he began his second lecture tour at San Diego. He spoke in Los Angeles, Seattle, La Crosse (Wisconsin), Grand Rapids, and Elmira (New York), before his return to the East Coast in mid-February, where he conducted two public debates with the British novelist Hugh Walpole.

Walpole, although only thirteen years older than Wilder, had been an established novelist since 1910. The two men had several qualities in common. Walpole had begun his career as a schoolmaster and had enthusiastically and cheerfully sought out every literary figure of consequence in England, including Thomas Hardy, Virginia Woolf, and Henry James. Walpole liked Wilder and described him with an astonishing acuteness:

> Wilder said some lovely things [during the debates]. Found him a charming companion. He is a real student, loving erudition, culture, quiet backgrounds. In the middle of his kindliness there is a little core of sharp malicious humour. He watches everything.

After the Walpole debates, Wilder resumed his lecture tour, and he was in Morgantown, West Virginia, on Friday, February 21, when *The Woman of Andros* was published. His good fortune seemed to be holding. The first (and most important) reviews appeared two days later in the Sunday book sections of the *New York Times* and the *New York Herald Tribune.* The *Tribune* had given the novel the place of honor on the right hand column of the first page with Wilder's picture occupying the center two columns. The headline over the book's title was WILDER'S THIRD AND BEST. The reviewer was the distinguished author of *Contemporary American Novelists* and editor of the *Cam-*

*bridge History of American Literature,* the redoubtable Carl Van Doren himself. No novel in 1930 could be launched under better auspices. The headline, "Wilder's third and best," paraphrased Van Doren's closing assertion that *The Woman of Andros* was superior to both *The Cabala* and *The Bridge.* The *Times* placed its review (unaccountably unsigned) on page four. But the review and Wilder's picture filled all five columns and most of the length of the page. The headline read:

THORNTON WILDER'S NEW TALE
HAS CLASSIC BEAUTY
In Its Perfection of Form, "The Woman of Andros"
Surpasses His Previous Work

And the closing sentence was virtually identical with Van Doren's judgment. "All things considered, 'The Woman of Andros' is the best book we have had from him." A few days later, writing his review in the publication that he edited, the *Saturday Review of Literature,* Henry Seidel Canby reinforced the *Times*'s and *Tribune*'s judgments by averring that although *The Woman of Andros* "will not be so popular [as *The Bridge*], it will be as much approved." Moreover, Mr. Canby linked Wilder and Hemingway as "the bell wethers of the oncoming generations. They are more alike than they seem. Each has powerful sentiment under the restraint of his form. Each stands mightily for an intense perfection of his expression. Hemingway has only one utterance—of the vernacular—and shapes that with an eloquent simplicity which seems to be the voice of yesterday but actually has some of the accent of all time in it. He is a journalist trying to make art out of intensity. Wilder is a scholar and a moralist in whose ears literature is always murmuring. . . ."

About one thing, at least, Canby was right. The sales of the book, though they were excellent, never approached those of *The Bridge.* Boni ran off an initial printing of 60,000 copies which sold quite rapidly. Then he printed an additional 30,000 copies which did not sell, so that even today in secondhand bookstores of New York mint-fresh copies of *The Woman of Andros* are still obtainable.

But with reviews like those from the high priests of what Dwight Macdonald later labeled Mid-Cult, Wilder's fortunes did not seem to be declining. If *The Woman of Andros* was not a runaway best seller, its sales—for a serious and compressed work of fiction—were impressive and gratifying. Published on the same day and reviewed in the same book section were two novels that did not sell as well. One was John Dos Passos's *The 42nd Parallel*; the other—more fateful for Wilder—was by a thirty-six-year-old left-wing naturalist writer named Irving Granich who, under the pen name of Michael Gold, had just incorporated his ideas about "the proletarian novel" in *Jews Without Money*. In February 1930, the stock market crash was five months old and a great depression was beginning. Given the state of the economy when the books were published, *The 42nd Parallel* and *Jews Without Money*, whose impact would presently be felt, were perhaps a year too early; *The Woman of Andros* was a year too late. And publishing this book was to provide Wilder with the most harrowing and humiliating experience of his lifetime.

In the spring of 1929, however, no clouds were visible on Wilder's horizon. He reached the end of his lecture tour in Oak Park, Illinois, on March 7 and officially began his residency on the campus of the University of Chicago on April 1. Before taking up his teaching duties, Wilder published the following announcement in the university student newspaper: "1. I shall reside in Hitchcock Hall during the Spring Quarter 2. I shall be offering two courses and they will not be snap courses."

One of the two was a humanities survey, a large lecture course in which Wilder spoke on some of the major works in world literature. His other offering was a small seminar, limited to ten, to be devoted to student writing of fiction. Wilder chose the privileged ten on the basis of personal interviews. One student whom he accepted was Harry Thornton Moore, who was to become a well-known figure in the academic world through his exhaustive biography of D. H. Lawrence and through his editorship of the prestigious *Cross Currents* series; Moore applied for admission even though he was still a freshman. He arrived for the interview with a manuscript, which he handed to Wilder, while explaining that it was a novel about a farm boy in Indiana. "Why Indiana?" asked Wilder, and began to read. As he read, he giggled and shuddered over the sheer ineptness of it all. But he accepted Moore. Others in the class included Robert Ardrey, who later became a playwright and the author of successful books with anthropological themes; Lloyd Davidson, a transfer from Harvard; Louis Engel; Hannah Wallen; Frances Stevens; Ruth Ziev; and Dexter Masters, the son of poet Edgar Lee Masters. The class met in the Gothic-style Wieboldt Hall, Room 102, just inside the main entrance. The atmosphere of pointed arches and casement windows served Wilder's purpose. He was unsympathetic to writing that was emotional or extravagant in tone. Having set up a traditional standard, he would ridicule—as he read student writing—in a kindly, but severe, manner anything that did not conform to his classic notions. Moore felt that Wilder's inflexible attitude served most of the students as a good corrective for their stylistic self-indulgences. Meeting the writing students at eleven, after his lecture hour, Wilder would give them a hard time; storming up and down the platform, he would roar with mock rage when he encountered a cliché: "Imagine how fresh and wonderful it was when someone first said, 'Another Indian bit the dust!' " Notwithstanding, no one missed the class because Wilder was—apart from the havoc he wreaked upon their exercises—extremely genial and helpful in all things. He accepted, with disarming enthusiasm, all invitations extended by the writing students, of whom he would say: "Once a student of mine, always." And he thought he meant it. Even after the end of a term, they were free to return to the class when they had a new story to present. Wilder's relationships with students continued for years—as long as the relationship remained student and teacher, as long as there was no real demand for a relationship based on equality.

The Chicago faculty's attitude toward Wilder, especially before he took up residence, was hostile, particularly among the members of the English Department. Chicago's faculty was a distinguished one, and the standards of the university were at least the equal of Harvard's at the time. Hutchins's arrival was received with mixed feelings and his appointment of Wilder was deeply resented. Wilder's academic credentials—for a department of scholars like Chicago's English faculty—were nonexistent. The department included men with international reputations: W. A. Craigie, who before coming to Chicago had completed the definitive dictionary of the English language, *The New English Dictionary* (generally called the *Oxford English Dictionary*); J. M. Manly, the Chaucer scholar; Charles Read Baskervill (Elizabethan drama); G. E. Bentley (Shakespeare); Ronald Crane (eighteenth-century poetry); George Sherburn (Pope); Robert Morss Lovett (literary history); and others. But after a year or two of exposure to Wilder, the department's resentment dissipated. From the beginning, Wilder treated his colleagues with genuine respect, maintaining at all times the air of a modest, good-natured neophyte. In fact, so modest was he that, although the professors came to accept him and like him, they never took him seriously as a member of the department. Over the years his title was transformed from "Lecturer on English" to "Professorial Lecturer." But naming Wilder to a professorship was out of the question.

The cool reception Wilder received from his new colleagues did not greatly trouble him; his successful first quarter with the students at Chicago more than justified, for him, his having accepted the post. Then early in his second quarter, in October 1930, without warning, Wilder was subjected to the most extraordinary and violent critical attack that any American writer had sustained in the twentieth century. The attack did not originate in Chicago, but came via the *New Republic* in New York.

Wilder's assailant was Michael Gold, exponent of the proletarian novel and left-wing critic, whose own *Jews Without Money*, appeared at the same time as *The Woman of Andros*. Gold was a leader of the proletarian school of criticism, standing at the other end of the spectrum from the group called the New Humanism with which Wilder was associated. Both schools have long since mercifully been abandoned and forgotten; but, in 1930, they were not only flourishing, but claimed among their adherents passionate men. Although a large number of American writers at that time were personally committed to left-wing causes, or subscribed to socialist ideologies, few of them—if they were writers of fiction or of poetry—explicitly injected political ideology into their imaginative work. Rather, they served on committees, signed manifestos, or staged protest marches in Boston Common or in Union Square. Although writers like Jack London and Upton Sinclair were openly didactic in their intentions, the emerging generation of left-wing writers, John Dos Passos, Edmund Wilson, and Dorothy Parker, among them, generally avoided explicit political attitudes in their imaginative writing. But two influential writer-critics, Michael Gold and John Howard Lawson, passionately believed that literature should serve humanitarian ends and help bring about social reform through a forceful overthrow of the capitalist system; their judgment of literature was, to a considerable degree, an appraisal of its effectiveness in advocating social justice. One novel that elicited their admiration was Dos Passos's *Manhattan Transfer,* but as Marxist critics they felt that even this book, in its ending, fell short of their ideal because of a lack of "militancy."

Opposed to Marxist critics such as Gold in the United States and Christopher Caudwell in England, were the New Humanists, a group of largely New England conservatives led by Irving Babbitt of Harvard and Paul Elmer More of Princeton. Reinforced to a degree by T. S. Eliot, the school found its leading apostle in Professor Norman Foerster. The New Humanists' aim was to

> Commend to man the study of his own humane tradition, and summon him to take up the racial torch and hand it on—in any case (they) place man's hope not upon what nature, whether within or without, may do for him, but upon his making himself more completely human. (*The Cambridge History of American Literature,* 4:481.)

The New Humanists emphasized the classical restraint they associated with the Greek and Roman tradition, but they also required that a Christian ethic permeate a work of literature. Good literature dealt with a "proportionate standard which consists of the *normally or typically human.*" They preached that unlike the irrational and disturbing works of the romantic writers, or the idealistic excesses of the proletarian writers, or the irrationality of the naturalists, truly humanistic writing embodies "restraint or control" and that it, like religion, "enjoins the virtue of Humility."

While the New Humanists analyzed and defined important elements of some of the great literature of the past, the movement's relevance to the literature of the twentieth century was slight. Actually, Wilder's work was the only contemporary writing of consequence which the humanists could point to as embodying their position. Not having given the matter the deep study that George Santayana gave it,* Wilder had no objection to being included in the New Humanists' camp; in fact, he cheerfully called himself a humanist, with little deep commitment, as some time later he was to regard himself as an existentialist.

The left wing, seeing in the New Humanist movement a threat and a challenge, produced symposia and diatribes against it that identified this predominantly Protestant New England group with the forces of reaction and oppression. It followed that Wilder, chief among contemporary humanist writers, would become the most likely target. Michael Gold launched the attack with his contribution to the fall literary issue of the *New Republic* (October 22, 1930), with an article entitled "Wilder: Prophet of the Genteel Christ." Gold discussed Wilder's three published novels and the collection of three-minute plays. Such was the nature of Gold's attack—like "an explosion in a cesspool"—that Edmund Wilson, then in his Marxist period and generally sympathetic to Gold's position, described Gold's comments on Wilder as "harsh and scurrilous." In the perspective of today, the essay emerges as at best patently wrong headed and at worst malicious and factitious.

The piece begins with a contemptuous dismissal of *The Cabala* on the grounds that the cabala who are the novel's main characters perform no useful function in "the world that feeds them." Gold's summary dismissals of *The Bridge of San Luis Rey*, *The Angel That Troubled the Waters*, and *The Woman of Andros* are equally contemptuous for related reasons: that they do not comment on contemporary social problems.† This quick, devastating statement about characters and their situations, typical of Gold's method, is an example of hit and run criticism. It is not, of course, really literary criticism at all.

Why, then, was Gold's article taken so seriously and how could it have affected Wilder adversely? For one thing, Gold, after damning Wilder's work, not very subtly shifted his attack to Wilder himself. Gold constructed an image of his victim that was poisonous and false; he

---

* The New Humanists were dealt a harsh blow in 1931 by Santayana who effectively destroyed their position in his essay, "The Genteel Tradition at Bay." He condemned their absolutism as falsifying and unperceptive, the fruit of a decadent attitude, since "only a morality frankly relative to man's nature is worthy of man."
† Using this yardstick, one could safely have predicted Gold's reaction to, let us say, Jane Austen, Thackeray, or Proust.

portrayed Wilder as an effete apologist for—and, simultaneously, a stylist panderer to—the corrupt tastes and degenerate values of upper-class Anglo-Saxon Protestants.

> Mr. Wilder remains the poet of a small sophisticated class . . . our genteel bourgeoisie. His style is their style; it is the new fashion . . . Wilder is the perfect flower of the new prosperity . . . he has . . . the air of good breeding, the decorum, priestliness, glossy high finish as against intrinsic qualities, conspicuous inutility, caste feeling, love of the archaic, etc. . . . This Emily Post of culture will never remind [the parvenu class] of Pittsburgh or the breadlines. He is always in perfect taste; he is the personal friend of Gene Tunney. . . .
>       Let Mr. Wilder write a book about modern America. We predict it will reveal all his fundamental silliness and superficiality, now hidden under a Greek chlamys.

Gold's criticism of *The Cabala* and of *The Bridge of San Luis Rey,* both novels with origins in the imagination of a conscientious artist, was irrelevant and irrational. If both novels are flawed (and they are), Gold fails to describe their flaws; one wonders if he could have. But as far as *The Woman of Andros* is concerned, there was unfortunately a kernel of truth in Gold's denunciation. In thrashing about, he exposed a nerve in Wilder's subconscious. The essential failure in the novel has its roots in a weakness in Wilder himself; and Gold was not too far off the mark in identifying it.

Wilder's personal inadequacies, perplexities, and contradictions, even, one might say, the empty places in Wilder's inner life, were reflected in the writing of *The Woman of Andros*. (In justice, one should add that the book also bears the stamp of his affirmative and enthusiastic response to life and his high-mindedness and sense of justice). The novel is the work of a discontented, but hopeful, young man trying, first, to reassert his waning Christian faith to a congregation of suspicious deacons and then attempting to communicate an urgent sense of life to a legion of the uncertain young.

Using Terence's *Andria* as a springboard, Wilder explored two entirely different themes, neither of which had anything to do with the literature of ancient Rome. Both themes were viable and vital in 1930 and, for that matter, remain so, Gold notwithstanding. The first is a variation on the myth of Venus and Adonis. In this instance, a well-born Greek youth has come under the spell of a hetaira (the woman of Andros) who nightly entertains the unattached young men of the region with a banquet and readings from the Greek classics of an earlier epoch. The Andrian woman, thirty-five years old and already aware of her imminent death, is a saint who provides a haven for a collection of waifs and strays; she is also silently and secretly in love with the young Greek,

Pamphilus, whose thralldom to her is—presumably—not sexual, but spiritual and intellectual. The second theme enters when Pamphilus accidentally comes upon a crowd of adolescents about to ravage a young girl, a stranger to the island, whom he rescues. The remainder of the novel deals with the situation of the two young lovers, whom custom would bar from marriage. The two stories are united by the girl's being Glycerium, the younger sister of the woman of Andros, who dies after she learns of the affair between the two young lovers.

Wilder handles the first theme with a humanist's control and restraint. The hopeless love that the woman of Andros suppresses is counterbalanced by her dignity, by her compassion for all men and women who suffer, and by the calm and self-knowledge which her study of Plato and the literature of Greek tragedy have given her. She is, in fact, an idealization of the great actress, the woman who can become in life the tragic heroine she portrays on the stage. The portrait is, finally, an image of every woman of beauty, talent, and charm who, looking in the mirror one day, must say, "It is time . . . to forswear love and life." Wilder's making the woman a courtesan, superimposing Camille on the Marschallin, was perhaps excessive. But the imperatives of the plot, presumably, gave him no choice.

The reader's interest in the first theme comes from involvement in the full characterization of Chrysis, the woman of Andros. The second theme has to do with caste and class, money and property, mores and tribal customs. The family's and community's opposition to Pamphilus's alliance with Glycerium has its counterpart in every Western community, particularly when a leading family is involved. Whether in New York, New Haven, or even Hartford, the scion of a prominent clan does not contract an alliance with a young woman, however pretty, if she is déclassé; the fact that she has been made pregnant by the young man serves merely to emphasize her undesirability. The point that Wilder makes is that a young man and woman in love—whatever their antecedents or community ties—have the right to fulfill their own destinies. Not a very original observation, but it is a subject that Wilder dealt with earnestly and persuasively. Most relevant, Wilder's point of view in the matter is clearly that of an American committed to New World attitudes; and thus the whole moral issue—the issue of prenuptial intercourse—he utterly ignored. The sexual pleasure the young lovers took in one another, Wilder implies, was as natural as holding hands, and as innocent.

Unfortunately, he felt that he had to introduce a third theme, one which both Edmund Wilson and R. P. Blackmur recognized as both gratuitous and fatal to the point of view of the novel. The opening and concluding paragraphs of the book make clear that Wilder was asserting that a pagan civilization which had reached a high level of development could only grope uncertainly and hesitatingly because it wanted the example of Jesus Christ to give it focus and direction. In the novel, we encounter a few individuals on the island of Brynos who have intimations of the true Christian spirit: Pamphilus, Chrysis, and a young priest of Aesculapius and Apollo. But since they were not Christians, these characters were to be denied the ultimate peace which passeth all understanding. It seems incredible that a rational, serious, and perceptive intelligence operating in the third decade of the twentieth century could solemnly indite this kind of twaddle. But Wilder, seriously alarmed that his two major themes should prove offensive to Professor Phelps, Amos Wilder, and other worthies of their generation—some of the subject matter will disappoint and displease you, he told Phelps—introduced the theme of the wistfulness of the pagan soul for the coming of Christ in order to allay the suspicions of those who might feel that he was as depraved as the author of the scandalous *A Farewell to Arms,* which had come out the previous year.

Having pacified his elders, Wilder made possible the Gold review, neatly characterized by Hart Crane as "the recent rape of *The Woman of Andros.*" The religiosity of the work made it possible for Gold to write:

> Mr. Wilder wishes to restore . . . the Spirit of Religion in American Literature. . . . But what is this religious spirit Mr. Wilder aims to restore? Is it the crude self-torture of the Holy Rollers, or the brimstone howls and fears of the Baptists, or even the mad, titanic sincerities and delusions of a Tolstoi or Dostoievsky?
>
> No, it is that newly fashionable literary religion that centers around Jesus Christ, the First British Gentleman. It is a pastel, pastiche, dilettante religion, without the true neurotic blood and fire, a daydream of homosexual figures in graceful gowns moving archaically among the lilies. It is Anglo-Catholicism, that last refuge of the American literary snob. . . .
>
> Wilder has concocted a synthesis of all the chambermaid literature, Sunday-school tracts, and boulevard piety there ever were. He has added a dash of the prep-school teacher's erudition, then embalmed all this in the speciously glamourous style of the late Anatole France. He talks much of art, of himself as Artist, of style. He is a very conscious craftsman. But his is the most irritating and pretentious style pattern I have read in years. It has the slick, smug finality of the lesser Latins; that shallow clarity and tight little good taste that remind one of nothing so much as the conversation and practice of a veteran cocotte.

The tone and substance of Gold's bullying invective (he was in person a mild little man) shocked and offended the literary world. For two months, the controversy remained heated in the *New Republic.* Wilson tried to take a middle ground in an unsigned editorial published five weeks after Gold's article appeared. But his published position merely fanned the flames. Henry Hazlitt, literary editor of the left-wing *Nation*, was among the more notable of Wilder's defenders. Hemingway, hospitalized in Montana, stayed out of the public controversy, but finally wrote Wilder, assuring him that he, Hemingway, was in Wilder's corner.

Wilder himself, although he carefully refrained from making a public statement, was wounded and visibly shaken. A day or two after receiving a copy of the October 22 *New Republic,* Wilder's attention was directed by some of his students to an article in the *Daily Maroon* in which an undergraduate had criticized another. As Wilder read what had been intended as a good-natured piece, he grew red with fury. He turned to the writer and with a choking voice sputtered:

> You shouldn't have done that. You shouldn't write that way about someone else. I'm sorry I've ever said anything bad about anyone. Now I know how it feels.

Apart from that outburst, Wilder passed over the whole matter in silence. But Michael Gold had materially changed Wilder's life. The wretched piece may have caused Wilder great pain, but as it turned out, the article had a most salutary and liberating effect upon its victim. "Let Mr. Wilder write a book about modern America," Gold had written. "We predict it will reveal all his fundamental silliness and superficiality." Very deliberately, Wilder took up the challenge.

# VII

## Up off the Floor or:
## Getting Gertie's Ardor

*"Of all forms of genius, goodness has the longest awkward age."*
—THORNTON WILDER, "THE WOMAN OF ANDROS"

Finishing up his first year's teaching at Chicago, Wilder realized in the late fall of 1930 that not only was *The Woman of Andros* a failure (notwithstanding the *New York Times* and the *Herald Tribune* and the *Saturday Review*), but that his reputation had been seriously damaged. Despite the reasoned and judicious defenses in opposition to Gold's position, Wilder understood that the onset of the 1930s—the depression years—had changed the climate of American cultural life. The day had passed when, with stylistic elegance, he could brood reflectively over the vagaries of the heart and ironically set down the anguish of the unloved and the unwanted. His books had mirrored his own loneliness, his own disappointments, his desire to give in a situation where there were no takers, and his eagerness to take when there were no givers. That whole decade of his life that ought to have been the fulfillment of the romantic dreams of adolescence had been a wasteland of rejection and indifference. The only flowering things that had emerged had been his three novels; and these had finally been trampled on, despised, and nearly uprooted. The old section of his garden, then, would lie fallow; he would cultivate

84

something different, in another place. He might go back to playwrighting; his potential as a novelist, for the time being, was exhausted.

Wilder had already experienced failure as a playwright with the plays he wrote for Boleslavsky's American Laboratory Theater which had been rejected, discarded, and forgotten. His only produced play, which Boleslavsky had put on in the winter of 1926–27 was badly received by the critics and soon fell into oblivion. The little plays of *The Angel That Troubled the Waters* were not designed for a stage. A return to playwrighting was hazardous; and he proceeded with caution.

In the next several months, Wilder wrote six one-act plays. They were not produced on Broadway; they attracted no great attention in professional theater circles; they failed to bolster his diminished reputation. But, of the six plays, three are strikingly innovative; one of them according to Wilder was the finest one-act play ever written by an American and the work he was to choose, in 1942, as representing his best.

The six plays, published jointly in November 1931 by Yale University Press and Coward-McCann as *The Long Christmas Dinner & Other Plays in One Act* were, in the order in which they appear in the volume: *The Long Christmas Dinner, Queens of France, Pullman Car Hiawatha, Love and How To Cure It, Such Things Only Happen in Books,* and *The Happy Journey to Trenton and Camden.* Three of the plays are in a conventional mode. *Such Things Happen Only in Books* looks back to the ironical short plays of Susan Glaspell, whose work it strongly resembles. In the piece, all kinds of melodramas are taking place in an old house in a New Hampshire village unbeknownst to the young novelist living there with his wife. The novelist is busy rejecting conventional plots because they are unlike real life; but the play makes the ironical point that the happenings in real life are more incredible than those that are set down in books. The idea reflects a slight variation on one of Wilder's favorite notions: that the novelist has to invent stories because the plots and counterplots of real life are too incredible and complex for fiction, that the fictionist and playwright have to simplify and distill actual experience. *Such Things* is the weakest play of the lot, and Wilder himself expunged it from a subsequent edition of the collected plays. It clearly lacks his stamp.

*Love and How To Cure It,* despite its conventional form—an episode involving four people in an otherwise deserted London music hall—expresses a major Wilder theme, the Proustian theme of the earlier novels: that we despise those who desperately offer us their love and yearn after those who withhold it. The play, in fact, is almost an attempt to condense *Swann's Way* into twenty minutes. Linda (Odette), a "beautiful, impersonal, remote, almost sullen girl of barely sixteen," a ballet dancer, is obsessively pursued by the wealthy and elegant Arthur War-

burton (Swann), a university student. They had mét at the soirées of a
Madame Angellelli (Mme. Verdurin). But Wilder ends the play with a
New Haven Wilder family twist: once Arthur is made to see that his
infatuation is merely a plea for attention, a form of self-love, he leaves
Linda unharmed so that she can moon after an offstage Mario who
"doesn't even seem to notice you when you're there." . . . *And the
curtain falls.* Biographically speaking, the play is interesting: the curious
admixture of Proustian irony and New England dismissal of a passionate
attachment as an attention-seeking device is suggestive of Wilder's life
style. Dramatically speaking, the play has not remained very active in the
repertory.

The third of the conventional plays, *Queens of France,* was to prove
the hardiest among the three; it finally had a professional production in
New York in September 1966. The play's protagonist, an amiable swin-
dler-attorney, was suggested by Thomas Mann's confidence man, Felix
Krull. The theme of both Mann's story and Wilder's play suggest that
even the swindler, if he pursues his occupation with the grace, the
dedication, and the craft of an artist exercising his imaginative faculties,
brings to his victims not unhappiness, but pleasure and release.

> No scenery is required for this play. Perhaps a few dusty flats may be
> seen leaning against the brick wall at the back of the stage. . . .
> The STAGE MANAGER not only moves forward and withdraws the few
> properties that are required, but he reads from a typescript the lines
> of all the minor characters. He reads them clearly, but with little
> attempt at characterization, scarcely troubling himself to alter his
> voice, even when he responds in the person of a child or a woman.
> As the curtain rises the STAGE MANAGER is leaning lazily against
> the proscenium pillar at the audience's left. He is smoking.

The stage directions here look very familiar. Perhaps more people
would find them more familiar than the stage directions for any other
play ever written. And virtually every such person would be astonished to
discover that they are the directions to a play they've never read or seen.
For they introduce Wilder's *The Happy Journey to Trenton and Camden,* which is about an American mother of the lower middle class and
the journey she takes from Newark in the family car, driven by her
husband and accompanied by her two children. Michael Gold had challenged Wilder to write about modern America, and this play is the first
installment of Wilder's answer to the challenge. It demonstrates the
emptiness of Gold's predictions. Indeed, no short play had ever captured
so faithfully and so movingly the emotional and tonal rhythms of a large
segment of American society. This was the play that Wilder singled out
as his best; assuredly it is his best one-act play and the one against which

all other American short plays must be measured. It clearly prefigures *Our Town,* just as *Pullman Car Hiawatha*—a play in which a train car of passengers speeding simultaneously across Ohio and through the cosmos —anticipates *The Skin of Our Teeth. The Long Christmas Dinner* also reveals Wilder's new preoccupation with man's short space on earth in relation to the countless generations that have preceded him and that— in the 1930s, at least—could be predicted to follow him.

Moving into his midthirties, Wilder had become more detached from people. Or he thought he had. His determination to rid himself of emotional involvements, to avoid, under any circumstances, giving his heart away, is clearly reflected in the fascinating trio of plays, two of which are "stage managed" by an objective observer, who understands everything but stands apart from the action, and one of which recounts the endless rituals of birth, marrying, feasting, and dying.

The three plays, *The Long Christmas Dinner, Pullman Car Hiawatha,* and *The Happy Journey to Trenton and Camden* were the evidence that although Wilder's reputation had been diminished by the literary establishment, he was functioning with an unremitting vitality. Rather than attempt to recapture or reconstitute *The Bridge,* his one great success, he appeared to have taken off in a new direction. These little plays did not, of course, establish Wilder as a dramatist of consequence; but to serious workers in the theater (such as Jed Harris), the plays made clear that he was a dramatist of significance. Four of the plays had their premiere in New Haven under the auspices of the Yale and Vassar dramatic societies in late November 1931. A few days later, the University of Chicago showed three of the plays, including the first performances of *Queen of France.* The final premiere, that of *Pullman Car Hiawatha,* took place on December 11, at Antioch College in Yellow Springs, Ohio.

Neither the college productions nor the publication of the plays recovered for Wilder his former prestige; at thirty-four, he was becoming regarded, particularly in academic circles, as a literary holdover from the 1920s who was comfortably berthed in a safe teaching position at a wealthy institution from which he could compose minor plays for little theaters.

Wilder was in residence at Chicago for no more than six months out of the year. He devoted the other half to writing, traveling, and working in Hollywood studios—he was asked by Samuel Goldwyn to work on film scripts. During the year that followed the one-act plays (1932), his only finished piece of writing was the translation of Andre Obey's *Le Viol de Lucrèce (The Rape of Lucrèce),* an assignment he undertook on behalf of Katharine Cornell. Opening in December at New York's Belasco Theater, the play was Wilder's first Broadway venture (the

American Laboratory production of *The Trumpet Shall Sound* being what came to be called Off Broadway). The auspices could hardly have been more distinguished: the first lady of the American theater was directed by Guthrie McClintic, with settings by Robert Edmond Jones, music by Deems Taylor, and choreography by Martha Graham. Miss Cornell was supported by Brian Aherne and Blanche Yurka. For reasons that may have had nothing to do with Wilder's translation, the production was a fiasco. Stark Young—who had befriended Wilder ten years before—called it, in his *New Republic* review, "feeble, uncertain and unglamourous." A woman wrote to the *Saturday Review* denouncing Wilder for having betrayed Obey. Clearly, Wilder's Broadway apprenticeship had hardly begun.

But life for him in Chicago was considerably more than tolerable. As one of Hutchins's chief counselors, his mentor and confidant, a friend of the family and good natured "uncle" to the Hutchins children, Wilder was securely established in the power center of the university. Whatever position the faculty took in respect to him was irrelevant; he taught what he liked when he liked, and the students flocked to his classes. While there was a difference of opinion among the students about the value of the course content, it was universally agreed that Wilder put on a good show. He was amiable, he was accessible, he was intense, and he was sincere. In short, he was popular. And popularity is the traditional alternative to scholarly renown. There were many, even at Chicago, who achieved neither. One incident that a number of undergraduates recall about Wilder took place during the period when he was living in the men's residence hall. An emergency developed when a foreign student committed suicide by throwing himself out the window. In the resulting hubbub, there was no one to man the dormitory switchboard and for a few hours Wilder successfully bridged the gap. For those who saw or heard about Thornton Wilder at the switchboard, the act symbolized his deep commitment to the university community, his unpretentiousness, and his preference for service over being served.

And he did, indeed, place himself at the disposal of his students. There were several hours each week when he was available for conversations, counsel, and evaluation, not only to students enrolled in his classes, but to strays who happened to wander by. Anyone who could find space was allowed to audit not only the lecture course, but the writing seminar. The future novelist Marguerite Young drifted in and out of his course in writing fiction, although years passed before she got up the courage to speak to him. Wilder attended meetings of a poetry club presided over by Gladys Campbell; he hovered over the dramatic society.

Of the several important collegiate friendships he established with undergraduates, one, in particular, reveals Wilder's classic pattern of advance and withdrawal, as well as his extraordinary generosity and patience toward the young. Students in his lecture course in the classics in translation routinely submitted papers for Wilder to read. He was struck one day by the exceptional quality of a paper written by a student named John Vincent Healy on the subject of Robinson Jeffers' version of the Oresteia, *The Tower beyond Tragedy*. Upon inquiring, Wilder discovered that Healy was totally deaf and that a student sitting next to him transcribed Wilder's lectures for him. Moved by the boy's disability and captivated by his perceptions, Wilder decided to befriend Healy, a project that was not easy. While the boy's talents, both as a poet and critic of poetry, were prodigious, association with him presented two problems. In common with the speech of many deaf persons, Healy's was difficult to understand; complex and subtle ideas about literature cascaded from him in a bewildering rush. The other difficulty for Wilder was that Healy was no docile and reticent adolescent; on the contrary, he was a proud, arrogant Irish youth from a wealthy South-Side Chicago family who, though he welcomed Wilder's interest in him, stood not at all in awe of his teacher. In fact, Healy found Wilder's tastes in poetry naive and dated. Wilder's "modern" poets were Robert Frost, Elinor Wylie, and his two friends, Edwin Arlington Robinson and Edna St. Vincent Millay. Wilder was either antagonistic to or unfamiliar with the poetry of Jeffers, T. S. Eliot, Pound, and Yeats, the poets whose work meant most to Healy.

Despite all this, Wilder pursued his friendship with the gifted young man. He visited the Healy home which was situated close to the Chicago campus; he even helped Healy with his articulation of sounds, the first help Healy had received since his mother had worked with him in his childhood. In later years, it was Wilder's attempt to improve Healy's speech that the younger man remembered above all his kindnesses. But Wilder's affectionate regard for Healy was not sentimental pity for a handicapped youth. Wilder himself had written poetry, but his verses though grounded in deep emotion had been academic and sterile, never quite coming off as anything except admirable exercises. Healy, at seventeen or eighteen—the age when Wilder was writing his verses—was achieving what Wilder had not been able to do. Moreover, Healy could communicate to Wilder his enthusiasm for the great contemporary poets whose stature was only beginning to become apparent. Wilder's appreciation of Yeats, which developed over the coming decades, began with his knowing Healy.

The friendship between Wilder and Healy continued after the younger man's graduation from Chicago in 1932. Healy went on to Harvard where T. S. Eliot was lecturing. Eliot, too, was impressed with Healy to the extent that he criticized and annotated several of the young man's poems. Healy, who had published some of his poems in *Poetry* while he was still an undergraduate, began appearing in the prestigious little magazines throughout the United States and in the *Saturday Review*. Over the years, he continued to write poetry and criticism and established himself as a foremost Yeats critic, until he suddenly gave up writing in 1940 and withdrew to Maine, where he brought up a family and earned a living as a farmer.

Although he had left Chicago, Healy kept in touch with Wilder, principally through the mails. Possessed of an acute social conscience, Healy denounced Hutchins and so provoked a quarrel with Wilder; essentially, the incident ended their friendship although a desultory correspondence continued and there were occasional meetings. Even these encounters ended completely when Healy gave up writing and retired to his Maine farm.

There is nothing particularly remarkable about Wilder's friendship with Healy; the pattern of their association repeated itself in Wilder's life a number of times, with students, with young poets and young writers, and even with the younger professional men whom Wilder met in the natural course of events. What the relationship with Healy reveals is that at thirty-five Wilder began taking on some of the autocratic and despotic characteristics of his father. Beneath his mask of geniality, he came to enjoy molding, guiding, counseling younger men and women— so long as they unquestioningly yielded to his intellectual authority. Although Wilder was genuinely touched by Healy's affliction and impressed by his talent almost from the very start, he was unnerved by Healy's challenge. Poetry was not Wilder's strong suit and in that area he had more to learn from Healy than he had to teach. Healy's antagonism toward Hutchins was, of course—although it seemed justified to the idealistic young man—a vicarious attack on Wilder.

Months before—in failing to reply to Healy's letters, in avoiding meetings that would have been convenient—Wilder demonstrated that the relationship had become wearisome to him. Doubtless, Healy's brilliance and insights about modern poetry could have earned him a longer friendship with Wilder had the younger man been submissive and tactful. But Wilder was irritable and brooked no challenges from his acolytes. And when Healy followed up his attack on Hutchins with a charge that Wilder had based his lecture on Euripides on the material in the *Encyclopaedia Britannica,* the rapport between them ended. The loss, of course, was principally Healy's and he was sad to lose Wilder's friendship. What he failed to see was that he had allowed himself to be maneuvered by Wilder, who had prepared the grounds for a break by demonstrating that Hutchins (his best friend) had been infamously and unfairly attacked by Healy. (But did Hutchins need to be defended

against Healy when two-thirds of the Chicago faculty were already opposed to the president's policies? Was it necessary to place the vulnerable
younger man so clearly and irrevocably in the wrong?) In a final letter,
Wilder defended Hutchins against Healy's allegations (which charged
Hutchins with overweening ambitions and callousness concerning the
welfare of a college groundskeeper). He concluded his communication by
coldly breaking a dinner engagement with Healy, by stating that there
was too much antagonism between them and by expressing the hope that
sometime in the future they could meet and talk without trampling on
each other's sacred grounds. It was a peremptory dismissal, neatly justified by everything that had led up to it. Wilder had fallen into a pattern
that served him well henceforth: he invoked justice when he ceased to
care.*

Wilder's life as a member of the university community during the
first half of the thirties took him as far away from home as he had ever
been. He even came close to making Chicago his actual residence. After
living on campus for four years, he finally rented a comfortable off-
campus apartment at 6020 Drexel Avenue, near the Midway. Not only
did he become deeply involved with the Hutchins's administration of the
university and with the Hutchins's menage, but he also began to frequent the homes of wealthy Chicagoans, particularly socialites like
"Bobsy" Goodspeed and Margaret Ayer Barnes, high-minded women
who both wrote and supported the fine arts. He became a patron of
*Poetry* and he staged a production of Handel's opera *Xerxes*. Generally,
his life in Chicago in these years was a continual shifting from low gear,
to middle gear, to high. Mornings were devoted to preparing and delivering a humanities lecture and to teaching his writing class. The remainder
of the day he divided between his students and their activities, on the
one hand, and the high cultural-social life of Chicago's Gold Coast, on
the other. Harry T. Moore recalls meeting Wilder at a party on North
Michigan Boulevard in which liveried servants (this during the nadir of
the Depression) brought in trays of hors d'oeuvres. Glancing at the

---

* Healy, though he was banished, lingered on in Wilder's subconscious. Twenty years
later, when Wilder was composing *The Ides of March* (a novel which had as two of its
central figures Julius Caesar and the poet Catullus whom Caesar loved while Catullus
despised him), as we know he gave half the dedication to Lauro de Bosis "Roman
poet, who lost his life marshalling a resistance against the absolute power of Mussolini. . . ." One might see a parallel here to Catullus and Caesar. But such a reading
would be misleading. Mussolini is not at all the counterpart of Wilder's Caesar; nor
did Mussolini know or care about de Bosis. Moreover, de Bosis and Wilder were contemporaries and not antagonistic toward one another. One is much more persuaded by
the correspondences between the antagonisms of Wilder-Healy and Caesar-Catullus
than by any of the other young poets in Wilder's life, particularly since Wilder once
slightingly referred to de Bosis as "le martyre imaginaire" and because Wilder modeled
Caesar upon himself.

waiters, Wilder said to Moore, "This makes one feel the grand seigneur."
But Wilder was just as likely to be seen at a spaghetti dinner in the
cramped apartment of a married—or quasi-married—student couple; he
cheerfully accepted whatever student invitations came his way; he dispensed good cheer, advice, and more tangible largesse with an open
hand. He virtually picked up Robert Wooster Stallman off the street
when Stallman arrived in Chicago without money but with the hope of
becoming a poet; and Wilder was partly responsible for saving Stallman
from starving to death by arranging for the president's office to parcel out
money which Wilder himself had secretly provided. Robert Ardrey, one
of Wilder's few protégés to succeed as a professional writer, sent his
teacher a friend who had made a girl pregnant. The distraught young
man returned to Ardrey after his discussion with Wilder more upset than
ever: "I told him the situation and Wilder grappled with the problem by
discussing Plato! . . ."

In truth, Wilder was happier and more content in Chicago than he
had ever been in his life. On campus he was a personage and off campus
he was a celebrity. And quite deservedly. He brought to his lectures on
the classics fresh and original insights of a creative imagination. So
far as the city of Chicago was concerned, he was its outstanding literary
figure in residence—eager to throw the weight of his prestige behind the
city's energetic cultural impulses. The difficulty with Chicago was that
although he could live happily there, the one thing he could not do was
write.

But his commitment to Chicago covered only half the year; the rest
of the time he led a different kind of life. Alexander Woollcott had
become his intimate friend. Wilder had encouraged Woollcott to collect
and publish as a book the best of his miscellaneous essays. Then he
suggested ideas and recommended revisions when the essays were written.
He urged Woollcott to undertake research on his family's involvement
with a communal experiment in the previous century. In all these efforts,
he was giving Woollcott the impression that he took the bulky man's
slender talents seriously. Wilder recognized that when a journalist-
observer is successful, he wants to be more than read; he wants to be read
with respect. He wants, in short, to be regarded as a writer.

Intimacy with Woollcott had its reward: acceptance by the luminaries of the New York theater world. Wilder met Helen Hayes and
Charles MacArthur, Lynn Fontanne and Alfred Lunt; Ruth Gordon and
Jed Harris (an unwedded couple); the Ben Hechts; Alice Duer Miller;
the Sidney Howards; Hope Williams; and Ethel Barrymore. Perhaps, one
should say acceptance by *some* of the luminaries. The writers among
Woollcott's friends—mostly playwrights or writers of popular fiction—

were frequently indifferent to Wilder, or, as in the instance of George S. Kaufman, downright hostile.

Why this should have been is hard to say. As playwrights, for example, they did not accept him as a professional man of the theater; and as popular, work-a-day writers, they felt Wilder was highbrow, overeducated, and unworldly. The actors and actresses, on the other hand, were more tolerant; they invited him for weekends and for dinner parties. Actually, they were not quite so friendly and admiring as they seemed, as Wilder was ultimately to discover. But, in the early thirties, when he first made their acquaintance, he was dazzled by their apparently warm acceptance.

Two members of Woollcott's circle did become genuinely close to Wilder. One was Jed Harris, who was not so much intimidated by Wilder's erudition as he was convinced that Wilder was something more than a writer of plays for little theaters; Harris was patiently waiting for a full-scale theater work from Wilder on which he could expend all the energies and directing genius none of his previous plays had consumed. The other friend of Woollcott who became an intimate of Wilder was Ruth Gordon. Possessing neither the beauty and carriage of an Ethel Barrymore, the voice of a Katharine Cornell, nor the sheer virtuosity of a Helen Hayes, Miss Gordon came to the theater with little more than a superhuman will to succeed. Among her physical disadvantages were her knock-knees; when skirts rose, through the vagaries of fashion, and exposed actresses' legs, this incredible woman went to a surgeon and had both legs broken so that they could be reset straight. What drew both Woollcott and Wilder to Ruth Gordon was her intelligence and her sense of humor, rare qualities for a lady in the acting profession. Eventually, her intellectual powers bore fruit in several successful stage comedies, as well as stories and memoirs. Woollcott and Wilder took "Ruthie" under their respective wings and counseled and coached her; Wilder, at least one time after she separated from Jed Harris, lent her money. He predicted to all who would listen that Ruth Gordon was destined to become the leading actress of the English-speaking stage, and the augury momentarily seemed a real possibility when she scored a great success in both London and New York in Wycherly's *The Country Wife*. In the long run, out of all his conquests in the Broadway theater, Wilder's friendship with Ruth Gordon was the only relationship to survive.

During the 1930s, Wilder reveled in his sense of being a part of the glamorous hierarchy. Mary Pickford had become his friend! And Woollcott, during the years between 1932 and 1935, was as close to an intimate as Wilder ever had. Friendship is based, as Plato wrote and Wilder knew, on equality; and, intellectually, the two men were far apart. But they

shared a tremulous love for the theater, for fine actresses, and for redoubtable old ladies. They loved to divine talent in the young, to
encourage and nurture it, as they did with Ruth Gordon's gift and later
with Orson Welles's—Wilder discovered the young genius in Chicago
and sent him on to Woollcott. Perhaps, above all, they loved gossip, the
more malicious the better. It was no accident that Alice Roosevelt Longworth ("If you have anything bad to say about anyone, come over and sit
by me") was a great friend of Woollcott. During the years when their
friendship was closest, Wilder and Woollcott would write each other long
gossipy letters about trifling matters. Woollcott's, of course, were full of
news; wherever he happened to be was a communications center.
Wilder's responses, while less newsy, were seldom earnest, since he was
cautiously aware that the contents of his letters would surely be shared by
half a dozen of Woollcott's intimates. But occasionally, something deep
within him would come through; and perhaps his most important and
telling revelation to Woollcott appeared in a letter written on a January
night in 1934. Wilder describes his "working" day in New Haven: he had
spent a whole morning on a difficult crossword puzzle in the London
*Spectator;* at home and in his study, he read a book about South America
and worked a little on *Heaven's My Destination;* then he went back to
Yale for tea at the Elizabethan Club and a stint at the university library
reading critiques of Paris plays; later he looked into the *New Yorker*
"hoping to find Woollcott," but instead had to read Benchley and
Fadiman with distaste. After a few more details of this kind, Wilder
describes how, with self-loathing, he dragged himself upstairs to his study
to resume work on his novel. There, instead, he began the letter to
Woollcott that took him well over an hour to write.

Thus, on his own description, Wilder's existence was divided into
three self-contained spheres: his life at Chicago—all-consuming; his social life in New York and New Haven, interspersed with lectures and
forays into Broadway and Hollywood; and writing. It was, of course, the
last that made him nervous, despondent, and sometimes almost suicidal;
it had always been writing which had those dark effects upon him.

One of the nagging questions in Wilder's mind was whether the new
work, his first novel since *The Woman of Andros,* would reestablish him
with those critics of fiction whom he respected, whose good opinion every
serious writer to some degree hopes for. The novel that he was writing
was especially important to Wilder for a number of reasons: it would
stand as his response to critics like Gold who accused him of an incapacity to write about life in contemporary America; the book was also
directed to Hemingway's attention, partly because Hemingway's earlier
enthusiasm for Wilder had metamorphosed into a patronizing commiser-
ation. The novel was—at least Wilder stated so—partly influenced by

what he admired in and learned from Hemingway. But *Heaven's My Destination* was not composed in order merely to reestablish its author as a literary force; he was using the writing as a means of working out some of his own problems. Twenty years later, Wilder stated that the book represented "an effort to come to terms with pious didacticism and narrow Protestantism" of his childhood and adolescence. "The comic spirit is given to us in order that we may analyse, weigh and clarify things in us which nettle us, or which we are outgrowing, or trying to reshape. [*Heaven's My Destination*] is a very autobiographical book. . . ."

Not *very*. But it was certainly something of a counterstatement to the religiosity he had expressed in earlier years. It may also owe something to the kind of liberating influence exerted upon him by the freethinking and irreverent Woollcott. Certainly, it was an exorcism of strictures imposed upon his childhood and adolescence. By the time Wilder wrote *Heaven's My Destination,* he had already become a heavy smoker and drinker, both practices that had been abhorrent to a younger Thornton Wilder; and while there had been no period in his life when he quite achieved the priggishness of the novel's hero, George Brush, one can hear the accents of a Lawrenceville housemaster in many of this character's sentiments. Wilder said many times that he based George Brush partly on his father, partly on his brother Amos, with influences also from Gene Tunney and himself. In truth, what he borrowed from the others is of no great importance, mere surface details. Without becoming tendentiously psychological, one can deduce that George Brush is autobiographical in the sense that he is the idealized image that Wilder had once created of himself: Brush is athletic, mechanically and otherwise handy, "tall, solidly built," ruggedly handsome, adept at self-defense, and possessed of a fine tenor voice so beautiful and well-trained that it captivates any and all audiences. Wilder, of course, did not possess such attributes to any extent! Some he possessed not at all. Nor is there any evidence that the adventures and misadventures of George Brush ever befell Wilder.* (On

---

* The absence of some other parallels is fascinating: George Brush was committed to chastity, sobriety, and piety; he, on the one hand, cut himself off from his family because he had nothing in common with them, but he longed to be married and the father of several children; he accumulated no money, deciding that the earning of interest was evil; he was a pacifist and refused even to defend himself when physically attacked. By way of contrast, Wilder's family ties were never severed; he prudently invested his money in banks, or in stocks and bonds; he did not marry and raise children; he drank and smoked; both as a young man and again in middle age he volunteered for military service. The outstanding difference between George Brush and Wilder is that the fictional character was unconventional and indifferent to the opinions of others. George Brush rebelled, not against what people believed, or paid lip service to, but against what people *did*; Wilder, though he was always capable of the kindnesses performed by George Brush, was never a rebel; on the contrary, he has always been liked for his tact, his tolerance, and his understanding of other points of view.

the other hand, some of them may have happened to Jed Harris, who had—after dropping out of Yale—become, like George Brush, a traveler selling text books. Harris also emerges in the novel as a character named Burkin.)

One must be aware of Wilder's ambivalent relationship to his priggish and irritating hero in order to understand the basic weakness of the novel and its critical failure. John Chamberlain, in his January 2, 1935, review in the *New York Times,* summed up much of the critical reaction:

> The reason why "Heaven's My Destination" is not good satire probably resides in Thornton Wilder's own ambiguous attitude toward his chief character. One gathers that Wilder likes George Brush and would like to approve of him. Yet the palpable idiocies which Brush believes cannot be part of Wilder's own mental equipment. The matter is rendered more complicated by the fact that Brush's "crazy" theories have tucked away in them several kernels of truth. . . . Mr. Wilder's intelligence and his emotions very probably conflicted all through the writing. . . .
>
> A novel that is cast as a morality play and yet leads to no system of morals can succeed only as a satire on human fallibility. A satire, however, demands something more than mildness of method, something more than scenes that are almost skeletal in their presentation of conflict. George Brush and his friends and his antagonists say and do many things that are essentially vulgar, yet the sums of their speech and their actions do not add up to anything very hearty. Mr. Wilder is not vulgar enough himself to simulate vulgarity in others. . . . (his attempt to be vulgar is, paradoxically a little prim. . . .)
>
> The question which Mr. Wilder has not answered involves Mr. Brush's "goodness." Can the species Closed Mind ever be "good," even with the sanctions of Protestant tradition behind it? If Mr. Wilder had tried to answer this question before writing. . . . "Heaven's My Destination" might have been less enigmatic. And instead of being mildly amusing, it might have gathered impetus from certainty and moved forward into something positively zestful.

Read in the context of today, *Heaven's My Destination* is thematically more relevant to the 1960s than it was to the critics of thirty-five years ago. George Brush's commitment to *Ahimsa* (the Oriental doctrine of refraining from harming any living being) was recently more prevalent among scores of thousands of young people than it was in the thirties when the pacifistic ideal was counterbalanced by the threats of Fascism, Nazism, and Communism. Our ambivalence (exasperation and admiration) toward George Brush has its counterpart in our feelings about youth movements, student uprisings, and communes on the deserts of New Mexico. Wilder's novel, moreover, treats such concerns with a firm control that shades from irony to satire to farce. Wilder's immense comic gifts were intimated in both *The Cabala* and *The Bridge of San Luis*

*Rey* (though they were not much in evidence in *The Woman of Andros*); but *Heaven's My Destination* is that rare example of a period piece whose comedy is more apparent and delightful a generation or two later than it was at the time of its first appearance. A sturdy contribution to the fiction of the thirties, the work emphasized to Wilder and to those who valued it that Wilder's comedic genius cried out for further exploitation and that the lyric-philosophic mood of the earlier novels could, with impunity, be abandoned . . . or temporarily laid aside.

But the reactions of the serious critics to *Heaven's My Destination* disappointed Wilder. Except for a long and respectful piece by the aging Desmond MacCarthy in London's *Sunday Times,* the novel was largely ignored in the important critical journals. The most academic of the critics to review the work was R. P. Blackmur who, writing in *The Nation,* set the whole tone of his unflattering piece in the opening sentence:

> Perhaps the great bulk of the immediate readers of this romance will be among the subscribers to the Book-of-the-Month, of which this is the January selection. . . .

In short, although the new book did not provoke the obloquy heaped upon *The Woman of Andros,* neither did it restore Wilder to the ranks of America's foremost novelists, ranks which had been augmented in the early thirties by Thomas Wolfe, John Steinbeck, James T. Farrell, and John O'Hara. An old-fashioned picaresque novel about an innocent young man in quest of his sainthood was not what the urban culture centers were ready for. *Heaven's My Destination* had been slowly and lovingly composed; but despite the exhausting months lavished upon it, it seemed to Wilder as though he had produced, despite the imprimatur of the Book-of-the-Month, another failure.

A noteworthy detail in the publication of this book is that it was the first of Wilder's work to come out under the sponsorship of the house of Harper (later Harper & Row). The whole matter of Wilder's shift from A. & C. Boni is rather curious. Albert Boni said thirty years after the event that Wilder never informed him of his intention to abandon the firm; that, in fact, Boni's first intimation that he was losing his best-selling author came through the rumor grapevine. *Heaven's My Destination,* by contractural agreement, belonged to Boni but he sold the rights to Harper and Brothers, reserving only the book-club rights. In losing Wilder, A. & C. Boni, publishers of Marcel Proust and D. H. Lawrence, lost the will to continue and Wilder's defection essentially ended Boni's career as a publisher of new books and new writers.

The entire matter is puzzling. It is not uncommon for writers to switch publishers or for publishers to induce authors to make changes.

What is most odd about Wilder's move is that he planned it for at least five years without, according to Boni, informing him. Cass Canfield, the chief editor at Harper & Row, has written that he received Wilder's commitment to Harper's in the spring of 1928, that is to say within a few months of the initial success of *The Bridge of San Luis Rey*. Canfield's recollection is corroborated by a postcard Wilder sent to Hemingway on June 7, 1928, where Wilder urges Hemingway to join him at Harper's. At that time, Wilder was obligated to deliver his next two novels to Boni and it was not until 1934 that he finished the second of the two. His secretiveness in promising a book to Canfield may have had its origin in a sense of guilt. Wilder visited Boni several months before he ended the connection with his firm to ask the publisher to draw up a contract that would bind him to A. & C. Boni for life. Boni immediately replied that such a contract would be unethical and that he "would not do that to his worst enemy." Wilder, obviously, was attempting to nullify his Harper commitment. Why should he do that?

From Wilder's letters we know that he was uneasy and distrustful of A. & C. Boni, almost from the very beginning. As we have seen, he believed that his contract with Boni was unfair. A. & C. Boni was, of course, a small firm, a partnership, which published important but not very profitable European authors like Proust, D. H. Lawrence, and Huysmans. In the same year that they published *The Bridge of San Luis Rey*, they also published *Oil* by Upton Sinclair, which was banned in Boston. In response, Boni covered the offending pages with a fig leaf and Sinclair personally sold copies of the book on Boston Common. The book finally sold over 90,000 copies in this country, 250,000 in England, and 500,000 in Germany. Then, in 1928, Boni published Sinclair's *Boston*, which dealt as critically with the Sacco-Vanzetti case as *Oil* had dealt with the Teapot Dome scandals. Wilder may have had no misgivings about the firm's strong leftward tendencies but it was obvious to him that his father, a conservative Republican, would take no pleasure in the fact that his son's publishing house was an enterprise engaged in polluting the body politic with the scabrous works of Upton Sinclair. Another source of concern was that Boni had sold *The Bridge* to the movies and the film version did not please Wilder.

Against these considerations lay the ineluctable fact that Albert Boni, through Lewis Baer, had sought out Wilder when he was all but unknown, had counseled and encouraged him to transform the shapeless "Memoirs of a Roman Student" into a publishable novel, and had advanced him the money that enabled him to complete *The Bridge of San Luis Rey*. Boni had published the novel even though such acute editors as those at the *Atlantic Monthly* and Carl Van Doren of the Literary Guild, after reading the manuscript, had turned it down as unsuitable for serial publication or book club selection because they felt there was no public for a story about eighteenth century Peru. Given Wilder's lack of initiative and experience working in the novel form, Wilder might very well, in 1934, have still been teaching French at Lawrenceville, occasionally contributing short works to the little magazines, and writing theater pieces for Mrs. Isaacs's *Theater Arts Monthly*— if it had not been for Albert Boni. Wilder lacked the professional ruthlessness of successful and ambitious men. It is true that like George Brush, he hated ingratitude

> *more in a man*
> *Than lying, vainness, babbling drunkenness*
> *Or any taint of vice whose strong corruption*
> *Inhabits our frail blood.*

And, though thirty-five years later Boni would still regard Wilder's defection as an inexplicable act of ingratitude, we must remind ourselves that Wilder scrupulously fulfilled his contractural obligation in delivering his first four novels to A. & C. Boni. Without question, Wilder's was a sound decision. The arrangements he made with Harper's were fairer than those he had made with Boni. And, equally important, his rapport with Cass Canfield was to remain stable and congenial for nearly half a century.

When *Heaven's My Destination* was published (the English edition in December 1934 and the American in January 1935), Wilder was already back at Chicago for the fall and winter terms. Four years had passed since he had become a member of the Chicago community and since the publication of *The Woman of Andros*, with its shattering aftermath. While he was clearly established as a novelist, he privately questioned whether he had truly found his métier. His having begun his professional writing career as a novelist was, as it were, an accident, and the recognition he found so quickly also represented a combination of happy circumstances. Seven years after the publication of *The Bridge of San Luis Rey*, he could no longer have doubts about his vocation as a writer; but the cool reception accorded *Heaven's My Destination* intensified his long-standing suspicion that he should abandon fiction and continue to develop himself as a dramatist. Conscious of his big streak of gregariousness, he knew that his imagination was quickened when it anticipated an eventual collaboration with actors and actresses, set designers, directors, and responsive audiences.

At thirty-seven, Wilder had reached a crossroad in his life. He had the choice of moving about comfortably between Chicago, New Haven-New York, and Hollywood—teaching, writing an occasional novel or an occasional screenplay, and enjoying the hospitality of the Hutchinses in Chicago, Charles MacArthur and Helen Hayes in Nyack, and Mary Pickford and Douglas Fairbanks in Hollywood. Or, as an alternative, he could evolve a new way of life. . . .

The agent who was to determine the redirection of Wilder's career appeared in the person of a short, heavyset woman, an American expatriate from France, newly arrived in Chicago, with a monk's coiffure, the eyes of a sibyl, the nose of an imperial Caesar and a Gioconda smile. The visitor—the best-known and least-read woman writer in the world—was making a triumphant return to her native America after a thirty-year exile. This colossus of the Rive Gauche, genius or mountebank, nourisher of or nourished by half the artistic talent of Europe and America, in coming to Chicago was to acquire the last, but not the least, of her distinguished devotees: and she would modify and mold him so that he would be different from what he was before. That December, Wilder met Gertrude Stein; within a month she was to pronounce *Heaven's My Destination* the American novel.

# VIII

## The Long Happy Journey
## to Grover's Corners,
## New Hampshire

*"The third act of that little play was based on Gertrude's ideas, as on great pillars. . . ."*

The fame of Gertrude Stein, when she returned to her native United States in 1934, was far greater than the recognition her name evokes today. All the world loves a mystery, and to those who were even only peripherally interested in literary matters, both she and her work were a grave mystery indeed. College professors, newspaper columnists, subscribers to the book clubs, and the rest of what could be called the American literary world were looking for a sign, some proof that Miss Stein was either the towering, though unappreciated, literary talent of the generation, or else a gigantic hoax whose capacities for self-advertisement had deluded even the most responsible of her camp followers. Samples of her writing were taken out of context and reproduced as evidence that she could write only semiliterate gibberish. But writers like Sherwood Anderson, Scott Fitzgerald, and Ernest Hemingway were, or had been, numbered among her impressive band of disciples.

Always ready to oblige an uncertain and grateful public, Henry Seidel Canby, editor of the *Saturday Review of Literature*, sought to relieve the general uneasiness about Gertrude Stein, pontificating thus:

> If this is literature or anything worse than stupidity, worse than madness, then has all criticism since the beginning of letters been mere

101

idle theorizing. If it is literature, then alas! for literature. Thank
Heaven, that there are still Professor Lowes and Harvards to conserve
tradition and guide taste, and to make the world unsafe for eccen-
tricity. To raise the grotesque and the absurd to the plane of the serious is to render a disservice to literature. More, it is to render an
insult to intelligence and evoke a curse on criticism.

In other words, Stein could be accepted as nothing more than an
amusing and engaging comedienne. But the academic people were unwilling to accept Canby as their avatar; word drifted across the seas and
continents that T. S. Eliot, while making clear that he disapproved of
what Gertrude Stein wrote and represented, had declared himself impressed by her methods and "immensely interested" in whatever of her
work he had read. Some of the avant-garde at home, like William Carlos
Williams, were similarly equivocal; they would refuse to make a value
judgment about her writings, but they would just as stoutly refuse to
dismiss it as the nonsense a great many people hoped it would be
adjudged.

The publication, in 1933, of the witty and thoroughly readable
*Autobiography of Alice B. Toklas* settled nothing; it was a brilliantly
executed memoir, but it was not a representative piece of Gertrude
Stein's imaginative writing; similarly the opera *Four Saints in Three Acts*
which opened in New York several months before her arrival there (but
whose Chicago premiere coincided with her arrival *there*) was a great
romp and highly praised in conventional circles. But it was, after all, a
libretto for music by Virgil Thomson, and it did not have to be judged
on its own merit as a work of literature.

Long before her arrival in Chicago, Wilder found himself facing the
question of Gertrude Stein. Since he "had never gone to Paris," had
never been a part of the coterie of resident American artists there, he had
never been taken to her home—in fact had never met her. He knew of
her through several of her friends and acquaintances. But by the time
Wilder became friendly with Hemingway, the latter had already
loosened his ties with Gertrude Stein. Glenway Wescott had also been
rejected by her; she said of him that although he possessed "a certain
syrup, it just doesn't pour." Katherine Anne Porter, gravely respectful
about *The Making of Americans*, wrote with less propriety about Gertrude Stein's person, describing her as "looking extremely like a handsome Old Jewish patriarch who had backslid and shaved off his beard."

The fact that Gertrude Stein was of Jewish blood further complicated Wilder's reactions to her. Unlike his father, Wilder was not anti-
Semitic. He had easily associated with Jews all his adult life, had warmly
responded to Edith Isaacs and Amy Wertheimer, was indebted to Lewis
Baer and Albert Boni, alternately fascinated and repelled by Jed Harris,

and had been enthusiastically helpful to Yale graduate Geoffrey Hellman, whom he commended to the editors of the *New Yorker*. If there was a vestige of anti-Semitism lingering in Wilder's subconsciousness, however, it was his notion that Jews are, after all, a separate species who should not only maintain their differences, but also insist on them. Of course, a great many American Jews subscribe to the same idea. But some, Gertrude Stein among them, believed that Jewishness was an accident of birth, a state of being that an individual could choose to embrace or ignore—in a society, that is, which allowed such a choice. Wilder, incidentally, unlike Henry James, Edith Wharton, Scott Fitzgerald, T. S. Eliot, Ezra Pound, or Ernest Hemingway never, in any of his work, included a phrase, or even a word, that denigrated Jews or Negroes, or any other minority group. His Christian bias in the early novels is evident; his distaste for Jed Harris's brand of rationalism is revealed in the portrait of Burkin in *Heaven's My Destination*. Up to 1935, Wilder believed Christians should be Christian; Americans, American; Jews, Jewish.

And so it was that, in 1933, Wilder was valiantly struggling with the mystery of Gertrude Stein by reading—or trying to read—*The Making of Americans,* a work commended to him by the French critic and intimate friend of Gertrude Stein, Bernard Faÿ. Wilder wrote Woollcott that he could barely endure the small portion that he had forced himself to read. He points out that not only does she fail to mention that she is a "Jewess," but she also fails to identify the family who are the subject of the novel as being Jewish. For Wilder, the most important thing about the Hersland family was that they were Jews. This odd notion was a lapse of judgment on Wilder's part and a rare lapse of taste. In a little over a year (after becoming a friend of Stein), in another letter to Woollcott, he reversed himself abjectly and utterly. Many who professed disdain for Gertrude Stein and all her works capitulated to some degree upon meeting her. Even Hart Crane. Even Henry Seidel Canby. But no one was to be more thoroughly conquered, converted, and saved than Wilder. And no one was more generously and consistently to acknowledge his debt.

Gertrude Stein, together with Alice B. Toklas arrived in Chicago early in November 1937, the guests of Mr. and Mrs. Charles Barnett ("Bobsy") Goodspeed.* Mrs. Goodspeed, president of Chicago's Arts

---

* Mrs. Goodspeed, née Elizabeth Fuller, was president of the Arts Club from 1931 to 1940. The importance of the Arts Club to the cultural life of Chicago can best be understood by pointing out that the first exhibitions of Soutine and Mondrian in America were held under its auspices; the club held the first Braque retrospective and was the first in this country to show Picasso's *Guernica*. Mrs. Goodspeed, one of Wilder's intimate friends throughout his Chicago years, first brought Wilder and Gertrude Stein together at a dinner she gave at her home for Miss Stein.

Club and largely responsible for Chicago's primacy in the exhibition of important European painters, had visited Gertrude Stein the previous summer; her encouragement had helped Stein to decide to make the American tour. One especially persuasive prospect was the opportunity to see *Four Saints in Three Acts* during her time in Chicago.

Gertrude Stein's first lecture in Chicago was given at the Arts Club on November 25. Eight days later, she addressed an audience of 500 (her inflexible limit), under the auspices of the Renaissance Society at the University of Chicago. A few days before her début at the university, together with Miss Toklas, Wilder, and the Goodspeeds, she was a dinner guest at the Hutchins home, even though Robert Hutchins was not present since he and Mortimer Adler, were holding their Great Books session with a group of selected students. After dinner, the company adjourned to the upstairs sitting room when Hutchins arrived with Adler, the guiding genius of Great Books at Chicago, and Hutchins's chief counselor in matters of philosophy and education. Gertrude Stein was interested in hearing about Chicago's Great Books program—a system of liberal education in which the students read the original documents in the major areas of learning: philosophy, political science, economics, anthropology, physical science, and mathematics, instead of textbooks and secondary sources. In response to Miss Stein's questions, Adler sketched out the ambitious and extensive reading program. After listening for a while, Miss Stein asked whether the students were not reading materials which were, for the most part, nineteenth century translations. Assured that they were, Miss Stein inquired whether it was not indeed a pity that some of the best students at one of America's leading universities were spending the greatest part of their time reading such bad prose. Adler immediately responded,

> But, Miss Stein, we are concerned not with belles lettres but with the communication of ideas, the important ideas of the centuries. Surely you can see that there are more ideas in one chapter of *The Wealth of Nations* than there are in all of Milton's *Paradise Lost*?

To which Miss Stein heatedly responded,

> Not at all! There are more ideas in one *page* of *Paradise Lost* than in all your *Wealths of Nations*. Now I don't want to argue this any further. You're narrow. And I can tell by the narrow shape of your head that you're a born arguer. You could prove anything to me but you'd be wrong. . . .

Wilder, who up to this point had been stretched out on a chaise longue, interposed himself between the two principals and reassured them that each was misunderstanding the other. Wilder succeeded in restoring a harmonious atmosphere for the moment, but irreparable damage had been done. Gertrude Stein had affronted Adler, and, in doing that, she earned the enmity of his most faithful ally, Maude Hutchins. President Hutchins had been contemplating offering Stein a generously endowed chair at the university, an offer she would have been pleased to accept. (Gertrude Stein was then sixty and, despite her fine collection of paintings, she was without more than modest financial resources. At that moment of her life and because she was moved and fascinated by her return to America, the post at Chicago would have suited her perfectly.) But the friction that an appointment for her would have produced in Adler and Maude Hutchins, to say nothing of a largely conservative faculty, persuaded Hutchins to forego the invitation. He did, however, invite her to meet with the students in the Hutchins-Adler seminar; she proved herself to be an effective teacher, eliciting more discussion from the students than Hutchins and Adler could ordinarily generate.

The contretemps between Gertrude Stein and Adler secretly delighted Wilder. He opposed Adler's educational attitudes, and resented the influence he exerted over Hutchins. He felt that Adler had received an appropriate comeuppance at the hands of Gertrude Stein, that she had indeed struck a blow for humanistic freedom. (For years after, Wilder—whenever he was in the company of young people—would recount the story; his imitation of Gertrude Stein came to be a choice item in his dramatic repertory.) The incident, in fact, transformed Wilder from an antagonistic skeptic to an affectionate aficionado, over the few days between their first meeting at Bobsy Goodspeed's dinner and the brouhaha at the Hutchinses. He persuaded Hutchins to extend another invitation to Miss Stein to return to Chicago in the spring and conduct a lecture-seminar series on writing for a group of students whom Wilder would select.

Within a few weeks of this first visit to Chicago, *Heaven's My Destination* was published and Gertrude Stein procured a copy of the book. She promptly wrote Wilder that it was *the* American novel, an overstatement that he welcomed in the light of the tepid reactions that were drifting in from other sources. One might even suspect that he viewed Miss Stein's verdict as reinforcing evidence that she was indeed the wisest, most perceptive, most authoritative critic of English writing in the world. On January 15, he wrote her at great length, beginning with a depreciation of his modest talents. For the length of her seminar at Chicago in the spring, he offered the two ladies his newly acquired Drexel Avenue apartment—an invitation which they accepted. (Wilder moved into one of the college's residence halls.) The letter is fascinating because, although Wilder had known the Misses Stein and Toklas no more than six weeks and could have had no more than three or four encounters with them, he was writing with an intimacy and openness rare for him. He refers to family matters; to the state of affairs in the Hutchins menage; to the profoundly religious implications of Bach's *B minor Mass;* and to his own missed potentialities as a religious thinker. He calls Stein's attention to some concealed nuggets in *Heaven's My Destination* and casually declares his love for a (unidentified) student, at the same time as expressing his admiration for the genius of Handel and the Baroque. Though remarkable, the letter is altogether character- istic of the letters Wilder wrote Gertrude Stein and Alice Toklas for several years—until the fall of France. They are among the finest ex- amples of Wilder's epistolary efforts; and although he maintains much of his characteristically cautious reticence, these letters provide a superb glimpse of a man moving into his maturity, both as an artist and as a person.

The immediate rapport between Wilder and his two new friends (Alice Toklas was no mere appendage, as Wilder shrewdly grasped) is further documented by Wilder's next letter, when he gave the women instructions about moving into his apartment. He exclaimed how won- derful it was to be rich again (*Heaven's My Destination* was selling briskly) and said he had gone out and bought two new pair of shoes and two new suits at the same time.

In a sense he was joking; no money would be coming in from royalties for months. And Wilder didn't require big book sales to get some clothes and shoes. Nevertheless, for some time Wilder had been suffering some financial difficulty. In addition to maintaining two house- holds, his own and the family one in New Haven, Amos Wilder's grave illness was a severe drain upon his resources. Also, money that Wilder put aside for his own use was apt to be squandered on students; when a dozen of them accompanied him to a bar or restaurant, Wilder would imperiously pick up the check. And to assuage their self-respect, he tried to give the impression that this supply of money was inexhaustible. Yet, his comment on being rich again may have had a different kind of practical basis: He may have felt that since a true friendship between himself and Misses Stein and Toklas seemed to be developing it was necessary for all three of them to understand that apart from Wilder's and Gertrude Stein's small capital, all three of them were equally obli- gated to work for a living—as best they could. Friends must understand such matters, particularly in a world where Maecenases are constantly sought to underwrite private printings or to subsidize unappreciated painters and unpublished poets.

Judging from the tone of the letters that Wilder was writing in the early months of 1935, and from the recollections of those who were his friends at the time, the conjunction of Wilder and Gertrude Stein was one of the happiest accidents of his life. Not only did she renew his sense of his artistic worth, but her urgent sense of life revived his own. Within days of his first meetings with her, he was writing Woollcott with unabashed delight that "Gertrude Stein and I are that-way-now." He wrote Glenway Wescott (presumably in reply to a congratulatory letter about *Heaven's My Destination* since they had been out of touch for four years) that he had become weary of teaching the humanities, bored with listening to what had become stale from his own lips. Yet a week later he jokingly described himself to Stein as talking on the *Iliad* with the tongues of men and angels.

Wilder was not teaching during the winter quarter of 1935, although he was in Chicago for most of the time. The end of January marked the fruition of his staging of Handel's *Xerxes*. The opera was performed by the music department of the University of Chicago largely because Handel was one of Wilder's great enthusiasms. Not only did Wilder volunteer to direct, he retranslated the Italian libretto into an idiomatic and contemporary English and assumed a small part (of a soldier) which required his singing a single line. The entire venture provided him an opportunity to indulge his passion for devising, directing, and performing in a stage work—an opportunity that had been largely denied him since his adolescence. *Time,* in their review of the effort, made no comment upon the merits of the revival, but devoted most of its space to Wilder's contribution. It even showed Wilder in his soldier's costume; but, in cape, baggy pants, and an outrageous headpiece he managed to look as much like a soldier as Calvin Coolidge, in a feathered headdress, had looked like an Indian. Later in the winter, after a few weeks at home in New Haven and a fast lecture in Brooklyn, he returned to Chicago in time to serve as interlocutor for Gertrude Stein's writing lecture-seminar at the university. During this time, Woollcott, understandably curious to see Stein in action, journeyed to Chicago. Wilder gave a student party at his apartment to which he invited Woollcott; the party's raison d'etre was to celebrate Robert Ardrey's being summoned to New York by Charles MacArthur and Ben Hecht, who were interested in one of young Ardrey's plays.

The four student guests at the gathering were those Wilder considered his most promising students at Chicago; and he predicted that by 1950 each one would have become "a big splendid figure in the American world." One of the four was a painter; one was a storywriter; one was a playwright; one was a philosopher. Actually, of the four, only one achieved the fame that Wilder predicted for him—Ardrey. But although Ardrey did achieve some recognition as a playwright, his main impact came later as a popular anthropologist, author of *African Genesis* and *The Territorial Imperative*. Another guest, Robert Davis, the student-philosopher, had written a paper on Plotinus and Freud that impressed Gertrude Stein so greatly that she invited him to visit her the following summer at her home in Bilignin, France. Unlike Wilder, Miss Stein's training in philosophy was extensive, and she was willing to play Goethe to Mr. Davis's Eckermann.

Wilder was devoted to these four young men; like the woman of Andros, they caused him to "praise all living, the bright and the dark." But of the four he was most devoted to Robert Davis; just as he had been instructed by John Vincent Healy in modern poetry, now he planned to be tutored by Davis in classical philosophy. And with that end in view, he invited Davis to accompany him during the summer and fall on a trip to Europe, enabling the young man to renew his acquaintance with Gertrude Stein, and begin some graduate study in Vienna.

Wilder took a leave from the university beginning in April 1935: his plans included travel, writing, and lecturing. Before sailing from Montreal on the S. S. *Arcania* at the end of June, he attended the wedding of his brother Amos. Leaving Robert Davis to explore England on his own, Wilder arrived in Paris on July 6 where, for a few days (he wrote Gertrude Stein), he saw no one but got drunk twice a day on the half a carafe of wine he took with his noon and evening meals.* He confessed to being vaguely disturbed to be finding a happiness in biochemistry alone. But within a few years, he was no longer disturbed; drinking became very much a normal part of his life.

He brought with him to Paris the publisher's dummy of Gertrude Stein's *Narration,* based on her lectures to the University of Chicago seminar group. Wilder had agreed to write a foreword and, in response to her urging, agreed further to sign a special edition of the volume. The work was published by the University of Chicago Press, and it contained a four-page introduction by Wilder, the first of three such services he was to perform for works by Gertrude Stein. Because Wilder was devoted and eager to serve, Miss Stein was not at all reluctant to find him practical chores; she besought him to discover publishers for her manuscripts; she urged him to sell *The Autobiography of Alice B. Toklas* to the movies;

---

* Anyone who had an opportunity to see Wilder at close range over a span of almost forty years was aware of his consistently heavy drinking pattern. Generally he took four or five martinis before the evening meal, with plenty of the appropriate wines during the meal, and not much less than a third of a bottle of whiskey in the long evening that followed. The effect of all this was not particularly remarkable. Liquor simply intensified—slightly—the rush of words, the emphatic gestures, the overall enthusiasm. In short, liquor seemed merely to stoke the fires of his personality. Wilder himself declared that "I drink a great deal, but I do not associate it with writing." He did not drink during his working hours; most assuredly he was not an alcoholic, although he was certainly dependent on alcohol.

she insisted that he write a commentary on *The Geographical History of America*. But she discovered that Wilder, truly devoted though he was, genuinely obliging in a hundred different ways, could only be pushed in certain directions. He would *not* provide a commentary; he would **not** collaborate with her in her writings. Anything else, but not that. Uncharacteristically, she accepted this rebuff without reprisals of any kind. And, indeed, her relationship with Wilder remained one of the most—and one of the few—completely harmonious associations of her lifetime, although it was suddenly interrupted by Germany's conquest of France.*

Prior to going to Gertrude Stein's country place in Bilignin, near Belley in the Rhone Valley, Wilder and Robert Davis—who had quickly wearied of London—spent several days investigating Paris and its environs. There were few things that gave Wilder more delight than revealing a favorite city or locality to a younger person who was seeing it for the first time; Davis was Wilder's ideal in such a role, for the young man was all attention, appreciation, and comprehension.

In fact, Wilder was commencing what seems to have been a most exhilarating and satisfying summer, despite the cloud of family worries that was hanging over his consciousness. He had to be concerned about conditions at home: his mother and Isabel were carrying the intolerable burden of attending the wants of Amos Senior, hospitalized by a series of strokes from which there was no hope of recovery. Amos Junior was no help; he had just married. And Charlotte, now living in New York's Greenwich Village, trying to eke out a living as a poet-essayist, was manifesting signs of an incipient nervous breakdown. No one in the family had suggested that there was anything more for Thornton to do beyond providing financial support. Yet, they were there while he was traveling in Europe. These thoughts were disquieting; but he had sufficient judgment to realize that his presence at home would serve no purpose, that the death watch is somehow a woman's work, that his travels in Europe and visits with Gertrude Stein (and, subsequently, with Freud) were essential both to his growth and to the renewal process essential to men of his vocation. And so he explored the inexhaustible riches of Paris and, still accompanied by Davis, visited Fontainebleau for long walks in the woods and elevated reading before they began the trip south to Gertrude Stein's summer home.

The visit was not a disappointment. Wilder emerged from the experience exhilarated, but also somewhat shaken, somewhat changed.

---

* Gertrude Stein, possessor of one of the most subtle and interesting minds of the century, was a political ignoramus and, unfortunately for herself and Miss Toklas, didn't realize it. Influenced by her close friend, Bernard Faÿ, later disgraced for having collaborated, Miss Stein misread every portent in the 1930s. Her failure to leave before the fall of France in 1940 resulted in her sustaining physical privations for four years, and the war experiences may have contributed to her sudden decline and death in 1946.

Writing to Woollcott, he described conversations on the mind and the passions, theories that sent religion and the idea of "human nature" into thin air. He acknowledged that Miss Stein had a tremendous mind, but described it as ultimately abstract to the point of inhumanity. The truth of the matter was that for the first time in his life, Wilder was meeting, on equal terms, a first-class literary-philosophical mind. Stein understood his own ideas, sympathized with, respected, and encouraged them; and, most important, she enabled him to throw overboard the religious deadwood that he had been dragging around for years. Now his more deeply felt themes could be fused directly and organically with his artistic sensibilities. Academic critics have written from time to time about Gertrude Stein's "influences" upon Wilder's later work. Actually Gertrude Stein was not so much an influence—neither on Wilder, nor Sherwood Anderson, nor Hemingway, to cite her best known disciples— as she was a catalyst. She had the inspired teacher's gift of understanding what was already there and what latent strengths needed encouragement and development. In Wilder's early novels, particularly *The Bridge of San Luis Rey* and *The Woman of Andros*, Wilder, somewhat uncomfortably, had to devise complicated stories as a means of explaining *why* things happen or fail to happen. Then, in *Heaven's My Destination* and in three of the one-act plays, he had already forsaken plot and conventional dramatic action; he was, in other words, moving from valuation in sequence to instantaneous cognition. Decades before, Gertrude Stein had renounced plot and dramatic action in her own novels and plays. She was more interested in the *how* of things than in the *why;* it was the ritual of human life she sought to dramatize, to express human emotions as they are, rather than in the heightened and strained state produced by the conventional dramatic situations. In discussing these matters with Wilder, she planted seeds that were ultimately to bear some remarkably choice fruit. The encounter had an immediate effect on Wilder's choice of literary form; he left Bilignin more determined than ever that he would write plays—plays, moreover, that would bear his unmistakable and individual stamp.

With Robert Davis he headed toward the Italian Alps where the plan was to take a walking tour from Cortina d'Ampezzo to Bolzano to Merano, an ambitious project for a man in his late thirties who was habitually engaged in sedentary occupations. Wilder, however, was so spiritually exhilarated—and in such excellent physical condition—that he had no hesitation about tackling the steep and twisting roads and trails that such a journey would have entailed. But the more rugged Robert Davis, confronted by so frightening a prospect of making his way on foot from one mountain town to another developed a host of symptoms and collapsed into a series of maladies. Wilder thereupon took

Davis back into Austria by train where with the help of aspirin he made a speedy recovery. A few days later they were in Salzburg.

The Salzburg festivals of the 1930s preceding Hitler's takeover of Austria have become legendary in retrospect. And with good reason. In a single week, the audiences could hear successive performances conducted by Felix Weingartner, Bruno Walter, Wilhelm Furtwängler, and Arturo Toscanini. Singers such as Lotte Lehmann, secure in their maturity, shared the stage with emerging prima donnas like Zinka Milanov. Max Reinhardt staged drama from the classical repertory. But the glory of Salzburg was opera, the music of Mozart, Beethoven, Verdi, and Richard Strauss. Nothing to be seen and heard in the whole world could more wholly have delighted and absorbed Wilder. For music was the only passion to which he wholly surrendered himself; his truest ecstasies were experienced only at great performances of music. And the music he heard in the summer of 1935 came in a series of breathtaking performances: in a ten-day period, he heard a symphonic program performed by the Vienna Philharmonic conducted by Maestro Toscanini; Mozart's *Don Giovanni* (with Bruno Walter); Beethoven's *Fidelio* (Toscanini and Lotte Lehmann); Verdi's *Falstaff,* twice (Toscanini); Strauss's *Rosenkavalier* (Lehmann); Mozart's *Marriage of Figaro* (Weingartner); and Goethe's *Faust* (twice) directed by Max Reinhardt.

The holiday provided other diversions. At Salzburg, there were old friends to see, including Bobsy Goodspeed and Katharine Cornell; and Fritz Kreisler, the eminent violinist, told Wilder the story of his life, while Max Reinhardt invited him to his *schloss* to meet the Thomas Manns. Throughout the journey, the companionship of Robert Davis, earnest, grave, and enthralled by a succession of discoveries, remained for Wilder a source of constant pleasure. Every now and then, Wilder said later, they fell into conversations in which each man surpassed his usual self and a sort of mystery took place.

That same summer Wilder had a reunion with an Englishwoman who metamorphosed from a notable acquaintance into an intimate friend. This was the celebrated London hostess Sibyl, Lady Colefax, at whose London home, Argyll House, Wilder had first been presented to her and with whom he had maintained a correspondence since. In 1935, Sibyl Colefax, the wife of Sir Arthur Colefax, a barrister and erstwhile member of parliament, was an extraordinary woman of sixty. Her lineage, though it was more than respectable (James Wilson, founder of the *Economist,* was her grandfather and Walter Bagehot, her uncle) was deeply rooted in the middle class. Her husband, Sir Arthur Colefax, though he had greatly prospered before World War I, was by this time no longer wealthy. Nor was Lady Colefax accounted one of England's great beauties; although in any case she had observed throughout her life all the conventional proprieties. Yet, without wealth, distinguished lineage, or physical allure, she presided for three decades over London's most distinguished salon. Statesmen, cabinet ministers, journalists, artists, writers, musicians, and actors from England, America, and the Continent daily visited her drawing room. Even before her home had become an acknowledged shrine, Henry James, Bernard Shaw, and H. G. Wells had frequented Argyll House. By 1935, Mrs. Wallis Simpson and the Prince of Wales had made her their confidante. Sir Harold Nicolson's diary reveals that he visited her daily.

In 1928, Wilder had met both André Maurois and Arnold Bennett at a tea given by Lady Colefax. Her home provided a glimpse of England's legendary foreign secretary, Sir Austen Chamberlain; on later occasions, he was to meet Noel Coward and John Gielgud. In the early years of his acquaintance with her, Wilder could only account himself a minor American satellite of Lady Colefax's extraordinary circle. But owing to his friendship with Woollcott (who was Lady Colefax's American viceroy), Wilder's respectful awe had transformed itself into an affectionate camaraderie which all but rivaled his friendships with Gertrude Stein, Alice Toklas, and Ruth Gordon. By 1935, Lady Colefax had demonstrated an interest in Wilder and in his work that transcended the merely casual and polite; their meeting at Salzburg initiated a relationship between them that endured until 1950, the year of her death.

Like the other ladies in his life, each of whom provided an attentive, comprehending, sympathetic ear and an admiration of his artistic gifts, Sibyl Colefax could be, with impunity, the recipient of Wilder's ardent devotion and affection; yet, he could move in and out of her life at will. Unlike his mother and Isabel, whose claims and demands—because they were never articulated—were as binding as steel, Sibyl Colefax was a mother-sister of unrivaled elegance; and her list of intimate friends made the Wilders' modest New Haven circle of professors, together with their various wives, daughters, mothers, sons, and in-laws, appear hopelessly provincial. Even Wilder's Chicago matrons, Mmes. Claire Swift, Margaret Ayer Barnes, and Bobsy Goodspeed could not compete with "dear and excellent Sibyl," to whom Wilder addressed a great number of the very best letters he ever composed.

After the happy weeks in Salzburg where the concerts and reunions with friends had been followed by salubrious long walks in the Salzkammergut and serious reading and writing, Wilder and Davis went on to Vienna. The high point of this visit for Wilder was a series of meetings with Sigmund Freud. It is commonly assumed that Wilder's meetings with Freud had as their purpose a psychoanalysis, but Wilder, in fact, sought out Freud principally because the older man's work fascinated and absorbed him. During their talks, Wilder did informally consult Freud about his sister Charlotte's mental condition. When Wilder described her symptoms, the physician could only concur that a breakdown seemed imminent and inevitable, a prognosis which unhappily was all too well substantiated.

Freud had read all Wilder's novels in German and found them much to his liking with the exception of *Heaven's My Destination*. He considered Wilder more *ein Dichter* (a poet) than a mere *Romanschriftsteller* (storyteller) and he regarded Wilder's latest novel as shamefully prosaic and sordid—an evaluation that provides more insight into Freud's literary tastes than it does into Wilder's artistic capacities.

Perhaps the most bizarre aspect of the Freud-Wilder meetings was Freud's astonishing conclusion that Wilder would make an excellent husband for his daughter Anna. With characteristic middle-European practicality, he envisaged an excellent match for a couple no longer quite young, but intelligent enough to value each other's virtues and capacities. Wilder tactfully sidestepped the issue, but he was sufficiently struck by the situation to confide Freud's proposal in a letter to Gertrude Stein.*

Returning to the United States in November 1935, Wilder brought back with him drafts of several plays in various states of completion. The draft on which he had made most progress was his reworking of an old play by the Viennese farceur, Johann Nestroy, *Einen Jux Will Er Sich Machen (He'll Have a Good Time for Himself)*. Having talked with Reinhardt in Salzburg, Wilder had high hopes that the renowned master director would stage his *jeu d'esprit* in New York. This little Viennese farce would, in its various incarnations, turn out to be his most disastrous failure and a quarter of a century later his greatest popular success.

The winter of 1935–36, however, was far from prosperous for Wilder. Not only did he support his two households (his own in Chicago or wherever he hung his hat, and the family home on Deepwood Drive) but for the third year he was paying his father's costly hospital expenses. He continued work on the plays, commuting between New York and New Haven before resuming his midwinter lecture tour, which would end just before he was to begin teaching at Chicago. He had come to regard lecturing as an intolerable burden, hardly less oppressive than teaching, which he described in letters both to Sibyl Colefax and Gertrude Stein as an enterprise which for him had become a shame and a bore, since he had lost conviction in what he was saying.

Shortly after resuming his teaching duties at Chicago in April 1936 and assuming that his father's death was imminent, Wilder filed his

---

* Wilder authorized the publication of the letter, long after Freud's death, in Donald Gallup's edition of letters to Gertrude Stein, *Flowers of Friendship*.

resignation from the university, effective September 1, 1936. Everyone expected Amos Wilder to die in the spring, when the effect of the strokes had darkened his mind, but his death did not actually occur until July 2. According to Isabel, among the five Wilder children, Amos had most alienated Charlotte and Thornton. Even so, Charlotte, eking out a living as a writer in Greenwich Village, came to the funeral. Wilder's teaching duties at Chicago rendered it impractical for him to attend.*

It cannot be said with finality that Wilder hated his father, although such feelings can be inferred both from letters and from his remarks to intimate friends. What is apparent is that he never forgave his father for his sternness and lack of sensitivity, either privately or publicly. In print, there is barely a reference that he ever existed; in private letters, he describes his father in a tone that can best be described as savage irony.† In the 1950s, while speaking to this writer, a sudden memory of his father called up in Wilder an uncharacteristic rage, an outburst not entirely unlike that in the penultimate scene in *The Skin of Our Teeth* when the son-actor and father-actor nearly kill one another on stage.

As the day of his liberation from teaching duties approached, Wilder was in a state combining exhilaration and confusion. Having already worked on a movie for producer Samuel Goldwyn (the film was Tolstoi's *Resurrection,* released under the title *We Live Again,* and featuring Fredric March and Anna Sten), Wilder entertained thoughts of spending several months in Hollywood before commencing his final lecture tour in January and February. Instead, during that fall of 1936, he traveled, somewhat frenetically, and wrote, somewhat sporadically. He first settled for some weeks in St. Thomas ensconced up in the hills at Bluebeard's Castle. Finding afternoons in the Virgin Islands too hot, he thought next of permanently settling in Berkeley, California (where there was, he wrote Gertrude Stein, the resources of a large library and the opportunity for long walks). Returning from the Caribbean he turned up at Berea College, Kentucky, to visit its president and Mrs. Hutchins, old friends from his Oberlin days and Robert's parents.

During the months of freedom following his father's death and his release from Chicago (but interrupted by the January-February 1937

---

* Curiously enough, in writing Gertrude Stein and Alice Toklas, Wilder withheld the fact that he was not present at the obsequies; in fact, he gave the impression that he was there—in contrast with Isabel's subsequent recollection that he arrived as soon as he could, but not in time for the funeral. Wilder did not conceal from Misses Stein and Toklas, however, that far from feeling sorrow, he was relieved that his mother and Isabel were spared any more of the strain and hardship which his father's protracted illness had imposed upon them.

† A Wilder letter to Woollcott in the early 1930s mercilessly derides his father's Puritan self-absorption.

lecture tour), Wilder worked on and thought about several long plays. Among them were at least three that he never brought to completion or at least never offered for production. But he continued work on the Nestroy-inspired farce, *The Merchant of Yonkers,* and he provided Jed Harris with an adaptation of Ibsen's *A Doll's House* for Ruth Gordon. Most important, using the techniques he had experimented with six years earlier in *The Happy Journey to Trenton and Camden,* lifting a scene from *The Woman of Andros,* and focusing upon some aesthetic principles he had derived from conversations with Gertrude Stein, Wilder had begun work on the play that was to prove as critical to his career as *The Bridge of San Luis Rey* had been a decade earlier. In early 1937, enough of the play was completed so that he was reading drafts of it to friends and neighbors and dispatching a scene or two overseas to Sibyl Colefax. By June, he was at the MacDowell Colony writing another draft of this newest work in progress, to which he had by now given the title of *Our Town.*

# IX

## Landscaping Shubert Alley

*"I saw it as a director's dream come true."*
—JED HARRIS

The man at work on *Our Town*, we must remind ourselves, was a forty-year-old novelist of a certain international celebrity who had had no critical, nor even popular, success for a decade. And, stagestruck since adolescence, Wilder ached for recognition and respect from the glamorous theater personalities whose acquaintance he had been cultivating since his first adventitious meeting with critic Stark Young in the early twenties. For Wilder, it was not enough to be merely a friend of the Lunts, Ruth Gordon and Jed Harris, Helen Hayes and Charles MacArthur, Noel Coward, and Alexander Woollcott and Mary Pickford; he wanted to be their working colleague, a bona fide man of the theater and accepted as such by George Kaufman, who seemed chronically incapable of remembering who Wilder was.

Robert Ardrey aptly summarized the fascination that writing plays held for himself, for the best creative talents among the students at the University of Chicago in the 1930s, and for Wilder, their teacher:

Viewed from its cheapest seats or viewed from its most expensive,
viewed in some provincial theatre or in the vicinity of Broadway's

116

electric glamor, the plays of the time cast an equivalent spell over the imaginations of incipient young writers, wherever they might be. Fortunately for me, in my senior year at Chicago Thornton Wilder joined the faculty. It was 1930. Wilder at that time had two Pulitzer Prizes yet to go, but he had just won his first for *The Bridge of San Luis Rey*. When it was announced that he would teach a course in creative writing to a class limited in number to fifteen, Chicago became the scene of a struggle for survival unrivalled since the earlier years of Capone gangland massacre. Students fought among themselves. North Shore hostesses fought for entrance not only to the class but to the University. No trustee's arm was left untwisted. No eminent faculty member was left unassaulted for recommendation. Intellectual mayhem, character assassination, well-placed rumors of fakery and plagiarism, that the brilliant short story by So-and-so published in the literary monthly had been in truth written by somebody else, became the weapons of the moment.

I make no apologies, but I have an inexplicable gift for survival under conditions of jungle warfare. I wound up a member of the Fifteen Chosen. And at the first meeting of the class Thornton Wilder—not that much older than we were—looked about at us through his horn-rimmed glasses, rubbed his mustache and laid a question before us.

"There's something I need to know," he said. "We're going to discuss creative writing. But I'd like a show of hands. What *form* of writing appeals to you most? If you're granted the condition that make for final success, what is it you'd most like to write? Novels?"

One hand went up. The reader must remember that our class was facing, in splendid awe, a young author whose rocket-like rise had been associated with nothing but the novel. Yet there was only one hand. Wilder seemed quite unastonished and surveyed the hands in laps. The short story? No hands. Poetry? No hands. The play?

Fourteen hands went up. Wilder snorted. Then the someday author of *Our Town*, *The Skin of Our Teeth* and *The Matchmaker* lifted his hand too.

No other literary genre, it would seem, could offer so many rewards: money, of course, and fame; but also the collaboration of gifted men and women—actors, directors, producers, designers. And actresses. And a successful Broadway playwright was assured a seat at the Algonquin's famed Round Table.

As Ardrey's story illustrates, even though Wilder had already achieved most of the material benefits that come to an established author, he yearned, like Henry James before him, and as much as any fledgling author, for success in the theater. Between Wilder and the others, however, there was a difference. Given his literary prominence, as well as his aesthetic discussions with Gertrude Stein he could now court success as a playwright on his own terms. His plays would have nothing in common with the prevailing modes. S. N. Behrman, Philip Barry, Robert Sherwood, Sidney Howard, Eugene O'Neill, Noel Coward, Sidney Kingsley,

Clifford Odets, George Kaufman and Moss Hart, Owen Davis and Maxwell Anderson could rest easy; Wilder was not in competition. Not with
Ibsen. Not with Chekhov. Not with Strindberg. And most particularly
not with Shaw.

Wilder's first exposure to professional theater, we noted, coincided
with his adolescence in Berkeley when he attended the mindless melodramas, farces, and romantic comedies performed by the stock company
at the Liberty Theater in neighboring Oakland. Absorbed as he was by
these performances, he inevitably turned to reading Shakespeare and
Ibsen to satisfy his maturing sense of what drama could be. By the time
he was eighteen and a student at Oberlin College, he had become so
fascinated by drama and the theater that he had not only begun writing
the three-minute plays, but he had also written a prize essay, "The
Language of Emotion in Shakespeare," one sentence of which reads:

> Ibsen overcame the obstacle [of rhetoric] by the use of symbols which
> move like great clouds behind the ordinary parlor conversations.

A dramatist who materially influenced Wilder in the impressionable
years of his late adolescence was Theodore Dreiser. In 1916, Dreiser, who
was known as a novelist in the naturalistic tradition, had composed seven
one-act plays of quite a different sort, which John Lane published under
the accurately descriptive title *Plays of the Natural and Supernatural.*
Three of the seven plays are good, workmanlike examples of their period,
in the tradition of Susan Glaspell and the Provincetown Players (who
did, indeed, later produce Dreiser's full-length tragedy, *The Hand of the
Potter*). But it was not the naturalist plays that excited the young
Wilder. Rather, it was the four "supernatural" plays whose influence can
be traced in Wilder's dramatic work from the early three-minute plays
through the one-act plays of the early thirties to *Our Town.* In both,
theme and technique, Dreiser was the first modern playwright to begin
the expansion of Wilder's dramatic imagination.

In one of his plays, *The Blue Sphere,* Dreiser lays before us an entire
section of a village called Marydale. And though the play has as its focus
in the kitchen of the Delavan home, the audience (or more properly, the
reader) sees the exterior yard, the front gate, the sweet pea vines, and
trumpet flowers that separate the Delavan house from the Minturn house
next door. As the play progresses, the reader is taken to the main street,
to the outskirts of the town, and finally to the railroad crossing where the
fast mail enters the village and kills an infant child. Dreiser made no
attempt to indicate a solution to the production problems of *The Blue
Sphere;* presumably, he did not intend it as a stage work at all. But
Wilder, fascinated by the idea of recreating the interiors and exteriors of

two two-story houses adjoining one another, of adding Main Street, the school yard, the village drug store, the choir loft, the church, and the village cemetery—all scenes of continuous and even simultaneous action —was enabled, over a score of years later, to place a setting like that of Dreiser's play.* Wilder was absorbed by more than Dreiser's free-floating, expressionistic technique on the stage. Wilder was to make use of two of Dreiser's themes in his novels: the ecstasy of being alive, as seen through the eyes of those who no longer have life, and the repetitive, cyclical history of mankind. Later, he elaborated upon these themes and fully orchestrated them in *Our Town* and *The Skin of Our Teeth.*

Another early influence on Wilder's mature dramas was Mei Lan-fang, a celebrated Chinese actor whom Wilder saw perform in New York in 1930, whose effective use of pantomime influenced *Our Town.* And Richard Boleslavsky, who produced Wilder's *The Trumpet Shall Sound* in 1926, trained his actors to perform without props, a technique that interested Wilder.†

The innovation in *Our Town* that provoked the most critical appro-bation as well as later imitation was Wilder's use of the Narrator-Stage Manager, part of whose ancestry lies in the Chinese theater but whom Wilder borrowed mainly from his own earlier play, *The Happy Journey to Trenton and Camden.* Without the Narrator there would be no *Our Town;* and the Narrator as Wilder conceived and employed him has no real precedent in European-American theater. The character has roots, of course, in a number of literary works of the past, for example, the author-commentator of *Vanity Fair;* the Chorus in Shakespeare's Henry V; and the Coryphaeus (chorus leader) of the Greek classical tragedies. But Wilder's Narrator has a more Protean essence: he is at once cracker-barrel philosopher, village druggist, Congregational minister, puppeteer, prop-erty man, stage manager, and ageless seer god. He is, in effect, a com-

* Wilder is said to have derived some of his staging ideas from the published writing of the French playwright Alfred Jarry whose stage directions for *Ubu Roi* (1896) prescribe a bare stage with a single backdrop and a Stage Manager who is to appear from time to time with a placard informing the audience where the action is taking place. Jarry's influence on Wilder, however, would have required Wilder's poring over several volumes of Jarry's *Oeuvres complètes;* only in volume seven does there appear the letter from the playwright to the director about the staging. Whether Wilder actually had Jarry in mind when he was writing *Our Town* is a moot question. More important to *Our Town* was Wilder's seeing one of the first performances of Pirandello's *Six Characters* in Rome in 1921, where the audience entering the theater were con-fronted by a bare, half-darkened stage.
† The legendary French troupe, La Compagnie des Quinze of Jacques Copeau (1913– 24), performed on a very simple stage: with bare walls, little scenery, and a concrete floor. One of the plays in their repertory was a revival of Prosper Merimée's *Le Car-rosse du Saint-Sacrement,* the ancestor of Wilder's *The Bridge of San Luis Rey.* Wilder saw Copeau's production of the Merimée during at least one of its two New York seasons 1917–18 and 1918–19.

posite of what Wilder himself, by 1937, was becoming—or at least what he was role playing.*

Wilder's aspirations for his play challenged those of any other American playwright. *Our Town,* he hoped, would revolutionize or at least drastically modify dramatic form. Further, he intended the play to refocus his countrymen's consciousness of the American myth by reenacting in ritual fashion birth, initiation, courtship, marriage, and death, as those rites occur in the context of an idealized turn-of-the-century village in New England, physically and spiritually removed from industrial filth and turmoil, racial strife, urban crimes, and social inequities. Rather than attack, undermine, or denigrate the latter-day Puritan ethos, the play would uphold and reinforce it. Wilder understood that Eugene ONeill's and Sinclair Lewis's successes in their respective satires of American Puritanism (a tradition that neither writer understood very clearly) stemmed precisely from America's irrevocable commitment to its Puritan ideas. Indeed, it is difficult to satirize something unless it is already deeply embedded in the matrix of the national consciousness. Wilder's play was to be a celebration of the egalitarian ideas and Puritan attitudes associated with his childhood upbringing. Neither China nor California nor Rome and neither sojourns in the capitals of Europe nor association with the intellectually gifted men and women of the world's great cities could wean him away from his American Puritan heritage. The experiences of his adult years merely enabled him to view that heritage—like the play's Narrator—with a certain ironic detachment mingled with pride. But Wilder's commitment to it was steadfast.

Because he sensed that his "little play," as he referred to it in letters, was potentially a masterwork, Wilder worked on it slowly, patiently, and lovingly. He had begun serious work during his 1936 fall stay at Bluebeard's Castle in the Virgin Islands. By January 1937, he was far enough along to read an early draft to Edward Sheldon, now blind and bedridden, but still the oracle, counselor, and friend to a number of the New York theater personalities. Sheldon immediately grasped the play's importance. He wrote Wilder these words of encouragement:

> . . . You broke every rule. There is no suspense, no relationship between acts, no progress but every seven minutes—no every five minutes—you've supplied a new thing—some novelty—in the proceedings, which is at once a pleasure in the experience, and, at the same time, a contribution to the content of the play. Most plays progress in time, but here is progression in depth. Let us know this town more and more.

* Wilder did, in fact, play the Narrator many times: first on Broadway, as Frank Craven's replacement; in summer stock; and on television. Although Wilder essentially lacked the professional actor's temperament, he enacted the role with a definitive authority and style.

Before setting forth in February on his final lecture tour, Wilder spent the 1936–37 winter season shuttling between New Haven and New York, working on three plays and renewing old friendships. He loved being in New York. Woollcott invited him to dinner with Gerald Murphy, John Gielgud, and Ruth Gordon. The Lunts invited him to "just a small party": the guests included Hope Williams, the Sidney Howards, Sibyl Colefax, and Woollcott. Wilder wrote Gertrude Stein and Alice Toklas that his dearest hope was that within five years they might all be living in New York, "the greatest city in the world," together with "Alick" and Ned Sheldon and the Hutchinses and Ruth Gordon. In the same letter, he predicted that Robert Hutchins would become president of the United States "in eight or ten years."*

The notion of bringing Gertrude Stein and Alice Toklas back to New York as permanent residents obsessed Wilder. Having succeeded in establishing his parents and sister in the big brown house in Connecticut, he now dreamed of acquiring one or two of the red brick houses on Washington Square North and setting up a commune. The prospective inmates varied from time to time, but the Wilder-Stein-Toklas nucleus remained constant in his mind.

One of Wilder's prominent women friends who was actually sojourning in New York that winter was Sibyl Colefax. Her husband, Sir Arthur, had died in the previous autumn and, as a consequence, this formidable London hostess had had to relinquish Argyll House after the decades of success and happiness there. With characteristic generosity, Woollcott had invited Lady Colefax to visit New York, underwriting all of her expenses and incidentally enabling Wilder to reinforce the friendship that had truly flowered only the previous summer at Salzburg, although their acquaintance had begun in 1928. And Wilder was genuinely attentive; when he was not actually seeing Lady Colefax, he was sending her "piccoli bolletini: frammenti d'uno diario." Most of the extant 120 odd letters that Wilder wrote to Sibyl Colefax are distinguished for their spontaneity and openness, comparable to his concurrent correspondence with Gertrude Stein and Alice Toklas. In a letter dated January 18, for example, he describes to Lady Colefax leaving the Lunts' dinner party with Woollcott who, after an acidulous attack on Sidney Howard, went into an abject description of self-indulgent pleasures (not specified by Wilder) that he would abandon himself to, if he could. Wilder describes his reaction to Woollcott's maunderings as "half-horrified curiosity." Changing the subject, Wilder summarizes a recent all-night talk session

---

* Five years later, Gertrude Stein and Alice Toklas were struggling for survival in Nazi-overrun France; Woollcott was dead; Hutchins was politically dead; Wilder was in uniform; Ruth Gordon was everywhere. Only Edward Sheldon, perforce, was in New York.

with Jed Harris—who is troubled by bad dreams and whose psychic problems Wilder analyzes as comparable to those of Maude Hutchins. Then he moves on to a fulsome panegyric on the Lunts, as expiation, presumably, for the indiscreet comments he had made about them in a widely circulated letter to Lady Colefax in 1933.*

Writing to Lady Colefax a few days later, Wilder provides a detailed account of an early morning visit to the celebrated dinner club, Twenty-One on Fifty-second Street. Arriving there at 3:15 A.M., he dances in turn with the wife of an actor and then with a well-known professional dancer, Anita Page. He describes being accosted by "walk-ons" (first a fraternity brother, then an aspiring actor who had been a secretary to Woollcott). Next, he has a long conversation with Madeline Sherwood, formerly the wife of Marc Connelly and subsequently married to Robert Sherwood; they discuss Sherwood's work habits "with awe." Leaving Twenty-one at 4:35 A.M., Wilder encountered Sherwood himself at the stairhead. Presumably the men had just met for the first time. Sherwood, a kindly and generous man, said some words of praise about the final paragraph of *The Woman of Andros*, which several years earlier he had reviewed for *Scribner's*. Nervous at the encounter, Wilder tactlessly dismissed the lines Sherwood so sincerely appreciated, saying that they were merely an imitation of the closing paragraph of James Joyce's "The Dead." Sherwood, in turn, was embarrassed and the two writers awkwardly parted, Wilder furious at himself for having acquitted himself so badly.

Wilder's gracelessness and awkwardness in the presence of Robert Sherwood has interesting ramifications. Whatever self-doubts he may have harbored about his own artistic achievements and capacities, he had no doubt whatsoever that they were superior to those of Robert Sherwood. At that time Sherwood's plays included *The Road to Rome, Waterloo Bridge, Reunion in Vienna, The Petrified Forest,* and *Idiot's Delight,* none of which Wilder regarded as possessing any real literary or artistic merit. He had written Sibyl Colefax, in fact, that he felt that the Lunts were dissipating their talents by appearing in plays like Sherwood's *Reunion in Vienna* or Noel Coward's *Design for Living.* Why, then, had Wilder fallen on his face in the presence of Sherwood?

The answer lies principally in Sherwood's being at that moment the most fashionable and consistently successful playwright in New York. Within five years, he had written three long-running plays and had adapted a fourth, *Tovarich,* from the French pen of Jacques Deval. In

* The letter, still a legend among the older generation of Broadway and West End luminaries, was never published. A parody of it by Woollcott that he sent to Lady Colefax was included in Woollcott's selected letters (edited by Beatrice Kaufman). Noel Coward circulated the contents of the Wilder original, now in this author's collection.

the same period, he had turned out a succession of motion picture scripts for Metro-Goldwyn-Mayer, Samuel Goldwyn, United Artists, Alexander Korda, and Warner Brothers—films based on both his own and other people's work. Sherwood enjoyed a certain kind of Broadway-Hollywood réclame that Wilder would not have entirely rejected for himself. For, from the point of view of Sherwood's associates, Wilder's role was essentially peripheral; he was not in the center of the theater world like the Lunts and Gertrude Lawrence and Gilbert Miller and Noel Coward—and Sherwood. Nor were the calls from Hollywood loud, clear, or frequent.

Wilder was intimidated even more by something besides Sherwood's professional eminence. Sherwood was New York Society, or more accurately, a man who through his own achievements had been graduated from the Social Register into more general prominence. His forebears, far from being a succession of genteel New England divines, were commercial and legal worthies firmly anchored in New York and Westport. Sherwood's grandmother, for example, had been a formidable social arbiter whose intimates and acquaintances had included the Vanderbilts, the Morgans, the Roosevelts, Robert Browning, Oscar Wilde, and Lord Randolph Churchill. She had received a diamond pin from Queen Victoria, audiences from Queen Marguerite of Italy, and the Legion of Honor from the French government. Moreover, Sherwood, only a year older than Wilder, had left Harvard at the end of his junior year and, when he was rejected by the United States Army for military service because he was underweight, had enlisted in July 1917 in Canada's famed Black Watch Regiment. By February 1918, he was in France and served in the trenches for five and a half months before he was wounded, gassed, and hospitalized. Confronted by Sherwood, socialite-playwright, alumnus of Milton Academy and Harvard, veteran of overseas combat, a six-foot-seven-inch giant successively married to two beautiful actresses, a man's man and friend of Douglas Fairbanks, Will Rogers, Ring Lardner, and Robert Benchley—confronted by this casual, gentle, and self-accepting man, Wilder could establish no camaraderie, no community of interest, no real friendship.

Sherwood's world was the sphere of Broadway playwrights where everyone was a professional. Despite the occasional incursion of an Edna Ferber or a Lillian Hellman, it was a man's world. Neither novel writing nor teaching the young held any cachet in an atmosphere so permeated by cigar smoke, whiskey, profanity, and male assertiveness as the playwright's world in which Sherwood held a commanding position. Yet, despite his sense of alienation from Sherwood's environment, Wilder was determined to be more than a mere camp follower.

Work on *Our Town* continued through the late spring and early

summer of 1937. Simultaneously, Wilder was able to turn over to Jed
Harris his adaptation of a translation of Ibsen's *A Doll's House,* continue
work on the Nestroy farce, and sketch out a third play. In June, the
winter lecture tour having been followed by spring in New York and
New Haven, he retreated to the MacDowell Colony; there, work on *Our
Town* went well and before leaving Peterborough, he felt sufficiently
confident to offer Woollcott the dedication.

On July 3, Wilder sailed for France on the S. S. *de Grasse* as
American delegate to the Institut de Cooperation Intellectuel of the
League of Nations, the first of several occasions in which Wilder functioned as a distinguished citizen in the service of his country. Why should
Wilder have begun accepting time-consuming and exhausting assignments as a delegate to international conferences and seminars, as special
envoy for the Department of State, or as military intelligence officer in
the Army Air Force? Few men, of course, can resist the distinction of
being named a representative of their country or even of their profession.
The tradition of men of letters serving as public servants is as old as
history itself, with Sophocles, Vergil, Dante, Chaucer, Milton, and
Goethe among the names one can adduce. Neither Wilder's sense of civic
duty nor his patriotism were at all diminished by the memory that his
father's watchword was duty, honor, country. On the other hand, although Wilder's own patriotic commitment was profound, like that of
Faulkner and Hemingway, he might—like Faulkner—have reasoned that
he could best serve his country by writing as much and as well as he
could. But Wilder's extraordinary gregariousness, that element in his
personality which almost neurotically attracted him to any collection of
talented and worldly people, drew him to Paris. His writing was temporarily set aside.

Once in Europe, Wilder first refreshed himself with visits to Parisian
theaters and museums. He attended a performance of Giraudoux's
*Electre* which he considered a great deal of adorable pirouetting under
the great vaults of that fearful story, that "mixture of matricide and high
spirits" as one critic had described Sophocles' version. Curiously, a letter
to Gertrude Stein written that same week contains a postscript, heavy
with irony, in which he describes the Venus de Milo as entirely worthy of
Baedeker's three stars, "a very good statue."

Also, in Paris, he briefly saw Sibyl Colefax and made an arrangement
for a more extended rendezvous in Salzburg the following month. Perhaps without intending to, Lady Colefax imposed upon Wilder a frus-
trating disappointment: the Duke and Duchess of Windsor—the most
glamorous newlyweds of their epoch—had somehow learned that Sibyl
Colefax planned to inaugurate her August holiday in Salzburg in
Wilder's company. Inviting her to visit them in their nearby hideaway,

they bade her bring Wilder. But having passed on the invitation to the stupefied Wilder, Lady Colefax added that she did not recommend his accepting unless he were going merely out of curiosity. As she put it, the Duke and Duchess didn't speak their language, the language of literature and art.* There was no way for Wilder to accept, given the circumstances in which he was proffered the invitation—particularly since Lady Colefax may have had private and unspoken reasons for not wishing Wilder to accompany her. But he was grievously disappointed at having been offered so tantalizing a glimpse of so rich a feast and then being denied the opportunity to approach the table. Only eight or nine months had passed since Edward's abdication, and there was nobody who was not avidly curious about the former king and "the woman he loved."

The agenda for the Paris conference, as drawn up by Paul Valéry, included such matters as the impoverishment of vocabularies in modern languages; the decay of syntax; the inability of the moderns to understand long sentences; the effect of radio listening upon literary forms; the question of who would support the serious literary artist when there were no longer patrons nor an elite interested in the work of an Ezra Pound or a James Joyce. Wilder chose, as the subject of his contribution to the discussions, a defense of American English, of American reasons for refashioning the language to suit the needs of a great continent. His address elicited the delighted approval of Gilbert Murray, E. M. Forster, and Valéry himself, none of whom realized that Wilder was paraphrasing Gertrude Stein's *Lectures in America* and *Narration*.†

Replacing E. M. Forster, who resigned on the grounds that he was unaccustomed to committee work, Wilder was drafted to serve on a committee formed to draft a resolution furthering the circulation of good books and the support of distressed and impoverished authors through an international royalty agreement. The resolution ended:

> La comité constate enfin que le destin prochain des lettres dépend essentiellement de la liberté de penser, et de l'independence economique laissée aux esprits créateurs. (The committee declares that the future of letters depends essentially on liberty of thought and economic independence granted to creative spirits.)

* Harold Nicolson confirms this notion in relating how Edward, when he was king, left a party given by Sibyl Colefax while Artur Rubinstein was playing the piano; then, having interrupted the music, His Royal Majesty returned to the party when Noel Coward replaced Rubinstein at the piano. Actually, in the situation described by Nicolson one can sympathize with King Edward. "Mad Dogs and Englishmen" is more appropriate to parties than Chopin ballades, if only because one need not listen to the former, even out of politeness.

† In letters to Gertrude Stein, Wilder painstakingly and deliberately acknowledged his indebtedness. But he felt that there might be awkwardness if he were to declare his source publicly. The question could have been raised: why was the United States represented by Wilder and not by Gertrude Stein, herself?

Germany, not being a member of the League, was without representation. But Italy, represented by Signori Ojetti, Guiliano, and Pavolini, objected to the resolution. Wilder, partly because he didn't trust his French, but also because he felt the resolution was vaguely worded and meaningless, kept silent. In matters political, although he inclined toward liberalism, he was usually reluctant to make his position public, as though he somehow feared the censure or disapproval of his father, of William Lyon Phelps, of the Chicago Gold Coast ladies—or of Gertrude Stein, whose political philosophy was firmly grounded in that of the McKinley administration. The resolution, however, was firmly supported and defended by MM. Jules Romains, Duhamel, and Focillon and by Señor Madariaga, and it prevailed.

After visiting Gertrude Stein and Alice Toklas at Bilignin, Wilder went on to Salzburg for the Festival where he delighted in Toscanini, Bruno Walter, Weingartner; *Fidelio, Magic Flute, Falstaff;* and Goethe's *Faust,* directed by Reinhardt. For company there were Sibyl Colefax, Erich Maria Remarque, Carl Zuckmayer, Hugo von Hoffmansthal, and Frederic Prokosch. Once again Salzburg's music and drama, its architecture and sculpture, its residents and visitors all combined to intoxicate Wilder's senses. But, alas, this was the end of Salzburg's golden age; in a few months Salzburg was to be absorbed by the master of nearby Berchtesgaden. Max Reinhardt and Bruno Walter became exiles; Toscanini was never to return.

The Salzburg experience, which Wilder described to Gertrude Stein as sheer pleasure, seems to have been the ideal preparation for finishing *Our Town.* In Paris and Salzburg, Wilder had temporarily exhausted his need for excitement, for mingling with the writers and thinkers in Paris, for attending performances of music and drama by the world's great interpreters, and for all night conversations with brilliant and gifted friends, acquaintances, and pickups, all of them ending after curfew in the third-class waiting room of the railroad station. Now, the Festival over, his friends dispersed (Sibyl Colefax going on to her rendezvous with the Windsors) Wilder proceeded, by way of Innsbruck to Zurich and St. Moritz to resume writing, renewed and refreshed.

He began work on the second act of *Our Town* in Innsbruck during the first week of September. At the same time he came upon a novel, *Der Kampf um Caesar's Erbe* (The Battle Over Caesar's Legacy) by Ferdinand Mainzer; this was a significant encounter since the novel lingered in Wilder's mind and led, a decade later, to Wilder's own novel about Caesar.

Meanwhile, correspondence with Sibyl Colefax entered into new layers and folds of intimacy; having already read to her as much of *Our Town* as he had written, Wilder included in his letters to her that fall

copies of new scenes as he wrote them and detailed summaries of what
was to come. She, in turn, wrote about her visits to the Windsors and to
Bernard Berenson; her visit with her former sovereign lasted from lunch
until the early hours of the following morning. The Duke and Duchess,
she said, were completely happy and he was physically and mentally
abounding in good health; between lunch and tea, the Duke joined the
haymakers in the valley and took a scythe and cut the best swath of all.
In his reply, Wilder confided that he was outraged to receive the
Hutchinses' postcards from England, which contained no return addresses,
because they were in terror lest he call on them. The same letter summarizes the wedding scene of *Our Town,* including a passage (later excised
from the text) where George Gibbs, just before the ceremony, turns on
his father and knocks him down, at the same time reviling his mother.
His letter of September 4 contains an early version of the stringbean
scene in Act I, where Emily asks her mother, "Am I pretty, mama?" In
this early version, the dialogue lacks the spontaneity and conviction of
the scene as it was ultimately to emerge. But *Our Town* is already all
there; and this earlier version reveals how much care and artistry went
into the writing of what appears to be a simple, artless play.

The ten or twelve weeks in Zurich that Wilder spent writing and
rewriting *Our Town* may very well have been the most self-disciplined
and concentrated effort of his career, even though he kept up his regular
routine of long walks, an extensive correspondence, a careful reading of
the daily papers, and the reading of books, many of them sent by
acquaintances and total strangers who hoped for and received painstak-
ing criticisms of their new works. At the age of forty, Wilder's energies
seemed inexhaustible. The surge of creative and physical energy filled
him with happiness, the only kind of satisfaction that seemed possible for
him to attain. When he wasn't at his desk, he would prowl about in
Zurich's old town, or wander along the shores of Lake Zurich with its
Alpine views, or visit the zoo. Animals and small children delighted
him.

On September 13, a Monday, he wrote Gertrude Stein and Alice
Toklas, and revealed to them, at long last, that he was writing a play
called *Our Town,* that he had completed two acts and would have the final
act finished by the following Friday. The third act, he stated, was based
on Gertrude Stein's aesthetic and philosophic ideas (though elsewhere he
was to declare in several instances that the third act was based on Canto 8
of Dante's *Purgatorio,* a most tenuous connection, hardly visible to the
naked eye). As for Wilder's indebtedness to Stein, it does indeed exist.
Her scientific rationalism and cold indifference to religious fervor undoubtedly contributed to a diminuendo in Wilder's Christian commitment. Moreover, Gertrude Stein had been writing plays since 1913. It was

her conviction that plays are not unlike landscapes, in the sense that both landscapes and plays provide a representation of physical expanses whose terrain is composed and laid out for the absorbed examination by an audience. She did not believe that plays should tell stories, but rather that they should contain random people whose random conversations we overhear, whose movements and ritualistic acts we observe as the dramatis personae move to and fro across their expanse of earth symbolized by a theater's stage. To a considerable extent, Wilder employed these technical ideas in *Our Town:* some of the dialogue, such as the three conversations forming the coda of Act I, contribute nothing to the "story line" of the play; the pantomime of the two mothers—starting the fire in the kitchen stove and preparing breakfast, shelling peas, and stringing beans—suggest the ritualistic acts of all mothers, not only in this particular play but in the universal continuum which the play hopes to evoke. In short, *Our Town* is at least as descriptive as it is narrative; in that respect, Wilder, the playwright, was disciple to Gertrude Stein.

In mid-October 1937, Wilder journeyed to Italian Switzerland to get some sun and cure a cold. He would have preferred Italy proper but his outrage at Fascism (whose spirit reminded him of his father) prevented him from crossing the border. A few days later, he returned to Zurich. By the last week of October, he had completed the full drafts of *Our Town* and of the farce based on Nestroy's play, now entitled *The Merchant of Yonkers.* Jed Harris, in London, having been apprised that Wilder's year-long efforts had borne fruit, called him in Zurich and the two men arranged a meeting in Paris at month's end.

The meeting was momentous. Jed Harris—dynamic, professional, intelligent—Broadway's *Wunderkind* of the 1920s, was now in his late thirties, still possessed of the fierce magnetism that had drawn Wilder to him in their first chance meeting ten years before. Most recently, Harris had produced and directed Wilder's adaptation of *A Doll's House.* Starring Ruth Gordon and a brilliant cast, the production had already achieved high critical praise even before its New York opening scheduled for late December. Wilder had thought of giving Harris his choice of *Our Town* or *The Merchant of Yonkers,* but for Harris there was no choice. He was drawn to *Our Town* because the play fulfilled all his dreams as a director: its spaciousness was for him a liberation, freeing him of furniture, props, drawing rooms, and doors—in fact, the whole three-hundred-year-old Western theater tradition. The play would enable him to work exclusively with language, gesture, movement, light, and shade. Wilder's great doubt about the plays revolved around the very basic question: Were they practical theater? Harris's unequivocal judgment that they were indeed and that he wished to begin production of *Our Town* immediately exhilarated Wilder to a manic pitch. All at once, the two men began thinking about an actor to play the Narrator. In those first exciting moments, their enthusiasm led them to Sinclair Lewis, a choice not entirely bizarre since Lewis had successfully appeared as the small-town editor in the dramatization of his own novel, *It Can't Happen Here*. Eager to commence, Harris, as he later reported, "tore the hand-written pages of *Our Town* out of Wilder's looseleaf notebook, stuffed them into his pocket and departed on the first available ship for New York." Wilder joyfully returned to Zurich for another work stint on an uncompleted play about Haroun-al-Raschid. But, after two weeks, he received a cable from Harris:

> Dear Thornie Please If You Possibly Can Do Sail This Week As I Need You Very Badly For About Two Weeks Work Before We Go Into Rehearsal Casting Provisionally Underway Cable Opinion Of Frank Craven For Stage Manager Affectionately Jed

Wilder left Zurich immediately. After short visits to Sibyl Colefax in London and Gertrude Stein and Alice Toklas in Paris, he sailed from Cherbourg on the *Queen Mary* in the last week of November and arrived in New York as the month ended; he was awaited by the impatient Jed Harris and the little band of play watchers curious to see what "the professor" had finally—all on his own—concocted for the Broadway stage.

# X

## Success Enough for All
## Normal Purposes

The actors preparing their roles for the production of *Our Town* said later that it was a transcendent experience, differing from anything they had undergone before or afterward. It was not just a matter of working under Jed Harris's direction, or that they were breaking new ground in theater technique. Instead, they felt the play's uniqueness. They were awed by an intensification not only of their manhood and womanhood but of the joy and pain of being American.

The establishment of an American theater (that is to say, the performances of plays by American dramatists) antedated the Declaration of Independence by a decade. Since that time, although theater in America had more or less flourished up to 1938, American dramatic literature had not. Of all the plays by American authors written in the eighteenth and nineteenth centuries, not a single one survives either in the regular theater repertory or in the school and college textbooks. Richard Moody's anthology, *Dramas from the American Theater 1762–1909*, contains twenty-seven plays; half a dozen titles are identifiable to the general scholar and only one—*Uncle Tom's Cabin*—is known to the general reader. The most admired play in the collection, William Vaughn Moody's *The Great Divide*, a success in 1906, has not been given a professional performance in New York since 1917.

In 1938, the year of *Our Town*, American dramaturgy possessed a tradition of a little more than twenty years—dating from O'Neill's debut with the Provincetown Players. There was, in other words, no real tradition, no American playwright whose reputation had been tested by time, no national play. The American situation stood in contrast, of course, with the European countries' experience; each of them had produced at least one play that somehow expressed the nation's aspirations, mirrored the nation's image, or reflected a significant aspect of national character. Russia had *Eugene Onegin* and *The Cherry Orchard*. Norway, *Peer Gynt*. Germany, *Faust*. Italy, *Mandragola* and Verdi's operas. Austria, *The Magic Flute* and *Fidelio*. France, *Le Cid* and *The Misanthrope*. Spain, *Life Is A Dream*. England, *Hamlet* and *Henry V*. In contrast with these monuments, *Our Town* is a modest work, modestly conceived by its author who consistently referred to it as his "little play." But in the tradition of Whitman and Emily Dickinson, the play celebrated the commonplace, the not unusual, the daily life. It defined the dissatisfactions, the empty places, the frustrations inherent in American living, but it also illuminated our democratic vistas and provided a sense of national identity. The actors rehearsing in *Our Town* knew, in short, that their participation in the premiere was to earn them a tiny share of immortality. A quarter of a century later, every surviving actor from the production maintained, through a round-robin letter, communication with the others.

Arriving in New York from Europe early in December 1937, Wilder was met by Jed Harris with a list of proposed revisions and emendations. Harris installed Wilder at once in a Long Island cottage where he could revise uninterruptedly. Harris had suggested adding what was to become the wedding breakfast scene in Act II. At the outset, Wilder willingly acceded to Harris's suggestions and, except for a brief excursion to New York to dine with Sinclair Lewis at the Century Association before a performance by the Lunts of Giraudoux-Behrman's *Amphitryon 38,* he worked conscientiously and well. But after several days, with the new scene added and other scenes rearranged, Harris began cutting and pruning the script in preparation for rehearsals that were to begin on December 29. As Wilder conceded in a letter to Sibyl Colefax on January 2, he realized that Harris's cuts helped the play; nevertheless his amour propre was wounded by Harris's cavalier treatment of him and his manuscript; and he began building up a deep resentment against his producer. As Harris later reported the interchange, the first break between them came during the first company reading of the play. The cast, seated on the stage, began their reading with Harris seated in the orchestra and Wilder behind Harris. Harris was puzzled and dismayed by the actors' uncertainties, fumblings, and hesitations until he discovered that Wilder was visibly manifesting dissatisfaction by much headshaking, wincing, and grimacing. Harris forthwith banished Wilder from the theater until such time as the actors had learned their parts and the play was set. Wilder was furious, but Harris had his way. There was nothing for Wilder to do but to withdraw to the genteel precincts of the Century and resume work on *The Merchant of Yonkers,* which he had now resolved to present to Max Reinhardt.

Once *Our Town* was rehearsed to the extent that the actors had established their interpretations, Wilder was allowed back into the theater. He was relieved, even exhilarated by the actors' performances. His early misgivings about Frank Craven (the Narrator), Evelyn Varden (Mrs. Gibbs), and Helen Carew (Mrs. Webb) were wholly dissipated; he was joyous about Martha Scott's Emily. In general, his faith in the genius of Jed Harris was restored, so that his chief dissatisfactions now lay in word changes that Harris or the actors had made during the rehearsals; it turned out that everyone was amenable to restoring the text to more or less what Wilder had written and, for a few days, harmony prevailed—until Princeton.

The first performance of *Our Town* was a one-night stand at the McCarter Theater in Princeton, New Jersey. The seats were sold out, and Wilder's earlier ties with Lawrenceville and Princeton created anticipatory good will. But the performance was not a success. The failure was due partly to the fact that the play was inadequately lighted. (Ultimately, seventy-five hours were required to "light" the play.) Also, the acoustics of the theater were poor so that a number of the lines were lost to an audience who were already confused by the absence of scenery. Faced with a cool reception for the play, Wilder panicked. Harris reported that he turned on the producer, all the weeks of his resentment and humiliation boiling up into a fury. Over the heads of people who gathered around Harris to express their admiration, Wilder screamed: "You simply do not understand my play!"

More confident than the author and more experienced in the vagaries of the theater, Harris ignored Wilder's attack and calmly readied the production for its move to Boston. But Boston was also not reassuring. When *Our Town* opened there on Tuesday, January 25, 1938, box office sales were poor and the critics who ought to have favorably responded to this New England idyll were diffident and uncertain. Given so unusual a play, they dared not commit themselves without New York reviews to guide them. Again, Wilder's faith in Jed Harris ebbed, particularly when poor attendance forced Harris to cancel the second week and move up the date of the New York opening from the second week in February to the first.

Was the production doomed? On the disheartening Saturday-evening closing in Boston, in the midst of the unexpected preparations for the return to New York, Harris received a despondent telephone call from a woman staff assistant asking for personal and emotional reassurance. Harris gently remonstrated. He said, in effect, that yes he understood her state of mind, that of course she had his highest regard. But with all he had to do, he couldn't talk at length. He had an obligation to the production, to the play, to the company. Everything would be all right. He asked for her patience and understanding. . . . A few hours later, early that Sunday morning, the woman, a well-born society matron, wife and mother, committed suicide. The cast was stunned. Harris was grief stricken, tormented by guilt. Surely he could have prevented the tragedy, had he been more concerned—he told himself. The shock freed Wilder from all his resentment; he felt that the play's survival depended on his allaying Harris's guilt and sorrow. For a few days, Wilder and Jed Harris grew closer than they were ever to become again, united by their sense of loss and by their determination to keep *Our Town* afloat.

Nor was Harris one to allow personal matters to threaten a venture to which so many had given of their best. Having rejected the Shuberts's offer of the dilapidated Forty-ninth Street Theater—the only theater available—Harris had persuaded Gilbert Miller to let him use the Henry Miller for the one week before Miller himself would require it for an Ina Claire vehicle. Harris reasoned that the Forty-ninth Street Theater would insure a disaster. The play required a suitable theater and the Henry Miller suited. If the play was a success, another theater would somehow materialize. During the final days before the Friday night opening, the cast and lighting crew were devotedly working at the Henry Miller to bring the production to its highest possible level of excellence. During that week, Harris was lunching at the nearby Harvard Club with Brooks Atkinson, drama critic of the *New York Times*. Harris, foxlike, proceeded to bait Atkinson.

"Your trouble," he said to the genial New Englander and Thoreau biographer, "is that you're not really involved with theater. My Uncle Abe haunts the Second Avenue Yiddish theaters. When he comes home, my family hangs on his every word. He has seen everything, he understands everything that has taken place. We really see through his eyes."

Atkinson good naturedly took the bait. How could he improve himself?

"Get into a theater where everyone's at work. See how a play is put together," Harris suggested.

But, Atkinson demurred, no director would allow him in a theater during a working rehearsal.

"Nonsense," exclaimed Harris, "come over to the Henry Miller and watch my company working. No one except me will even know you're there."

The two men walked down the street and Atkinson saw *Our Town* at a working rehearsal, the cast and crew entirely unaware of his presence. Harris had taken a shrewdly calculated risk. By giving Atkinson the leisure to reflect upon and to absorb this complex "little" play, he had made certain that the dean of theater critics would exert his most deeply considered and thoughtful judgment; but could any play be appreciated in an empty theater? On the other hand, if Atkinson saw it at the opening with only ninety minutes to puzzle the whole matter out at a typewriter, he might communicate more puzzlement than enthusiasm to his readers. Under the conditions Harris had brought about, Atkinson had ample time to ruminate.

For Wilder, opening night, Friday, February 4, 1938, was a nightmare. The Princeton and Boston experiences had demonstrated that failure was a real possibility. Glenway Wescott, emerging from the stage door after having congratulated an actress who played a small part (won through Wescott's intercession with Wilder), encountered Wilder that night in the theater alley in an old trench coat looking distraught and exhausted, "as though he had walked for miles in haste." As Wilder nervously questioned Wescott about his reactions to the play, Wescott gently took him by the arm to clear the way for visitors clustered around the stage door; Wilder was all atremble. Responsive to Wilder's acute but controlled anxiety, Wescott praised the work without qualification. Then he added that he felt that its high quality might forestall immediate popular acceptance, that a play of such excellence might be caviar to the general. In the instant of having made that observation, Wescott immediately regretted it. Too late, he grasped that what Wilder wanted at that moment more than anything was popular acceptance of his play. And then Wescott was relieved to realize that Wilder had paid no attention to the gloomy prognostication. In spite of all unfavorable auguries—the half-empty theater and the Boston critics, the suicide, the "borrowed" theater, the absence of first-night enthusiasm, ebullience, and excitement—Wilder still clung to his faith in the play . . . in Jed Harris and his actors . . . in a world that rewards diligence, patience, and humility.

Although *Our Town* was to emerge in the next thirty years as the work of American dramatic literature that has attracted the greatest number of audiences and readers in this century, the immediate response was moderate. Fortunately, Brooks Atkinson's glowing tribute insured a respectable run. The Morosco theater magically became available. A Wilder interview appeared on the first page of the *Times* Sunday drama section. But critical opinion was divided. John Mason Brown of the *New York Evening Post* and Joseph Wood Krutch of the *Nation* aligned themselves with Atkinson. But Richard Watts of the *New York Herald-Tribune* and the *Time* and *New Yorker* critics contained their enthusiasm. John Anderson, the very capable and scholarly reviewer for Hearst's *New York Journal-American,* refused to consider *Our Town* a play and described himself as uninvolved in the experience, a view shared by other reviewers including Miss Wilella Waldorf of the *New York Post.*

The New York reviewers' mixed reaction to *Our Town* was reflected three months later when they assembled to choose the Drama Critics Circle Prize for the best American play of 1938. On the final ballot, John Steinbeck's dramatization of his novel *Of Mice and Men* was awarded the prize on the basis of twelve votes to four for *Our Town.* Among the critics who voted against *Our Town* were two of Wilder's earliest supporters in the theater, Stark Young and Mrs. Edith Isaacs. (Had Wilder failed to keep his fences mended?) Others who preferred the Steinbeck play were Robert Benchley of the *New Yorker,* Richard Watts, George Jean Nathan, Burns Mantle, John Gassner, and Richard Lockridge.* Atkinson, John Mason Brown, Krutch, and a Mrs. Ruth Sedgwick held firm for *Our Town.* And Edmund Wilson, never an "accredited" drama critic, privately wrote Wilder his unqualified admiration.

The whole long drawn-out experience—the rewritings, the rehearsal contretemps, the quarrels with Harris, the suicide, the tryouts, the struggle for a theater—all so depressed and exhausted Wilder that the fact that he had survived on Broadway failed to exhilarate him. Sick with a cold, he was eager to leave New York behind for the warm dry air of Arizona. By mid-March he had made the break, taking a small apartment in Tucson where he continued work on *The Merchant of Yonkers.* The comparative isolation of Tucson, its health-restoring ambience, and a regular work routine all combined to restore his good spirits. The disappointment of not winning the Critics' Prize was shortly thereafter assuaged by *Our Town*'s receiving the 1938 Pulitzer Prize. The award not only prolonged the play's run well beyond the summer, but transformed the published text of the play into a best seller.

The acute worsening world situation was causing Wilder grave concern. Hitler had annexed Austria. Wilder described to Gertrude and Alice how Sigmund Freud, aged eighty-two, tried to calm his family while storm troopers ransacked the Freud home in Vienna, and he expressed to

* John Gassner, then editor of *One-Act Play Magazine* was subsequently to become a leading drama historian, an eminent critic and a Sterling Professor at Yale. In 1954, he published *The Theater in Our Times,* subtitled "a survey of the men, materials and movements in the modern theater." In the six hundred page text, there is not a single reference to his 1938 choice for the best play, *Of Mice and Men.* Wilder receives eleven entries including an intelligent and appreciative analysis of *Our Town.*

the two ladies his anxiety about their remaining in France. To the North American Committee to Aid Spanish Democracy he contributed the manuscript of *Heaven's My Destination*. To Max Reinhardt, a refugee in Hollywood, his property and possessions seized by Hitler, Wilder offered *The Merchant of Yonkers,* when he finished it.

Wilder returned from Tucson in May with the new play completed. Isabel, who had been in Europe, met Wilder in New Haven and the two set out for Hollywood to confer with Dr. Reinhardt. Isabel was traveling as her brother's secretary, but with the technical training she had received at the Yale Drama School, Wilder hoped that she would somehow become a part of Reinhardt's entourage.* Much of the summer they spent in Hollywood. But Isabel grew bored once Reinhardt had made clear that he had no use for her services. To divert her, Wilder took his sister for two weeks to Taos to visit Mabel Dodge Luhan, since Reinhardt had been forced to postpone production of *The Merchant of Yonkers* until late fall. After Taos, she returned alone to Hamden, determined to write movie scenarios which she tried to market with her sister Charlotte's assistance, but without success. By the end of summer, Wilder still had no firm date from Reinhardt, and he used the time to map out a new play, *The Alcestiad,* which he ultimately brought to completion seventeen years later and presented to Tyrone Guthrie for production at the 1955 Edinburgh Festival.

Festivals were on his mind. Salzburg was out, but he now envisaged a Saratoga Springs Festival which, in 1940, would present an old play by Goldoni and two new plays by himself—plus Mozart and Schubert chamber music performed by the Budapest String Quartet. He had even more ambitious dreams for 1941: The Philadelphia Orchestra and the Budapest String Quartet would perform the Beethoven symphonies and quartets and the Saratoga theater would stage Calderon's *Life Is a Dream* along with two additional new plays by himself. Saratoga Springs fascinated him and he often visited the place, usually out of season. But, although the Springs were to present many seasons of play repertory, Wilder never did participate or give them a new play of his.

In September 1938, *Our Town* was still running on Broadway and for the middle two weeks of the month Wilder replaced Frank Craven as the Narrator. Still piqued at Jed Harris, he agreed to perform providing

---

* Wilder's hope that Isabel could achieve economic and spiritual independence was never to be realized. Her destiny was to remain, successively, nurse to their mother; guardian of the Hamden-New Haven house the *Bridge* built; Thornton's personal secretary; emissary to Broadway and to his publisher during his absences; late in life, Wilder's traveling companion. It was an arrangement that both came to resent with considerable force, he, because he felt trapped; she, because she was forced to live her life exclusively in the shadow of her brother. Ultimately, in their old age, both accepted the arrangement with resignation and relief.

certain conditions were met, one of which was that Harris not enter the theater while he was on the stage. Harris's response to Wilder's ukase read:

> Dear Thornton: I received your latest communication and like all others I ever get from you it is a characteristic blend of fatuousness, vanity and superb unconscious buffoonery. . . .

No one else in the world, except perhaps Wilder's sister Charlotte, would have addressed Wilder in such a fashion. Oddly enough, Harris's message had no effect upon the relationship between the two. A grudging mutual respect persisted. Wilder's performances in the role were eminently satisfactory; some responsible viewers preferred his interpretation to that of Frank Craven. In any case, he won his membership in Actors' Equity, and he carried his membership card for a long time thereafter.

Despite hopes that *Our Town* might run in New York through the 1939 World's Fair, the play closed late in October in preparation for what was to have been an extended national tour with Dorothy McGuire replacing Teresa Wright in the role of Emily, first created by Martha Scott. (All three young women were to become motion picture stars.) But the tour lasted only twelve weeks, ending its run in Chicago on February 10, 1939, because during eight of the twelve weeks the play operated at a financial loss to Harris.

Even so, *Our Town* had run for over a year. The play had won the Pulitzer Prize. Wilder had achieved success in the New York theater. He had, in fact, both written and starred in a Broadway production—a feat equaled by a mere handful: George M. Cohan, Noel Coward, and Mae West. For Wilder, it was all a salutary experience. He would never again become so intimately involved with the working theater, nor be so exposed to the humiliations that a strong-willed and experienced director like Jed Harris could subject him to. He had learned the valuable lesson that in the theater there is a division of labor: that he couldn't write the play, then direct it, and then play the leading role. He saw that in the commercial theater he had to accept the idea of a director's controlling the production. For someone who had for years been good naturedly but strenuously bullying students and neophyte writers, the lesson administered by Jed Harris was hard to swallow. But Wilder swallowed it and absorbed it into his system. He gave the directors of his subsequent plays no trouble at all.

What he also learned was that a play could achieve a respectable run of forty weeks and still not be a smash hit—like such contemporary attractions as Clare Boothe Luce's *The Women,* or Kaufman and Hart's *You Can't Take It with You,* or Rachel Crother's *Susan and God.* Even after

*Our Town,* George Kaufman still failed to recognize Wilder in their encounters in lobbies and elevators. Nor did Hollywood besiege Wilder with five-thousand-dollar-a-week offers for his services or with the promise of a king's ransom for the screen rights to his play.

Yet Wilder had made his point: *Our Town* showed that realistic-naturalistic theater had pretty much exhausted itself and that realism now properly belonged to the realm of films and radio plays. Further, it was clear now that legitimate theater, if it were to survive, would have to address itself to a smaller, more discriminating audience and devise new modes of representation. The models of drama which were rooted in the nineteenth century and whose heights were reached by Ibsen and Chekhov would have to give way to newer (and older) modes; moreover, plays by Americans ought to have their roots in the cultural soil of America, not in that of England or Germany or France.

At the time, not many people were greatly impressed by Wilder's play or his ideas. Broadway still regarded him as an amiable eccentric who by a stroke of luck had succeeded with a freak play whose appeal lay mainly in a combination of novelty and sentiment. One of the few to grasp the implications of *Our Town*'s success was Jed Harris. Harris wanted to continue producing Wilder's plays. But the two men had separated; and by the time Wilder was ready to return to Harris, Harris had withdrawn from Wilder.

When *Our Town,* after scraping along for forty weeks, quietly left New York for its twelve-week tour of cities which gave it lukewarm support, it seemed as though the play was heading toward oblivion. Yet, thirty-five years later, the text of *Our Town* has been reproduced in over two-hundred anthologies, putting the play in the hands of millions of school and college students. Along with *Hamlet, Macbeth,* and *Romeo and Juliet, Our Town* is known to most Americans. Every day of the year it is being performed somewhere in the United States. Since 1938 it has had three important revivals in New York, the most recent in 1969. Another noteworthy revival, under Alan Schneider's direction was undertaken at Washington's Arena Theater in 1973. *Our Town* has in effect become our national play—or come as close as any play has come thus far.*

Admirers of *Our Town* who know little about Wilder's life assume the play is autobiographical. The facts of his life would seem to contradict such an assumption. Wilder's youth was spent not in a New England village, but mostly in Madison, Wisconsin, and Berkeley, California. Nor was there in his life anything like a teen-age courtship or a marriage and

---

* Of the dozen plays chosen to help commemorate the American bicentennial at the Kennedy Center in Washington in 1976, *Our Town* will be the first of the plays to be given.

the death of a young bride. Wilder's father bore little resemblance to the easygoing, mild, and relaxed Editor Webb or to Dr. Gibbs; his mother was not an obedient and conventional housewife. There are virtually no parallels between George Gibbs and young Thornton; or between Emily and Wilder's sisters, Charlotte and Isabel.* In short, there is virtually nothing in the play that at first glance parallels people or events in Wilder's own family life. It would seem to be a wholly imaginary projection. But not entirely.

Wilder's parents were both of New England stock (approximate contemporaries of the Gibbses and the Webbs) and they manifested the same dry, unemotional tricks of speech, the matter of factness and understatement as the parents in *Our Town*. There was the same unspoken assumption that young people would fulfill conventional obligations and that they would adhere to accepted modes of conduct. Daughters were not told they must not wear makeup or dresses whose collars revealed too much of the neck; nor were sons warned against chasing after girls who were "fast." Such instructions would have been supererogatory. Mrs. Webb's response to Emily's question, "Mama, am I pretty enough to get somebody?" Wilder has attributed to his mother. "Now stop it! You're pretty enough for all normal purposes." In fact, it is difficult to see how the play could have been written by anyone who had not spent—as Wilder had done—most of his childhood and adolescence in a household where he was surrounded by females.

The females of *Our Town* are much more fully achieved than their male counterparts. Emily's burgeoning sexuality is clearly drawn. Both mothers allude to the trauma of wedding nights. By contrast, George's sexuality is entirely covert—as thoroughly concealed as that of the Rover Boys or Frank Merriwell. Nor does either of the two fathers figuratively— or in any other way—unbutton himself. To the extent that *Our Town* deals at all with sexual matters, they are dealt with in the framework of conventional nineteenth-century American Victorian notions:

> that the shameful subject of sex not be discussed between members of different generations nor between a man and woman who are not married to one another;

> that sexual intercourse is initially a horror endured by every decent young bride and that it is subsequently an unpleasant duty, like housework and changing diapers;

> that anyone whose sexual drives are not satisfied in the nuptial bed is headed for alcoholism, disease, scandal, divorce, or suicide.

* The third sister, Janet, was not a part of Wilder's youth, having been born when Wilder was nearly twenty.

These ideas, while they could not represent Wilder's conscious views on the subject when at the age of forty he was writing the play, constituted, nevertheless, some of the context of ideas about sex that he had unconsciously absorbed in his formative years and that were to remain as a kind of permanent residue in his subconscious.

Much of what happens in *Our Town*—getting ready for school on winter mornings, afterschool games and chores, evening homework, choir practice, birthdays, weddings, and funerals—all these distillations of Wilder's experiences fuse easily into the remembered experiences of the millions for whom the play is an exercise in nostalgia. Just as Wilder looked back thirty odd years to his own childhood, successive generations have looked back and found their own correspondences in the play. Yet, not long ago in the summer of 1969, the *Times* reported that some children in the Harlem area of New York staged *Our Town;* the thirteen-year-old girl who played Emily said that the role seemed unreal to her, "it doesn't have much to do with me." The thrust of the article—an attitude shared by the *New York Times* drama critic, Clive Barnes—was that the play is no longer relevant.

It is true that the play is not directly relevant to current social conditions, but neither was it relevant in 1938. No one in Grover's Corners is addicted to anything stronger than coffee, no one seems to sustain any disease worse than whooping cough; crime seems unknown, and the poor Polish families across the tracks seem to know their place. The village life described by Wilder, however, although it avoids the depiction of the mean, petty, ugly, and sordid, is no sentimental idyll: the church organist hates the town and commits suicide; the young Gibbs boy dies of appendicitis on a camping trip; mothers and fathers and sons and daughters go through life taking one another for granted; the most promising young man in the village, after winning a scholarship and graduating from M.I.T., is among those killed overseas in a remote war; Emily dies in childbirth. Nevertheless we can see how from the point of view of the young girl interviewed by the *Times,* from the point of view of a great many of those who were coming of age in the late sixties and seventies, *Our Town* has become irrelevant in a basic way.

*Our Town,* essentially, is a play about belonging—belonging to a family, of course, but even more so, to a community and to a nation. George Gibbs is wholly at one with Grover's Corners, New Hampshire. He has no wish to leave it, even when there is the opportunity to go away to the state agricultural college. The only circumstance under which George would leave would be the coming of a war; he would leave then as his forebears had left forty years before "to save the Union." George is not intellectually curious nor imaginative; he doesn't even share the characteristic restlessness of so many of his countrymen who left the

Corporal Thornton Wilder, aged 21.

Amos Parker Wilder. (*Yale University Archives*) Isabel: "Oh, Richard, it's scary how Thornton has become the image of father!"

Wilder in New Hampshire, 1925. (*Courtesy the late Amy Wertheimer*)

In the summer of 1928, newspapers both in
New York and England were agog at the
prospect of the Tunney-Wilder walking tour.
(*London Daily Mail*)

Fall, Mont Blanc.

Wilder's first appearance on Broadway was in 1932 in his adaptation of Obey's *The Rape of Lucrèce,* which starred Katharine Cornell and Brian Aherne. *(New York Public Library)*

Robert Hutchins, Mrs. Claire Swift, Wilder and Maude Phelps Hutchins. *(Courtesy Mrs. Gilbert Chapman)*

Wilder and Alice Toklas at "Bobsy" Goodspeed's. *(Courtesy Mrs. Gilbert Chapman)*

Wilder and Gertrude Stein at Bilignin. *(Yale Collection of American Literature)*

John Craven and Martha Scott as George Gibbs and Emily Webb looking out their respective bedroom windows in *Our Town*. *(New York Public Library)*

Mrs. Webb (Helen Carew) and daughter Emily in *Our Town*. *(New York Public Library)*
"Am I pretty enough to get anyone?"
"You're pretty enough for all normal purposes..."

Jed Harris directing *Our Town*. *(New York Public Library)*

Thornton and Isabel Wilder
at Deepwood Drive. *(Yale
Collection of American Literature)*

Wilder with Mabel Dodge Luhan. Mrs. Luhan
held intellectual soirées at her lower Fifth Avenue
apartment. At this one, Wilder explicated James
Joyce. *(Yale Collection of American Literature)*

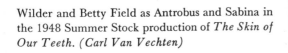

Wilder and Betty Field as Antrobus and Sabina in
the 1948 Summer Stock production of *The Skin of
Our Teeth. (Carl Van Vechten)*

Wilder as Antrobus, Third Act, 1948.
(*Carl Van Vechten*)

In 1955 the State Department sponsored a world tour of *The Skin of Our
Teeth*. Helen Hayes and Mary Martin
as Mrs. Antrobus and Sabina. (*Rod-
erick McArthur*)

Wilder, aged 45, entered the Army Air Corps as a captain. *(Courtesy Janet Cohn)*

Wilder at Richard Goldstone's apartment in Greenwich Village, talking to singer Doda Conrad, 1960. *(David Noakes)*

Wilder at 74. *(Barbara Kruch, Zurich)*

farms and villages for the big cities East, North, South, and West. But George and the denizens of Grover's Corners, regardless of whether their natures determine that they remain in their region and their state, or move on to Boston or Ohio or California, never question the allegiance they pledge to the flag and the republic. Like Wilder himself, who eagerly offered his services to the armed forces in 1917 and 1941, the people of his play are more American than they are Christian, more patriotic than they are religious. Like their British ancestors, they are more likely to be emotionally stirred by the flag passing by than by a representation of virgins or crucifixions. For Wilder, for the people of his play, for the audiences to whom the play was directed, being an American was a source of pride. Not that America was a sceptered isle, a precious stone set in a silver sea on whose far-flung dominions the sun never set; nor was it either one of the two continental powers of western Europe ferociously trying to establish hegemony; nor was it an impoverished Mediterranean country stirred up by a leader recalling to his people ancient grandeurs and glories. The American pride was based on the limitlessness of land and resources, the invulnerability achieved after little more than a century of independence. In the schools, the children of the thirties sang of their country's "spacious skies . . . amber waves of grain . . . purple mountain's majesty above the fruited plain." To be sure there was economic, social, and racial injustice. But from the time of Teddy Roosevelt at the turn of the century down to Franklin and Eleanor Roosevelt in the 1930s, the litany was reiterated: just as Americans had ended the tyranny of a foreign monarchy and had eliminated slavery, so could they end the range of injustices that still prevailed. Encouraged by such assurances and despite depressions, industrial strife, and vast pockets of wretched poverty which rendered somewhat discordant the strains of "America the Beautiful," Americans in general continued to love their country and to foresee a future when even the Negroes would have enough to eat. The American dream was not a discreditable one; and somehow, for millions of Americans, *Our Town* came as a reassurance. In purging the American past of most of our travails and squalor; in eliminating from our consciousness our colossal debts to Negroes and Asians, Irish, Italians, Poles, Mexicans, and Jews; in viewing the typical American community in terms of a decent, clean, hardworking New England village, the play somehow provided hope and promise for the American future. Its inherent optimism derived from its native soil.

And so the life of *Our Town* has been determined by a people with faith in itself, in the nation's capacity to survive, in the principles that accompanied the nation's coming into being. When the faith, the survival,

the principles go, presumably another nation will come into being, and
it will have its own play.

At the end of the *New York Times'* account of the Harlem *Our
Town* with the young actress's comment that the role of Emily "didn't
have much to do with me," there is an indication that her audience
didn't agree:

> The audience of 350 Harlem children clapped with a gusto dreamed
> of only by the most successful Broadway producer.

What could have evoked so favorable a reaction from the children of
Harlem? They were responding to the spontaneity, the spirit of improvisation that pervades the play. They believed, as Wilder intended, in
what was taking place. That is not to say that all of the children believed
it was an actual wedding, or that George and Emily were really doing
their homework, although some of the less sophisticated among them
accepted everything as reality. What was real to all the children was that
the actors had at this moment in time assumed their roles and prompted
by the ingenious and ubiquitous stage manager were convincingly enact-
ing them.

Those qualities of spontaneity, of ease, of joyful improvisation are
the essence of Wilder's achievement as a dramatist. They are qualities
that distinguish his stage work from the novels that preceded *Our Town*.
While Wilder was a member of the University of Chicago faculty, there
was in residence a graduate student who happened to be an accomplished pianist. The young man was sometimes prevailed upon to give
semipublic performances, a few of which Wilder attended. Asked on one
occasion if he were not impressed by the pianist's technique, Wilder
agreed that his command of the piano was indeed formidable. "But," he
added, "I don't enjoy his playing, it irritates me. The way he sits at the
piano, the way he attacks the keyboard says to me: 'See how truly
remarkable I am!' The sense of self-importance he communicates, that
very quality of *performer* makes it impossible for me to hear the music."

On rereading his books, Wilder had come to find something of that
*performer* quality in his own fiction. Earlier, he had been overly aware of
his audience, and then he learned from Gertrude Stein that this was
undesirable in a writer. Both Wilder's admirers and his detractors had
called him a *stylist,* with reason. His first three novels had been written
with a French elegance, characterized by quotable apothegms ("Style is
but the faintly contemptible vessel in which the bitter liquid is recommended to the world") and fine turns of phrase. His fourth novel,
*Heaven's My Destination* was a further demonstration of Wilder's virtu-

osity: inspired by Don Quixote, he conceived a picaresque novel and composed it in the idiom of the American Middle West.

In *Our Town* there is nothing of the virtuoso visible. The author, in fact, has utterly disappeared; only the dramatis personae comment and grasp the implications of the action. The play, moreover, avoids delicate ironies and edged satire. Wilder never patronizes his New England villagers, who are never quaint, narrow, or absurd. Each has his dignity, his individuality, his reason for being. While Wilder makes no effort to plumb their depths, neither does he present them as types: the Village Drunk; the Doctor; the Gossip; the Housewife; the Boy; the Girl. This is no play about the meanness of small town life, nor about the pathos of the disadvantaged. The play does not expose social ills or reveal the corruption beneath the skin. Rather, it depicts the outward behavior of some unexceptional people in a rural American community around the turn of the century. In describing little more than what they did, said, and thought aloud, Wilder—eschewing plot, complication, conflict, scènes á faire, climaxes and catastrophes, substituting *how* for *why*—provided insight into the human condition and helped his countrymen to see precisely what it is to be an American. For the characters in the play resist classifying and stratifying human beings; they resist the idea of limiting anyone's opportunities and scope; they reject both tribalism and a state religion. In short, for all that *Our Town* could not and would not encompass, it provided (and perhaps for a little while longer it will continue to provide) that shock of recognition to all of its heterogeneous audiences, enabling them to see that we are, in fact, a nationality and a people.

# XI

## Bombs: At Home and Abroad
## (1938–41)

A few days after the end of *Our Town*'s New York run in the fall of 1938, Max Reinhardt arrived from the West Coast to begin rehearsals of *The Merchant of Yonkers*. This play, based on Nestroy's mid-nineteenth-century farce, *Einen Jux Will Er Sich Machen,* Wilder had given to Reinhardt partly out of friendship and admiration and partly because he was furious over the cavalier treatment he felt Jed Harris had accorded him. The venturesome Herman Shumlin, a respected Broadway producer, had got the production ready so that Reinhardt could begin rehearsals immediately. The cast Shumlin and Wilder had selected included Percy Waram as the merchant of Yonkers; June Walker as the milliner; Nydia Westman as Minnie Fay; and Tom Ewell as Joseph Sweeney. And in the leading role of Dolly Levi was a veteran actress, Jane Cowl, a star of a certain magnitude whose greatest successes had coincided with Wilder's adolescence and who had been "at liberty" for many months. In her middle years, Miss Cowl had developed into a cross between "great lady" Katharine Cornell and "high comedienne" Ina Claire. Wilder's first choice for Dolly had been Laurette Taylor, who indignantly rejected the role when Shumlin asked her to appear for an audition.* But Miss Cowl was available, and Reinhardt, who knew

*Herman Shumlin told this writer that this report by Miss Taylor's daughter (in *Laurette*) is inaccurate. He was unable to hire Laurette Taylor because he feared that her periodic incapacities at that time would imperil the production.

nothing about American theater was satisfied with the choice. But as rehearsals progressed, Wilder became more and more certain that Jane Cowl's Dolly would sink the play; and his instinct told him to replace her with Ruth Gordon. Yet he failed to act on his idea, partly out of deference to Reinhardt, partly out of natural timidity.*

Actually Ruth Gordon, who had prophesied that Reinhardt was wrong for Wilder's new play, called the turn. When the play opened, the direction failed to evoke the spirit of New York in the 1880s and Miss Cowl's performance helped not at all. The customers simply didn't come and the combined prestige of Reinhardt, Wilder, and Jane Cowl could keep the production going for no longer than five weeks after its New York premiere on December 28, 1938. Even before the show closed, Wilder had fled to Mexico, hurt and exhausted by the experience. Unable to admit it to himself, he was ultimately to blame for the fiasco; he had chosen Reinhardt and he had accepted Jane Cowl. He got a modicum of comfort in a letter of condolence from Woollcott who predicted that the play would be successfully revived, a prediction Wilder fiercely clung to for the next decade and a half; it was, indeed, Wilder's long term faith in the play that saved it from oblivion. Under a new title, in fact, it was to undergo the most extraordinary rehabilitation of a stage work in theater history.

After months in and around New York, dissipating his creative energies in socializing and participating in the complicated process of mounting a Broadway play, he felt the need for a place of retreat like Mexico, which would afford him complete isolation from everyone and everything familiar. Wounded by the contemptuous reception accorded *The Merchant of Yonkers*, he did not want to encounter any more commiserations, sincere or insincere. Instead, he asked for nothing more than to be able to work without distraction upon the new play that was taking shape, his partial adaptation of Euripides' *Alcestis*.† Sailing from New York on January 20, 1939, abroad the S. S. *Siboney*, he took with him extensive notes on all the classical material he could find that dealt

---

* Why Ruth Gordon, Wilder's long-time friend for whom he maintained a passionate enthusiasm, was not engaged at the outset is unclear. Jed Harris told this writer (in 1970) that Miss Gordon was never invited to audition for the role perhaps because of her close personal relationship with Harris at the time. Wilder elsewhere claimed that she turned down the part because she mistrusted Reinhardt's capacities as a director of so American a play. But Wilder's assertion seems to be contradicted by a reference he made elsewhere to a quarrel with Miss Gordon, which originated in her not being offered the role of Dolly Levi, and by Edward Sheldon's letter to Wilder recommending Miss Gordon for the role and affirming that she wanted it badly.

† Never published in the United States, Wilder's *Alcestis* was worked on, put aside, worked on, put aside, completed, put aside, and finally offered to the 1955 Edinburgh Festival where it was given its only English language performances. But its post-World War II history was considerably more extensive than that.

with the Alcestis legend; he slowly made his way to the Yucatan and its Mayan ruins. His plan was to settle finally for ten or twelve weeks in Cuernavaca, not far from Mexico City, where he hoped to make uninterrupted progress on the play.

But Mexico, as it turned out, was wholly unsuitable for him. Having disembarked at Progresso and inspected the ruins that lie nearby, he made his way to Mexico City and from there found accommodations in Cuernavaca, close to Mount Popocatapetl. Absorbed as he was by Mexico's ruins, temples and pyramids, overwhelmed by the beauty of its bougainvillea and oleanders, distant mountains veiled in blue and purple, and volcanoes topped at sunset by rose-hued snow, he found that he could not work in his surroundings. The altitude kept him awake at night; alkali dust exacerbated a cold he'd not shaken off since leaving New York; the blazing sunlight caused his eyes to ache; the food for him was indigestible. In addition to the physical discomforts, he was dismayed by the plight of the Indians whose poverty he observed on his daily walks through their villages or in Mexico City. In contrast to what he felt was the hopeless, patient nobility of the Indians, he found himself offended by the Mexicans who seemed to him immoral, sharp, and vulgar. He observed endemic graft and commonplace cruelty. His sensibilities outraged, he cut short his visit and headed North for home by way of Corpus Christi, San Antonio, Knoxville, and Washington.

Part of his dissatisfaction with Mexico was a reflection of his most troubling problem with *The Alcestiad:* how were the legendary gods and goddesses, heroes and heroines to speak? In blank verse? In the stately English of a Gilbert Murray translation? In contemporary American idiom? In a rhetoric that Wilder would somehow devise for them? Wilder was uncertain that he could bring off a play in the classical tradition—as the French playwrights seemed to do so easily—particularly since he was handicapped both by inexperience in writing verse and by little knowledge of Greek. Faced with the possibility that he might never complete *The Alcestiad,* he remained determined, nevertheless, that none of his future plays should be naturalistic in construction, decor, or theme. Ideas for new plays crowded his mind and absorbed his thoughts. By spring of 1939, he had returned home. Back in Hamden, much of his creative energy was dissipated by his fleeing from the good women of Deepwood Drive to New York and fleeing his friends in New York back to Deepwood Drive.

He loved the socializing in New York. Having become acquainted, through Woollcott, with the witty Alice Roosevelt Longworth, he was now an occasional houseguest of her brother, Theodore Roosevelt, Junior. Writing Sibyl Colefax from the Roosevelt home at Oyster Bay (and on their stationery, a practice he derided in others, once asserting that playwright Herschel Williams accepted a weekend invitation from the Henry Luces *only* so that he could write all of his friends on Luce stationery), Wilder listed the other houseguests: Mr. and Mrs. George S. Kaufman, Joseph Alsop, Mrs. Longworth, Woollcott, Henri Bernstein, and Eve Curie. Wilder's agenda for the same week included a musicale at Ruth Draper's (whom he didn't like) ; a dinner at the Henry Luces's (neither of whom he liked) ; a lunch at the Samuel Barlows'; a Condé Nast tea; and attendance at several banquets for causes (which bored him).

By this time Wilder had decided to spend May and June in England and France despite the threat of an outbreak of war. (In April Hutchins had advised him that war would break out within a month, a prophecy based on a telephone conversation with Henry Morgenthau, secretary of the treasury, who needed a Chicago professor in preparation for the incipient crisis.) Despite the possible hazards—or because of them— Wilder booked passage and sailed from New York in the first week of May.

In London, Wilder encountered dozens of distinguished refugees from now-occupied Austria. Among these were Stefan Zweig whose silken manner Wilder compared to that of André Maurois; many of the Austrians, men of letters for the most part, came to Wilder for assistance in getting visas to the United States. He energetically did what he could. The plight of these men augmented his comprehension of the monstrousness of the Hitler regime and its threat to the very existence of sanity and civilization. He was thrown into a state of despair over these good, brilliant, and gifted humanists—homeless, penniless, and jobless—in a country where their chief talent, their command of German, was useless.

His most devastating encounter was with Freud, Austria's towering exile—now eighty-two, in pain, only three months removed from death. It had been four years since Wilder and Freud had last met and, in that time, Freud's whole world had collapsed: his home, his books, his journals, his possessions had been confiscated; and now his body, stricken by a fatal cancer, was disintegrating. Despite all this, Freud's mind was keen, his spirit as generous as ever. Recalling their earlier encounters in the fall of 1935 when he had expressed his disapproval of *Heaven's My Destination*, Freud's first question to Wilder when he appeared at five in the afternoon of June 21 was,

> You are not angry at me for the harsh words I said about your novel . . . the one about the good fool? [George Brush] You see, I am no seeker after God.

And after describing to Wilder something in his upbringing, of his mother and father, he cited Heine's phrase *mein unglaubengenosse* (my

agnosticism), adding: No, I am no seeker after God; but I love the gods.
And he pointed to the Greek, Roman, Etruscan, and African images in
their glass cases, household gods which he had been allowed to bring out
with him from Vienna.* The two men talked until Freud, exhausted, lay
down on a sofa while Wilder and Anna Freud, the doctor's favorite child
and herself an eminent analyst, continued talking over tea. The experience filled Wilder with awe and veneration for the indomitable grand
old man and his Judith of a daughter. Among the things she told him was
an account of the day the Storm Troopers burst into the Freud household,
arrested her, and brought her to Gestapo headquarters for an entire day
only to allow her to return miraculously home at suppertime.

Also during this London visit, Wilder discussed with the young
director, Michael St. Denis, the possibility of his producing *Our Town* in
England. But the idea of presenting the play with English actors became
more and more distasteful to Wilder and the project was abandoned.

Across the channel, Wilder took his leisure in Paris and Fontainebleau and visited Gertrude Stein and Alice Toklas again at their summer
home in Bilignin. However much he pleaded with the two ladies to
return to America while they could, they obdurately insisted on remaining in France. Miss Stein's sources assured her that the chances of war
were not very great and, incredibly enough, she believed them. Giving up
on this project for the moment, Wilder tried to enjoy the visit; he
purchased a painting by Sir Francis Rose of Gertrude and Alice with
their poodles, Pepe and Basket.

One of the most memorable weekends of the visit was a Henry
Jamesian pilgrimage Wilder took with Lady Colefax to the Manor House
at Mells, presided over by the venerable Lady Horner. The occasion was
apparently a perfect English country weekend, and it so greatly impressed Wilder that he described it all in great detail to Gertrude and
Alice and, subsequently, referred to it in a number of his letters to Lady
Colefax after the outbreak of the war. During the summer Wilder also
visited Sir Max and Lady Beerbohm, and he received an invitation to
dinner from Lord Beaverbrook. But he could not accept since it came
just as he was leaving for Paris. At a lunch with Henry and Clare Luce,
Wilder arranged for them to visit Gertrude and Alice. Subsequently,
Gertrude Stein wrote Wilder,

> We saw a lot of the Luces and we did like them we had a very good
> time together.

* When Freud fled from Vienna in 1938, he left behind the bulk of his personal
library. The following year, an American book collector saw an advertisement placed
by a Leipzig bookseller offering a collection of esoteric psychological texts. Correctly
surmising that the collection was Freud's library, the American made an offer. The
books were shipped to New York and are now housed in the library of the New York
Academy of Medicine.

Wilder's relationship with Henry Luce extended over a period of fifty-five years. The association was never close, but each man alternately fascinated the other. Despite the similarities in their backgrounds— China and Yale and strict Calvinist upbringing mingled with strong doses of chauvinism—Luce and Wilder were in temperament, talent, and personality natural antagonists. Wilder despised Luce who was, in turn, contemptuous of Wilder. So it had been when they were schoolboys together at the Inland Mission School at Chefoo and the mutual antagonism was reinforced at Yale, although each had begun to have intimations of the other's latent powers. Now, in 1939, both distinguished successes in their early forties, the two men accorded one another respect, cordiality, and deference. Wilder was an occasional dinner guest at the Luce townhouse in New York or he went to luncheon at Luce's private dining room at the Time-Life building. They had long earnest conversations and consultations about the state of the world, about the state of arts and letters. Part of Luce's success lay in remaining always educable; Wilder's magnetism derived from his perennial eagerness to educate. Yet despite the superficial good feeling that had built up between them, Wilder would still sometimes characterize Luce as gauche and ruthless or would describe Clare Luce as silken and feline. It seemed to him that they had both made disastrous successes of their lives. Nor did Luce always take pains to conceal his visceral conviction that Wilder lacked the moral and spiritual toughness that Luce so greatly admired in Wilder's father, Amos. A typical interchange between the two took place a year or so before Luce's death in 1967, at their forty-fifth Yale reunion, when Wilder—perhaps unconsciously, perhaps deliberately—infuriated Luce by suddenly interrupting a private conversation they were having in a small room at Dean De Vane's home to pay court to an elderly lady of his acquaintance who, by chance, had wandered into the room where the two men were talking.

Considering their mutual dislike, why then over their fifty years of acquaintance did they seek each other out, maintain the appearance of old school friends, and make thmselves useful to one another, even if only in ways of no real importance? The initiative for sustaining the relationship came from Wilder. Even as an adolescent he was impressed by power, that is to say, by the men who wielded power. He liked to be close to the powerful though his own ambitions along those lines were more modest: he enjoyed exercising power, as he was to say of the wives in *Our Town,* indirectly. In those terms, we can understand his long and intimate relationships with Hutchins and with Woollcott. And, in the same context, we can understand his relationship with Luce who, in 1953, finally made Wilder the subject of a *Time* cover story. Wilder's cultivation of Luce was motivated less, however, by what Luce could do for him than by what Luce could *do,* by what, in fact, Luce *was:* one of the three most powerful publishers in America.

And what was the basis of Luce's interest in Wilder? If for Wilder, Luce was the incarnation of power, Wilder was for Luce the incarnation of success. Each week and each month Luce published millions of words (some of them his own) , ephemeral words, out-of-date almost before the ink had dried, forgotten before the paper they were printed on was thrown into the incinerator. All the words in *Time, Life,* and *Fortune* combined, for example, could not defeat Luce's mortal enemy Franklin Roosevelt in his bid for a second, third, and fourth terms. But Luce, we recall, had long yearned to write something more permanent than editorials and messages of moral uplift. As a young man, before his commitment to journalism was complete, he wrote verses both in English and in Greek that were not wholly contemptible. But he had long since come to understand that nothing he would ever write was imperishable, that his words were written on the slipstream of progress, that even his most reasonably thought out and carefully drawn up pronouncements were read or weighed without even the attention accorded the daily lead editorial in the *New York Times.* In contrast, Wilder's writings were secure between the hard covers of books, books that circulated into and out of public libraries, books that counted as part of a nation's literature.

At the time of their meeting in June 1939, despite Wilder's public allegiance to Luce's bête noire Roosevelt, the two men found common ground in their mutual concern about a war whose imminence was unmistakable. Wilder educated Luce in the true nature of Hitler, the potential destroyer of Western civilization, or at least dramatized for him the full scope of the Nazi evil. Having had access to the most articulate and responsible victims of Nazi cruelty and viciousness, Wilder was able to communicate reports of Hitler's Reich with an immediacy, a conviction, and a passion that the best of Luce's own reporters might have envied. And Luce was to value Wilder's observations and listen intently to the words without ever really respecting the man who gave them utterance.

Before sailing for New York on the *Île de France* in late June, Wilder arranged to pick up Gertrude Stein's *Two Hundred Stanzas in Meditation,* portions of which he arranged for publication in *Poetry.* Despite his admiration for their author, Wilder refused to write a prefatory note; he explained to George Dillon, a friend from his Chicago years and editor of *Poetry,* that he did not understand Stein's verses even though he subliminally felt their authority. And then, Wilder added in his letter to Dillon that his latest enthusiasm (and one sees the sequence of thought) was the recently published *Finnegans Wake* of James Joyce which Wilder characterized as a great, beautiful, deep book. This work was, in fact, to haunt and even obsess him for the next twenty years. Indeed, it played a major part in making of Wilder a world-famous dramatist.

The summer months of 1939 Wilder mostly spent reading *Finnegans Wake* and performing the role of the Narrator in *Our Town* at summer theaters in Stockbridge, Massachusetts, New Hope, Pennsylvania, and Dennis on Cape Cod. In a letter to Woollcott he ruefully contrasted his previous weeks in London, Paris, and Bilignin where he had conversed with Jean Cocteau, Max Beerbohm, Hugh Walpole, H. G. Wells, Desmond MacCarthy, Harold Nicolson, Christian Berard, Louis Jouvet, and Gertrude Stein with his life in Stockbridge where he could chat with Dennis King . . . and where he did not attend performances of the Boston Symphony at nearby Tanglewood.*

As the summer of 1939 drew to an end, twenty-five years after the guns of August had signaled the outbreak of World War I, the Germans invaded Poland, thereby releasing a tension that had become almost unbearable. The first several days saw Hitler's blitzkrieg of Poland; England and France declaring war on Germany; and Russia annexing eastern Poland. Wilder was transfixed in horror and disbelief. Would the agonizing convulsions that gripped the world of his adolescence repeat themselves on an even vaster scale? His first thoughts were for his compatriots Gertrude Stein and Alice Toklas who, no longer young, were physically ill-equipped for the inevitable hardships that lay ahead. As an inducement for their return, Wilder asked his lecture agent, Lee Kendrick, to set up a new American tour for Gertrude. His first word from them after the outbreak of hostilities was barely reassuring:

> . . . except for one or two moments of scare not about bombs but about our beloved France we are hopeful . . . we are staying on here another month and then back to Paris, after that we do not know, we have settled down to go on, Alice is type-writing Ida I am writing, Basket and Pepe are asleep the rain is raining Giraudout [sic] is very popular in his job. . . . Madame Pierlot [a neighbor in Bilignin] says three wars are too many, well so are two. . . . Betty Leyres who is here with her three months old baby said about the book *The World Is Round*, I hope when Johnny is old enough to read it the world will still be round, well we all hope so. . . .

---

* Wilder's musical tastes were undergoing profound changes. Though he continued to absorb himself in the work of Palestrina and in music of the Baroque, he had lost interest in what is regarded as the standard orchestral and operatic repertory, preferring modernists like Berg and Bartók. In the 1950s he collaborated with composers Paul Hindemith and Louise Talma, each of whom wrote opera scores to librettos based on Wilder plays.

In the meantime Wilder was casting about for a place to work. He first tried Washington, moving on to Atlantic City where a convention of Shriners provided him with the background of the second act of a new play that was taking shape in his mind; finally in November he rented an apartment for four months at 81 Irving Place, a few steps removed from Gramercy Park in Manhattan. During the first months of the war, he found that he could not properly work on the plays that were filling his mind. Instead, he produced an adaptation for Brian Aherne of Farquhar's restoration comedy, *The Beaux' Stratagem;* for the Limited Editions Club, he devised an introduction to *Oedipus Rex;* for the Federation of Jewish Charities, he contributed an epilogue to an entertainment that climaxed their annual fund-raising dinner; and on behalf of Gertrude Stein he made strenuous attempts to get a publisher for *Four in America,* lecture dates, and publication of her poetry. On his own behalf, he entered into negotiations with Sol Lesser, an independent Hollywood producer who had secured the film rights to *Our Town.* Wilder was dissatisfied with the screen treatment that Lillian Hellman had provided for Lesser and, consequently, had offered to compose the screenplay gratis. In the fall–winter of 1939, long consultations and lengthy correspondence with Lesser led to Wilder's screenplay for *Our Town.*

But persisting in the back of his mind during that same time was the idea for an unusual play, "high, wide, and bold," as he apprehensively referred to it. Part of the concept grew out of *Finnegans Wake;* the idea received additional impetus from the outbreak of World War II; he was said to have received additional inspiration from a visit to the New York production of Olsen and Johnson's *Hellzapopin.* Wilder was unequivocally stimulated by a return, on behalf of Reinhardt, to Pirandello's *Six Characters in Search of an Author,* of which he attempted a new adaptation. The classic, measured sequences of *The Alcestiad* were set aside as the new comic-strip play—as Wilder described it, funnier than the Marx brothers, graver than *Paradise Lost,* and more topical than Robert E. Sherwood's latest—began to take shape in his mind.

For Christmas, Sol Lesser, in appreciation of Wilder's unremunerated screenplay of *Our Town,* gave Wilder a new Chrysler convertible. Thornton and Isabel were nonplussed: Thornton had no license and barely knew how to drive. But he finally blurted out to Isabel, "It was very generous of him." "Generous!" exclaimed Isabel, "If you had an ounce of business sense and received the payment due you for the weeks and weeks you've worked on that movie script, you could buy a dozen cars and hire a chauffeur to drive them." Wilder decided to take driving lessons, to get his license, and to drive off in his new car in April.

And so he did. Relinquishing his New York apartment in March after a winter spent in a close examination of *Finnegans Wake* (he explicated some pages of it at a soirée given by Mabel Dodge Luhan in her tower apartment at One Fifth Avenue) , he dropped off Isabel and his mother at Williamsburg, Virginia, proceeding alone in the Chrysler toward Saint Augustine, Florida, to begin work in earnest on the new play. His sojourn in Florida was not very long. Within a few weeks, he was driving back to New England in time to attend the May 23 movie premiere of *Our Town* in Boston.* From there, he returned to the MacDowell Colony and resumed work on what he continued to call his comic-strip play. It was during his stay at the MacDowell Colony in June 1940 that Hitler's armies overran Western Europe and drove the forces of Great Britain back into the sea. Wilder's anguish was profound. He gathered up first editions, manuscripts, and a precious long-cherished letter from T. E. Lawrence and sent them off to Sibyl Colefax so that they could be auctioned off for British War Relief.†

Work on the new play alternated with close readings of *Finnegans Wake,* about which Wilder sent detailed progress reports to Edmund Wilson at Wellfleet, Massachusetts. But the writing was interrupted during the summer by Wilder's returning to summer stock to play again in *Our Town*. With two difficult and ambitious plays in progress, why did he resume acting, an activity which not only took up a great deal of time but exacted a prodigious expenditure of his psychic energies? It is obvious by now that Wilder simply loved being on stage. As an adolescent he had had to be satisfied with small parts or small audiences. In *Our Town* he was the star of his own play. Moreover, he enjoyed the theater, being with actors, scenery painters, apprentices hoping to become actors, actors hoping to become directors, and directors determined to become playwrights. The George Gibbs in the production at Amherst, for example, was played by Wilson Lehr who, in time, became the director of a venturesome college theater in New York City and professor of dramatic arts at both City College and Brooklyn College. Scores of such young men and women who met Wilder on the summer circuit have remembered with gratitude his generosity, encouragement and good

---

* The film version of *Our Town*, after its Boston premiere, enjoyed a first run in New York at the Radio City Music Hall, and it launched the film career of William Holden who played George Gibbs. But it did not make motion picture history. Only one work by Wilder was successful in films; this was a screenplay he wrote for Alfred Hitchcock, demonstrating that he had a sure grasp of cinematic writing, a craft which interested him only intermittently.

† Wilder's generosity is one of the most attractive facets of his personality. To the consternation of his family (and of the Yale Library, beneficiary of his memorabilia) he gave away precious holographs, manuscripts, and fair copies of his work to worthy causes—indifferent to the fact that what he was giving was of considerable monetary value. John Hay Whitney was interested in purchasing the manuscript of *The Bridge of San Luis Rey*. Wilder handed it to him as a gift!

counsel. There was, of course, another reason for Wilder's taking on these assignments in summer stock: for his performances he was paid more than adequately. In addition to his salary, no negligible sum, these performances increased his royalties and augmented Wilder's almost marginal income.

Before setting out for another work stint, this time in Quebec, Wilder had a number of chores in the early fall of 1940 that required his attention. One was political. In his own words, Wilder was "fanatically for Roosevelt," because he felt that Roosevelt, more than any other influential man in America, saw clearly what America could and must do for the Allies and that he could put such measures into effect, by skillfully driving through the formidable opposition. As a consequence of his convictions, Wilder became one of a group of prominent writers invited to Hyde Park for a nationwide broadcast supporting Roosevelt's reelection to a third term. (The only well-known writers supporting Roosevelt's opponent, Wendell Willkie, were Booth Tarkington and John P. Marquand*).

Wilder's next chore was occasioned by the fiftieth anniversary of the First Congregational Church in Madison, Wisconsin—the church the Wilders attended at the turn of the century. Wilder accepted an invitation to speak on the subject of "Literature and Religion." Before departing for Madison, however, in conjunction with Padraic Colum, he actively worked on a petition to the Nobel Prize committee urging that its award for literature go to James Joyce, "destitute in southern France." Among those supporting Joyce were Van Wyck Brooks, James Bryant Conant, Robert Hutchins, Aldous Huxley, Sinclair Lewis, Archibald MacLeish, Eugene O'Neill, Dorothy Thompson, and Edmund Wilson.†

In Madison, escorted by graduate student Robert Stallman, whom he had befriended when Stallman was starving in Chicago in 1933 and who was now completing his doctoral studies at the University of Wiscon-

---

* Wilder's assessment of Roosevelt is worth recording: That he was not a great man but that he was disinterested, tireless, instinctively active, and creative so that his bravery in action did not look like bravery; that Roosevelt was free from fanaticism, without spite or retaliation. . . . FDR laughed at the discomfiture of his opponents like a boy who has played a practical joke—not like the snarl of an injured brooder. Wilder's affection for Roosevelt was deepened a year or so later when the Commander-in-Chief refused to tender the necessary papers to Henry Luce who was eager to visit the war zones.

† At this time, Joyce was indeed a refugee in a village near Vichy, ill and living off contributions from his friends. He succeeded, after many difficulties, in returning to his World War I haven, Zurich, but within weeks after his arrival there, he died. He had been furious that the war had prevented people from giving their full attention to *Finnegans Wake*. The Nobel Prize committee did not award him its prize; no prizes were awarded in 1941, or for the next four years.

sin, Wilder was invited to lunch with the English faculty. Arriving at the Faculty Club, he looked in vain for the two men he most wanted to meet, Miles Hanley, the Joyce scholar, and William Ellery Leonard, the poet and classicist. Both were notorious for their unconventional manners and had not been invited; but, at Wilder's insistence, both men were found: Hanley upstairs in the quarters and Leonard in his house across the street. Later that day, Wilder tried unsuccessfully to find the house where he had lived forty years earlier. Sinclair Lewis was temporarily on the English faculty that fall—though he soon thereafter precipitously ended his connection with the university—and Stallman, who had been informally designated as guide to distinguished visitors, arranged for Wilder and Lewis to meet in a downtown hotel bar. According to Stallman, Lewis was arrogant and competitive, where Wilder was amiable, but not submissive. At one point, Lewis truculently produced his Actors Equity card, whereupon Wilder triumphantly displayed his own. The tension of the meeting undoubtedly had its roots in the fact that Lewis had already grown restless and uncomfortable teaching at the university. In any case, the meeting seems to have ended another of Wilder's literary friendships, though his association with Lewis had never been particularly meaningful nor rewarding for either.

Wilder went on to Chicago, where he was scheduled to lecture on "True and False Realism in the Theater" at the university. Robert Hutchins had invited eighty Chicagoans to a supper after the lecture and forty-nine of them accepted. The invitation list reveals that no one from the department of English was invited, that Mr. and Mrs. Mortimer Adler declined, and that among those who accepted were a Chicago attorney and his cultivated wife, Mr. and Mrs. Adlai Stevenson. The guest list was otherwise made up of affluent Chicagoans whose benefi cence to the university was nourished through occasions such as this. Loyal to Chicago and to Hutchins, Wilder was thoroughly complaisant in fulfilling his role.

By mid-October, Wilder had installed himself in the Chateau Frontenac in Quebec and was hard at work on the new play. He described it to Sibyl Colefax as a slapstick account of mankind stumbling, childlike, hard pressed, absurd, and sublime, surviving ice ages, floods and the jungles within his own breast, murder and self-murder. In the letter, he stated his intention of dedicating the play to the beleaguered Lady Colefax who, at sixty-seven, was desperately coping with the sufferings of the victims of bomb-stricken London, arranging free midday concerts for the poor and music-starved Londoners, and continuing to provide a comfortable meeting place for the powerful men in government where they could "unbutton" and relax with their peers in a quiet drawing room.* Although Wilder was exhilarated by the progress he was making with the play, he continued to be distracted and anxious about European developments and England's fate. He was, moreover, concerned about the presidential election, Roosevelt's bid for a third term: in the most embittered campaign since the Civil War, the country witnessed venomous street corner exchanges, assembly hall debates and even vitriolic radio addresses. Wilder was dismayed at a broadcast by Clare Boothe Luce to whom he privately awarded a celluloid rose—to share with her husband—for public fatuity and nonsense. Ruth Gordon wrote Wilder about the same broadcast that Mrs. Luce sounded like a congenital idiot from high society; she was particularly outraged by Mrs. Luce's calling Roosevelt and his advisers "the Hyde Park Gestapo."

By Christmas, Wilder had completed two acts of the play and was home briefly before starting off for an extended stay in Washington. The Department of State had invited him to visit Colombia, Ecuador, and Peru during March, April, and May, 1941; his mission was to create an atmosphere favorable to the United States among the intellectuals and creative people of those countries. Before leaving on this goodwill mission, Wilder spent several weeks in Washington learning Spanish and getting briefed on his mission.

At about the same time, Wilder was asked to provide appreciations in memory of the recently deceased Sidney Howard and Scott Fitzgerald, the latter request coming from Edmund Wilson. Wilder, understandably, refused both requests. He felt that his contribution would necessarily have to reflect the truth about his feelings toward the writings of both Howard and Fitzgerald; since he had reservations about their work he preferred to say nothing. But on the occasion of Joyce's death in January, he immediately accepted *Poetry* editor George Dillon's invitation to write a memorial piece. Published in the March 1941 issue of *Poetry*, Wilder's essay on Joyce was subsequently reprinted as a monograph in 1944; it was an eloquent and incisive statement about Joyce's achievement and stature.

In Washington, his study of the Spanish language and his work on Act III of his war play continued. He took great pleasure in making the acquaintance of France's former chief of protocol, Alexis Léger, who, under the name of St. John Perse, had written a considerable body of poetry which was subsequently to win him a Nobel Prize. It was also during this Washington sojourn that Robert Hutchins delivered an

---

* When Sibyl Colefax finally got to see an unfinished version of the play a year later while Wilder was in London for a brief official visit, she expressed certain reservations about it which Wilder interpreted as a rejection of the dedication. As a result, the published version of *The Skin of Our Teeth* is without a dedication. *Our Town* was dedicated to Woollcott and *The Merchant of Yonkers* to Max Reinhardt.

address, broadcast nationally, which materially altered Wilder's relationship with him.

Ever since Wilder's resignation from Chicago four years before, the friendship between Wilder and Hutchins had undergone a certain deterioration. In the summer of 1937, we recall, when the Hutchinses dispatched their picture postcards to Wilder, they never provided an address where *they* could be reached, and Wilder was convinced they were trying to avoid a meeting. Then, in 1940, the Hutchinses arrived in New York for what was to have been a two-week visit. Maude Hutchins seemed to Wilder to have become difficult. Earlier, Wilder could envisage Hutchins becoming president of the United States; now he believed that Maude was injuring her husband's chances of any kind of political future.

But something even more basic than Maude's behavior was emerging to slacken the bonds of friendship between Wilder and Hutchins. Wilder's commitment to the Allied cause was total. He regarded Hitler as a virtual incarnation of the devil, particularly in his cruelty and in his contempt for the human spirit. Moreover, he passionately supported Roosevelt's efforts to render every possible assistance to the Allied effort. When in the spring of 1940 the war erupted in a series of German conquests, Wilder determined that sooner or later he would personally take up arms against the Germans. Then, in July, he expressed the hope that he would be in uniform before New Year's 1941. In the crisis in Europe, in short, Wilder saw Western civilization at bay, the barbarian at the gates. Never in his life had he been so passionately involved; all the women he cared about, Gertrude and Alice, Sibyl Colefax, his own mother and sisters, were all threatened. After the fall of France, it was clear to Wilder that only American involvement could save the world from the scourge of Hitler's armies.

He was terribly dismayed when on January 23, 1941, Robert Hutchins made a nationally broadcast address advocating American neutrality and warning his countrymen against involvement in the European conflict. In one stroke, Hutchins gave enormous additional credence and respectability to the America First Committee and its chief spokesman, Charles Lindbergh.

Although Wilder was not taken by surprise, he had been clinging to the illusion that if only he and Hutchins could meet and talk they would find "at three in the morning" that they were of the same mind. Out of respect for their long association, Wilder concealed his disappointment from Hutchins, and only weeks after the speech did he acknowledge that they were poles apart. He did, however, communicate his outrage to Gertrude Stein and denounced Hutchins's logic, asserting that Hutchins had doubtless provided the University of Chicago trustees and other Chicago millionaires with raptures of delight. Most Americans, Wilder added, ranged in their reactions to Hutchins's speech from shock to contempt. Thus Wilder's adulation of Hutchins, at the end of a quarter of a century, fizzled out at this moment when Hutchins had dug his political grave. For Wilder and for intellectual leadership throughout the United States, the stature and the charisma of Robert Hutchins simply vanished overnight; at forty-two, the boy philosopher, visionary, and educational reformer had turned himself into another midwestern isolationist. Ten years later, he divested himself of the troubled Maude, married his secretary, and left Chicago for California to administer some of the millions amassed by Henry Ford. After January, 1941, Wilder would speak privately about Hutchins, with a baleful shake of his head, as a man who, out of some kind of self-indulgence, had failed to fulfill his great potential.

Still, on the surface, the relationship between the two men seemed unchanged. Later in 1941, Wilder returned—for the last time—to teach a summer session at Chicago. The two men's letters included assurances of affectionate regard. Each continued to refer to the other as his best friend even when they didn't see each other for years at a time and when their correspondence had trickled down to an exchange of Christmas cards. Each, having long since exhausted the need for the other, perceived that the relationship was a hollow shell. Out of nostalgia or pride or stubbornness they allowed the shell to remain, a memorial to their lost youth and their extraordinary expectations.*

Wilder's Latin American trip coincided with another personal blow. His sister Charlotte, for the past several years, had been courageously subsisting in New York's Greenwich Village as a writer and had published one single volume of her poems. Now past forty, she had lost her struggle for independence and self-identity and had succumbed to mental illness, a condition from which she was never to emerge. Thornton and Charlotte, at least in their adult years, had not been close; but because Wilder was involved with his family and sensed that his own successes

---

* Why Hutchins chose to take a public position identifying him with the extremist elements in the country—the Right, the Left, the German-American Bund, the Anglophobes—is a question not easily answered. The reasons are undoubtedly complex: he was certainly giving voice to his deeply felt pacifist convictions, but he had also been living in Chicago too long. And Hutchins, also, had an aversion to being on the same side as most intellectual opinion; he treasured the role of maverick. The fact remains that he was one of the few widely known and respected spokesmen of the intellectual world to champion isolationism at the very moment when Hitler's legions seemed invincible. Wilder was only one of the tens of thousands who were sickened and saddened by Hutchins's position . . . or by the manner in which he announced it, in a broadcast.

had somehow contributed to Charlotte's breakdown (as they may very well have done) , her plight weighed heavily upon him.

March, April, and May were spent respectively in Colombia, Ecuador, and Peru where Wilder attempted to win over the intellectual communities. Foreseeing that in a short time the United States would be engaged in all-out war with Germany and perhaps with Japan, Roosevelt was eager to alleviate some of the bitter anti-American feeling in Latin America. Wilder was well qualified for his mission: although he was strikingly different from the South Americans in temperament, tastes and appearance, he nevertheless achieved a rapport with them that few members of our diplomatic corps could muster. Combining a sure sense of tact with an aura of affectionate intimacy, Wilder, the author of *The Bridge of San Luis Rey,* astonished and delighted the intellectual élite of the countries he visited. Gratified by his fine showing, Washington officials expressed their interest in his touring the remainder of South America— an assignment Wilder was not eager to accept. His sights were set on a European mission.

It was during his visit to Bogota, Colombia, in March 1941 that his sister Janet, the youngest Wilder (young enough to be Wilder's daughter) , having earned a doctorate in the biological sciences from Chicago, married a prosperous Massachusetts attorney, Winthrop Saltonstall Dakin. Although he missed the wedding, Wilder, in his letters to Hutchins, Gertrude Stein, Woollcott, and Sibyl Colefax, expressed a proper bourgeois satisfaction in the alliance.

In June, Wilder began his summer assignment at the University of Chicago, a chore that he undertook with weary reluctance and carried forward with a well-concealed bored distaste. Mornings he lectured on Homer, Sophocles, Dante, and Cervantes; on two afternoons a week, he saw student-writers during office hours. The experience exhausted him, kept work on his new play at a standstill, and left him exasperated with himself and with Hutchins who had urged the assignment upon him. Behind these feelings lay the undeclared, but deeply felt, estrangement from Hutchins, whose unhappy marriage, Wilder felt, had drained him and rendered him intellectually incapable of thinking through the problems he faced. Having broken with Hutchins in his own mind, Wilder felt he must act as though nothing between them had changed. The return to Chicago, though only for a summer, would at least give credence to the idea that their friendship had survived the ideological split between them. Wilder may even have felt that Hutchins needed him around during this personal crisis. In addition, Wilder had to earn some money. The recent South American tour had been undertaken with virtually no financial support from the government beyond transportation and a niggardly six dollars per diem. After three months in Bogota,

Quito, and Lima, Wilder was out of pocket ten times the amount of his allotment. And, in addition to the dependence of his mother and Isabel, Charlotte was now incapacitated and her medical expenses were considerable.

Shortly after completing his teaching duties at Chicago, Wilder, together with John Dos Passos, was invited by the International Committee of PEN, the world writers' organization, to attend a writers' congress in London. Although the visit to England meant a third postponement of the play, which by now Wilder had about decided to call *The Skin of Our Teeth*, he avidly accepted the invitation. After the previous summer's graphic accounts of the bombing and fire damage inflicted upon England's cities in general and London in particular, Wilder was eager to see the devastation at first hand and to experience personally the consequences of all the destruction.

And experience it he did. As he walked through the blacked-out streets of London, the silence was for him as loud as bombs. The destruction (not yet as extensive as it would be later on) appalled him; it was, after all, his first direct encounter with pure havoc. He visited a bomber base and broadcast to a Western Europe now almost entirely overrun by Nazis. Introduced by H. G. Wells, he addressed a luncheon meeting of the English-speaking Union. And with Dos Passos he represented the United States at what he was later to describe as the futile and acrimonious proceedings of PEN; he aligned himself with Rebecca West and E. M. Forster in the humanist camp, rather than with those delegates who were proposing that the membership devote themselves exclusively to propaganda for the Allied cause. Wilder was cordially greeted by a number of minor British officials, by publishers Robert Longman and Hamish Hamilton (the latter having sponsored Wilder's visit), and by the master of Trinity College, Cambridge. But, prickly as he was in such matters, Wilder took offense when on the occasion of meeting Harold Nicolson (for the fourth time) at a PEN reception, he was given little more than a peremptory nod. Wilder's love for England did not extend to British upper-class males who—in this regard like George S. Kaufman —somehow put him down.

By early October, having flown via Portugal back to New York, Wilder was ready to resume work upon *The Skin of Our Teeth*. His hopes for the play were high. Jed Harris, who had seen Acts I and II in the previous spring, had expressed enthusiasm, proposing this actor and that actress for the principal roles. (Ruth Gordon had been rejected for the role of Sabina on the grounds that she was too short to be a proper seductress.) With all distractions out of the way—or almost—Wilder, acting upon suggestions made by Sibyl Colefax in London that allowed him to resolve other problems in Act III and in a final spurt of energy, completed the text of *The Skin of Our Teeth* at three o'clock on New Year's Day, 1942. He was exhilarated and eager to rush the play into production so that he could properly serve his country which for the past three weeks had been—at long last!—in a state of war with the Axis powers.

But, in a very short time, Wilder's eagerness and exhilaration would give way to disappointment and frustration. He was to discover that getting into the uniform of a soldier at the age of forty-five was easier than getting his play produced on Broadway.

# XII

## Skinnegans Wake

*". . . certain charges ought not to be made. . . ."*

*The Skin of Our Teeth* was the climax of Wilder's literary rehabilitation. His career, which in 1927–28 had brought him international renown, three years later found him with a greatly diminished reading public and virtually no critical supporters. His novels (together with the mercifully forgotten allegorical drama, *The Trumpet Shall Sound*) had reflected Wilder's twin Puritan preoccupations, religionism and sexual frustration. These early works, while they revealed an unmistakable artistry, were nevertheless shot through with a pervasive ironic melancholy which the general public mistakes for high-minded tragedy and which serious critics finally pass over in bored silence. Michael Gold's essay, for all its essentially wrong-headed notions and deplorable vulgarity, was a coup de grace that almost buried Wilder's literary reputation and forced him to reconsider both his thematic concerns and his very vocation as a novelist. The happy end result of Wilder's long self-examination was that he transformed himself from a Christian tragedian to an eclectic comedian, from an all too empathetic narrator to a crisply objective dramatizer. In short, he moved the setting of his work out of the international salon and into the American home where, artistically at least, he more truly belonged. The transition to comedy that had begun with the 1931 one-act plays and *Heaven's My Destination* reached its fulfillment in *The Skin of Our Teeth*.

In completing *The Skin of Our Teeth* so soon after the attack at Pearl Harbor, that is to say at a moment when with an untrained army and a crippled navy the United States was at war with Germany and Japan whose combined land and sea forces were superior to our own— Wilder felt that he had written a play that was perfectly in key with the historical moment. Exhilarated by the sense of having struck a blow for freedom, he immediately communicated with Jed Harris who, newly married to a young actesss named Louise Platt, was in Hollywood organizing his household. Wilder expected that Harris would produce and direct the new play and that Alfred Lunt and Lynn Fontanne would enact the roles of Mr. and Mrs. Antrobus. A third leading role, that of seductress-maid of all work Lily Sabina, remained uncast in Wilder's mind. Woollcott had urged him to offer the role to Ruth Gordon, but again Wilder rejected her because he felt she was physically unsuited to the role. His first choice, he was later to declare, was Fannie Brice; but he resolutely refused to accept Miss Gordon. This refusal could have been based on reasons other than her lack of physical charms. Wilder surely understood that since Miss Gordon and Jed Harris had broken up their menage, a professional collaboration might be awkward for either or both of them.

Wilder assumed that not only would Jed Harris direct but he also would arrange the financing, cast the play, engage a designer, and take charge of the production. But after he sent Harris the concluding third act early in January, he waited in vain for a response. Harris remained incommunicado for weeks and Wilder found himself engaged in a correspondence with Harris's secretary, Eddie Goodnow, who reported that Harris was busy finishing a script for the Army; furnishing a new home in Santa Monica; had not had time to read Act III; and had misplaced Acts I and II. After three weeks, Wilder was thoroughly exasperated. Though none of Goodnow's letters included a categorical refusal from Harris, Wilder abruptly terminated the negotiations—if that is the correct description—with a curt telegram informing Harris that he, Wilder, was making other arrangements for the production.

Harris's response was, first, a telegram:

LETTER MAILED TODAY HAPPY NEW YEAR BEST REGARDS JED.

His letter was, for the most part, an attack on the play. After praising the first act, Harris described the second act as a faulty and confused restatement and the third act as utterly trivial. But having damned two-thirds of the play, Harris urged Wilder to come to California, discuss revisions with him, and postpone production until after he had directed a play by Dorothy Heyward—then he would be ready to direct an improved version of *The Skin of Our Teeth*.

But Wilder had made an irrevocable decision. Despite his admiration for Harris's extraordinary capacities, a conviction that never deserted him, he was resolved that Harris would be replaced, that the play would be produced and directed by someone else. But his disappointment over Harris was intensified by another rejection. In the midst of the maddening silence from the West Coast, on January 9, he had received a letter from Lynn Fontanne in Wisconsin reporting that she and her husband were comfortably resting and that they had no commitments. At the moment that Wilder broke off with Jed Harris, he offered the direction of the play to Alfred Lunt together with the roles of Mr. and Mrs. Antrobus for himself and his wife. Their immediate response was most favorable, asking Wilder to forward a copy of the play as soon as possible. Then, five days later, on the same day that Harris announced that he was directing Mrs. Heyward's play, Wilder received a telegram from Lunt expressing grave reservations about *The Skin of Our Teeth*. A subsequent letter from Lunt made clear that he was reluctant to direct or participate in the production.

In the last week of January, however, Wilder took one important and fateful step. He found a producer, an unknown and wholly inexperienced young man named Michael Myerberg, son-in-law of the singer Margarete Matzenauer and for five years manager of conductor Leopold Stokowski. The news of Wilder's decision was reported in the January 30 issue of the *New York Herald Tribune* as follows:

'SKIN OF OUR TEETH,'
NEW THORNTON WILDER PLAY,
TO GET PRODUCTION IN APRIL

The new Thornton Wilder play, "Skin of Our Teeth," described as a combination of realism and allegory, has been acquired by Michael Myerberg for production here in April after a short road tour. Mr. Myerberg, who has been Leopold Stokowski's manager since 1936, expects to start rehearsals in ten days. The producer received the completed script on Tuesday evening. He said yesterday that the play was of "all time, all places and all people. It examines the problems of the human race against the background of Mr. and Mrs. George Antrobus, of Excelsior, N.J."

Mr. Wilder's last play here was "The Merchant of Yonkers," produced in December, 1938, by Herman Shumlin at the Guild Theater. It ran for thirty-nine performances.

The first sentence of this story was very nearly the kiss of death. Any play described to potential investors as a "combination of realism and allegory" was not likely to attract much cash. Myerberg's experience as a theatrical producer was obviously nonexistent. And the announcement's grim reminder of Wilder's previous entry into the Broadway sweepstakes was hardly reassuring. The few people who knew Myerberg were puzzled by Wilder's choice. The two men had met, it seems, some years earlier at Mabel Dodge Luhan's. Wilder had confided to Myerberg his intention of writing for the commercial theater and Myerberg, from that time on, periodically reminded Wilder that an admiring, high-minded, and energetic producer was standing in readiness to produce Wilder's plays. Myerberg came forth with just such a reminder at the moment that Wilder decided to give up on Jed Harris. The younger man's earnestness and intelligence seemed to him to be a reasonable alternative to the producing talents of Jed Harris, particularly since Harris was unavailable.

Wilder's choice, however erratic it appeared to the Broadway theater people, was not entirely as impulsive as it seemed. He was eager to get the project moving as quickly as possible and none of the established producers were falling over themselves to get the play; the word going around was that the play was a disaster. Fortunately, Myerberg's lack of experience was balanced by his belief in the play, and by his determination to see it successfully produced. Within three weeks after he took charge, he and Wilder had secured Fredric March and his wife, Florence Eldridge, for the roles of Mr. and Mrs. Antrobus. In addition, they engaged as the play's director an unknown young actor from the Group Theater who had staged two plays, only one of which had reached Broadway. The young director, recommended to Wilder by Robert Ardrey, was Elia Kazan.

*The Skin of Our Teeth* was making progress, except in the matter of financial backing. Thirty-seven astute and discriminating theater people expressed an interest in financing the production—until they were given the script to read. A thirty-eighth, Mr. Lee Shubert, listened to the first act and agreed to give Myerberg one-tenth of the production cost provided he didn't have to listen to acts two and three. Ultimately, seventy percent of the capitalization came from Myerberg's personal investment, the only other investors of consequence being Fredric March and S. H. Fabian, a motion picture theater owner; a small group of idealist-intellectuals, such as Irving Rosenthal—at that time a marginally paid instructor at City College—put up moderate sums toward an aggregate amount that constituted the final ten percent of the production costs.

Wilder's participation in the production virtually came to an end when it became necessary to postpone staging from spring to fall; the

Fredric Marches had film commitments until later in the year. Once he had made some revisions in late January and early February and turned over the completed script to Myerberg, Wilder's chief occupation was finding a place for himself in the armed forces. Unwilling to do what a number of professional writers had already done—offered their services to Archibald MacLeish, now an assistant secretary in the Roosevelt cabinet who could provide patriotic authors with offices in Washington where they might spend the duration of the war writing memos to one another—Wilder was eager to join a combat unit. Aged forty-five, but in excellent health, he volunteered his services to the military authorities. He was determined that if they could not make use of him he would apply for work in a factory, an alternative he was to be spared.

Wilder spent the spring of 1942 waiting for a call to arms. He filled the time, and they were suspenseful weeks for him, writing scripts for government films (*Manuelito Becomes an Air Cadet; Your Community and the War Effort*), consulting with Myerberg and tinkering with the playscript, visiting the ailing Woollcott at his island home in Vermont, and all the time waiting for Washington's decision. In mid-March he received a telegram from Max Reinhardt asking for the rights to produce *The Skin of Our Teeth;* remembering that the petitioner was once the most venerated theater man in the world, Wilder with a heavy heart replied that he had completely settled arrangements. He discovered the letters of Simon Bolivar, thanks to his recent acquisition of the Spanish language; and he rediscovered the poems of Robert Frost whose genius he now apprehended, declaring in a letter to Woollcott that Frost was better than Wilder's old friend from the MacDowell Colony, Edwin Arlington Robinson.

In the midst of all this marking time, the matter of finding an actress to play the part of Lily Sabina remained unsettled. In desperation, Myerberg, with Wilder's reluctant permission, sent the script to Helen Hayes. According to Miss Hayes's published recollections, she assumed that she was being considered for the role of Mrs. Antrobus, the role she was ultimately to play in subsequent revivals in the 1950s; her published recollection also records that Wilder himself sent her the script at the moment that he finished it. The facts are somewhat different; her letter to Woollcott dated July 2, 1942, reveals that Myerberg sent her the script with the suggestion that she play Sabina. She went on to say that she felt that Ruth Gordon would be better suited to the role, and that she wouldn't dare attempt it because she would be haunted by the thought of Miss Gordon's delivery. After considering the role for several months, she decided to take instead the starring role in a play about Harriet Beecher Stowe. Miss Hayes's aesthetic principles were tempered by practical considerations: *The Skin of Our Teeth* was an experimental play and

Helen Hayes did not regard herself as an experimental actress, anymore than did the Lunts. In the midst of the whole dilemma of who would play Sabina, Mrs. Fredric March (whom Wilder once described as a perennially uninteresting actress) somehow had intimations that Helen Hayes would turn down Sabina and offered herself for the role, a proposal that was received without comment.

But all the production problems abruptly ended for Wilder when he received a call to Washington early in May inviting him for an interview which might lead to a commission in Air Force Intelligence. After being subjected to a searching interview, he was scheduled for a physical examination on May 18. He passed both examinations, and on May 19, he left for a screen-writing assignment in Hollywood, where he awaited receipt of his commission as Captain of Air Force Intelligence.

Wilder's abrupt departure for Hollywood came about because of an offer from Alfred Hitchcock inviting him to compose a screen play based on an anecdote that had come to Hitchcock's attention; the story had to do with an attractive psychopathic murderer who takes refuge in the bosom of his married sister's conventional home in a conventional small town. The screen treatment was admirably suited, Mr. Hitchcock felt, to the talents of the author of *Our Town*. Wilder unhesitatingly accepted the assignment, certain that his military role would be an extended one; he was eager to leave some extra money behind, not only for his mother and Isabel but also to help defray the costs of Charlotte's now clearly indefinite hospitalization. He worked steadily with Hitchcock on the screenplay, whose title was to be *Shadow of a Doubt,* until the receipt of his orders placing him on active duty. The orders arrived on June 16th directing him to report to the Officer Training School at Miami Beach, Florida no later than June 29. But by June 24, the day that Wilder had to entrain for Florida, the script was still not finished, and so Hitchcock accompanied him on the journey across the continent and the screenplay was completed en route.*

Wilder spent his first six weeks at the Officer Training School where he was given a general indoctrination and subjected to a moderate amount of physical training. That he was able to survive the drill, the marches, and the hour and a half long formations in the blinding Florida sun of July is evidence of his excellent physical condition. A number of his classmates had to be returned to civilian duty; several of the officers in training actually perished from their exertions in the tropical heat. For a

---

* *Shadow of a Doubt,* released in the winter 1942–43, enjoyed a great critical success and was, in fact, the most successful film that Wilder ever worked on. Its co-star, Teresa Wright, had succeeded Martha Scott as Emily in *Our Town* four years before. An important segment of the Hitchcock canon, *Shadow of a Doubt,* is frequently revived in art theaters, in museum repertories, and on television.

man of forty-five, the Miami Beach experience was an achievement; it was that, in fact, for men half his age. On August 10, Wilder was transferred to the Intelligence School at Harrisburg, Pennsylvania, and upon graduation on September 19, he was assigned to the headquarters of the 328th Fighter Group, stationed at Hamilton Field, California. Within weeks after joining his combat unit, Wilder said that he was happier and healthier than he had ever been. His sole recreation was a day and a half spent every two weeks in San Francisco; yet, he managed to provide Myerberg with a number of important changes in the text of *The Skin of Our Teeth* and even continued to work on the several-times attempted and discarded *Alcestiad*.

Meanwhile, back in New York, Myerberg proceeded with the production of *The Skin of Our Teeth*. Helen Hayes finally rejected the role of Sabina, but, in doing so, she recommended that the part go to Tallulah Bankhead. The script was dispatched to Miss Bankhead who was between engagements at home in Connecticut; she shrewdly and immediately recognized that the role presented her with her finest opportunity since *The Little Foxes* four years earlier. What she did not know was that Wilder had considerable misgivings and had to be persuaded to accept her. It took the combined efforts of Ruth Gordon, Helen Hayes, and Edward Sheldon, plus the desperate importunities of Myerberg and Kazan, to persuade Wilder that this tragic-glamorous actress who specialized in tarnished ladies' roles had the comic gifts that would enable her to play a part envisaged for Fannie Brice. But the signing of Miss Bankhead marked the end of the major casting obstacles. The Marches were now available and rehearsals began early in September for a New Haven opening on October 15.

Kazan had assembled an inspired supporting cast: for the Fortune Teller he selected the veteran Florence Reed; for the Stage Manager, E. G. Marshall; Morton Da Costa and Stanley Prager played small roles. The children's sculptor in papier-mâché, Remo Buffano, not only built the dinosaur and the mammoth but also played the dinosaur so engagingly that, in succeeding decades, theatergoers continued to recall the creature's charm. Finally, persuaded by the playwright Robert Ardrey, Kazan selected the virtually unknown Montgomery Clift for the pivotal role of Henry. But despite the brilliance of the cast, rehearsals turned out to be a nightmare for Kazan and for certain members of the company.

The chief problem was Tallulah. Almost immediately, an antagonism developed between her and Florence Eldridge; and the two ladies stopped speaking to one another and remained enemies for the length of their respective engagements. Moreover, Tallulah had scant respect for Kazan's directorial talents, and she proceeded to ignore his suggestions and devised a performance that was her own very original and personal interpretation. Finally, she loathed Myerberg, whom she regarded as a cheap, penny-pinching incompetent upstart. Certain other members of the cast viewed him in the same light and welcomed Tallulah's championing of their cause against the producer. Tallulah, in short, was divisive, rebellious, and unmanageable. But as matters turned out, she saved the play.

Another problem was Myerberg. His moods alternated between black hysteria and megalomania. At one point, on the evening of the Philadelphia opening, he hysterically offered to sell the entire production to Fredric March for $35,000, an offer that March was ready to avail himself of, except that Myerberg changed his mind the next morning when he read the favorable reviews by the Philadelphia critics. Myerberg, moreover, was continually attempting to make changes in the script, but his meddling was frustrated by the combined opposition of Isabel Wilder and Tallulah who had formed a powerful alliance against the producer.

Wilder, out in California, was bombarded by letters and long-distance calls from all the principals involved, each of whom regarded him as a court of appeal and the soul of reason and enlightenment. To him went letters from Tallulah, champion of the integrity of the written script and of the actors playing minor roles; from Florence Eldridge who wrote even lengthier letters complaining about both Myerberg and Tallulah; from Myerberg and Kazan about Tallulah's refusal to accept direction. Finally Woollcott, who wished to become a part of the cast and play the part of the Newsreel Commentator, heard but not seen, wrote that Tallulah was entirely incompetent and that the role should be given to Ruth Gordon.*

And yet, despite the backstage dissension—one actress undercutting another, a director who could not control his leading lady, an author who could be reached only by long distance, a producer who had alienated his entire company, a play whose techniques were innovative and whose theme was obscure—the rehearsals went on, and the opening took place in New Haven on schedule. Four days later, on October 19, the play began a week's run in Baltimore and then moved on to its Philadelphia opening on October 26. Wilder arrived in New York in time to see a run-through two days before the New York premiere. What he saw did

* Because the role of the Newsreel Commentator is an amplified offstage role and Woollcott actually recorded the lines so that he would not have to be present at performances, an arrangement that greatly pleased Myerberg principally because it enabled him to dispense with the services of Morton Da Costa, who had been cast in the part, and thereby cut down on overhead. Miss Bankhead, who despised Woollcott, dispatched an account of these shenanigans to Wilder and pointed out that the recording was unintelligible and that the audience was so confused by the familiarity of the voice that even if it were clear they would have paid no attention to the words. The Woollcott recording was scrapped and Da Costa was rehired and given back his part.

not wholly displease him: Tallulah Bankhead's performance, although it was not what he had envisaged when he wrote the play, was clearly a tour de force that did not, to any appreciable extent, invalidate the play as a whole. He was more disappointed and concerned over Florence Eldridge's performance which he regarded as inadequate in the face of Miss Bankhead's very spirited antics. In general, he was gratified and relieved by the high level of the performances, but dismayed by the direction which he felt failed to suggest the idea of spontaneous improvisation that he had so intensely hoped his script might evoke. But, above all, he wanted the play to *go,* and it seemed to him as though it might.

And so it did. In the face of the dire predictions from Broadway's soothsayers and savants, the play was a bewildering success. The performances following the November 18 opening brought standees to the Plymouth Theater throughout the winter. Within hours of its opening, *The Skin of Our Teeth* became the most talked about production of the season; it had chic, it had flair, it had style, and no one with pretensions to sophistication or taste could afford to miss it.

The play's success with the public was, to a certain extent, due to the critics' favorable response to Wilder's play and to Kazan's direction. The *New York Times,* the *New York Herald Tribune,* the *New York World-Telegram,* the *New Yorker,* and the *Nation* responded enthusiastically both to the play and the production. The dissenting critics, Louis Kronenberger of *PM,* Wilella Waldorf of the *New York Post,* John Anderson of the *New York Journal-American,* and Burns Mantle of the *News,* were generally ineffective when it came to the matter of box office sales. Readers of the *Daily News* were not patrons of serious theater; and readers of *PM* were more likely to be swayed by Krutch of the *Nation* or by Atkinson of the *Times* than by the young Kronenberger. But the overriding attraction that brought people to the Plymouth Theater was the news of Tallulah Bankhead's outrageous performance as Sabina. The amount of direction she accepted was minimal; she saw the role as a travesty of all the performances she had ever given, on and off the stage. And while that was not exactly what either Wilder or Kazan had in mind, it worked. Nor could anything deflect Tallulah from her very personal interpretation. Wilder had deliberately written a play that sounded like an improvisation; and of all the principal actors, Tallulah was the only one who really appeared to be making things up as she went along. The audience believed that her asides, her confidences, her "ad libs" were of her own devising, even though she never, in fact, altered a word of Wilder's dialogue. Her Sabina, which appalled and embittered Kazan, dazzled the critics and captivated the audiences. She was the focus of the reviews. Even the stately and scholarly Krutch found her capers "delightful," and he attributed the popular success that the play enjoyed to the cavortings of Miss Bankhead. It remained, in the minds of those who saw it, one of the genuinely memorable performances in the theater; and all subsequent interpretations of Sabina were merely hollow reminders of what Tallulah had done. Once before, she had placed her authoritative and ineradicable stamp upon a characterization when she played the role of Regina Giddens in Lillian Hellman's *The Little Foxes*. Now she had done it again.

It was Tallulah's archenemy who lavished upon the play itself (and upon its fabricator) the ultimate in praise. Never noted for the profundity of his criticism, often influenced by his personal relationship with the author or actor, Woollcott nevertheless correctly identified *The Skin of Our Teeth* as a classic American play whose influence and impact would outlast the decade. Writing for the March 1943 issue of the *Atlantic Monthly*, he summed up his impressions as follows:

> ". . . here is a theatrical craftsman every bit as bold, as impatient as ingenious and as sovereign in his field as Frank Lloyd Wright . . . there is the sound of rending wood at the back of the auditorium and the ushers come down the aisles bringing torn-up seats for the Antrobus fireplace. . . . But long before this, even with the rise of the first curtain, there had been another rending noise, the sound of Mr. Wilder . . . briskly shattering all those comfortably familiar conventions of the theater which would only be in his way. . . .
>
> It is not easy to think of any other American play with so good a chance of being acted a hundred years from now. . . . Of course it is a war play. Only those who had forgotten *The Trojan Women* would have thought it impossible that a play *could* be at once so topical and so timeless.

These words of high praise from his old friend were sad words for Wilder. By the time they appeared in print, Woollcott was dead. But they were a fine legacy; Wilder was not so fatuous as to take seriously the comparison with Euripides. But he was to say a few years later that Woollcott was right in calling it a "war play" and in understanding that the techniques were something more than mere novelties.

Woollcott's death had been a sudden one; he was stricken after a broadcast in January and died almost immediately. In losing him, Wilder lost a powerful ally and someone who came very close to being a long-term friend. He had long since lost his awe of Woollcott and had scant regard for his talents; but he had developed a genuine affection for Woollcott, not only because the older man spared Wilder the sting of his barbed wit, but because Woollcott deferred to Wilder and, in fact, displayed a kind of intellectual dependence. With Woollcott's passing, Wilder had sustained a loss, the first serious loss of his life excepting, of course, that of his unlamented father.

Now that *The Skin of Our Teeth* was successfully launched, Wilder might have expected that nothing further would distract him from his military duties. But, in less than a month after the opening, Wilder found himself in the center of a controversy comparable in magnitude to the one provoked by Michael Gold's attack twelve years before. Henry Seidel Canby's *Saturday Review of Literature* in its December 19, 1942, issue ran in a feature article the stunning accusation that Wilder had pilfered James Joyce's *Finnegans Wake* to produce *The Skin of Our Teeth*. The authors of the article, Henry Morton Robinson and Joseph Campbell, did not charge Wilder with outright plagiarism, but they contended that the Joyce work formed the basis of the play and that Wilder was culpable in withholding from the public an account of his sources.

The publication of the article in America's only mass-circulated literary publication came as a bombshell. The success of *The Skin of Our Teeth* was still fresh news. Now its author, the eminently scholarly and respected Thornton Wilder, honorably employed in the service of his country, was being charged with literary theft. Newspaper reporters dashed down to Washington where Wilder was on detached service from his California-based bombardment group. Wilder's response was terse and not at all helpful: persons concerned with the question of his plagiarism should read the two works and make up their minds for themselves. It was a typical Wilder reaction: eminently reasonable, patrician—and infuriating. His observation on the matter clarified nothing at all; the intellectually lazy were frustrated and the intellectually inept were confused. What was wanted from Wilder was a denial of the charges or a confession of guilt. Instead, he had rested his case on the two works in question and that, as the journalists would say, was dirty pool.

Joyce's *Finnegans Wake* had been a work in progress for seventeen years prior to its publication in 1939. The book bewildered most of the reviewers, and the attention that it might have received was quickly diverted by the advent of World War II. Many of Joyce's most devoted admirers found their master's final work incomprehensible; the number of readers in the United States who were absorbed by *Finnegans Wake* in those first few years after its publication was pitifully small. The novel made tremendous demands upon its readers and presupposed a knowledge of several of the Indo-European languages, European and Irish history, geography, anthropology, and psychology. Those who tackled the book in earnest were principally college professors who, together with a few critics like Edmund Wilson, turned their attention to the work, partly for the pleasure of it, partly out of a sense of professional obligation.

Wilder was one of the few "amateurs" who plunged into *Finnegans*

*Wake* for the sheer excitement of the experience. Another "amateur" who took up the formidable book was a senior editor of the *Reader's Digest* and the future author of a popular novel, *The Cardinal*. This editor-journalist, Henry Morton Robinson, was fascinated by the academic world where he had briefly resided when he was an English instructor at his alma mater, Columbia University. He also yearned to be a man of letters, but his poems and stories had thus far brought him neither money nor fame. He viewed Wilder as the darling of the gods: Wilder's fiction had made him famous; he had been on the English faculty at the University of Chicago; his essay memorializing Joyce had appeared in the prestigious pages of *Poetry;* he had given public lectures on *Finnegans Wake;* and now he was establishing himself as a leading American playwright. Robinson, a truculent and envious man, viewed himself as Wilder's nemesis.

In collaboration with another Joyce scholar, a young Sarah Lawrence professor, Joseph Campbell, with whom he was preparing a key to *Finnegans Wake,* Robinson composed his accusation for the *Saturday Review* article, which was entitled: "The Skin of Whose Teeth? or The Strange Case of Mr. Wilder's New Play and *Finnegans Wake.*" The lead sentence set the tone:

> While thousands cheer, no one has yet pointed out that Mr. Wilder's exciting play, *The Skin of Our Teeth,* is not an entirely original creation, but an Americanized re-creation, thinly disguised, of James Joyce's *Finnegans Wake.* . . .

Without using the word plagiarism, Robinson and Campbell gave the impression that Wilder had somehow dramatized the substance of Joyce's novel and had failed to acknowledge the play's origins. And for those readers unfamiliar with Joyce's novel, that is to say, for virtually all of their readers, Robinson and Campbell provided some sketchy, but credible, documentation. The parallels do exist: the overall structure of the play resembles the novel in two critical aspects: both are circular in form so that the last word of the novel and the last speech of the play are also their respective beginnings; structurally also, both avoid chronological development so that the respective characters exist simultaneously in diverse epochs and eras. The protagonists of both works, Joyce's Earwickers and Wilder's Antrobuses, are prototypes both of mankind's progenitors and of the parents of every middle-class family group. Lilith, who is the "other" woman—Lily Kinsella—in Joyce's novel, is fleshed out into Wilder's Lily Sabina.

But Wilder wasn't in the least secretive about these resemblances, and, lest any Joyceans fail to notice the relationship between the two works, he deliberately interpolated a line from *Finnegans Wake* into the text of his play: Sabina, speaking of Mr. Antrobus's past, quotes almost verbatim from *Finnegans Wake* (33) :

> . . . what I think is that there are certain charges that ought not to be made, and I think I may add, ought not to be allowed to be made . . .

Another explicit reference to Joyce's novel is made by Mrs. Antrobus in the second act when she displays the bottle she will throw into the ocean, a bottle containing a letter describing all of the secrets a woman knows and has never told to any man. The two references, neither of which is of any organic importance to Wilder's play, are significant and highly developed episodes in Joyce's novel. No reader of *Finnegans Wake*, seeing or reading *The Skin of Our Teeth*, could fail to receive Wilder's signals, just in case the connection had not already been established.

But, in their broader charges against Wilder, the fact is that Robinson and Campbell were wrong. Wilder indeed loved the novel so well that he paid it the most flattering homage one author can pay another; but *The Skin of Our Teeth* is no "Americanized, thinly disguised recreation" of *Finnegans Wake*. Robinson's and Campbell's further charge that *The Skin of Our Teeth* is "not an entirely original creation," was eminently unjust; the play is at least as original as Shaw's *Saint Joan* and it is considerably more original than Shakespeare's *Antony and Cleopatra*. *The Skin of Our Teeth* is, in fact, as original as a good play ought to be and more original than any significant American play written since *Our Town*. Joyce's novel, as a novel, was unique both in form and content. And so was Wilder's play, as a play. Apart from the ocean that separates the themes of the two works, the basic *generic* difference makes comparison absurd.*

Mr. Robinson and Dr. Campbell displayed an almost willful disregard of the creative process. Every work of literature is inspired by and indebted to work that has preceded it. And although Wilder's intimate familiarity with *Finnegans Wake* inspired and determined both the overall scheme and the principal dramatis personae of his play, the play remains Wilder's work. Moreover, Robinson and Campbell's erudition did not enable them to recognize that, as indebted as Wilder was to Joyce, *The Skin of Our Teeth* is equally indebted to *Six Characters in Search of an Author* and to *Tonight We Improvise*. We recall that

---

* At least two dramatizations of portions of *Finnegans Wake* have been successfully produced. In addition, a film version by Mary Ellen Bute was displayed at the 1965 Cannes Film Festival. None of the dramatizations bore the remotest resemblance to Wilder's play.

Wilder had attended one of the premiere performances of Pirandello's masterpiece during his Roman sojourn, 1920–21, and in 1941—during the composition of *The Skin of Our Teeth*—he was actually revising *Six Characters* for Max Reinhardt. A great many of Wilder's most hilarious effects, together with its climactic scene in the third act—the confrontation between Antrobus and his son—are pure Pirandello. But such is the history of art: the artist takes what he needs from what has gone before to create his own work from within himself. Literary creation proceeds from the crucible of the imagination, thousands of elements fusing into the making of the new.

Unfortunately for Wilder, sensational charges of dishonesty against an established and respected writer provide more interesting subject matter for newspapers and periodicals than a hard look at the aesthetics of artistic creation. Nor did the drama reviewers cover themselves with any distinction in the controversy; all of them, with the exception of Krutch, who uncharacteristically remained silent and finally joined those of his colleagues who censured Wilder in a curious manner, were intimidated by Robinson and Campbell. The reviewers had not read Joyce's novel, and most of them had not even made any effort to do so. In no position to refute or confirm the allegations, they took refuge in discreet silence and the hope that someone other than themselves would resolve the entire matter.

A few responsible observers did come to Wilder's defense. The first was an unidentified writer for *Time* who stated, after summarizing the accusations of Campbell and Robinson:

> . . . The few initiated stalwarts who had both read *Finnegans Wake* and seen the play, were of the opinion that Campbell & Robinson were trying to make headlines out of what should have been footnotes, were confusing influences with imitation. According to Michael Myerberg . . . Wilder got his idea when a chicken landed on his lap at *Hellzapoppin*.

A Mr. Carl Balliett, Jr., writing in the January 2, 1943 issue of the *Saturday Review*, intelligently made the distinction between the Campbell-Robinson charge and the whole matter of literary influence—he alluded to the fact that Joyce had structured his *Ulysses* upon the Homeric epic and concluded his defense with the observation that Wilder "has always needed some slight catalytic agent to bring his creative powers and his fine craftsmanship into play." Finally Edmund Wilson, instead of his colleague Krutch on the *Nation*, devoted to the discussion a full article entitled "The Antrobuses and the Earwickers" (*Nation*, 30 January 1943, pp. 167–68) :

. . . The general indebtedness to Joyce in the conception and plan of the play is as plain as anything of the kind can be. . . . He has written and lectured on *Finnegans Wake;* is one of the persons who has been most fascinated by it and who has most thoroughly studied its text.

This derivation would not necessarily affect one way or the other the merits of Wilder's play. Joyce is a great quarry, like Flaubert, out of which a variety of writers have been getting and will continue to get a variety of different things; and Wilder is a poet with a form and imagination of his own who may find his themes where he pleases without incurring the charge of imitation . . .

These three responses to Robinson and Campbell ought to have put an end to the discussion and cleared Wilder of any opprobrium. And, in fact, for the next three months the controversy seemed to have ended. But on April 13, the Critics Circle convened to select the prize play for 1942–43. The proceedings, according to the written testimony of more than one critic present, were not wholly estimable. Present or voting by proxy were

> JOHN ANDERSON, *Journal-American*
> KELCY ALLEN, *Women's Wear Daily*
> GEORGE FREEDLEY, *Morning Telegraph*
> JOHN GASSNER, *Direction*
> WOLCOTT GIBBS, *New Yorker*
> ROSAMOND GILDER, *Theater Arts Monthly*
> HOWARD BARNES, *Herald Tribune*
> JOSEPH WOOD KRUTCH, *Nation*
> LOUIS KRONENBERGER, *PM*
> WARD MOREHOUSE, *Sun*
> BURNS MANTLE, *News*
> GEORGE JEAN NATHAN, *Esquire*
> LEWIS NICHOLS, *Times*
> ARTHUR POLLACK, *Brooklyn Eagle*
> WILELLA WALDORF, *Post*
> STARK YOUNG, *New Republic*

Burton Rascoe, of the *World-Telegram,* arrived late and did not vote on the first ballot. This delay was important; if he had not been late, the final result might have been greatly different.

On the first ballot, Anderson, Krutch, Nathan, Young, Pollack, and Freedley awarded their votes to Sidney Kingsley's play about Thomas Jefferson, *The Patriots.* Morehouse, Miss Gilder, Barnes, Gibbs, Nichols, and Gassner voted for *The Skin of Our Teeth.* The other votes were scattered. The vote was thereby tied six to six and, at that point, the adherents of Wilder's play were called upon to defend their choice in the light of the charges leveled by Robinson and Campbell! Astonishingly enough, none of the men had done his homework and no defense was forthcoming; finally Miss Gilder—ignoring the whole question of the provenance of *The Skin of Our Teeth*—defended her choice on the basis that it was the only play worthy of the critics' prize for that year.

Six ballots later, through defections by Morehouse, Gibbs, and Gassner who were joined by Waldorf, Allen, Mantle, and Zunser, *The Patriots* was awarded the New York Drama Critics Circle Prize for the best play of the 1942–43 season. The resulting flak was considerable. Burton Rascoe publicly attacked his colleagues in his column in the *World-Telegram* and divulged the fact that some of them, most notably Wolcott Gibbs, were pressured to switch their votes because they could not counter the charge that Wilder had been guilty of plagiarism.* Lewis Nichols, standing in for war correspondent Brooks Atkinson, also denounced the decision, though in milder terms than those of Rascoe. Rosamond Gilder reserved her indignation for a personal letter to Isabel Wilder; and Howard Barnes revealed, in his column in the *Herald Tribune,* that John Anderson and George Jean Nathan were the two critics who browbeat colleagues into making the switch.

The aspersion thereby cast upon Wilder's professional reputation was somewhat mitigated three weeks later when the Pulitzer Prize committee met and voted its award to *The Skin of Our Teeth.* Lewis Nichols, writing in the Sunday Drama Section of the *New York Times* quietly, but tellingly, observed how the Pulitzer Jury had righted a wrong and, in effect, had made fools of the Critics Circle. Ironically, the critics' organization had originally been formed to weaken the impact of the Pulitzer Prize. The Pulitzer Jury's action effectively ended the whole controversy, as Edmund Wilson's article ought to have done, but didn't. It is true that fourteen years later, in the columns of *Esquire* (March 1957), Robinson, this time without the collaboration of Professor Campbell, revived his charges against Wilder, adding that everything that Wilder had published was based on something else; on the second attempt, Robinson's effort to discredit Wilder drew no fire and the whole matter of examining Wilder's sources and influences fell to the lot of interested German scholars.

How did the whole sorry affair affect Wilder? While, on the one hand, the publicity probably helped the play's run, the attention did not augment Wilder's prestige. In the years that followed, long after everyone

---

* Wolcott Gibbs's role in the entire controversy was eccentric. His first reaction to the Robinson-Campbell charges was to compose a satiric counterthrust published in the *New Yorker;* but, being insecure because he really did not know *Finnegans Wake* beyond the first page or so, he was intimidated into changing his vote from Wilder's play to Kingsley's. Immediately after having done so, he published in his *New Yorker* column an apology and explanation. He apologized for having voted for an inferior play and explained that Wilder's refusal to deal with the charge caused him to abandon his first choice.

had forgotten the details of the controversy, a number of reasonably well-informed men and women involved with literature and the theater retained the impression that Wilder had been somehow guilty of something unsavory in connection with *The Skin of Our Teeth*. Harold Clurman, for example, described Wilder as a playwright who was adept at arranging flowers that had been grown by others.* At a 1955 press conference in Edinburgh that preceded the premiere of *A Life in the Sun* (as *The Alcestiad* was titled during its run at the Edinburgh Festival there), a British reporter questioned Wilder about his reputation for making use of other works of literature. The literary public has a long if inaccurate memory, particularly if the matter at hand is scandalous or improper or even mildly discreditable. Considerably more print has been devoted to Hemingway's humiliating sparring match with Morley Callaghan than to his winning of the Nobel Prize.

Wilder himself was not so gravely shocked or concerned this time as he had been twelve years earlier by the Gold attack. Feeling inwardly secure because he knew *The Skin of Our Teeth* to be the fruit of his own exertions, he at first dismissed the Campbell-Robinson article and its initial aftermath as, in his own words, a tempest in a teapot. It was not until he lost the Critics Circle Prize that he understood that the teapot tempest had inflicted more extensive damage to his reputation than he had realized. Ultimately, he directed the main thrust of his anger against Henry Seidel Canby, editor of the *Saturday Review of Literature*. He felt that Canby, as a professor at Yale and a former enthusiast for Wilder's work, had displayed irresponsibility and perhaps a certain maliciousness in opening the pages of his magazine, giving his imprimatur so to speak, to what Wilder regarded as reckless and mischievous charges. This grievance against Canby and the *Saturday Review of Literature* was not entirely unjustified; years later, the editor Harrison Smith—who had composed an editorial in the *Saturday Review* that endorsed the Campbell-Robinson attack on Wilder—candidly admitted that stimulating literary feuds enlivened his magazine and increased reader interest. What gave credence to the charges against Wilder was not the prestige of Robinson and Campbell, but the prestige of the *Saturday Review of Literature*, which, according to Smith, received considerable mileage from the controversy it had deliberately provoked.

And yet, one cannot escape the conclusion that the chief architect of Wilder's misfortune was Wilder himself. It is clear that Wilder, through the text of the play, was nudging all diligent Joyce scholars lest they fail to notice the parallels; this kind of academic high jinks is standing operating procedure when one is producing fiction, poetry, or closet

---

* Clurman had some reason to harbor a grudge against Wilder because of an offhand remark by Wilder that appeared to reflect his distaste for the work of Clifford Odets.

drama for a publisher like James Laughlin's New Directions. But when one has written a Broadway play starring a Hollywood matinee idol and a glamorous and internationally celebrated actress, the indebtedness of the play to Joyce's *Finnegans Wake* is likely to be obvious only to a slender proporton of any given audience. Under such circumstances, Wilder could easily have included a program note in which he paid homage to James Joyce—just as Brahms or Beethoven or Chopin did when they used a Haydn or Mozart theme as the departure point for elaborate compositions of their own. So simple and appropriate a gesture on Wilder's part probably would have forestalled the Robinson-Campbell article and certainly would have rendered it innocuous and unnewsworthy.*

It is possible that a program note was considered and rejected, either because of the objections of the producer or because Wilder felt it immodest on his part to appear to inflate his own work by linking it with one of larger proportions. But, there was still another means of putting an early quietus to the issue raised by the *Saturday Review:* when the Robinson-Campbell charge appeared, reporters went down to Washington (where, in December 1942, Wilder was on temporary duty) to inquire about the facts or, at least, to be enlightened about what to them was a very difficult matter. Wilder chose not to enlighten them at all; instead he fell back upon the old schoolmaster's response to a student's question: go look the answer up yourself. According to *Time,* Wilder brusquely stated: "All I can say is to urge those who are interested to read *Finnegans Wake* and make up their minds for themselves."

This of course is a kind of *hubris,* schoolmaster's *hubris.* Had Wilder been dealing with a group of university graduate students participating in a Joyce seminar (and such already existed in 1942), his response to the question would have been entirely in order. But he was faced with members of the working press. Men at the top of their profession, such as George Jean Nathan, Woollcott, and Anderson, had been intimidated by *Finnegans Wake.* Neither the reporters—nor indeed most of the drama critics—had any intention of completing Wilder's homework assignment. They chose, instead, to bide their time.

Wilder's handling of the reporters was a tactic that he never repeated. And it reveals one of the less engaging facets of his personality. Shy, withdrawn as an adolescent, yearning for recognition and respect as an undergraduate, at the age of twenty-four, he suddenly was placed in charge of adolescent boys where he necessarily played the role of benevolent tyrant, partly to maintain discipline, partly to conceal his own sense of inadequacy. (His French, at that time, according to one of his stu-

* Wilder did finally make the gesture in the foreword to *Three Plays* (Harper, 1956).

dents, Monroe Stearns, was barely serviceable.) And between the age of twenty-four and forty, Wilder almost continuously occupied the platform as either teacher or lecturer. He was not accustomed to exploring knowledge with his students; he was accustomed to explicating, explaining, interpreting, and performing. Before the 1960s, this was not unusual for most teachers, but it produced in Wilder the teacher's occupational disease: treating people as if they were in need of enlightenment. Asked a question about literature or music, or even paintings, about which he did not know a great deal, he would make unequivocal responses or immediate judgments even when he was uninformed or unprepared. Without a moment's hesitation, he was capable of attributing to Guido Cavalcanti lines out of Dante's *Divine Comedy,* or bristle if a student challenged one of his animadversions. Scholarship was not his vocation, but he was an amateur scholar for whom scholarly pursuits constituted a hobby—like double crostics, anagrams, and four-hand piano playing. So it seemed to him in December 1942, in the middle of World War II, that if the journalism fraternity was curious about the connection between his play and *Finnegans Wake,* it was their responsibility to dig the matter out for themselves. That was, after all, their *assignment.*

The aftermath, the loss of the Critics Prize and the consequent shadow on his reputation, taught him to be more diplomatic in his dealings with the gentlemen and ladies of the press. At that Edinburgh interview of August 1955, for example, when the old question was raised about his borrowings from other writers, he gracefully and happily met the indiscreet question face on. Even though a majority of the newsmen were audibly dismayed by the question and created a hubbub of protests, he gestured to quiet them: "Gentlemen," he exclaimed, "it's perfectly true. The implication of your colleague's question is true. I do borrow from other writers, *shamelessly!* I can only say in my defense, like the woman brought before the judge on a charge of kleptomania, 'I do steal; but, Your Honor, only from the very best stores.' "

Wilder's experiences with *The Skin of Our Teeth,* like his previous involvements with the New York stage, were largely unpleasant and unsettling. Those whom he had thought of as *good* friends had regarded his play, before its success, as they might a loathsome disease and refused to participate in it as actors, actresses, directors, or producers. He finally understood the bitter paradox of the theater world: that the world whose denizens most generously and openly shared their feelings, their emotions, their secrets, their homes and apartments, their money, energies, and time, was also a world where friendship counted for nothing at production time; no one in the theater, unless he was starving for money or attention, would associate himself with a play that seemed destined for failure—not for his mother or daughter—or best friend. It seemed to Wilder that those actors and directors and producers who had achieved the most success and the greatest reputations were the least venturesome, the least encouraging, the least capable of risking failure. For years, he had shared a part of his life and his psychic energies with the warm, irresistible, egomaniacal world of theater people—at their worst, adorable but exasperating children, fascinating and boring, loving and greedy. Mingling with them for Wilder had been like going to a party when the work day was over. He had envisaged *The Skin of Our Teeth*—putting the play on, that is—as a delightful romp with his dearest friends as the main participants. As it turned out, he was better served by strangers.

Wilder's disappointment in his friends in the theater followed by the attack on his artistic integrity might have gravely depressed him if he had not been by this time absorbed in his duties with the Air Force, a responsibility which for the next three years distracted him from contemplating the vicissitudes that underlie the life of a Broadway playwright. Nevertheless, it is clear that the first half of Wilder's adult life was an irresistible turning toward the theater and the high life symbolized by New York. The second half of his life was to be a turning away. The Second World War marked the great divide between the halves of his career.

*The Skin of Our Teeth* outlasted the memory of its original production and, since then, has enjoyed a number of notable presentations without the brouhahas and the frenetic actions of publicists and press agents. Before the war had ended, the play was well mounted in England; the production was directed by Laurence Olivier, with Vivien Leigh as Sabina. (Olivier subsequently played Antrobus in a production that toured Australia.) The play's impact on postwar Germany was extraordinary. Not only did every German city of consequence, while digging itself out of its rubble, stage the play, but *The Skin of Our Teeth* created an interest in both itself and Wilder that after a quarter of a century has not yet abated. More academic scholarship concerning Wilder's writings has been produced in Germany than in the United States.

In the late 1940s, *The Skin of Our Teeth* was revived on the West Coast by John Houseman. Two subsequent productions sponsored by the State Department were sent abroad; the first, in 1955, was directed by Alan Schneider and featured Mary Martin as Sabina and Helen Hayes as Mrs. Antrobus. A similar production, again with Helen Hayes, toured abroad in 1961. In 1968, there was an "updated" production for Britain's Chichester Festival: the play was transformed into the format of a television performance, with predictably disquieting results. And, of course, through the first thirty years of its existence, the play has remained a staple of summer theaters and repertory-university companies throughout the United States.

Like *Our Town, The Skin of Our Teeth* has become fixed in the tradition of twentieth century dramatic literature, regularly performed on the stage, and read in the schools and colleges here and abroad. Its vitality stems from its retreat from naturalism into the freer theatrical forms that characterize post–World War II drama. And related to those techniques (which no longer startle today's audiences) are the high-spirited improvisational effects that emphasize the human comedy: man's cliff-hanging capacity for survival, endurance, and renewal. Though *Our Town* would seem to be America's favorite play, there are many who prefer *Skin*'s broad comic sweep to *Our Town*'s admixture of nostalgia, irony, and *lacrimae rerum.*

Nevertheless, there were critics who expressed serious reservations about *The Skin of Our Teeth,* the most notable of whom has been the *New York Times*'s Walter Kerr, who observed that Acts II and III are merely restatements of the basic dramatic situation of Act I. Kerr's comment, which has been frequently echoed, has a surface validity, but it fails to consider that despite the repetition of the first act situation, the play nevertheless achieves a dramatic progression. In Act I, the human family, though it appears to be safely installed in twentieth-century Excelsior, New Jersey, is really confronted by two sets of dangers: those suffered by the pioneers and the natural cataclysms and catastrophes that the cavemen survived in the Ice Age. The characterizations are correspondingly simple and basic: Antrobus is "American-vulgar," an ingenious, open-hearted, and blustery family provider; Mrs. Antrobus is not easily distinguishable from *Our Town*'s Mrs. Webb; nor are her children, Gladys and Henry, far removed from their older counterparts, Emily Webb and George Gibbs, despite Henry's unfortunate propensity, like Cain's, for the slingshot. And Sabina is a conventional hired girl whose comic effects are mainly achieved when she steps out of character into the role of Miss Somerset, the actress who is purportedly playing Sabina. The first act, in short, depicts the plight of man subject to the caprices of his physical environment, such as erupting volcanoes, tidal waves, earthquakes, avalanches, famine, and plagues of locusts. Actually, in Wilder's play it is glaciation that threatens the life of man. The human family of Act I carries no oppressive burden of guilt; for them, nature's perilous turnabouts are purely adventitious events. The refugees who gather toward the conclusion of Act I are explicitly pre-Christian inhabitants of the earth: the nine Muses, Homer, and Moses. Together with Adam, Eve, Cain, and Lilith, they all stand in geologic time desperately hoping to stave off cold and starvation as Act I ends, with Mrs. Antrobus (Eve) repeating in English the Hebrew text spoken earlier in the act by Moses, "In the beginning God created the heavens and the earth," Gladys, her daughter, continuing, "And God called the light day." The curtain falls on Act I with Sabina's exhortation to the audience, "Pass up your chairs everybody. Save the human race."

Although the structure of the second act superficially resembles the first act, the Antrobus family has progressed beyond its state of relative innocence. In having achieved dominion over sea and land, Mr. Antrobus has become the supreme politician, with a strong flare for unabashed hypocrisy; Mrs. Antrobus is detestably smug; the nubile Gladys begins to manifest sluttish tendencies; Henry's vicious streak is getting out of control; and Sabina has developed into a highly professional adventuress. The chorus of gentle refugees of Act I metamorphoses into a drunken and profligate horde of "Conveners." In general, the relatively stable moral society of Act I, which had been threatened by an impersonal natural disaster, changes in Act II into a social order both corrupted and corrupting, a world that a wrathful Jehovah must purge through storm and flood.

The final act discloses that neither the cataclysms of nature nor the punishments of the Supreme Judge can threaten the life of man on this planet as dangerously as his own self-destructive impulses. Mankind's tensions combined with the lethal artifacts of contemporary civilization have set up a conflict between the ego and the id that comes close to being irreconcilable. The outward manifestation of this conflict is global war and the opposing forces are led respectively by the rational George Antrobus and the irrational Henry. In this final act of the play, the principals, having survived the war, either as victors, or as vanquished, undergo a kind of metamorphosis: Mr. and Mrs. Antrobus take on a new dignity; Sabina, pathos; and Henry, credibility. The play ends on a note of quiet and restrained optimism, reminiscent of a late Beethoven quartet.

Yet, despite the play's intention of being a comic-strip account of mankind's struggle for survival down through the ages, like Wilder's other successful plays, *The Skin of Our Teeth* has as its focus American family life. These plays contrast with the first three novels which turn around the Proustian theme of the gentle lover in fruitless pursuit of an unworthy or unattainable beloved. Wilder once wrote (to Amy Wertheimer) that he had profoundly suffered the pangs of disprized love, but that he had come to regard love as a sort of cruel malady through which the elect are required to pass in their late youth and from which they emerge, pale and wrung, but ready for the business of living. As child and adolescent, however, Wilder found security, reinforcement, and respect at home from his mother. Even though there were long separations from his father, who could not conceal his disappointment in his second son's "weaknesses" in character and intelligence, that father always displayed an abiding concern for his son's proper development and well-being.

Thus, the novels recorded Wilder's emotional privation in accepting a destiny given over to the single life and, finally, burlesqued his earlier anguish, his religious zeal, his attempts at self-improvement in *Heaven's My Destination*. In the plays, he celebrated the only permanent and meaningful emotional realizaton he could lay claim to—his position as son and brother, a member of a family.* To assert that Wilder's plays developed out of his involvement and concern with his own family is not to imply that there are concrete biographical correspondences between the plays and the Wilder family. Unlike O'Neill, who dramatized his family again and again, Wilder never used his plays to exploit the very real drama of his own household, nor depicted recognizable character traits of members of his family. An objectivist and a philosopher by temperament, if not by training, he was too deeply absorbed with the American family as representative of the human family to particularize in his plays about any specific family he knew, least of all his own.

Nevertheless, elements of his father, his mother, and himself reveal themselves in *The Skin of Our Teeth,* as they did in *Our Town.* Amos Wilder and George Antrobus, for example, shared an obsessive concern about their respective children's formal schooling, but they bungled the matter of their children's sociopsychological and sexual development; any manifestation of sexual curiosity or precosity (such as a daughter's using cosmetics or wearing any article of clothing that drew attention to the existence of her sexuality) would throw both worthies into a state of fierce rage or icy contempt. Wilder's lifelong resentment of his father, which was given no explicit expression in the earlier plays, erupts in the final scene of *The Skin of Our Teeth.* Unlike the Henry/Cain character, Thornton was a docile, respectful, and compliant son. But inwardly he raged against his father's unwavering self-absorption, his sense of moral superiority, his Olympian judgments, and his irrevocable decisions. Even when he reached his thirties and his father had entered into a physical decline, Wilder would gibe at the image his father had created of being

* Wilder's apparent unconscious choice of a familial relationship over a liaison reveals itself in the succession of older woman friends who occupied his life from his twenties to his fifties. Wilder's mother could not express by word or gesture the profound affection she felt for her younger son. And though she was an intelligent and well-read woman, she provided no source of intellectual growth for Wilder once he had reached his majority. Wilder's surrogate mothers were several, and the most important of them —Edith Isaacs, editor of *Theater Arts Monthly,* Amy Wertheimer, Lady Colefax, Gertrude Stein, and Alice B. Toklas—all dispensed an admixture of intelligent appreciation of his work, as well as intellectual stimulus and affectionate warmth.

*sans peur and sans rapproche.* This image cast so long a shadow in New Haven that it blighted Thornton, by giving him a feeling of ineffectuality and unworthiness that he could never forget, or forgive.

Mrs. Antrobus's unwavering protectiveness toward the unredemptive Henry reflects Isabella Wilder's cool, unemotional, and steadfast defense of Thornton. Though Henry's deficiences were certainly concrete and harrowingly real—in contrast with Thornton's which were negligible—both mothers, the real and the imagined, shared a maternal ferocity concerning the well-being of their offspring which, combined with devotedness, caused Wilder to compare each of these ladies to the tigress caring for her young.

Wilder said repeatedly that in this play he was transforming Joyce's Everyman and Wife into an American comic-strip couple: Antrobus, brash, confident, enterprising; Mrs. Antrobus, frigid, smug, possessive, and managerial. The personae of the Antrobuses were not at all like the darkly complicated and intelligent parents of Thornton Wilder. But, in their implicit attitudes, evaluations, and assumptions, the Antrobus and the Wilder families merge into one of those representative families of provincial America who, with their vaguely transcendental New England world view, played so important a role in our history before the aftermath of the Second World War.

The assumptions of *The Skin of Our Teeth* are pervasively moralistic: man's significance and survival derive from his adherence to a set of ethical values conveniently framed for him by Hebrew prophets, Greek philosophers, and Judaic-Christian synthesizers. The Antrobuses, denizens of a New Jersey suburb of New York—that is to say, neither urban nor rural dwellers—are unmistakably and characteristically inheritors, not only of their own American tradition but of the better part of European culture. Mr. Antrobus, inventor of the wheel and of the alphabet, becomes "president," just as Wilder's father or his best friend, Robert Hutchins, might have. For one of the things that Wilder dramatized in *The Skin of Our Teeth* was the American boast that any man, any white Protestant at least, with the values of an Amos Wilder— his view of America's destiny, his moral earnestness, idealism, and self-assurance—*might* and, indeed, often *did* rise to a position of authority and leadership. George Antrobus, composite of Amos Wilder, Thomas Edison, Henry Ford, Theodore Roosevelt, and Warren Harding, is not so much Everyman as Everyman's leader in the battle for survival. Unfortunately, there is nothing in the portrait that provides for a glimpse of a Gandhi, a Juarez, or even a Lenin, who in the minds and hearts of his followers was also a champion of man's survival—survival that lay outside of or endured in spite of the Protestant ethic and the American image of itself.

# XIII

## The Soldier

*"One of the benefits of military service,* one *of them, is being thrown into daily contact with non-artists, something a young American writer should consciously seek . . ."*—WILDER IN "PARIS REVIEW" INTER-VIEW, 1956

During the six months between the attack on Pearl Harbor and his entry into the armed services, Wilder was prodigiously busy. He not only completed the writing of *The Skin of Our Teeth* and concluded the complicated arrangements for its production, but also, in a bewilderingly short time, composed the successful screenplay *Shadow of a Doubt* for Alfred Hitchcock and was making considerable progress on a new play, *The Alcestiad*. In short, he seemed to be on the verge of becoming, on his own terms, a professional playwright and screenwriter; a New York man of the theater subject to calls from the West Coast.

Why then, at the very moment of his life when he might have committed his most productive energies to the world of stage and film, did Wilder, aged forty-five, actively seek out military service and irretrievably cut himself off from all literary and dramatic pursuits for the duration of what was clearly to be a long war? Fourteen years after the fact when he was asked this very question, Wilder said: "I felt very strongly about [the war]. I was already a rather old man, was fit only for staff work, but I certainly did it with conviction . . ."

About Wilder's sincerity on this point there can be no question. Men of his generation, background, and conditioning held a deep sense of patriotism. Wilder and his coevals, Scott Fitzgerald, Faulkner, and Robert Sherwood had all volunteered for service during World War I. John Dos Passos served in the Ambulance Corps; Hemingway, still in his teens, was an ambulance driver on the Italian front. Wilder's classmates at both Oberlin and Yale had rushed en masse to the colors; even the maverick Robert Hutchins had volunteered for duty with the ambulance service overseas.

By World War II, however, among Wilder's contemporaries, Fitzgerald had died the year before Pearl Harbor; Faulkner, unable to procure a commission, sequestered himself in Oxford, Mississippi, doggedly pursuing a writing career that seemed to be going nowhere and making occasional forays to Hollywood for cash assignments; Hutchins had taken the isolationist road to oblivion; Robert Sherwood had joined the White House staff as chief polemicist for the Allied cause. Even Hemingway had avoided an outright military commitment; like Dos Passos, he established himself as a correspondent and accompanied the armies as a kind of journalist-mascot.

Moreover, recruitment officers were not eager to enlist middle-aged writers. Had it not been for his access to Archibald MacLeish and to Robert Lovett, a Yale alumnus serving in Roosevelt's war cabinet, Wilder's chances of wearing a uniform would have been remote. The armed services were deluged with applications from bankers and brokers, actors and artists, dentists and doctors, all in their forties and fifties, eager to procure commissions and outfit themselves at Brooks Brothers and Rogers Peet. By 1942, the officer corps was not very exclusive, but nevertheless incorporation into its ranks had suddenly become the only membership that mattered. Many an aging member of Skull and Bones, Porcellian, and Ivy would have traded his class ring and club key for a captain's or major's insignia. Henry Luce was not only denied an officer's commission (by Roosevelt), he was not even given permission to leave the continental limits of the United States. Roosevelt similarly revoked Charles Lindbergh's air corps commission; and Colonel Bertie MacCormack was never invited by his presidential cousin to leave the publisher's offices in the Chicago Tribune Tower.

Wilder, it turned out, was the only established American writer of consequence to be commissioned and assigned to duty with a combat force, precisely the assignment he sought. But again, why? Was it a matter only of conviction? Or did Wilder still suffer, like Hemingway and Fitzgerald, from both public and personal impugnations of their essential masculinity? Did the uniform invest Wilder finally with the manhood that his Yale classmates had denied him twenty-five years earlier and that his father had openly despaired of his son's ever achieving?

Obviously at a moment when a nation's existence is in danger, men wear their uniforms with pride and satisfaction, the older the man, the greater being the satisfaction. But Wilder's induction into the Air Corps was motivated by something more than conviction and masculine pride. During the first seventeen years of his life, we must remember, all but two were spent in a household where females predominated; during six of his adolescent years, neither Wilder père nor brother Amos was at home to alleviate the female ambience pervading the Wilder household. From his mother, Wilder had received a most devoted interest and from his sister Isabel a fascinated adulation, but his two years at schools in Chefoo and at Ojai were failures, so that he returned to his mother's house in Berkeley in the midst of his wounded adolescence with a sense of exhausted relief. In his nineteenth year, he left home to attend college in Oberlin where he encountered and was befriended by a new group of older women. And after two years in Ohio, he rejoined his family in New Haven where, ultimately, he constructed for his mother, his sisters, his father, and, of course, for his brother and himself "the house the *Bridge* built." The ties that existed between Wilder and his mother and sister had become indissoluble. ("Blessed be the ties that bind . . ." was the refrain of *Our Town*.) Unlike Hemingway and Fitzgerald, Wilder never ceased to be a grateful, devoted son and brother. He dedicated *The Bridge of San Luis Rey* to his mother and a late novel, *The Eighth Day*, to Isabel. But at the age of forty-five his several attempts at removing the yoke that bound him to the women at home frustrated him to the point where he had come to believe that they had blighted his life.* He had never, he felt, been free of them; never, because of them, had he managed to enter fully into a man's world. Lawrenceville had been populated by adolescents and aggressively athletic schoolmasters who viewed him—a bachelor teaching *French*—with subliminal hostility and suspicion; his years at Chicago were divided between postadolescents and society ladies and relieved by dinners at the Maude Hutchins-dominated president's house. And the five years since he had left Chicago had been principally spent in alternating periods at home with his mother and Isabel and

---

* Those who knew Wilder best doubted that they hindered him. Men who remain a part of their mothers' households, particularly those who are economically free to do otherwise, do so because that is their deep-seated wish. Wilder liked to believe that there were pressures exerted to keep him at home; these existed, of course, but he could have ignored them without any cataclysmic results.

lonely creative bouts in remote hotels and pensions: Quebec, St. Thomas, Zurich, Cuernavaca, Long Island, and Arizona. Military service, accordingly, exerted upon him the irresistible pull of a world in which he could at long last function as a man among men, where his competence, his craft, and his ingenuity could mesh disinterestedly with the capacities of other men, all of whom were singlemindedly intent upon the pursuit of a common goal.

Military service presented to Wilder not only an escape from his only ties—his blood relations—but a relief also from the profession of writing. It was not that Wilder disliked putting pen to paper. On the contrary. But writing for him—as his father had both shrewdly and wrongheadedly asseverated—was something indeed not unlike "carving olive pits." For Wilder, the art of writing was, in turn, a joy, a fascination, an absorption—so long as it was not the means of earning a livelihood. But his last three plays, all conceived as commercial ventures, had psychically and physically exhausted him. *Our Town* had destroyed his friendship with Jed Harris and narrowly averted disaster through the good offices of the *New York Times'* critic, Brooks Atkinson; *The Merchant of Yonkers* had been a painfully embarrassing fiasco; and at the very moment of Wilder's decision to join the armed services, the fate of *The Skin of Our Teeth* lay in the hands of an inexperienced producer and an unknown director. All these anxieties of committing a play to commercial production had become intolerable for Wilder; and his "success" as a Broadway playwright was tenuous at best. He was not, he never would be, he never really wanted to be a Robert Sherwood, a Philip Barry, nor even, God save the mark, a Maxwell Anderson. The idea of wresting a living from the Broadway stage, of producing a successful commodity every year, dismayed and disheartened him. He had reached a moment in his life when he desperately needed a release from both family and professional commitments. This need was the same buried impulse that he had blurted out to Amy Wertheimer seventeen years before: the impulse to run away from Princeton, from studies, from family, from the novel he had promised Albert Boni. And now, finally, he could run with honor, not from, but toward something; and, in the running, he could gain the unreserved approval of friends and acquaintances; from his Yale classmates, envy without rancor; and from the women at home . . . what could they bestow upon the only male Wilder available to defend his country but their blessing, their resignation, and the hope that he would ultimately return safe to the house the *Bridge* had built?

The three principal branches of the armed services, the Army, Navy, and Air Force, were eagerly competing not only for the best available technicians, managerial executives, and diverse specialists, they were also enlisting and commissioning public figures.* Athletes, sportsmen, movie stars, and popular singers were the most prominent among the nation's celebrities to be called to the colors. The Army Air Force, the newest and most glamorous branch of the services, enlisted two of Hollywood's most prominent actors: Clark Gable and James Stewart. It also commissioned polo player Tommy Hitchcock, presidential scion Elliot Roosevelt, and baseball player Hank Greenberg. Moreover, having set up an office of management control under Major Charles Thornton (with assistance from the future Secretary of Defense Robert MacNamara), the Air Force succeeded in employing its talented recruits with astonishing efficiency. Clark Gable and Hank Greenberg, of course, were exploited purely for their publicity value. But Colonels Thomas Hitchcock and James Stewart capably functioned as Air Force group commanders, the most vital and difficult of all combat assignments. Elliot Roosevelt, who before his military career was widely regarded as the problem child of the Roosevelt offspring, pressed for, developed, and commanded the Aerial Reconnaissance and Photo Mapping Wing in Italy, an extraordinary and creative contribution to the war effort that was never acknowledged by a hostile press. Although young Roosevelt's being the son of the president cost him at least one general's star, it did not deprive him of the respect of his superiors and the affectionate admiration of the airmen who served under him.

Wilder's kind of celebrity was of no value to the Air Force, and his skills might seem to have been better suited to the Office of War Information. But his capacities and performance of duties favorably impressed the officers at the Pentagon. After he was commissioned a captain in 1942, Wilder staunchly weathered the ordeal of orientation—marching, drilling, and exercising in the tropical July heat—all of which was conducted within the framework of rigorous military discipline. Thinner than he had been since his adolescence, Wilder buoyantly shipped off to the Air Intelligence School at Harrisburg, Pennsylvania, for six additional weeks of training. Dispatched in early fall to Hamilton Field, California, near San Francisco and assigned to the headquarters squadron of the 328th Fighter Group, Wilder plunged into duties that he found both interesting and congenial. He reported that he was absorbed, busy, and healthy and in exactly the kind of unit he wanted assignment to. Weekends, he visited San Francisco and Berkeley and sought out the three houses he had lived in during his sad adolescence, that period when his father, according to Wilder in a letter to Woollcott, was enjoying the more innocent pleasures of Hong Kong and Shanghai. His training at this

* In 1942, the Air Force was technically still an adjunct of the Army; but directly after Pearl Harbor it began to function as a separate branch of the service, though it did not legally become an independent service arm until 1948.

point consisted principally in the briefing of air crews, interrogating them upon their return from a mission, interpreting aerial reconnaissance photographs, and coordinating with air operations. The air force group, comprised of four squadrons and a headquarters squadron, was the basic air force unit, comparable to an army regiment; command and staff officers invariably received their tactical training at the group level.

Unlike many civilians who were flung headlong into military life, Wilder acclimated himself to the new regimen without difficulty. He found the training for a combat intelligence officer sufficiently rigorous that for the first time in his life he cut himself off from his two great passions—reading and music. There was no necessity for his doing so: books and concerts were readily available. But having committed himself for the duration, he fixed his intellectual and physical energies upon his new vocation with a purposeful energy that evoked the admiration of the younger officers, who were, in fact, his superiors in rank and responsibility.

Wilder served in California throughout the fall of 1942. But, with the coming of winter, he was placed on detached service and sent to Washington. The ostensible reason for his "temporary" assignment was that he was needed to edit some military publications. Actually, after being installed in the Office of Management Control, he entered into the third phase of his apprenticeship.

It is necessary to recall that while Wilder was undergoing training at Hamilton Field in the fall of 1942, Allied forces in the European Theater were organizing their first land offensive. On November 8, British and American troops successfully landed in Morocco and in the Algerian cities of Oran and Algiers. The long-term Allied strategy was to gain full control of the North African coast, the principal objective being to secure Tunisia, the appropriate launching site for both sea- and aircraft whose targets would be Sicily and Italy. By the time Wilder arrived in Washington, the war in North Africa (between Rommel's Afrika Korps and the Allies) was being waged between evenly matched ground forces. Although the American and French forces lacked battle experience, their easier access to supplies and the capability of the British army provided an overall advantage; above all the Allies had vastly superior air support. The importance of close air support for the success of sea and ground action had become acutely clear to the Joint Chiefs of Staff. The strategists in Washington and London, confident that British-American Free French forces in North Africa would ultimately prevail over the Axis powers, began in the spring of 1943 to formulate plans for invasions of Sicily and southern Italy. By then it was obvious that the Air Force (though technically still an adjunct of the army) would have to participate in tactical deliberations on an equal basis. Thus, Wilder's assign-

ment to the Air Force Office of Management Control came about because
the air command staff, numerically few and inadequately staffed by
career officers, reached down into the ranks of its reserves for the best
available brains.

The central problem facing the Air Force concerned the deployment
of aircraft both in tactical and strategic situations. A wide variety of
puzzles needed to be solved. How could headquarters be daily informed
how many aircraft were operational? How many aircrews were available?
Where were the strategic targets located and how many of them were
within the range of medium and long-range bombers? How was it possible
to achieve a maximum effectiveness in the deployment of light aircraft
covering an invasion attempt? How could one calculate the rate of attri-
tion both for aircraft and crew members and provide for an adequate
system of replacement? How much fuel and ordnance would be required
for how many aircraft flying how many sorties and missions how many
times a day, a week, a month? It was in these areas of investigation that
Wilder found himself involved after becoming assigned to Air Force
Headquarters in Washington in early 1943. Wilder was not a great
arithmetician, tactician or strategist; but he possessed a first-rate intelligence and an extraordinary capacity for working well with others.
Moreover, he had spent long years resolving textual problems and word
puzzles which had rendered him peculiarly apt in his new and awesomely
responsible assignments.

Life in Washington during the 1942–43 winter was monastic; Wilder
worked hard six days a week at the Munitions Building, foregoing
concerts, recitals, museum openings, and the endless round of cocktail
parties which, in war time as in peace time, constituted the principal
cultural activity of the nation's capital. Woollcott's death in January
shocked and saddened him; but he was not encouraged by his superiors
to participate in the memorial service at Columbia University. Fortunately, his last letter to Woollcott had been filled with gratitude for the
*Atlantic Monthly* review of *The Skin of Our Teeth*. Wilder had lost one
of the few men with whom he had achieved a genuine friendship. And
yet, despite their many mutual enthusiasms and their host of acquaintances among the world's notables whom they knew in common and
shared with one another and despite the exchange of confidences and the
loneliness they both sustained, Wilder's chief loss was that of an influential supporter and, perhaps, the best disposed critic of his work. He did
not really respect Woollcott; in fact, he held him in some contempt. He
saw in Woollcott's impulsive enthusiasms and superficial judgments, in
his sentimentality and his starry-eyed adulation of actresses, in his inadequate reading background and his authoritative delivery, a distorted and
exaggerated commingling of his own deficiencies and potential weak-

nesses, which, for the most part, he had overcome or at least concealed from public view. In short, Woollcott *was* what Wilder had conscientiously avoided becoming. In the last few years of their acquaintance they saw one another infrequently although their correspondence kept them in touch. Woollcott had come to realize that Wilder grew quickly bored in his company and deliberately avoided situations wherein they would spend any protracted periods of time together. More capable of affection, more dependent on the company of others than Wilder, Woollcott was slightly bruised by the treatment he received; and Wilder was not unaware that over the years he had received more from Woollcott than he had given.

Also during Wilder's sojourn in Washington in 1943, Steven Vincent Benét died. Wilder and Benét had known each other since their undergraduate days at Yale, but no real friendship had developed. Neither Benét's verse nor his life-style occasioned any favorable response in Wilder; nevertheless, he was dismayed that still another of his contemporaries had been prematurely silenced and he wrote in the *Saturday Review:*

> We are grateful to Steven Vincent Benét . . . principally because he was the first of our poets who knew the whole country and used the poets' means for opening our eyes to all of it. He loved the United States singly and collectively . . . the entire continent was always present in his mind.

By an unfortunate coincidence, the same issue of the *Saturday Review* (March 27, 1943) carried an angry letter to the editor written by Karen Barrett, attacking Wilder's 1932 adaptation of Obey's *Le Viol de Lucrèce.* She held that Wilder had transformed Obey's "Lusty homespun play" into "banal, billowy English." And she charged Wilder with "having made off with a good copper cooking pot, leaving a brummagem pair of candlesticks (wobbly too) in their place." Although the letter simply restated the critical opinion Stark Young had voiced in a January 1933 issue of the *New Republic,* such an onslaught—if Wilder saw it—could only have reinforced his sense of well-being in a situation where the performance of one's occupation was not subject to the scrutiny of critics, reviewers, and self-appointed busybodies.

By the end of May 1943, having proved his capacities at command level, Wilder was ordered overseas to Air Force headquarters, North Africa at Constantine, Algeria. The long campaign to wrest control of Tunisia from the Axis forces had just been successfully concluded and the Pentagon plans to invade Sicily and Italy were about to be consummated. Shortly after his arrival, Wilder was transferred to Allied Force

Headquarters at Algiers under the command of General Eisenhower. During the ensuing summer months, Wilder played his most significant war role—formulating the air plans for the Allied landings at Taranto and Salerno.

For the rest of 1943, he remained with Allied Headquarters. When Mediterranean Allied Armed Forces, with its headquarters in Caserta, Italy, was formed, Wilder stayed with it for the duration of his overseas service. Assigned to Air Plans, Wilder became a staff officer under Major General Ira Eaker who commanded the Twelfth and Fifteenth Air Forces and the British Commonwealth air units in Italy and Sardinia. Among the several missions assigned to MAAF air force units were the bombardment of Rumania's Ploesti oil fields, the marshalling yards of Verona and Vienna, and industrial plants in southern Germany and Austria. In addition, the air forces helped provide arms and assistance to Yugoslavian partisans, immobilized the remnants of the Luftwaffe, and supported the invasions at Anzio and southern France.

Wilder's ultimate assignment to the very nerve center of a command which exercised extraordinary power over the myriads of officers, soldiers, and airmen in the Mediterranean Theater of War (along with the entire population of southern Italy) profoundly affected his creative imagination and subtly modified his personality. His literary works up to this point of his life had been set in a phantasmagoria of opulent palazzi, miladies' chambers, hetaeras' banquet halls, bucolic kitchens and side yards, genteel parlors and suburban living rooms—appropriate settings for a procession of good women, grotesque women, anguished women, anxious women, women of genius, women of sensibility, women of sense, feeling, courage, talent, vision, compassion, and durability. From *The Cabala* to *The Skin of Our Teeth,* he had portrayed a wide range of characters, but particularly women who had in common the circumstance that they exercised powerful influence, but wielded no real power.

And power, in Wilder's frame of reference, was wielded by men. The whole matter of power, from his earliest consciousness, was a concept and a reality that puzzled and absorbed, fascinated and repelled him, in turn. He had been brought up in a household in which a strong father overpowered a strong mother, in which an authoritarian figure prescribed the inviolable rules of conduct for his resentful but compliant children who drew from a strong-willed mother security, encouragement, and love. Amos Parker Wilder harbored political ambitions. He was not meanly ambitious, but messianically so. Well educated and of exemplary moral character, he saw himself as a natural leader of the people, a potential governor, senator, or even president. Dr. Wilder's dreams of glory were not entirely without a basis. He was, for example, a handsome man with a commanding presence—like William McKinley; he was a political scientist, a skilled analyst-polemicist, like Dr. Woodrow Wilson of Princeton; like William Jennings Bryan, he was a charismatic speaker. In short, during the fourth decade of Amos Wilder's life, in the decade that he was editor of the *Wisconsin State Journal* and had become the father of Amos Niven, Thornton, and the two girls, Charlotte and Isabel, he emanated the aura of a man of destiny, an aura of which his wife and small children were at least subliminally aware. But, his destiny, as it turned out, was to be failure and obscurity. His political instincts were inept; a poor man without wealthy supporters, he was incorruptible, inflexible, and self-righteous; with ideas firmly rooted in the nineteenth century, he completely misjudged the temper of his times. Settling in Wisconsin—of all states!—he antagonized La Follette and the Progressives so that the critical years of his career were spent in the boondocks, as an obscure consul in China. By the time he returned to the United States he was wholly out of touch with American political, economic, and social realities. In the last decades of his life he tyrannized his children, directed Yale-in-China and presided over the demise of a conservative New Haven newspaper.

Wilder's writings from *The Cabala* to *The Skin of Our Teeth* reveal male characters whose absorptions are principally cultural and aesthetic; only in *The Skin of Our Teeth* are there intimations of an interest in the exercise of political power. But the exercise of power had always lain close to the surface of Wilder's consciousness. During infancy and childhood his father was the very model of a power figure, a deferred-to member of the Madison community, seemingly destined for some office of distinction. During the years of his schooling, Wilder never got close to those students who were at the center of things; in China, at Ojai, and at Berkeley, he remained on the periphery, a muser and a dreamer, a kind of sleepwalker, as he described himself.

At Oberlin, we recall, he became a disciple of the freshman class president Robert Hutchins, son of one of the college's more prominent professors. Wilder immediately identified Hutchins as someone who would cast a long shadow, and as the friendship ripened, he became more and more convinced that Hutchins would eventually succeed to the presidency of the United States. Even as late as 1940, having been convinced by Wilder that Hutchins was a presidential possibility, Alexander Woollcott nominated Hutchins as Roosevelt's successor in 1944 on one of his Town Crier's nationwide broadcasts.

But Wilder's fascination with the matter of power was not explicitly reflected in his writing before the beginning of World War II. Even love, which he understood to be a powerful force of potentially brutal proportions, he preferred to depict rather as an edifying influence, a balm, a means of achieving grace. Wilder's chief characters were most often women who had surrendered some essential part of their being—for love. Even the male and redoubtable George Brush had long since surrendered himself to the loving will of God and God's commandments; even the indomitable Dolly Levi finally placed herself under the stalwart protection of Horace Vandergelder. And Emily Webb, having put her temporal future in the hands of George Gibbs, resignedly places her eternal future into the hands of calm and easeful Death.

But the abrupt ending to the 1918 armistice, signaled by Hitler's rape of Poland, redirected Wilder's creative energies as he began to see man as the victim not only of his own passions, torments, inadequacies, and self-absorptions, but also as the survivor of cosmic and universal upheavals and disturbances which lay nearly, but not quite, beyond the scope of his control. *The Skin of Our Teeth* had been Wilder's first creative response to the Nazi holocaust. He saw that to meet and withstand the merciless forces of either natural or man-contrived cataclysms, the forces of reason and goodness and courage and vision would have to join together into a powerful, irresistible fusion. Wilder's *Weltanschauung* made him certain that moral order would ultimately prevail over moral anarchy and this view is at the core of *The Skin of Our Teeth*. The confrontation between the father and son in its final scenes dramatically echoes the clash between God the Father and his fallen angel in Milton's *Paradise Lost:* the son vainly attempting to reduce man's world to chaos and annihilation. Whoever held the power, in Milton's words, could make a hell of heaven or a heaven of hell.

When he joined the armed forces, Wilder had no intimation that he would win a place at the war tables and that he would participate in decisions upon strategic and tactical operations which would determine the course of history. Placed in the very center of one of the three Allied war machines, he began to understand that the impact of his father's editorials, of Robert Hutchins's educational dicta, or even of Henry Luce's ubiquitous periodicals were less consequential than the edict of a head of state or the ukase of a commanding general. Somewhat astonished, he found that the professional military men respected his judgment, utilized his talents, and admired his style. One personal encounter with a commander did, however, leave him nonplussed and embarrassed. The circumstances were as follows:

Field grade officers (by 1944 Wilder was a lieutenant colonel) stationed at MAAF headquarters at Caserta were housed in small individual tents large enough to accommodate a cot, a folding chair, and a small table. These tents, strung out on a level field fronting the great palace of Caserta which contained the headquarters' offices and the field grade officers' mess, provided minimal protection against the elements; except that they warded off rain and snow, the tents were cold in winter and hot in summer. The only amenity they provided was sufficient privacy for an officer to separate himself from the sight if not the sound of his fellows. Behind the palace, however, was a vast terraced park containing at the summit of the terraces a wooded area partly cleared to accommodate a dozen or so mobile housing units—the living quarters of the various generals and air commodores. In comparison with the tents, these units were idyllically luxurious; each contained two comfortable beds, running water for both kitchen and toilet needs, armchairs, a desk, windows, and carpeting. Most miraculous of all, they provided adequate electrical illumination. By October 1944, as the nights began to get longer and colder, Wilder (particularly frustrated that the amenities of his tent made virtually impossible his nightly ritual of reading himself to sleep) received word that he was to report to General Eaker's quarters early the following morning. He climbed the exquisitely terraced gardens of the Caserta palace and found his way to the general's trailer. There he found Ira Eaker shaving in solitary grandeur. Asked what he thought of the quarters, Wilder, in all sincerity, called them the dream of his life. Whereupon, to Wilder's astonishment, Eaker revealed that a departing general would leave vacant one of the units, much like the one in which Eaker was billeted, and Wilder might be interested in moving in. General Eaker, it seems, had been asked by the *Saturday Evening Post* to record his war experiences and he felt that if Wilder were a next-door neighbor he might assist Eaker in the writing. The general even hinted that he would provide the material if Wilder could do the actual writing.

Wilder was gravely perplexed. Although he coveted a trailer in the sheltered enclave that would give him the privacy and creature comforts that he had been deprived of for two years, and although he dreaded exposure to an Italian winter that threatened him with pneumonia and the other respiratory infections that he was subject to, he knew himself wholly incapable of writing General Eaker's memoir of the war.* After a few days of hesitation, he informed Eaker that the assignment was one that he could not successfully negotiate. Nevertheless, Wilder received a directive to occupy the vacated trailer where he remained for the duration of his overseas assignment.

But General Eaker was not the only war leader whom Wilder had an opportunity to observe. In 1940, he had gone with a group of writers to meet President Roosevelt at Hyde Park in conjunction with the 1940 campaign. Later, there were opportunities to observe Generals Eisenhower and Mark Clark and Britain's Sir Henry Maitland Wilson and

* Ira Eaker, it should be pointed out, had already written one or two books. He was a graduate of the Columbia University School of Journalism and perfectly capable of writing for the *Saturday Evening Post*. But his military duties made it impossible for him to execute the assignment. His World War II memoirs, if they were ever written, were never published.

Harold Alexander. Sponsored by his immediate superior, a British Air
Commodore, Wilder was flown to Yugoslavia in the waning months of
the war to meet with Marshal Tito's partisan leaders. And though he had
no personal dealings with either Stalin or Churchill, Wilder's access to
secret and top-secret war materials and documents provided him with
insights into the operating procedures of both those heads of state.

But Wilder's absorption with the psychology of leadership and the
exploitation of power extended beyond his observation of contemporary
leaders. His mission to Colombia, Ecuador, and Peru in 1941 had
provoked an interest in Simon Bolivar so that by the spring of 1942 he
had read "thousands of letters" by Bolivar, which he described to Gertrude Stein as reflecting a mixture of complete despair and complete
hope. Late in 1944, he read through Philip Guedalla's life of Wellington,
as well as Clausewitz on War. Soon after the liberation of Rome in 1944,
he took a week's leave there to renew his acquaintance with the city itself
and also to refresh his recollections of the extraordinary life and achievements of Julius Caesar, about whom he began making systematic entries
in his journal.

Wilder's week in Rome early in December 1944 was his first respite
from military duties in over two years, and it came as a blessed relief.
Leaving Caserta for Rome on a mild and sunny day in an open high-
mounted command car, he leaned out of the vehicle like an Airedale as
he took in the sights and smells of the campagna. His orders billeted him
at the luxurious Albergo Maestoso, commandeered by the Air Force for
high-ranking officers. Rome, to be sure, was something of a ghost city.
The buildings were intact; architecturally, nothing much had altered
since, a quarter-century before, he had arrived for the first time as a
tremulous virgin, an unknown prepared to be ravished by the Eternal
City's beauty, history, traditions, and wickedness. Ravished he had been;
and out of the experience had emerged the novel that had determined
the course of his life. No other city had rendered up to him so many
riches: Rome's ruins and relics revealed through archaeologists' picks and
shovels were tangible reminders of his youthful infatuation with the
Latin poets. The medieval and Renaissance palazzi, basilicas, fountains,
and piazzi; the prisons, churches, walls, gates, and great flights of steps;
the clocks, monuments, and bells; the Raphaels and Michelangelos, the
villas and the vistas, the cypresses, ilexes, and palms—all these infinite
treasures overwhelmed and intoxicated him again, after twenty-four
months of austere military duty.

For all its beauty, never before had he seen Rome so plain. Except
along the Via Veneto with its clusters of importunate streetwalkers and
hungry soldiers, the city was virtually deserted. The avenues, the streets,

and the Corso itself were empty of public and private vehicles. Neither streetcars, buses, nor cars were to be seen. Even military vehicles were assembled mainly in parking areas. Virtually everyone in Rome was a pedestrian and most of the pedestrians were military personnel. The Romans themselves remained, for the most part, in their homes or their shops, tranforming Rome into a truly wide-open city, its vast squares and piazzi empty except for occasional groups of sightseers from the Polish Army. The result was that the masonry, the architectural configurations, the urban spaces alternating with the compression of structure on structure, the pines and fountains of Rome were visible, impinging on Wilder's consciousness as they had never done before.

He could not get his fill of Rome. Half in a daze, he performed errands of mercy (carrying a gift of money to an ancient writer, a message of hope and reassurance to some elderly ladies) with the recollections of what he had just seen of Rome mingling with the anticipations of what he would be seeing next. Some of Rome's choicest and most secret treasures he shared with the driver who had transported him from Caserta. As they passed the Cancelleria, which Wilder identified as the oldest model for the Boston Public Library, he suddenly pushed upon an unsecured door that opened into an archway leading to a courtyard; beyond that rose tier on tier of the elegantly carved woods of a Renaissance palazzo. The beautifully tended greensward of the courtyard together with the magnificently maintained dark woods and wrought-iron lattice work of the building itself had the effect of transporting the two Americans four hundred years back in time.

Daylight hours in Rome were not enough for Wilder. He would set out at ten o'clock at night with a flashlight (there were no street lights) to conduct eerie tours of the dark and silent city; he pointed out the Villa Medici or the Quirinale illuminated only by moonlight and the inadequate beam of an army flashlight. One afternoon, he came upon an exhibit of paintings culled from collections in Naples, Rome, and Florence and displayed in the former offices of Mussolini in the Palazzo Venetia. Among the masterpieces was Velazquez's portrait of Pope Innocent, but the painting that transfixed Wilder was a landscape attributed to Giorgione.

When he was not savoring the sights of Rome, he visited old friends and new ones. He made the acquaintance of the actress Elsa Merlini who had performed in the Italian premiere of *Piccola Città* (*Our Town*) and to whom he confided his plans for the unfinished *Alcestiad*. To a young American officer, Herschel Williams, a friend of Isabel's and the author of the comedy *Janie,* he recounted in some detail the structure of the burgeoning novel about Caesar. Making acquaintances or renewing them throughout the week, he rounded up a dozen people, including an OSI member—son of novelist Hermann Broch—and an ambitious young English music hall performer who believed that if she exercised her considerable charms upon Wilder, he would be persuaded to write and star her in a new play tailored to her talents. All these he invited to a black-market restaurant where he spent a small fortune providing them with an authentic Roman dinner. Bored finally with a revelry more contrived than spontaneous, Wilder detached himself at one in the morning over the urgent protests of his guests, and said to his driver as they drove through the silent streets of Rome: "Fleeting is the worldling's hour . . ." Wilder's capacity for bonhomie and frivolity was limited. But though he flew back next day to Caserta and his military duties, Rome remained on his mind. The city had reminded him of what he was and what he was not. Could another man be what he was and what he was not? Was Caesar, perhaps, such a man?

By early 1945, when the outcome of the war was no longer in doubt and the Italian campaign with its bombing missions from Italian bases was overshadowed by the thrusts into Germany by Eisenhower's armies and the Eighth and Ninth Air Forces, Wilder became more and more restless and uneasy. He was available to welcome the hordes of important visitors from the United States: Katharine Cornell, Rex Stout, Kay Boyle, Carl Carmer, and Leland Stowe. When stagings of *Our Town* began proliferating, Wilder agreed to serve as consultant for the Caserta production. He met again with Elsa Merlini who was planning performances of *Piccola Città* in nearby Naples. In spite of his heated quarters in the generals' preserve, he caught a severe cold intensified by flying in a nonpressurized aircraft to Yugoslavia, so that he was hospitalized for several days. By mid-April, a few days after the death of Roosevelt, he was enjoying a week's leave on the island of Capri, then an Air Force rest camp. The island had the same effect upon him as Rome four months earlier. Not only did the amenities of life on Capri make his military existence on the mainland seem drab and irksome by comparison, Capri also evoked imperial Rome, for even in Caesar's time it was an earthly paradise, and Tiberius's ruins studded the island.

The chief reason for Wilder's nervousness and malaise, apart from his exhaustion, was that he knew that his mission in Italy was coming to an end. His diplomatic talents had first manifested themselves in South America and had become again evident in his relations with British, Commonwealth, and French officers at MAAF; they enabled Assistant Secretary of State Archibald MacLeish to nominate Wilder for the post in liberated Paris as United States cultural attaché. The appointment was to take effect in the fall of 1945, when the European war, at least, would have ended. The gregarious element of Wilder's nature eagerly responded to the whole idea and to the prospect of a reunion with Gertrude and Alice and his several friends and colleagues who by then would have reestablished themselves in Paris. Facing the reality that he had grown bored with his military associates in the summer palace of the Neapolitan kings and queens, he longed for release to the City of Light and Enlightenment.

But Wilder was troubled by something even more profound. For three years, he had written nothing but letters and journal entries. He had three plays that waited to be written or completed; he had thought about them, talked about them, alluded to them in letters to friends around the globe. But they were not being written. He was, after all—was he not?—a professional playwright and novelist. And he was not, after all, either a military tactician or even a diplomat. Also, he was forty-eight. How many productive years lay ahead?

Uppermost in his mind was the Caesar novel, which in some involuted fashion had evolved from his whole war experience, from his thoughts about the achievement and exercise of power. It was Caesar whose conquests and visions formed the basis for the *Pax Romana,* the four-hundred-year period of order and consolidation in Europe, North Africa, and Asia Minor. The fabulous and legendary Julius Caesar—a legend firmly rooted in history—was a man of such fascinating motives and character traits that for two thousand years he continued to challenge the talents of historians and composers and poets and playwrights —Mommsen, Handel, Shakespeare, and Shaw among them. Now, Wilder felt that he too was ready to come to grips with the protean figure of Caesar of whom it was said he was all things to all men. . . .

Wilder had been back only ten days from his April idyl on Capri when, not unexpectedly, orders arrived transferring him back to the United States for reassignment. He was needed in Paris, but he would first have to terminate his military status and be briefed by the appropriate officers of the Department of State. Although the war in Europe was drawing to a close and Germany's surrender was momentarily expected, Wilder's feelings about returning to civilian life were strangely ambivalent. On the day that he turned in his equipment and settled his accounts at Caserta, dozens of officers, airmen, and WACS (most of whom he barely knew, even by sight) said their good-byes as though he were a member of a family, departing for a continent from which he would never return. After one of these emotional farewells, the officer accompanying Wilder on these ceremonial rounds asked him the identity of the young WAC clerk with whom he had all but exchanged heartfelt embraces.

"Haven't the slightest idea," Wilder breezily responded.

"But you parted as though you were dear friends," the officer protested.

"Well, y'know," said Wilder, "long ago I had to learn to be an actor."

An hour later, as Wilder was packing the gear that he would take back to the United States, he noticed that he had not turned in an army blanket stenciled "Major T. N. Wilder." He was about to offer it to the younger officer, then suddenly he changed his mind:

"I think maybe I'll keep this," he said quietly. "They can bury me in it."

A few hours later, Wilder and his Army blanket were aboard a military transport plane headed West. He was leaving behind a world and a way of life which in some ways had been the most satisfying he had ever known. A part of Wilder had always been drawn toward the company of men. But the company of men had rejected him, at first utterly— as at Chefoo and at Ojai. By the time he got to college he learned role playing and could ingratiate himself sufficiently to earn limited acceptance, but not, according to Henry Luce, "from the elite." He was tolerated by the Lawrenceville faculty and even liked by the more intelligent members. But Chicago's formidable English faculty (to which he was never more than an adjunct) initially resented him as someone imposed upon them by the authoritarian Robert Hutchins; later they patronized him as an amiable dilettante, as, in a department of such scholars, indeed he was.

In the Air Corps, however, his situation was different from what it had ever been before. For all of its hierarchical structure, its ceremonial and ritualistic distinctions between the ranks, its emphasis on instant obedience, and its reliance on command decisions, the army in general and the air corps in particular were profoundly egalitarian institutions.* The success of the (Army) Air Force was based in part on the circumstance that its leadership, from squadron to command level was virtually free of political, economic, or social preferment, the kind of social ranking that characterized most of the European military establishments. An American soldier's advancement and his level of responsibility were generally based on merit and performance. Exceptionally qualified officers brought in from civilian life, such as Jimmy Doolittle and Charles Thornton, were given extraordinary precedence over career officers as a matter of course. Highly qualified sergeants were transformed into majors, colonels, and brigadier generals. Like Eisenhower's, General Eaker's origins had been most humble and Eaker reached his eminence without even having attended West Point. His MAAF command was won

* Except in one respect: de facto racial segregation was endemic throughout the armed services during World War II.

through his qualities of leadership and his renown as a pioneer in aeronautics. Eaker's capacity to evaluate objectively an officer's performance of duty led him to confer upon Wilder the highest decoration for supportive service, the Legion of Merit; it symbolized the respect that Eaker and Wilder's colleagues tendered him during his tour of two years. Even the British officers, most of whom could ill-conceal their disdain for Americans, were likewise respectful of Wilder and they procured for him the Order of the British Empire.

Although, like millions of others, Wilder found military service uncomfortable, exasperating, tedious, and monotonous, in turn, he was profoundly satisfied to find himself accepted as *par inter pares,* an equal among equals in a company of men whose abilities and character he gravely respected. And, like a great many Americans being released from the service, eager to resume or begin their civilian occupations, he welcomed the release; nevertheless, he took off his uniform for the last time with a profound and involuntary sigh. On that day he told a friend:

> Glad to be a free agent, I guess, but I hate to be wearing civilian clothes when so many are still in uniform.

# XIV

## Soldier from the War
## Returneth

*". . . but I have no subject."*

Wilder's return from Italy to the United States in May 1945 found him hopeful but exhausted, eager but depressed. Although he viewed his imminent return to civilian life with relief, he had nevertheless some disquieting intimations: his next work as a writer he felt would both define his existence as a man and determine his future as an artist. For at forty-eight he was about to enter those fateful decades, a man's fifties and sixties, which for some prove bitter and empty, for others fruitful and climactic.

There was, moreover, the nagging matter of his assignment to our embassy in Paris. He had no doubt that he would be fulfilling a critical function as the American cultural attaché. Our relations with the newly formed government of France headed by General Charles de Gaulle and, indeed, with the French people in general required reconciliation and reconstruction. He had demonstrated, in his government missions and in his war experiences, a genuine talent for generating good will. But however absorbing and important the asignment might be, no matter how it would gratify the gregarious side of his nature, his acceptance would indefinitely postpone his return to his vocation. He was a man with a strong sense of duty and that sense was pulling him apart. Duty to his country drew him toward Paris; his sense of himself as an artist drew him toward the writing tables in isolated hotel and motel rooms. That summer, he agonized over his decision.

Like many returning servicemen, Wilder was initially unaware of the extent of his psychic and physical exhaustion. Not until he had spent several weeks floundering in the bureaucratic red tape of the Air Force Redistribution Center at Miami Beach did both he and the examining physicians realize that he was in no condition to plunge into diplomatic activities in Paris. And, having made the decision to become a wholly private citizen, he stood uncertain what to begin work upon—or where.

The several projects which had made him ebullient in Italy, now that he was free to work upon any one or all of them, seemed suddenly unworkable. The novel about Caesar, which the previous Christmas in Rome he had been able to outline to Herschel Williams in extraordinary detail, now presented unsurmountable difficulties. The three plays he had been juggling in his mind, the half-completed *Alcestiad*, *The Sandusky, Ohio, Nativity Play*, and *The Hell of the Vizier Kabaar* now appeared impossibly pretentious. Two months after his return, he described himself as sick in mind and body and predicted that his physical examination would bring "this cracking ship to light." At the same time, although he wanted to work in the comic spirit again, he discovered that he had neither a subject nor even a likely place to work.

What precisely was wrong? Was it fatigue, a delayed reaction? Or had something within him or something outside himself—he wasn't sure which—profoundly changed? Could it be that the second World War, like the first, had so abruptly altered the Zeitgeist that he was no longer in tune with the times? Had he been precipitously assigned to a generation whose voice and presence was no longer needed—or welcomed? Could such things have happened in the short time since he had been away?

The most successful new play on Broadway in 1945 had been written by a hitherto unknown playwright with the improbable name Tennessee Williams who, for more than a dozen years of privation and humiliation, had sought to persuade an indifferent society to accept him as a human being and as an artist. Wilder's reaction to *The Glass Menagerie* was mixed. Williams had patently been influenced by *Our Town:* he had incorporated a Narrator who like Wilder's Stage Manager walked into and out of the play at will. Like *Our Town*, *The Glass Menagerie* was a family play, unplotted, homely, and casual. And like Wilder's play it was set in the familiar past, a past capable of evoking the same nostalgia generated by *Our Town* seven years before.

Except that it didn't.

Williams's play employed a Chekhovian objectivity, and its people emerged as either victims or victimizers. The sensible, astringent Mrs. Webb of *Our Town* had been transformed into the self-deluded, egocentric, semidemented Amanda Wingfield who, if she were not so pathetically ineffectual, would have come across as a veritable monster. Williams's depiction of American family life contrasted markedly with Wilder's celebration of what it was and what it might have been. (There is no intended irony in the use of "Blest Be The Tie That Binds" as the leitmotiv of *Our Town*). But Williams was clearly expressing his contempt for the generation which procreated him; he had contempt for its ignorance, its complacency, its ineptitude, and its hypocrisy.

Viewing *The Glass Menagerie*, Wilder saw in its relaxed construction the triumph and vindication of his ideas about dramatic composition and production. But he was made uneasy by Williams's odd mixture of brutality and sentimentality, sensitivity and vulgarity, and idealism and disillusionment that lay very close to the play's surface. These qualities surely reflected the new temper of the times, and they were outside the scope and capacities of Wilder's aesthetic limits. Williams had achieved popular acceptance, just as Wilder had twice achieved it. But by 1945, Wilder's two great successes, *The Bridge* and *Our Town,* were already "classics," that is to say museum pieces, artifacts of a world that existed before genocide and cataclysm had become commonplace. The immediacy of *The Glass Menagerie* lay in its presenting two young people attempting to escape from a world that was both intolerable and maddening. A play celebrating escapism and a retreat from responsibility left Wilder alienated and estranged.

His brief sojourn in Hamden-New Haven was a nightmare of frenzied activities and social obligations; he felt stifled by the domesticity of Deepwood Drive. In desperation, he would take the train for New York, dine extravagantly but well at Twenty-One, Voisin, or The Colony. After the theater he would return to Twenty-One or to the Oak Room of the Plaza where money—as he himself described it—fell from his pocket like confetti and it all seemed to him "very fascinating and remote."

During that early summer of 1945, while he was attending rehearsals of a USO production of *Our Town* featuring Raymond Massey as the Stage Manager, word reached Wilder that Lawrence Olivier's production of *The Skin of Our Teeth* in London had achieved a great success. These tokens of the scale of his achievements in the theater merely served to exacerbate the present sense of failure and inadequacy. Not only was he depressed by his writing block, but he realized that in his forty-ninth year he was retrogressing into a life pattern hardly distinguishable from that of twenty years earlier. His only residence was still the home he had built for and shared with his mother. Together with his sister, she enveloped him, he felt, in a protective tyranny that threatened not so much to suffocate him as to diminish his adulthood. In Hamden, he was engulfed in obligations and responsibilities to relatives, neighbors, friends, well-wishers, and a segment of the Yale community. Isabel prompted him when he was insufficiently alert to his mother's needs and whimsies; his mother suggested ways and means by which he might ameliorate the hardships of Isabel's single state. However much he railed to his few intimates about fate forcing him into the role of head of household, he was gravely concerned because of his inability to detach himself from "the women at home," as well as from all the genteel teas and suppers, the cocktail parties on cocktail parties, and the gatherings at Yale's Graduates Club and Elizabethan Club—and detach himself, above all, from the interminable gossip which the Yale–New Haven community had elevated if not to a high art then at least to a major industry, successfully competing against both Princeton and Cambridge. Knowing that he should escape, that he *must*, Wilder somehow could not give up Deepwood Drive for an apartment in New York, Paris, or London. Glenway Wescott and Monroe Wheeler offered to find him secluded quarters at a discreet distance from their rural retreat in New Jersey or in Bucks County, Pennsylvania. Wilder consulted other friends, writers, and artists about a suitable retreat that could be both his home and his studio. But the cord that bound him to mother and sister, that tied him to the house on Deepwood Drive, five minutes drive from the Yale campus, where he was now a life fellow of one of the residence halls, was indestructible. A part of him bitterly and silently acquiesced in the realization that there was not to be any other home for him, even though for another decade and a half he continued to struggle against that acceptance. For years to come, he would pretend to himself and to others that a breakaway was possible, even imminent.

The summer of 1945, which for Wilder was filled with doubt and indecision, frenzied activities and psychic exhaustion, was played out, we must recall, against a background that included atomic bombings, the surrender of Germany and Japan, the deposition of Churchill, and the overwhelming necessity for reconstructing a traumatized, disoriented, and devastated planet. It is not difficult to see why Wilder stood irresolute and uncertain, groping for a subject that would not appear contemptibly trivial or pathetically out of date. After the restless summer, determined to restore order and purpose into his life, he decided to return to *The Alcestiad*, his free adaptation of the Euripides play, which he had half-completed before entering upon military service.

Adaptations, fantasias, orchestrations, and burlesques of Greek tragedy had always held a fascination for him, particularly those which had come out of France: Racine, Gluck, Offenbach, Cocteau, and

Giraudoux, each in turn had had an impact on him. A living repertory of French drama deriving from Greek tragedy flourished in Paris and throughout provincial France, *Phèdre, La Belle Hélène, Antigone,* and *Electre* among other titles. Even more than Germany, where Goethe and Schiller had transformed the Greeks into German literature, France had thoroughly absorbed Hellenic tragedy and myth into its cultural blood-stream. In the United States, only Robinson Jeffers and Eugene O'Neill had sought to rework classical tragedy. But Jeffers's *Tower Beyond Tragedy,* had not yet been dramatized in 1945; and O'Neill's *Mourning Becomes Electra,* based, like Jeffers's poem, on the *Oresteia,* served to illustrate Browning's maxim that a man's reach should exceed his grasp.

Although there was no real tradition in America for adaptations of Greek drama, Wilder decided to do what he had more or less always done: ignore the current literary trend and base the structure of his work upon solid work of the past. The reason he chose Euripides' *Alcestis* as the basis for his return to writing was a complex one. The times required, he felt, an artistic statement of a certain consequence. Since the disastrous failure of *The Trumpet Shall Sound* in 1926, he had never dared to immerse himself in a play with a religious theme. Yet his religious-philosophical preoccupations were part of his inheritance, a family tradition which his brother Amos was upholding, both as a teaching theologian and literary scholar annotating Christian symbolism in English poetry. Although Thornton had long since rejected, as he himself stated, his father's narrow Calvinism, he could not exorcise his sense of "the presence of the numinous," a term he had derived from the German theosophist, Rudolph Otto whose book *The Idea of the Holy* greatly influenced Wilder's thinking.*

In *Our Town* Wilder had dramatized "The Daily Life," "Love and Marriage," and "Death" in a play whose intention it was to show how people relate to one another (or fail to do so). In *The Skin of Our Teeth,* Wilder had emphasized man's relation to aspects of his environment. Neither play in retrospect seemed to him to carry the weight of a truly important dramatic work; so that, in 1945, he hoped that by dramatizing man's direct relationship to cosmic forces, as the Greeks had done, he could construct the kind of dramatic monument which O'Neill had attempted and failed.

Moreover, he had conceived the notion that for the central role of his play, that of Alcestis, he could obtain the world's most celebrated actress, Greta Garbo, who only three years before—in her midthirties, her

---

* Otto's book (Oxford, 1931) contains the same epigraph from Goethe's *Faust* (II) that later served as the epitaph for Wilder's *The Ides of March:*

Das Schaudern ist der Menschheit bestes Teil.
Wie auch die Welt ihm das Gefuehl verteuere,
Ergriffen fuehlt er tief das Ungeheure.

beauty intact—had retired from the films. Through intermediaries, he ascertained that Garbo was indeed available and interested in resuming her career in such a play as he was engaged upon.

Late in October 1945, abandoning an earlier plan for a vast continental swing to Acapulco via Chicago, New Orleans, and Texas, Wilder set out in the 1939 Chrysler convertible (the one given him by Sol Lesser) enroute to Florida to work on his play. But even as he worked on it, in Ponte Vedra, Florida, in Brunswick, Georgia, and Myrtle Beach, South Carolina, there were intimations that he was failing to bring his ideas to life. The Gallic genius of his French counterparts, which enabled them to breathe wit and contemporaneity into the mythic beings of an ancient culture, eluded him; Wilder lacked the skepticism and cynicism of a Giraudoux or a Cocteau. He found himself unsure of the appropriate *style,* he, who had been called America's leading stylist! The problem was to avoid the Scylla and Charybdis of pretentiousness and flippancy.

By late fall, he turned north so as to be home for Christmas. Having become uncertain about the play, he began to reconsider the Caesar novel and stopped off at Chapel Hill to reread Suetonius and other sources at the university library. By the time he reached Washington and later Princeton (where he had arranged successive reunions with Air Force friends from his overseas base), his spirits were at low ebb. The Washington reunion was unsettling; the charming, dazzling flight surgeon with whom he had spent so many hours month after month at the officers' mess now seemed preoccupied and uninterested in Wilder's concerns. Similarly, his meeting with his Air Force captain friend a few days later ended in a senseless quarrel involving literary judgments—with the result that Wilder felt impelled to apologize by mail to the younger man who had gone back overseas hurt and confused by Wilder's uncharacteristic hostility and derisiveness. Neither man, of course, to whom Wilder seemed the essence of self-assuredness, could have guessed that he needed the very reinforcement and direction that they had sought from him. He was reminded again that apart from the service life, a sustained friendship for him was all but an impossibility lying beyond his emotional means. All he could afford were Ruth Gordons, Alice Toklases, and miscellaneous other older ladies scattered over America and Europe who cost him nothing—and gave him nothing.

New Year's Day was usually an extraordinary occasion for Wilder. New Year's, 1938, for example, had coincided with his completing for Jed Harris the acting version of *Our Town.* On New Year's afternoon, 1942, he completed *The Skin of Our Teeth.* New Year's 1946 stood in sorry contrast with New Year's 1945, which had been one of the happiest days of his life: in Caserta, Italy, the day had materialized—almost miraculously—like a mild May day, the temperature in the high sixties, brilliantly clear, with a light characteristic of the Italian Mediterranean. Even though it was a Monday, the commanding general had declared the day a holiday and Wilder was free to roam the environs of Caserta; he accompanied an officer-friend on a command car ride up into the Appennines toward Benevento. It was quite enough to make any soldier happy. As the two men climbed the gentle hills of the campagna, the younger man sang and Wilder related an idea he had for a nativity play, one that would roll off his pen the moment the war ended . . . in three or four months' time. This part of the Italian landscape, which Wilder had never seen, wholly intoxicated him: the scenery, the camaraderie, the singing, the anticipation of writing a new play—several new plays and a novel about Caesar—all combined on New Year's Day, 1945, to transfigure Wilder into a literary artist of infinite potentialities, whose greatest decades of productivity still lay ahead.

Now, one year later, New Year's Day, 1946, found him surrounded by middle-aged and elderly ladies; he was profoundly depressed, writing without conviction, without pleasure, without confidence that what he was writing was any good at all. The Italian campagna seemed as far away as the sense he had had of being young, accomplished, indefatigable, and inexhaustibly productive. For a few more weeks he would continue his struggle with *The Alcestiad* before he laid aside the recalcitrant material. For almost a decade it remained at rest. And Miss Greta Garbo delayed her debut on the New York stage—indefinitely.

# XV

## The Ides of March

*". . . with all its incompleteness it asks to be loved. . . . It has been called frigid, when it is all for fun and all about the passions. . . . It has been called hard, when it is all attremble."*—WILDER TO GLENWAY WESCOTT.

In picking up the threads of his Caesar novel in the spring of 1946, Wilder knew that he was taking a calculated risk. His two most recent novels, both out of print, had not been critical successes. Moreover, he had announced in interviews and essays his disenchantment with the novel form and had explained why for him the play was a more congenial mode of expression. In the novel, he said the reader is confronted by what has taken place; while in the theater, whether the audience is viewing *Oedipus Rex, Hamlet,* or *Three Men on a Horse,* they are seeing events that are taking place at that moment. In addition, he contended, where a novel is principally an account of a series of unique occasions, plays such as *Agamennon* or *Lear* or *Our Town* describe a generalized act, which evokes our belief through drama's power to raise those performed individual actions into the area of the universal, the type.

Now Wilder proposed in his new novel to effect a compromise, a kind of dramatization: he would eliminate the author's voice telling

211

what had happened and provide the reader with only a series of documents: letters, memoranda, official directives, journal entries, bureau reports. These documents—all but one of which were devised by Wilder—would carry the entire burden of the narrative, thereby providing, he hoped, something of the immediacy of a play.* Furthermore, he arranged the materials not chronologically but in a pattern that was, as Glenway Wescott was to say, "hard to describe":

> . . . [The novel] is in four parts or 'books,' covering the same main events four times over, starting a little earlier in each part and ending later. By means of this odd recurring and expanding chronology . . . the reader is given an extraordinary impression of a fate running its course, a sort of bird's eye view constantly on the wing back and forth, and higher and higher; and the passing of the historic time corresponds to the gradual increase of our understanding of the great matters at issue. (*Images of Truth*, p. 257.)

The ingenuity that Wilder applied to devising the intricate schemata for his novel was matched by the preparation he gave to its thematic and philosophical content. He drew extensively upon his learning, his studies, his conversations with distinguished thinkers, and, at the same time, projected his imaginative capacities as he had not done since he wrote *Heaven's My Destination*. Into the writing of *The Ides of March* went the distillation of conversations with Gertrude Stein (What is true greatness in a man?) ; ideas gleaned from Sartre's newly published essays on existentialism; Wilder's own lifelong teleological speculations; the fruits of his wide-ranging studies of Rome's history, literature, and culture. In addition, woven into the narrative were Wilder's war experiences, those insights he had gained into the day-to-day, hour-by-hour administrative responsibilities of a supreme commander. For a number of the principal characters, Wilder borrowed from his wide acquaintance. Clodia Pulcher was modeled on the Tallulah Bankhead of the 1930s. Cicero's commentaries (all imagined by Wilder and not drawn from Cicero's extant letters) resembled both the style and point of view of Alexander Woollcott. The grace, melancholy beauty, and cultivated intelligence of Antony's mistress, the actress Cytheris, was reminiscent of the Austrian actress, Eleanora von Mendelssohn, who later figured in a roman-à-clef by S. N. Behrman. Catullus, as the book's dedication implies, was to some extent based on Lauro de Bosis, Wilder's friend from his year in Rome. Poppeia's epistolary style is recognizable to intimates of

---

* Jerome Kilty, a protégé of Wilder, who both acted in and wrote for the theater, fifteen years after the publication of *The Ides of March* contrived—with Wilder's active collaboration—a staged abridgment of the novel. Despite John Gielgud's taking the part of Caesar, the production was a failure.

Isabel Wilder. Cleopatra, though she was drawn largely from Wilder's imagination and owes something to Shakespeare's (but not Shaw's!) portrait, resembled Vivien Leigh with whom Wilder became acquainted, along with her husband Laurence Olivier, at the time he began serious work on the novel.\* Wilder's portrait of Caesar, however, owed nothing to Shakespeare. In a letter to Robert Hutchins, he stated that he was incorporating some of Hutchins's physical mannerisms, along with his capacity for understatement and his infinite patience into the portrait of Caesar. But little of Hutchins really comes through in the execution except, perhaps, the physical languor and deliberateness which served to conceal Hutchins's, and the character Caesar's, quick intelligence and decisiveness.

The Julius Caesar of *The Ides of March,* like the central figures in all Wilder's novels, is a consciously wrought projection of an aspect of Wilder's idealized self. Just as he had exploited himself comedically in *Heaven's My Destination,* he transmuted into a self-portrait as Caesar his tragic sense of self. That is not to say that *The Ides of March* is an autobiographical novel; on the contrary, it is a persuasive reconstruction of historical events and an elaboration on the life and times of Julius Caesar. For even though, as Wilder himself notes in his preface, he has manipulated time sequences and presented as alive, historical characters already dead in the time span of his novel; his portrait of Caesar embodies the known qualities and characteristics of the historical person with infinitely more accuracy than those of Shakespeare or Shaw.

Nevertheless, it is impossible not to detect parallels between important aspects of Wilder's own spiritual odyssey and that of Julius Caesar. His Caesar is one of the avatars of the existential hero in the literature of post–World War II fiction, the most fully achieved existential hero created by an American novelist.

Early in the novel Caesar writes in his journal:

> —Last night I sat down and wrote the edict abolishing the College of Augurs and declared that henceforward no days were to be regarded as unlucky. I wrote on, giving to my people the reasons for this action. When have I been happier? What pleasures are greater than honesty? I wrote on and the constellations glided before my window. I disbanded the College of Vestal Virgins; I married the daughters of our first houses and they gave sons and daughters to Rome. I closed the doors of the temples, of all our temples except those of Jupiter. I tumbled the gods back into the gulf of ignorance and fear from which they came and into that treacherous half-world where the fancy invents consolatory lies. And finally the moment came when I

\* Urged on by Wilder, the Oliviers subsequently appeared in New York in Shakespeare's *Antony and Cleopatra* and Shaw's *Caesar and Cleopatra.*

pushed aside what I had done and started to begin again with the
announcement that Jupiter himself had never existed; that man was
alone in a world in which no voices were heard than his own, a
world neither friendly nor unfriendly save as he made it so.

And having reread what I wrote I destroyed it. . . .

In myself I was not certain that I was certain.

Am I sure that there is no mind behind our existence and no
mystery anywhere in the universe? I think I am. What joy, what
relief . . . if we could declare so with complete conviction. . . .
How terrifyingly and glorious the role of man if, indeed, without
guidance and without consolation he must create from his own vitals
the meaning for his existence and write the rules whereby he
lives. . . .

Wilder, we recall, had moved away from the Christian humanism of
his twenties; his destination was a more venturesome teleology which,
while it rejected the ultimate existential insistence that man is directed
by no forces outside himself, incorporated a number of existential postu-
lates. His Caesar had achieved power and was determined to use power,
not because he required adulation, but because power provided him with
the kind of freedom that a man of his capacities required. In becoming
emperor, he wrested freedom from an indifferent universe by virtue of his
own self-discipline and energies and the prudent application of his extraordinary intelligence and gifts. Caesar defined his self-fulfillment in
providing every Roman citizen with the opportunity of obtaining the
measure of freedom he could exercise in a rational and constructive
manner. Caesar, the father of his country, would enable each of his
"sons" to become their own fathers . . . a course of action that he
understood would ensure his own violent death at the hands of a "son."

Wilder, as we have observed, superseded *his* father in every area but
one: like Caesar, Wilder never fathered a son. But he had early engaged
his mother's absorbed attention; he had acquired world fame, money,
and the responsibility for sustaining his family; he had been the recipient
of his country's civilian and military honors; he had played a role in
determining the destinies of a number of gifted young men and women,
by counseling, evaluating, guiding, and launching them. And this can be
seen as a kind of fatherhood. Orson Welles, Robert Ardrey, Geoffrey
Hellman, Montgomery Clift, Ruth Gordon, Garson Kanin, Marguerite
Young, Harry T. Moore, Glenway Wescott, Edward Albee, and Laurence
Olivier are among those who have called Wilder their discoverer, or their
mentor, their spiritual guide of their artistic conscience. Moreover, in
addition to his generosity to the young or inexperienced, in addition to
his assumption of familial and patriotic responsibilities, Wilder achieved
fatherhood through artistic creation, a creativity not wholly removed
from the kind of creativity Caesar displays in this novel.

Book I of *The Ides of March* deals with Caesar's deliberations over the exercise of power, in respect to public works in general and improvements of the general welfare. One of the chief forces that tie his hands, however, is the established state religion. Caesar says he has inherited an intolerable burden of nonsense and superstition which hinders the day-to-day operation of the executive, senatorial, and judicial branches of government and forestalls rational and deliberate reforms throughout the Republic. As other rulers—Constantine, Henry VIII, Robespierre, and Lenin—did over the next two millennia, Caesar yearned to provide his regime with a fresh start by abolishing the state religion and by declaring that Jupiter himself never existed and that man is alone in a world where the only voices are his own.

Although Caesar contemplates making such a declaration, he is unable to do it. Caesar, like Wilder, has since adolescence looked upon the traditional rituals and beliefs of his upbringing first with skepticism, then with doubt, and finally with nothing more than nostalgia. But because Caesar, like Wilder, cannot dismiss the possibility of a mind "in and behind the universe," that influences both man's mind and actions, he cannot close the temples; and Thornton Wilder could not deny God.

In Book II, Wilder develops the novel's second principal theme: aspects of love. In Book I, the Proustian passion of Catullus for the unworthy Clodia Pulcher had already been established, together with Caesar's having once briefly been Clodia's lover—long before the advent of Catullus. The intimation of the old affair provokes Catullus to a furious hatred toward Caesar. And finally, the reader understands that Clodia's resentment of Caesar stems from her realization that she cannot by any means reawaken Caesar's interest in her. The triangle is completed by Caesar's awakening love for Catullus's art and inevitably for Catullus—a love not explicitly accompanied by homosexual overtones.*

As Book II unfolds, a second triangle joins itself to the one already established. Paying a state visit to Rome, Cleopatra resumes her liaison with Caesar that had begun five years earlier. Out of sheer malevolence, Clodia persuades Antony to seduce the queen during the reception Cleopatra has arranged for the distinguished Roman gentry. During the seduction, Clodia leads Caesar and his entourage to the bower where Antony is attempting to force himself on Cleopatra, whose struggles—as described by Antony's mistress—lack conviction. This Tristan-like situa-

* Accusations of homosexuality were, in fact, leveled against Caesar by some of the ancients, charges which Wilder, in his novel, takes into account; but siding with the majority of classical historians, Wilder implies that the idea of Caesar's homosexuality is without basis. A number of notable Roman emperors, military heroes, and commanding generals were homosexual, but there is little evidence to support the idea that Julius Caesar shared that disposition.

tion reveals some further aspects of love: Antony's attempted seduction of Cleopatra is motivated less by his infatuation than by his unconscious resentment and envy toward Caesar, his "uncle" and benefactor.* Antony's act has less to do with love than with the primal impulse of the son wishing to supplant the father. Antony's own reason for his action is never expressed, but clearly he initiates the act of "love" as an act of bravado, defiance, and challenge.

Cleopatra's motivation is less clear. Her role is ambiguous. On the conscious level she may have fallen prey in all innocence to Antony's forceful seduction. On the other hand, Caesar in middle age could hardly have been a satisfactory lover for a twenty-four-year-old woman. His sexual ardor had been diminished not only by age, but by his duties as head of state, by his awareness of Cleopatra's personal ambitions, and by his self-control and essential lack of romantic passion. Antony is the only man in Rome whose military valor can be compared with Caesar's. He is, moreover, twenty years younger, a handsome, passionate, and reckless man, capable of arousing the interest of an erotic young woman. Wilder's point about Cleopatra is that while her eroticism may have masked for the moment her constant concern about the inherent uncertainty of being queen of a conquered nation, her genuine veneration for Caesar superseded her interest in Antony's sexual and physical vitality.

These aspects of love—love as an unworthy, or absurd, or fruitless or vain expense of spirit—filter through the consciousness of Caesar. The pursuit of love invariably leaves Caesar with a sense of his betrayal by Catullus, by Cleopatra, and even by his child-wife Poppeia. For Caesar, Cleopatra's apparent betrayal was the most tragic stroke of all; at the moment when he is confronted by the subject of his most extraordinary political and amatory triumph, struggling in the arms of his heir presumptive, Caesar is subjected simultaneously to anguish, disappointment, jealousy, public embarrassment, and the consciousness that his career as a lover has ended. Cleopatra had been, indeed, a morsel for a monarch and no one could replace her. Her wit, her intelligence, her ambition, her educability, and her nobility were fused with charm and feminine grace. Power, Caesar discovers, no matter what its extent, can command anything except what is most worth possessing: loyalty, love, and life itself.

Like Caesar, Wilder was attracted by those young men and women whom he could teach and whom he could admire for their creative, intellectual, natural, and spiritual gifts and for whom he could—on rare occasions—entertain some kind of infatuation (a condition whose symptoms Caesar describes in one of the letters he dispatches to Cleopatra).

---

* Antony was related to Caesar on his (Antony's) mother's side and was regarded by Caesar as his political heir, since Caesar's closest male relative, his grandnephew Octavian, was still in his teens.

But as Bernard Shaw averred in his preface to *Caesar and Cleopatra,*
infatuations are unworthy of serious and accomplished men. Wilder, who
preferred so many things to writing—for example, ruminating, rummag-
ing through periodicals, newspapers and *Variety;* gossiping; puzzle-
solving; examining musical scores; explicating literary texts, and dating
undated plays—shared Shaw's Puritan position that love-making and its
elaborate rituals were sinful especially because they occupied time that
might better be given over to serious and profitable endeavor. Wilder,
characteristically agonized over what both he and his father agreed was
his tendency to indolence; to compound indolence with time-consuming
seductions and affairs was intolerable. On the conscious level, this was
Wilder's rationalization for his lifelong attempts to avoid any emotional
involvements that transcended the ephemeral. Asked once by a colleague
at Lawrenceville why he had never married, Wilder responded: "Well—
y'know—I'm not one very much for passion." But like Caesar, Wilder
had passion enough. He had trained himself to control his capacity for
amatory passion and almost—but not quite—to bury it. Passion un-
leashed, Wilder understood, could earn him his father's (and later the
ghost of his father's) contemptuous scorn, his mother's indignant tears,
his Yale classmates' derision. Worst of all, passion could and inevitably
would bring down upon him the worst punishment of all: his own self-
hatred, self-contempt, and self-destruction. He had concluded, early on,
that no one he desired would desire him, that to give his heart was to
invite rejection. Somehow he, like Caesar, would in the end find his love
struggling (or not even struggling) in the arms of another lover. Youth
calls to youth, and Wilder himself was aware that he had progressed
directly from adolescence to middle age. . . .

But *The Ides of March* is concerned with a good deal more than the
aspects of love. Wilder was writing his novel for a public and for a world
wearied and exhausted by the effects of despotic rule. And Julius Caesar
was the first of the succession of Roman emperors; it was he who terminated the Roman Republic and thereby planted the seed both of Rome's
imperial glory and of her eventual doom. But unlike Hitler, Stalin, or
Mussolini, Caesar seized power—as Wilder interprets history—because
the Roman Senate was incapable of wielding power. Caesar wanted to
create a better world for all the Roman people, throughout Rome's
farthest conquests. He dreamed of a rational government encompassing
the whole of Europe, North Africa, and Asia Minor. Caesar does not
resemble closely any of the despotic dictators of the twentieth century,
except that nowhere in Wilder's novel does he contemplate reforms that
would enable the Roman people to govern themselves. Of course, for the
fictional Caesar to have thoughts like that might have done violence to
history. And yet, if Wilder could transform Caesar into an existential

hero, he might also have provided him with Jeffersonian intimations. Essentially what Wilder gives us is a portrait of the dictator as Anglo-Saxon intellectual. Indeed, it is possible to read the novel as Wilder's version of "If *I* were King."

Wilder's absorption with Caesar ultimately derived from the zeal he inherited from his father and perhaps from several of his New England clergymen-forebears. He had once been able to satirize (in *Heaven's My Destination*) the deep-seated impulse to reform and improve his fellow beings, their institutions, and their tastes. But in the dozen years since he had written *Heaven's My Destination,* Wilder's sense of himself had changed: his father's death in 1936 had placed him, rather than his brother Amos, in the position of head of the family; the United States government had assigned him a number of responsible missions during a time of national emergency, missions in which he had acquitted himself with distinction; his plays had brought him recognition as a dramatist of international stature. Deep down, he yearned to be, like Sophocles, a poet-statesman, a man who could be all at once *dichter,* moralist, and legislator.* Lacking the imperial mien of a Robert Hutchins, the presence of an Eisenhower, the casual self-assurance of a Franklin Roosevelt, Wilder could exert power only through the writer's art. But so strong was his sense of irony and so powerful his common sense that in the midst of his narration he could not refrain from observing that power is in a sense self-limiting; that the greater the power a man wields over a population, the less security accrues to himself. Caesars and czars, dictators, duces, and fuehrers—the well-intentioned or the malignant alike—are necessarily doomed by the very source of their power, force.†

*The Ides of March* was published in March 1948. Selected as a Book-of-the-Month Club selection, it showed gratifying sales and for a week or two, according to the *New York Times,* was the best-selling work of fiction throughout the country. The novel found its way into a respectable number of the better households of America and it promptly joined Wilder's other works on the shelves of public libraries across the continent. Yet, Wilder was crushed by its critical reception. This novel, his

* Faulkner suffered from a similar evangelical tendency that he could not always entirely extirpate from his novels, and that sometimes inspired self-satire. Faulkner's fervor, however, was mainly restricted to interviews he gave journalists and to letters he wrote to the newspapers.
† Wilder's implication that those who live by the sword necessarily perish by the sword is a postulate that all men of goodwill would like to subscribe to. In 1948, of all the world leaders in power during the thirties and forties, only Stalin, the supreme autocrat, had retained his power and outlasted his contemporaries . . . a circumstance that contributed to the opaque relevancy of *The Ides of March* to the world after World War II.

*best* novel, as he rightly considered it, was neither praised nor attacked, nor evaluated. It was maddeningly, heart-breakingly ignored.

To be sure the *New York Times,* the *Saturday Review,* the major newspapers, and *Time* reviewed the book favorably, and even, in a few instances, with enthusiasm. The Sunday *New York Times Book Review* assigned Brooks Atkinson, the *Times'* drama critic, to do the review, and the *Saturday Review* chose Elmer Davis, a well-known journalist and news commentator. Neither man was, strictly speaking, a literary critic. (The true critics, the influential figures at the universities and the little magazines—persons like Lionel Trilling, R. P. Blackmur, F. O. Matthiessen, Mary McCarthy, Philip Rahv, Alfred Kazin, Irving Howe, Robert Gorham Davis, F. W. Dupee, Henry Hazlitt, and Edmund Wilson—*all* ignored Wilder's novel. No mention of its publication could be gleaned from *Prairie Schooner,* the *Nation,* the *New Republic,* the *Sewanee Review,* the *Partisan Review,* the *Kenyon Review,* the *Antioch Review,* or the *American Scholar,* journals whose impact upon American letters greatly outweighed their modest circulations. These periodicals, and their galaxy of notable critics ignored *The Ides of March* as if it had been written by Thomas Costain or Mika Waltari. It was as if, Wilder felt, he had dropped a heavy stone in a well and there was not even the sound of a splash.

Why the stunning silence? It had nothing to do with the quality of Wilder's novel; each of the above-named critics was addressing his attention to works of fiction inferior to *The Ides of March.* Partly, one assumes the explanation had to do with Wilder's life style. Most of the New York literary establishment—"the family" as it was later characterized by Norman Podhoretz—recalled Wilder's alliance with the late Alexander Woollcott, whom, as a man of letters, they held in contempt. They knew that Wilder frequented the homes of Katharine Cornell, Mabel Dodge Luhan, the Alfred Lunts, Helen Hayes and Charles MacArthur, the Robert Sherwoods, and the Henry Luces. . . . Dupee was fond of recalling the occasion when he encountered Wilder waiting with schoolboy excitement in a Chicago hotel lobby for Mary Pickford. Like Dupee, Dwight Macdonald, who had been an undergraduate at Yale in the 1920s at the moment of Wilder's first great success, regarded him as a snob and a climber. Indeed, Macdonald in the 1950s consigned Wilder, in an influential article, to the eternal purgatory of Mid-Cult. Most of the critics believed Wilder to be wealthy, descended from a moneyed, aristocratic, and influential family. Most of the younger, emerging critics, Kazin, the Trillings, Mary McCarthy, Robert Gorham Davis, none of whom had ever met Wilder, knew him principally as a playwright, author of *Our Town* and *The Skin of Our Teeth* (cribbed from Joyce?). As a novelist, they remembered him from their adolescence as the author

of *The Bridge,* and, from their early adulthood, as the author of a novel
fiercely attacked by Michael Gold.

Even with Edmund Wilson, who had been a friend and mentor,
Wilder had lost touch during the years since the outbreak of World War
II. Early in his career, Wilder had cautiously kept his fences mended in
relation to the prevailing literary establishment of the 1920s, but had
incautiously allowed them to fall into a state of disrepair in the 1940s.
Despite his incessant travel across the United States and Europe, despite
his frequent incursions into New York for dinners at Voisin, the Colony,
and the Oak Room with Sartre or the Laurence Oliviers, Giraudoux or
Ruth Gordon and Garson Kanin, Wilder remained a stranger to the
literary ateliers of the Upper West Side or Greenwich Village. A New
Haven regular, still fascinated by actors and actresses, Wilder did not
mingle with New York writers, editors, or critics. He had long since
abandoned his association with PEN, the writers' association; he did not
even maintain an apartment in New York. One read of his visits to the
metropolis in Leonard Lyons's column, and the items were notable chiefly
because of their infrequency. Sensing his indifference to literary currents
and his aloofness to the struggles and intrigues of the literary quarterlies,
the critics, confronted by the March selection of the Book-of-the-Month
Club, chose to ignore it. Within three months of its publication, *The Ides
of March* had disappeared from view.

In retrospect, one can see that Wilder's sense of timing failed him in
respect to *The Ides of March,* as it had done with *The Woman of
Andros.* The planet had just survived a cataclysm initiated by a trio of
dictators. Yet, Wilder's Caesar was the dictator as tragic hero. Spring 1948
was too soon for Americans to embrace Julius Caesar, the first Roman
duce. Dictators, absolute rulers, and ruthless military commanders were
not, for the moment, eligible for sympathetic and respectful treatment in
the years immediately following the war. Three of the most successful
American novels in the period dealt harshly with authoritarian leaders:
Robert Penn Warren's *All the King's Men,* Norman Mailer's *The Naked
and the Dead,* and Herman Wouk's *The Caine Mutiny.* Given the
climate of expectation that nourished those three books, many readers of
*The Ides of March* were puzzled by the heroic portrayal of the man
whose very name evoked both czar and kaiser and whose namesakes were
historically associated with the massacres of Jewish and Christian
martyrs. The Hollywood moguls knew better; *their* Caesars and their
Romans (unless they became converted) were cast as brutes or degener-
ates (see, for example, *The Robe, Ben Hur, Quo Vadis*). Hollywood's
Julius Caesar was always portrayed by a Louis Calhern whose dissipated
air clearly justified his assassination. Perhaps Michael Gold's baseless
charge that Wilder displayed an aristocratic disdain for the sensibilities

of the common people vaguely echoed in the minds of the liberal and left-wing critics when they had their initial encounter with *The Ides of March*. Considering that Wilder was the first American novelist of consequence to create an existential hero, consciously and deliberately patterned after the ideas set forth by Kierkegaard and Sartre, one wonders whether the book's failure to receive a serious evaluation was a reflection upon the work, or upon the critical establishment.

The indifferent reception to his novel rendered a serious injury to Wilder's morale and to the mysterious source of his creative energies. By the early summer of 1948, aged fifty-one, he had the depressing sense that his day had come and gone. Writing to Alice Toklas at summer's end, 1948, he said that he had embraced Gertrude's "doctrine of indifference-to-audience" and that he would think no more about the critical reception to the novel on which he had built such hopes and to which he had given his best.

But few artists are truly indifferent to audience. Even Gertrude Stein, when asked what she wanted most in the world, unhesitatingly responded with outstretched arms: "Praise, Praise. Praise." And so did Wilder yearn for praise, or at least for the dignity of an analysis of what he had done, an evaluation of his achievement. That same summer, he encountered a friend who had just completed a year's stint at an undistinguished university in upstate New York, tenanted by an undistinguished faculty and attended by undistinguished students. To the teacher's astonishment, within minutes after their meeting, Wilder asked: "What are they saying about my novel upstate?"

They were saying nothing. And they were saying nothing at Harvard or Chicago or Princeton either. The book was not being talked about. In time, good things were said about it in Germany. But that was in another country and, by that time, the book was dead.

# XVI

## Fifteen Years of Uncertainty

*"I'm glad to be home but I don't take home seriously. I'm already dreaming of starting out again."*—WILDER TO A FRIEND

In the decade that followed the publication of *The Ides of March* in 1948, Wilder reverted to a way of life not greatly different from that of the years before the war: traveling between America and Europe, sojourning in remote parts of Mexico, working in libraries (on Lope de Vega), teaching, lecturing, publishing articles in literary quarterlies, and composing introductions to other men's books. But his own imaginative writing, at no time an unbroken stream, now diminished to a trickle. During his fifties, he wrote no fiction at all. He fashioned two new one-act plays which he gave to an American sponsored drama festival in West Berlin, and then he promptly withdrew them; they were consigned to the same storage place that housed *The Alcestiad* and an uncompleted Kafka-inspired play, *The Emporium*. In short, he committed to publication during those ten years nothing except a German translation of *The Alcestiad*.

Wilder was demoralized by the serious critics' indifference to *The Ides of March*. On comparable occasions in the past, he had somehow recovered. The Gold attack on *The Woman of Andros,* for example, had been publicly damaging and intensely humiliating. But Wilder had responded with six new one-act plays and the wonderfully comic novel about his alter ego George Brush. Similarly, the tepid critical reception of *The Merchant of Yonkers* failed to inhibit the writing of *The Skin of Our Teeth*; if Wilder could be cast down by a sense of failure, he had often shown his resilience in the face of it. Until now, it had never incapacitated him.

But at fifty-one, the fear of failure nearly put him out of action. And this time, the fear was deepened by a combination of other circumstances. In 1946, both Wilder's mother and Gertrude Stein died suddenly. Their deaths did not interrupt his work on his novel and, at the time, he seemed not to be staggered by the losses. Yet, each of the two women had provided him with a center of stability and, over the years, he had alternated between them—Mrs. Wilder provided a home base, Miss Stein an intellectual base. The pattern was central to Wilder's existence and, for several years after the two deaths, he still veered back and forth between Isabel at Deepwood Drive and Alice Toklas in Paris, the two surviving women becoming surrogates for the two whom they outlived.

Toward both his mother and Gertrude Stein, Wilder had entertained a curious ambivalence. The depth of his affection for them was great and neither remained out of his thoughts or conversations for very long. Nevertheless, he "neglected" both women in their last years. During his constant absences from home, he wrote his mother less frequently than he might have done; on one occasion, Isabel sharply reprimanded him for having failed to write felicitations on his mother's seventy-fourth birthday. After the outbreak of World War II, Gertrude Stein wrote Isabel that Thornton is faithless, not a letter, not a word, nothing, but then he is that way. She knew he loved them but he is that way. After her death (only weeks after his mother died), he was filled with poignant self-reproach and he communicated the feeling to Alice Toklas.

Actually he did not neglect either his mother or Gertrude Stein. Everything he could reasonably do to ensure health and well-being, he had done for his mother, although it was Isabel who provided the care and companionship. As for Gertrude Stein, she grossly miscalculated the actual situation in wartime Europe, and so remained abroad (despite Wilder's repeated pleas that she return to America), isolated for six years from him and virtually all her other friends. Although he never articulated the thought, Wilder understood perfectly that although he had given both women all that his financial, intellectual, and affectionate resources allowed, their needs were actually inexhaustible; they could, inadvertently perhaps, suffocate him or render him unproductive and ineffectual if he gave them all that they were capable of taking from him. Since early youth he had developed a capacity for self-protection and survival that rendered him invulnerable against everyone, most particularly against those to whom he was most committed. All in all, the loss of these two women deprived him of a sort of ballast. Gertrude's industry, as well as his mother's expectations of him, had been a part of his Puritan conscience. Their passing was a release, but not necessarily a salubrious one.

Another changing circumstance in Wilder's life was an improvement in his finances. A young attorney employed by the New Haven law firm of Wiggin and Dana, Thew Wright, took over the management of Wilder's financial affairs. So prudently did Wright invest Wilder's small capital that the income from it, together with income derived from the stock rights to the 1931 one-act plays (which brought in the astonishing total of $20,000 per year) and the royalties from *Our Town*, netted Wilder an annual amount sufficient to maintain not only Isabel and the invalided Charlotte, but also himself in reasonable comfort. The freedom that came from no longer having to support himself by writing was for Wilder a mixed blessing. On the one hand, he now had the benison of peace of mind; but he also suffered, in exacerbated form, the lack of discipline that had dogged him all his life. Wilder never developed the control and drive that impelled professional writers from John Milton to Henry James to go to their desks for so many hours a day, so many days a week, so many weeks a year—and write (or dictate) because that was what they *did*.

Also, in the 1950s, Wilder found himself being transfigured into an American institution. At fifty, with three Pulitzer Prizes behind him, a play and a novel known to or read by every schoolchild, Wilder was ready for apotheosis. Half a dozen universities in turn, including some of America's most prestigious institutions, conferred honorary degrees on him. The American Academy bestowed its Gold Medal. He was made Honorary Fellow of the Modern Language Association. The French government awarded him a Legion of Honor and something similar eventually came from a president of the United States. He was invited to serve on panels, act as judge of literary contests, travel on roving commissions, and represent the United States at a UNESCO gathering in Venice. Delivered to his home were manuscripts composed by friends, friends of friends, and total strangers. Hundreds sought his recommendation for Guggenheim and Fulbright Fellowships and travel grants. Hundreds more requested his help in getting themselves or their offspring into Choate, Princeton, or Harvard Graduate School. All these demands and requests, while they to some degree exasperated him, gave him the sense of being fully occupied. Did the students at a Tenafly high school dedicate their yearbook to him? They were able to incorporate his handwritten letter of thanks. Was Pace College producing *Our Town*? Its director would receive some cautionary stage directions. Was a school child in Maryland at work on a Thornton Wilder scrapbook? A handwritten contribution was forthcoming . . . and duly reported by the wire services.

The United States was too large a country to transform any of its writers into intimate public figures on the model of England's idolizing James M. Barrie and Bernard Shaw; but a Wilder letter to a young person would generally find its way into the *New York Times* and a commencement address at Harvard would occupy columns in Harry Luce's *Time*. Indeed, in 1953, *Time* made him the subject of its weekly cover story, even though Wilder had published nothing in five years. The magazine portrayed him as a zany and colorful personality, virtually ignoring his career as a serious writer with a corpus behind him, a sensitive artist of unimpeachable integrity who would, typically, refuse an offer to write thirty- to fifty-word captions for *Life* pictorials at $500 per caption.

Despite his fears, sorrows, and distractions, Wilder kept occupied during the 1950s, kept moving, and kept trying to write. His principal creative effort was a play inspired by the work of his newest literary enthusiasm, Kafka. And, just as he had worked arduously on *The Alcestiad* as a play for the talents of Garbo, now he was tailoring *The Emporium* for the young and successful actor Montgomery Clift. Sponsored by Robert Ardrey, Clift had scored his first Broadway success in *The Skin of Our Teeth* as Henry/Cain Antrobus; and through Ardrey, Clift and Wilder became friends. Like a great many young people of intelligence, along with a passion for literature and the theater, Clift hero-worshiped Wilder. Even after he became a Hollywood star, he pursued Wilder, never missing an opportunity to hear him lecture or to join him for a meal when the two of them were in New York. His intellectual regard for Wilder was, naturally, intensified by the prospect of assuming the leading role in *The Emporium*. Clift had never had a starring role on Broadway; his stage career, in fact, never progressed beyond an appearance in a Phoenix Theater production of *The Sea Gull* on the lower East Side, in which he played the part of Trepleff. For that, he had received no plaudits, and the production was a failure.

But *The Emporium* provided a magnificent role, or promised to do so. The play focuses on a young man, one of many whose life is spent in trying to secure a job in The Emporium, a vast and mysterious department store. Hundreds and, over the years, thousands have sought employment in this magical establishment whose hiring practices follow no discernible pattern and whose directors choose people with no discernible qualifications and reject those who seem most obviously qualified. No reasons are ever given. The management itself is never seen, but it transmits its decisions through modest agents. Obviously suggested by Kafka's *The Castle*, The Emporium represents the palace of art through whose doors many seek entrance but few gain admittance. Clift was fascinated; he waited years for Wilder to release the play—in vain. At length, the young actor lost his youth and his looks, and he died expressing his disappointment that Wilder had failed to provide him with what he regarded as the central opportunity of his career.

Wilder's failure to finish the play had nothing to do with his feelings toward Clift. He liked him well enough, even though he was more inclined to the friendship of actresses than actors. He admired Clift for his talent and good looks and was flattered by Clift's adulation of his talent and learning. Nevertheless, despite his good will toward Clift, Wilder abandoned the play in 1952 or 1953, as he had abandoned a number of others, out of a conviction that they were not quite good enough.

In the two years that Wilder worked on *The Emporium*, he spent an inordinate amount of time in libraries both in the United States and in Spain in connection with research into the chronology of the plays of Lope de Vega. He pursued this investigation with professional zeal; but very little of what he accomplished has ever been published, even though scholars in the field of the Spanish Golden Age were impressed by the character of his enterprise. Years later, he admitted with a sigh that his scholarly efforts were not so much a diversion as an escape from his vocation.

In 1948, Wilder departed for London to participate in the rehearsals for a new production of *The Skin of Our Teeth* which Laurence Olivier was again directing; he was also playing Antrobus to the Sabina of his wife, Vivien Leigh. This second British production was not intended for either the British or American theaters, but for Australia. But Wilder did have a play on Broadway in 1948; during the late winter, he enjoyed the belated premiere of his 1931 *The Happy Journey to Trenton and Camden*. Performed as a curtain raiser for Sartre's *The Respectful Prostitute*, Wilder's play evoked little critical interest and, shortly after its opening, it was replaced by another short play entitled *Hope Is a Thing with Feathers* by Richard Harrity. Still, his involvement with the theater continued during the summer of 1948 when he performed at the summer theaters in Bucks County, Pennsylvania, and Westport, Connecticut, in the role of George Antrobus. In contrast with his professional command of the role of the Stage Manager in *Our Town*, Antrobus was clearly beyond his capacities. He was convincing in the essentially comic portraits in the first two acts, but could not really cope with the greater dramatic demands of Act III. He himself understood this, so that although he continued to perform in *Our Town* in subsequent summers, he never again attempted the more difficult role in *The Skin of Our Teeth*.

In the fall of 1948, Wilder again departed for Europe, accompanied at various times not only by Isabel, but also by his brother, Amos, his sister-in-law, and their two children. By November, he had reached Frankfurt-am-Main, where he participated in a University of Chicago seminar, in deference to the wishes of Robert Hutchins, newly divorced from Maude. (Within a year Hutchins married, not, as some Chicagoans expected he would, the widowed Elizabeth (Bobsy) Goodspeed, but an attractive divorcée, his secretary.) From Germany he went on to St. Moritz, a place haunted for him by the ghosts of Robert de Montesquiou (Proust's Charlus) and some of Proust's great ladies. But he found it by this time a minor resort frequented by trippers and featuring at the Palace Hotel a fashion show of gowns by Marcel Rochas. Leaving Amos and his family behind, he headed toward Italy accompanied by Isabel to attend one of the Milan premiere performances of *The Skin of Our Teeth*. After some days at Portofino where he met the musicologist-biographer, Sir Francis Toye, he proceeded to nearby Rapallo where he attended a disappointing dinner with Sir Max and Lady Beerbohm. Then, leaving Isabel behind in Italy, he made his way by train to Madrid; to his pleased astonishment, the customs official at the Spanish border recognized his name, so that when his train reached Barcelona reporters were on hand to interview him. Once in Madrid, he pursued his Lope researches and returned to New Haven in early spring.

He interrupted work on *The Emporium* in order to prepare himself for the Goethe Festival organized by Hutchins at Aspen, Colorado, during the summer of 1949, to commemorate the two-hundredth anniversary of the German poet's birth. Wilder was scheduled to deliver a major address to guests and speakers who would include Albert Schweitzer, Jose Ortega y Gasset, and Stephen Spender. In addition, he was asked to deliver the English translations of Ortega y Gasset's and Schweitzer's addresses, and he called upon both men the evening before to pick up the text of what each planned to say the following day. It has been reported that Ortega y Gasset casually handed Wilder his manuscript; but Schweitzer, after presenting Wilder with the text of his remarks, insisted that Wilder provide him, there and then, with an acceptable translation.

By the fall of 1949, Wilder felt that he had pretty well completed his work on *The Emporium* and, in a letter to Sibyl Colefax, he implied that it was the best work he had done. Despite his professed optimism about the play, however, he must already have had misgivings. For in December, at the very time that he believed that the play was virtually finished, he accepted the post of Charles Eliot Norton Professor, an annual rotating lectureship at Harvard carrying a stipend of $10,000.

Clearly Wilder did not accept the invitation for its financial rewards. His gross income the past year had been over $100,000, and he was under no real money pressures. Perhaps he was gratified to occupy the post that T. S. Eliot had held in 1932–33; he may also have found himself harboring a nostalgia for the academic life, cut off from the "real" world. These were possible reasons, but they were hardly sufficient to impel Wilder to return to something which he had so emphatically abandoned when he resigned from lecturing at Chicago.

Actually, the Norton lectures made up part of Wilder's larger decision to break his ties to Isabel and Deepwood Drive with its large house, built originally to house a family of seven. Now, for long periods of time, Isabel rattled around in the house alone, her life dwindling down to keeping the house ready for Thornton's returns and departures. She had spent most of her adult life providing support for her parents; now she was spending it in the service of her brother. And the idea of consuming the remainder of Isabel's life dismayed Wilder. He felt that the only solution was to begin with selling the house, providing her with a home of her own, and fending for himself. But so radical a change, he believed, would distress her if it were undertaken too precipitously. The first step in the plan would be his physical removal to Cambridge—or at least that was Wilder's rationalization for his return to teaching.

Moreover, the Harvard year, he unconsciously divined, would provide him with another respite from the exercise of his creative faculties. Between preparing an undergraduate course and developing a series of lectures on some classic American writers—Thoreau, Emerson, Whitman, Melville, and Emily Dickinson—there would be no time even to think about plays or novels. Harvard was to be a reprieve from creativity. And so it was. By the time the year drew to an end, *The Emporium* was no closer to completion. Soon the play was securely laid away with other uncompleted and unproduced manuscripts.

The year at Harvard was not an unmitigated success. Wilder lived in Dunster House in a small, somewhat cramped suite. The other Dunster residents were mostly undergraduate students and a few faculty and graduate students who were friendly and hospitable, at least on the surface. But there was an undercurrent of superciliousness toward Wilder, that might be traced to a combination of envy and contempt— envy because Wilder was a bona fide celebrity "who knew everybody";

contempt because they felt Wilder had scholarly pretensions. Some of the proved local scholars, such as Hyder Rollins and Perry Miller, left no doubt that they did not take Wilder seriously.

Some of the resentment and concealed spite was unavoidable. The academic establishment is traditionally inhospitable to distinguished visitors, particularly if the visitor's distinction has been won outside of the university. But Wilder was further vulnerable to the sneers of the Harvard men because he did not behave with the traditional reserve and aloofness, of say, Mr. T. S. Eliot. With his compulsion to be liked, to be friendly with everyone within range, he dissipated an incredible amount of energy in being engaging and interesting, not only at the innumerable cocktail parties and teas that were going on about him, but even to the most casual stragglers who came clustering around his living quarters. Faculty resentment was not diminished when his first two lectures of the fall term, on Whitman and Thoreau, entitled, respectively, "Toward An American Language" and "The American Loneliness," were packed by enthusiastic Cambridge audiences. The lectures were well delivered and they were fresh and unconventional—and solidly based on Gertrude Stein. The administration proposed to Wilder that he offer an undergraduate reading course in the spring term based on great novels, and he went to work.

The year's venture ended badly. Toward the close of the second term, thoroughly exhausted, Wilder collapsed into the university infirmary with a debilitating back ailment and from there he was removed to Massachusetts General Hospital. Even after his release from the hospital, he was in considerable pain and was frequently obliged to lie on the floor to ease his discomfort—a palliative that a number of graduate students considered another of Wilder's "affectations." Moreover, his lecture on Melville was said to have aroused the ire of Professor Miller, who intimidated Wilder to such a degree that the lecture was never published. Nor did Wilder ever prepare for book publication his Charles Eliot Norton Lectures, 1950–51. The whole Harvard venture, he finally admitted, "was a foolish, foolish mistake."

It was during his first term at Harvard, late in 1950, that Wilder sustained another profound loss in the death of Sibyl Colefax. In the passing of his mother and Gertrude Stein, he had lost the two women who had functioned as his moral and intellectual consciences. But Lady Colefax had been something both less and more, resembling in few respects the inventive and productive Gertrude or the fiercely matriarchal, sternly Puritan Isabella Wilder. Wilder's first involvement with Sibyl Colefax had been conventional. He always responded to attractive, intelligent, and worldly women; moreover, knowing her was to know half the world's men of achievement. As a type, how could she have failed to fascinate the man who wrote *The Cabala* and *The Bridge of San Luis Rey*! But over the twenty-two-year span of their acquaintance, the relationship between the two transcended the usual tie between hostess supreme and literary lion. Throughout his life, Wilder's profound need both to give and receive affection was never adequately fulfilled. He loved and was loved by his mother, but any manifestation of the feeling was severely restricted. He expressed his undying devotion to Gertrude Stein and Alice Toklas, but the hard core of that relationship—intellectual, practical, and even calculated—gave the affectional dimension a limitation of its own. But, as time went on in the friendship between him and Sibyl Colefax, the quid pro quo element diminished and the affection increased, at least in Wilder's consciousness, and if his letters of the last years of her life are any indication, she became the supreme mother figure for him.

During the postwar years when Lady Colefax was in her seventies, her spirit indomitable and the loyalty of her friends unshaken, Wilder became more and more concerned about her failing health and her financial condition, which was reputed to be straitened. His letters to her from this period are masterpieces of kindness, generosity, perceptiveness, and tact. Echoing Woollcott's generosity of the 1930s, he urged her to accept his gift of a trip to the United States, financed—as he pointed out—by a surge of royalties from *The Ides of March*. When it became apparent that her health made so long a trip impossible, he invited her for a less-taxing sojourn in the warmth of Italy and southern France. And when he realized that she could no longer travel with him as they had done a dozen years before, he visited her in London as often as he could arrange to.

Even in the very last year of her life, Sibyl's affection for Wilder—her very intense *interest* in him, which by that time would hardly be feigned—moved her to assemble, for what turned out to be his last visit to her, a small but extraordinary group of guests: Noel Coward, Rose Macaulay, Archibald Wavell (the British field marshal and former viceroy of India), and T. S. Eliot, whom he had met several times before. With Eliot, Wilder was able to pour out his enthusiasm for Kierkegaard and, to Eliot's astonishment, Emily Dickinson; with Noel Coward, he felt that he had finally overcome his awe for the most stylish and successful playwright, wit, and man of the world that England had produced since Oscar Wilde. Only Earl Wavell, aged sixty-seven and in the last year of his life, proved too formidable a personage for Wilder to tackle.

A few months after meeting Eliot, he attended a New York performance of *The Cocktail Party;* a year or so before Eliot had described it to

Wilder as his first attempt at "a *real* play." Although his feelings toward Eliot were most friendly—he was reverential toward the foremost poet writing in English—his reaction to Eliot's play was actively and excitedly hostile. Wilder watched the play with tense absorption throughout because he felt it was asking important questions. And as the evening progressed, Wilder expected there would be important answers. But instead of answers or affirmations, what came through for Wilder was an ungenerous, fastidious, low opinion of human nature. In Wilder's eyes, Eliot posits that since people are stupid, egocentric, mistaken dolts, their only chance to escape their predicament is to be seized by a vaguely adumbrated quality of sainthood. For Wilder, such a view of the world was sadly lacking: just because an artist is offended by the limitations of human nature he does not withdraw shuddering from it; he does not divide mankind into the Yahoos and those who are in a state of grace. Wilder concluded that Eliot was wholly deficient in *caritas,* charity, which Jesus had called the greatest of all virtues.

Eliot, Wilder felt, was the victim of his own dogmatism, which had dried his heart and stopped his ears and rendered him inattentive to the true state of mankind. One whiff of Tolstoi would blow all of *The Cocktail Party* away. In one of his very last letters to Sibyl Colefax, Wilder took note of the widely circulated reports that she was the Julia of Eliot's play and vehemently denied the justice of the parallel and added that she was neither the babbling hostess of Act I nor the Ministrix of the Mysteries of Act II. He pronounced her rather the Fighting Spirit of the world in which we live and work and, with the aid of the Sibyl Colefaxes, learn our way. Eliot, Wilder was convinced, was morally, intellectually, and politically a snob; the ordinary working man and woman evoked in him little more than a shudder. Such a sense of man provoked in the heart of the author of *The Happy Journey* and *Our Town* a most deeply felt aversion.*

Sibyl Colefax's death did not seem to those who knew Wilder well to have a strong effect upon him. He was not a mourner: he spoke of the dead casually, even lightheartedly, as though they were next-door neighbors who had suddenly decided to take up residence in remote parts of the

---

* A year before Wilder's meeting Eliot at Lady Colefax's, he had gone to Saint Elizabeth's Hospital for the Criminally Insane in Washington where Ezra Pound was incarcerated. Just as he venerated Eliot for his genius, so did he respect Pound. But Pound's anti-Semitic frenzy and his "messianic omniscience on politico-economico-financial reform" dismayed and revolted Wilder. It was on this occasion that Pound astonished Wilder (who thought he was meeting the poet for the first time) by telling him that they had met once before at the home of Adolfo de Bosis in Rome, in 1921. Both men had extraordinary memories, but it would appear that Pound's was something even more than extraordinary. In any case, Wilder was among those instrumental in securing Pound's release from the hospital.

globe. Nevertheless, she was the last of his spiritual mothers, the woman in whom he had found a synthesis of all the womanly virtues. No American writer since James has written more effectively about women or better understood the subtleties and capacities of the woman's mind and spirit. It was to this quality of Wilder's genius that Sibyl Colefax responded. If she was not his ideal reader or his most perceptive critic, then she often seemed to be the one whom Wilder wanted most to please. To her he revealed his journals, his works in progress, and his evaluations of the work of his contemporaries. Not even to her, of course, did he ever truly open his heart. But he shared with her a great deal more than he shared with virtually anyone else. When she died, he had only Alice Toklas, and Alice was only an echo of Gertrude; also, Alice, too, was growing very old.* As for Sibyl, her death was a reminder of his own mortality; worse yet, she was the last important figure in his life in whose presence he felt youthful. Her decline and death were for him at fifty-three the ineluctable intimations that his own old age was imminent—a state he contemplated with more horror than death itself. If Goethe and Verdi were two of his chief heroes, it was, in part, because they had conquered their old age, an achievement he desperately wished to emulate though he was not quite certain how it could be accomplished.

By the fall of 1951, Wilder was no longer certain of anything. The Harvard year was followed by three years of wandering, indecisions, false starts, and sudden resolves combined with a profound unresolved restlessness. When he completed his year in Cambridge he went off to Europe, hoping to ready the Harvard lectures for publication. He saw Alice Toklas and many other old friends; Tennessee Williams invited him and Isabel to a spaghetti dinner. But in a very short time he was ready to return to America, though not to Deepwood Drive. Dispatching Isabel to Italy for the winter, he thought first about acquiring a cottage in Bucks County, Pennsylvania. But he was plagued by a persistent cold that chronically clogged his ears, and went off, instead, to Daytona Beach where he continued to struggle with the Harvard lectures. Finally, in the spring, he returned to Deepwood Drive, expressing his determination to secure a house in Brooklyn Heights overlooking New York harbor. There, an Italian couple could look after him and provide him with the Italian food he loved. These fantasies came from his obsessive determination to disentangle himself from the responsibility of providing a focus for Isabel. All his adult life he had been fighting off anything and anyone who restricted his sense of freedom. The house on Deepwood Drive

* Virgil Thomson has asserted—in one of his reviews for the *New York Review of Books*—that Alice didn't really like Thornton, but merely that she found him useful.

symbolized her dependence. Now past fifty, periodically incapacitated by neurological complaints, she required Thornton's financial support. *But he did not want to go on living with her.* And he was desperate to make the break.

Still, he didn't.

Why not? He probably never knew himself. Ruthless in preserving his independence, he was unable to be ruthless with Isabel who, whatever her deficiencies, was fiercely loyal and utterly vulnerable. His indecisiveness in this critical matter may have been a manifestation of his essential and instinctive kindness, his inability to be confronted by pain that he himself inflicted; or it may have been his own fierce loyalty to family, his ultimate inability to finally detach himself from it. Or perhaps he understood that he could not exist permanently separated, that he had to belong to something, that Isabel was really the only one there was, and that her demands were less than anyone else's might be. But at the age of fifty-five, he was struggling desperately to make a break; this final struggle, as unsuccessful as the several that preceded it, so utterly possessed him that it may account for his never completing either the Harvard lectures or *The Emporium.* And, together, these two projects occupied hundreds of hours of writing during what turned out to be three wholly unproductive years.

Between the summer of 1951 and the summer of 1954, Wilder worked in Cambridge (Massachusetts), the MacDowell Colony, Paris, St. Moritz, Munich, Newport, Key West, Princeton, and Daytona Beach. During that entire period, except for a few weeks when he served as the secretary of a UNESCO conference on the arts in Venice (September 1952), he was the master of his own time and place. Yet unproductive months succeeded one another; nothing emerged that he could either publish or produce upon a stage. Even a collaboration with the Italian film director Vittorio de Sica came to little. But, in July 1954, there arrived a respite from failure, a reprieve leading to the most ironic success of Wilder's entire life.

Tyrone Guthrie, the distinguished British stage director, was invited to produce a play for the 1954 Edinburgh Festival. He and Wilder joined forces, Wilder offering to rework his discredited and condemned *Merchant of Yonkers,* a play he believed ideal for Guthrie's comedic talents. For several weeks before rehearsals began, Wilder worked with Guthrie on the script, under the new title of *The Matchmaker.* Although a general impression existed that he had extensively reworked the older play, he, in fact, changed virtually nothing. Sixteen years had passed since the original version was written so that here and there it was necessary to bring an idiom up to date. In a few instances, dialogue was transposed or slightly rearranged. But the only significant differences in the two versions were doubling the length of Dolly Levi's monologue in the fourth act (a brilliant addition which provides her with a significant extra dimension) and adding some farcical stage directions, presumably as Dr. Guthrie's contribution. One final change was the addition of Barnaby's curtain speech in response to Mrs. Levi's directive that he tell the audience what the play had been about:

> Oh, I think it's about . . . I think it's about adventure. The test of an adventure is that when you're in the middle of it, you say to yourself, "Oh, now I've got myself into an awful mess; I wish I were sitting quietly at home." And the sign that something's wrong with you is when you sit quietly at home wishing you were out having lots of adventure. So that now we all want to thank you for coming tonight, and we all hope that in your lives you have just the right amount of sitting quietly at home and just the right amount of adventure!*

There is a touching irony in those lines: at the moment that Wilder composed them he felt that he essentially had no home, or that he would dearly like to disencumber himself of the house that he owned so that he could have a home of his own.

Thus, in describing *The Matchmaker* as a "rewritten version of *The Merchant of Yonkers*," Wilder was somewhat overstating the case; the newer play was a slightly augmented version of the original, which during the years of its obscurity Wilder often defended as his "best play." He worked with Guthrie in Stratford, Ontario, where the director was supervising a Shakespeare festival. Once the text was fixed, the manuscript was taken to Scotland and rehearsals began with a cast representing artists of both the English and the American theater. The smaller roles were undertaken by British actors, and only Eileen Herlie as Mrs. Malloy and Alec McCowen as Barnaby Tucker represented Britain in the major parts. The other principals were American: Sam Levene as Horace Vandergelder, Arthur Hill as Cornelius Hackl, and Ruth Gordon as Dolly Levi. Tanya Moiseiwitsch designed the sets, and the play had its premiere at the Royal Lyceum Theater, Edinburgh, on August 23. The production was so successful at the festival that it was transferred to London's Theater Royal in November with the same cast, and a New York production was considered for the fall of 1955.

Wilder did not remain in England for the London premiere. Instead he crossed over to France and in October settled for six months in Aix-en-

---

* Owing to a typist's error, published versions of this final speech are corrupt. Wilder sent the correct version to this author in a letter dated April 17, 1968.

Provence where he knew scarcely anyone and thought he would be able to work. But what play or plays he completed in Aix is uncertain. Undoubtedly, though, they included the two gloomy one-acters he offered to the 1957 festival in West Berlin, *Bernice* and *The Wreck of the 5:25,* neither of which was ever published. Wilder's sequestering of these two plays is regrettable, since they reveal a dimension of his thematic concerns not associated with any of his published plays. Both are about alienation and can be traced to Wilder's postwar preoccupation with existentialism.

In *The Wreck of the 5:25,* a mother and daughter are awaiting the return of the man of the house, a minor functionary in a New York bank. Their vigil is interrupted when a neighbor telephones that a man is lurking outside the living room window peering in at the two. The police have been notified. But moments later, the husband arrives. It was he, as he explains, who had been looking into his own house. Earlier that day, a regular client of the bank died leaving him a legacy of $25,000 and urging him "from beyond the grave" to look more directly at life. As a result of the dead woman's message, the man envisages a wreck on his commuter train and then goes on to imagine an all-out nuclear war—in short, the abrupt and total destruction of the world he had secretly and cynically rejected his entire life. The play ends with the man announcing his determination to live more actively and acceptingly in the heart of his family, after having seen them anew behind the glass walls of their home. But in the last line of the play we discover that the police *had* come, had searched him on his own grounds, and had confiscated the gun with which he had intended to take someone's life, presumably his own.

The play is conventional in form—it could have been written in the first two or three decades of the twentieth century—and, despite its content, it is wholly free of melodrama or self-pity. The play is rather brisk, humorous, and evocative (like Wilder's other plays), but it also creates a new tension that is released only at the moment when the audience discovers that the cheerful and energetic commuter has been on the verge of blowing up his own comfortable little world. The optimistic note that characteristically ends Wilder's plays is absent; rather we are left chilled and uneasy as the play comes to its abrupt, but inevitable, conclusion.

The second play, *Bernice,* is even more starkly alienated than *The Wreck of the 5:25.* This piece concerns a released convict, formerly a solid citizen, who had successfully embezzled a large sum of money. Now free to enjoy his illegally acquired wealth, he has returned to his home in a small, midwestern city. His wife and daughter have long ago moved away in disgrace, but the embezzler has engaged a black woman named

Bernice to clean the house and cook for him. She is already installed when he arrives from prison. As she prepares the man's first meal, she tells him that his daughter has been trying to get in touch with him because she wants to return to the house and look after her father. Bernice, realizing that the man is inclined to effect the reconciliation, confesses to her own past: she has also been separated from a daughter when she served a jail term for murder. And she too was tempted to upset her child's new adjustment to life, but realized, in time, that both she and her daughter could survive only separately and not together. Pointing out the similarity of her case to her employer's, she tells him that reconciliation with their daughters would mean that they have to come to terms with a society from which both she and her employer are permanently estranged. The play ends with the man asking Bernice to send away his daughter who will arrive momentarily. He has determined to finish out his life alone.

These plays, clearly enough, share several images. Both men return to a house, a longtime dwelling place, from which they have been absent either psychologically or physically for an extended period of time. In both plays, the protagonist has acquired a large sum of money, not through his own or legitimate effort. Both men are husbands, and each is the father of an adolescent girl. Their respective daughters adore them and would give up everything for them. Both men are guilty and defiant; there is an element of violence in each of them.

What is to be made of these plays, so different from anything that Wilder had previously released to the theater? A young Wilder critic, Malcolm Goldstein, in his study *The Art of Thornton Wilder,* reports being told by Isabel Wilder that the plays were poorly received at their Berlin festival premieres and that they were withdrawn as a consequence. This information suggests that Wilder was unwilling to risk failure in an American production. But one may also speculate that Wilder—once the plays were presented on a stage—may have become apprehensive about their biographical implications.

At first glance, neither the commuter nor the former convict shows much resemblance to Wilder, who had been neither a husband nor a father; and his modest capital had come to him neither through a freak inheritance nor through embezzlement, but rather through his own honest efforts. The humanist, playwright, and novelist seems to be wholly removed from the two prototypical American businessmen in the plays. But the links between Wilder and the two characters are unmistakable. The somber and deliberate embezzler, rational, prideful, and self-disciplined, is the mature Thornton Wilder with his genial mask removed. Scrupulously honest in money matters, Wilder nonetheless had been accused on more than one occasion of appropriating literary materials belonging to others. He had described himself not as an innovator, but as a rediscoverer of forgotten goods.* And there are other bases for comparing Wilder to the character in *Bernice*. Both men carry the stigma of guilt (of different kinds), and, moreover, Wilder, like most public figures, had been sniggeringly accused of a variety of scandalous acts and sexual improprieties over the years, of which he was, most unhappily, quite innocent. Both the stage character and Wilder himself return to a home in a moderate-sized community they detest (or think they do), although that home happens to be the only place they can go. Seen in this light, *Bernice* takes on the quality of a Wilder nightmare. In a dream, Wilder stands convicted and disgraced. His former friends, relatives, family, neighbors, and associates have uniformly turned away from him. There is nothing in his former community that holds the slightest interest for him. Yet, when he is released from prison and given his freedom, the house that had been his home for the whole of his adulthood draws him back, in spite of himself, inexorably like a magnet. In the dream he can visualize the house empty of all its former inhabitants, empty even of its imaginary daughter who adores him and wants nothing except to serve him; but he cannot wrench himself free of the house itself. The house, together with the hoard of money that can never be taken away from him, are the two elements in his life that are stable, permanent, and perdurable. They both provide him with freedom and make freedom impossible. For they constitute two vital elements of his identity, the house and the hoard. To cut himself loose from either would be to lose his identity. And as the commuter makes clear at the end of *his* play, changing your identity is the equivalent of putting a bullet through your brain.

The bouncy commuter is more recognizably the gregarious Wilder of cocktail parties and social gatherings, the Wilder who is torn between watching unseen the homely, familiar actions of homely, familiar people and becoming himself a part of that action. *The Wreck of the 5:25* poignantly dramatizes the central dilemma of Wilder's existence in the mid-1950s. Like the commuter of the play, he occupied a respected

---

* As was observed earlier in this study, no one could seriously hold Wilder culpable for the uses he has made of literature that preceded his own. What is important to reflect upon in connection with a consideration of *Bernice* is that members of the American community read in their newspapers and magazines that he had been accused of a (literary) crime: plagiarism or literary embezzlement. One of his critics writing to the *Saturday Review* demanded that Wilder turn over a share of his royalties from *The Skin of Our Teeth* to the estate of James Joyce, Joyce himself having predeceased the production of the play, which Wilder later stated was "deeply indebted to . . . *Finnegans Wake*."

position in his suburban community—and in the American community as well—which Wilder, except in dreams, realized had no interest in vague and insubstantial accusations of literary peccadilloes. If there had been a wreck of the 5:25, if Wilder had walked away from the train that would otherwise have delivered him to Hamden and 50 Deepwood Drive, if he had—as the commuter in the play had fantasized—inspected and chosen for himself a new community, then he could have fashioned for himself a new identity and written a new kind of play, or novel, or story. But there was no wreck of the 5:25. Wilder was irrevocably committed to his New Haven suburb and to writing whatever it was that his good neighbors and the Yale community regarded as appropriate for him to write. Since he lacked the will to erase his identity (or to put a bullet through his head), his only remaining choice was to take the train and get off at the right stop because no more catastrophes, like World War II, would prevent the New Haven Railroad from taking him to where he was supposed to go.

The images of the two houses in the plays underscore an ambivalence that threads through Wilder's life. As a writer, as an artist, and as a "criminal" (it was Thomas Mann—as Wilder well knew—who postulated the curious, but thoroughly sound, notion that literary artists are necessarily "confidence men"), Wilder dreamed of a house where he could live undisturbed, attended only by an impersonal housekeeper. The idea of someone else living there, who could single-mindedly and devotedly minister to his emotional needs, was a consideration that he turned over in his mind and finally rejected; he could not afford to support that kind of relationship and be free. The house he had built a quarter of a century before in Hamden might, in his reverie, have served such a purpose. It was isolated enough, it was comfortable, it was his. It is the house in *Bernice,* though emptied of Isabel and closed to incursions from friends, relatives, and neighbors. One part of him ached for such a refuge, and because he knew that the house on Deepwood Drive could never serve as such, he fancied it removed to Bucks County, Oakland, Tucson, Brooklyn Heights, or Newport.

The other house in Wilder's life was a real house, standing in the midst of a real community, visited by real neighbors, relatives, and friends, presided over by his mother and then by Isabel, filled with familiar household possessions, the accretion of a lifetime, a house whose modest grounds were regularly tended like scores of other houses in the Hamden–New Haven community. Yet the two houses in the two plays are evidently the same. That is to say, in his imagination having merged the two homes, Wilder separated them again as he had separated the private and the gregarious elements of his nature. Wilder's compulsion to belong was even stronger than his need for solitude. One must see the two plays as one single play in which dream is succeeded by fantasy, and fantasy by reality.

The two plays underscore another aspect of their author: a certain unexpected and unaccountable provinciality. From the very outset of his career, with the publication of *The Cabala,* critics have referred to Wilder's urbanity and sophistication. While there can be no question about his broad academic learning—no American playwright or novelist in three generations has read so widely as he—his urbanity is another question. Except for *The Cabala,* his work dealt exclusively with provincial life (Even Caesar's Rome reminds one more of New Haven than it does of Paris, London, or New York.) The locales of his work are centered, after *The Cabala,* in Lima, Peru; a Greek island; midwest America and the rooming house district of St. Louis; Newark and Camden; the French quarter of New Orleans; Grover's Corners; Yonkers and the little old New York of the 1880s; Excelsior, New Jersey; southern Illinois; and Newport, Rhode Island. Wilder never resided in large cities, he merely visited them. Even his five-year residence at the University of Chicago was temporary and fragmented. Half the year he was either lecturing, working in Hollywood, or domiciled in Hamden; his sojourn in Chicago was spent partly in a university dormitory, partly in a furnished apartment near the campus. Still, Chicago was the closest Wilder ever came to participation in urban life. His sojourns in New York, London, and Paris were visits; he knew some of these cities' most celebrated and representative inhabitants, but he was never part of any of them, as James once was part of London, or Hemingway of Paris, or Edith Wharton of New York.

It is a sign of Wilder's provincialism that his two closest friends in New York were Alexander Woollcott and Ruth Gordon, who embodied for him the glitter, the wit, and the knowingness of the cultural and financial capital of America. It was precisely because he was a visitor and not a denizen that he remained fascinated by the gossip about celebrities of which Woollcott and Miss Gordon had an inexhaustible store. But their dazzle and sheen also repelled him. The house in *The Wreck of the 5:25* had to be deep in suburbia because Wilder had always to return to his provincial refuge where well-read, well-behaved people, together with an extensive university library, provided him with all the security he required after his excursions with the irreverent, unconventional, sacrilegious, and ribald frequenters of the Oak Room, the Algonquin, and the Colony.

What Wilder seldom experienced in his visits to the great cities was the real life going on in the cities' homes. By his own choice, his meetings took place in restaurants, bars, theaters, and sometimes clubs. Though he knew almost by heart the work of Proust and James who draw the reader into the great houses of Paris, or New York or London, Wilder became, in his own writing, fixed in suburban living rooms, small town kitchens, and exurban dining rooms. It was, finally, his own impatience with a milieu he had evoked once too often that made him withdraw two of the best short plays written by a master of the one-act play.*

*The Matchmaker*'s success in Scotland and England in 1954 prompted David Merrick to bring the London production to New York. Sam Levene relinquished his role and, in New York, Loring Smith played Horace Vandergelder. The only other important cast change involved the part of Barnaby. The British actor Alec McCowen withdrew and was replaced by Robert Morse, whose successful career essentially began with this role. Eight years later, the musical comedy version of *The Matchmaker* earned Wilder a sizable fortune. *The Merchant of Yonkers*, which closed after twenty-eight performances, enjoyed a second reincarnation as the 1964 Broadway musical *Hello, Dolly!;* and for years that show earned Wilder more than all his other writings combined.

During the six months that Wilder spent writing at Aix-en-Provence during the winter of 1954–55, he revised and completed the play he had begun before World War II and had tried to complete in 1945–46 before he laid it aside in favor of *The Ides of March.* The play, of course, was *The Alcestiad,* promised to Tyrone Guthrie for production at the 1955 Edinburgh Festival. Wilder was present for the late-August premiere at a theater-in-the-round; Irene Worth played the demanding role of Alcestis, who, during the course of the play, metamorphoses from a teenage girl to an old woman. Wilder's hopes for the play's success were mixed. His first new stage work in thirteen years, *The Alcestiad* (rechristened by Guthrie *A Life in the Sun*), elicited a great deal of interest on both sides of the Atlantic. Reporters appeared from everywhere and Wilder was obliged to hold a news conference to brief correspondents and critics about the play that they were to see. But despite all of these encouraging portents,

* This charge of provincialism, brought by some of Wilder's most energetic admirers and friends, is not so much a criticism as it is a description. Some of the most respected writers in English, from Jane Austen to Emerson to Mark Twain are provincial rather than urban in their scope. But the writer who lives apart from his nation's cultural capital is apt not to be sensitive to or aware of the continuing moral, economic, political, sociological, and aesthetic ferment which the constant influx of "the new men and women" provides. Edward Albee's *The Zoo Story* or Leroi Jones' *Dutchman* would hardly have been conceived or executed had their respective authors occasionally visited New York from homes in Schenectady or Richmond, Virginia. In modern times (and for the most part in the ancient world as well), the breakdown, change, and realignment of a civilization is initially experienced in the capital cities, and there is a lag before the rest of a country absorbs the shock. His lack of commitment to city life may partly explain why Wilder generally chose to locate his plays and stories in the past.

Wilder felt that Guthrie had somehow bungled the direction; although the play was based upon classical sources and was predominantly philosophical in spirit, Wilder had envisaged a brisk, dry, sometimes ironic, sometimes farcical treatment of the materials. Instead, the play moved slowly and portentously on stage, coming across more like Hoffmansthal than Anouilh or Giraudoux. The first night audience confirmed Wilder's fears, delivering a response that was somehow barren of any genuine enthusiasm. The British newspapers that Wilder read during breakfast next day published reviews that ranged from polite, to tepid, to hostile.

Two devastating attacks on the play appeared in London's Sunday *Times* and in the *Observer*, in reviews written by Harold Hobson and Kenneth Tynan, respectively. Hobson described Wilder as "an excellent dramatist who, in ill-advised moments, seems to fancy himself as a thinker. This leads to a terrifying superficiality, and to dullness . . . efforts to explain why God chastens those whom he loves end only in confusion and boredom, a plethora of flamboyant speeches, uncommunicative gestures and much depressing coming and going, noise and screaming." Tynan's attack was even more deadly: he began by faulting the play's dramatic structure, described Alcestis as "that dramatic nullity, the perfect, changeless, humourless human being"; in addition to calling the play "dramatically lame and philosophically indigestible," he decried its failure of language:

> Mr. Wilder fatally embarks on a sort of bald "timeless" prose which reads like a translation, has too many sentences beginning with "And," and narrowly avoids the ultimate affectation of beginning a sentence with "For."

Wilder's disappointment was temporarily mitigated when Jed Harris came to Edinburgh to view the play and decide whether he would give it a New York exposure. A night or two after the opening as Wilder was walking back to his hotel from a concert, he told a friend—pointing to the theater where *A Life in the Sun* was being performed—"Jed Harris is in that theater right now watching my play. I want *him* to produce it back home." Somehow Wilder had staked his hopes on Harris's reactions. Alas, Harris's dismissal of the play confirmed all of Wilder's fears about its possibilities. He promptly withdrew the play after the conclusion of its Festival run. It became unavailable for either a London or a New York production.*

---

* Retitled *The Alcestiad* (actually *Die Alkestiade*) , the play was subsequently released to several German-speaking cities, notably Berlin, Frankfurt, Munich, Zurich, and Vienna. Translated into German by Herberth Herlitschka in 1960, the Frankfurt-am-Main edition of the play is the only available version, although Wilder has permitted

*The Alcestiad* was to be Wilder's last full-length play. During the next seven years his creative efforts were focused upon a project involving two cycles of one-act plays, one entitled *The Seven Deadly Sins,* the other *The Seven Ages of Man.* Of these projected fourteen short plays, only five have thus far been released for performance, and only one of them has been published. The five plays that have been staged include the afore-mentioned *The Wreck of the 5:25* and *Bernice,* together with three plays that were produced and directed by Jose Quintero at the Circle in the Square on Bleecker Street, in New York's Greenwich Village. The trio entitled *Plays for Bleecker Street* were *Infancy, Childhood,* and *Someone from Assisi. Childhood* was published in the November 1960 issue of the *Atlantic* and, together with *Infancy,* it has been shown on educational television. Another very short play, *The Drunken Sisters,* which in the classical Greek tradition is a comic postlude to *The Alcestiad,* was also published in the *Atlantic* (November 1957). In addition to the two published plays, Wilder's only other new published work for a dozen years after the 1955 failure of *The Alcestiad* was a long interview with this writer that appeared in the *Paris Review* series, *The Art of Fiction* (spring 1957), subsequently republished in *Writers at Work* (Viking, 1958).

For seven years after 1955, Wilder moved about restlessly, continuing to visit Italy, Austria, Germany, and Switzerland, always hoping to find in one of those countries the ideal site where he could settle down indefinitely and work. No such place ever materialized although he returned again and again to St. Moritz where the winters seemed to agree with him.

Also, during those seven years of wandering both in Europe and across the American continent with occasional forays into Mexico, Wilder indulged his lifelong interest in music by collaborating with two composers, Paul Hindemith and Louise Talma, for each of whom he provided an operatic libretto. The Hindemith work was based on Wilder's 1931 one-act play *The Long Christmas Dinner.* Hindemith, in addition to composing the score, translated Wilder's libretto into German, and the opera was given its first performance in Mannheim, Germany, on December 20, 1961. The opera by Louise Talma was a much more ambitious work, involving years of collaboration with Wilder. Their joint effort, extending over a period of about six years, culminated in a production of *Die Alkestiade* at the Frankfurt-am-Main opera house on March 2, 1962.

---

scholars from time to time to borrow the typescript. The German productions were not unsuccessful; it is the kind of play that fits into the long and honorable Germanic theatrical tradition of free translations and adaptations of Greek drama that reflect the philosophical concerns of an era.

Despite the participation of two of Germany's most respected singers, Inge Borkh and the late Max Lorenz, the opera was not well received, and it has shown no evidence in succeeding decades of being absorbed into the repertory of any opera company.

In perspective, one sees that in the fifteen-year period that followed the completion of *The Ides of March* Wilder developed as a public figure and declined as a writer. During those fifteen years, he released five short plays, one full-length play, a revised comedy, two operatic librettos, a long analysis of his own writing, and two or three feuilletons on *Finnegans Wake,* Lope de Vega, and the state of the nation. These fifteen years comprised the years of Wilder's life between fifty and sixty-five; since a number of writers, perhaps a majority, end their careers when they reach fifty, there is nothing exceptional about Wilder's diminished productivity. But he himself was tortured and exasperated by his sense of failure; he felt that as he achieved higher levels of understanding and added to his experience of life he ought to be capable of writing more and better. This was a line of reasoning thoroughly in keeping with his pragmatic, New England background. Work was holy and the enjoyment of leisure was a sin. Added to his burden of guilt was the family tradition that considered theological speculation man's highest attainment, a position shared by generations of impoverished eastern European Jews, the most dedicated of whom devoted their lives to interpreting their holy books. The principal theme that runs through Wilder's *Paris Review* interview is that his work became more and more philosophical as it became more mature, that it attempted to reflect the essence of the American spirit and the relation of man to an eternal force. Though Wilder seldom mentioned it, his world view was saturated with selective Emersonian thoughts; one might suspect that it was not old age, but Emerson and the New England tradition that crippled his talent and stifled his imagination.

Wilder was both an artist and a man of passion. The sexual passions, controlled in his daily life, dominated his first three novels. At thirty-three, having turned away from love, he began his long, ironic but affectionate examination of American family life. At fifty, with *The Ides of March,* his work abruptly attempted to transcend both sexual passion and affectional ties: his theme iterates that reason, wisdom, and disinterestedness necessarily fall victim to the forces of egotism, veniality, ambition, and brutality. An admirable and absorbing novel, *The Ides of March,* was nevertheless overlaid with a forbidding chill, a remoteness between writer and reader that characterized Wilder's work thereafter. Wilder's perception of the failure of *The Ides of March* had turned him

back to drama. But that same philosophic glaze that characterized the
novel limited the appeal of his Bleecker Street plays. By 1962, having
reached the age of sixty-five, Wilder made a double decision: to retire
from playwriting and to leave home.

# XVII

## The Eighth Day

The year 1962, when Wilder was 65, turned out to be a year full of honors. Although the Frankfurt premiere of the opera *Die Alkestiade* was a failure, the criticism was directed against the music and not the libretto. Some of the critics, in fact, lamented that the music was unworthy of the text and others described the event as a play with music. Wilder, together with Isabel, had been on hand for the opening and the Germans accorded him the respect they felt due a man of artistic genius. No other country held him in such great esteem as Germany, whose government decorated him and whose scholars awarded him the Goethe Plakette.

Several weeks before the Frankfurt opening of *Die Alkestiade*, the *Plays for Bleecker Street* had been favorably received by the New York critics; whatever tempered reservations the reviews might have revealed, the three plays settled down to a respectable run. Furthermore, on the occasion of a reception by President Kennedy for Nobel Prizewinners at the White House, Wilder, as a guest of the Cabinet, was invited to read from his work in the auditorium of the Department of State. The critical reception to the Bleecker Street plays, the German accolades for the operatic librettos (*The Long Christmas Dinner* had preceded *The Alcestiad* by only seven weeks), and the Kennedy invitation all served to reinforce Wilder's status as an institution. Among those writers who were

245

his contemporaries, only Dos Passos, Faulkner, Steinbeck, and Glenway Wescott were still alive; but Wilder's aura of intellectuality combined with his popularity endeared him to the American establishment. For them, he had redeemed his promise of becoming what an American writer ought to be.

But Wilder did not take kindly to the idea of having become an institution; nor did he enjoy contemplating the possibility that he had written himself out. He remained vigorous and enjoyed relatively good health, despite being subject to long winter colds that brought on temporary deafness. His once trim body had turned corpulent, but his intellectual capacities remained undiminished, and he resumed his explications of *Finnegans Wake,* by publishing an article based on that work, *Bruno's Last Meal,* in the spring issue, 1963, of the *Hudson Review.* The most significant change that came over Wilder in his sixties was temperamental. Having been described in his thirties by Woollcott as a gadfly (a description that in its classical reference was kindly intended), Wilder now became somewhat waspish, more obviously intolerant of the faults and deficiencies of others. As long ago as the twenties, Hugh Walpole had shrewdly noted a "little core of sharp malicious humour" in Wilder. Now, the quality of his malice, though it remained discreetly concealed from all but his intimates (of whom there were astonishingly few), could no longer be described as slight. Not even his best friends, Robert Hutchins and Ruth Gordon, not even the faithful Isabel, when they were out of sight (and sometimes when they were plainly visible) were safe from his barbs. As for the young scholars who paid him homage, writing theses and dissertations about his work, their efforts were contemptuously and even savagely dismissed. But never publicly, and not directly. Wilder as a pedagogue had usually managed to be interesting; but he had been more a lecturer than a teacher. Even when he was young, he listened to his students only long enough to note the immaturity or the incompetence of their ideas; but his criticism had charm and humor, affection and value. In his late years, there was less charm or humor or affection. His strictures became stern, intense, and sometimes deeply wounding. A few old friends, when he announced that he was going to disappear into the Arizona desert, were reminded of Timon of Athens.

He departed for Arizona on May 20, 1962, uncertain about the length of his sojourn. His principal aim was to isolate himself from the various worldly temptations that had, he believed, prevented him from writing well and successfully. He was prepared to remain in the desert for at least two years, and he envisaged for himself a small house, at easy driving distance from a town with a bar, and not too far removed from a university library. As it turned out, he found himself moving around from place to place and after a year in the Southwest he could bear it no longer. By the fall of 1963, he was back in New Haven where it turned out that his exposure to the desert sun had caused skin cancer on the face. He was successfully treated for the condition at the medical facilities in what finally and irrevocably had become his home town, Hamden-New Haven, Connecticut.

But he had not come back from Arizona emptyhanded. After fifteen years of frustration and disappointments, Wilder had made considerable progress on a major undertaking, a novel more ambitious in scope than anything he had previously attempted—and twice the length. The writing took four years. When the book was finally published in the spring of 1967 by Harper & Row, it achieved modest bestsellerdom, with book-club adoptions as well as continuing circulation as a paperback after its initial publication. The financial rewards meant little to Wilder; because of the income from *Hello, Dolly!*, the royalties accruing from the novel were an income tax embarrassment. To avoid turning over all the money to the United States Treasury, Wilder assigned the profits from the novel to its dedicatee, Isabel Wilder. (Isabel was the first member of the family to receive a dedication since their mother was named in *The Bridge of San Luis Rey*.) *

Of all of Wilder's work, *The Eighth Day* is the most difficult to analyze and evaluate. Its beginnings suggests that it is a mystery novel. And a mystery it is indeed with a construction (who killed X and why?) not greatly different from that of *The Brothers Karamazov*. And just as *The Brothers* is essentially Russian, *The Eighth Day* is essentially American, one of the most consciously *American* novels written in this century. Wilder's feeling for and about America, first manifested in *The Cabala*, was sounded again in *Our Town* and became fully developed in *The Eighth Day*. The idea that the United States is the last best hope on earth, in the light of current history, has a decidedly hollow ring. The central irony in *The Eighth Day* is that even at the turn of the century, when the main action of the novel takes place, the American Dream had already gone sour. This was the onset of the twentieth century when the United States entered into decades of gargantuan productivity and planetary influence, together with a resurgence of hope that the American example might lead man toward new horizons. In presenting the history of two American families, the Ashleys and the Lansings, Wilder provides some interesting clues to the reasons for America's potential success and its actual failure; he contrasts John Ashley, who combines the New England transcendentalism of an Emerson with the ingenuity of a

---

* Of Wilder's thirteen published books, five of them carry no dedication at all. *The Cabala* was inscribed to his fellow students at The American Academy at Rome; *Our Town* to Alexander Woollcott; *The Merchant of Yonkers* to Max Reinhardt; *The Ides of March* to Lauro de Bosis and Edward Sheldon.

Ford or an Edison, with the profligate Breckenridge Lansing, a man who foreshadows a Warren Harding or a Richard Whitney. As both subject and theme, the failure of America is thoroughly absorbing. But Wilder's approach to his theme in 1967 was sadly mistimed. *The Bridge of San Luis Rey* was in tune with the American psyche of 1927, but *The Eighth Day* coincided with riots in the Black ghettos of American cities and with the fury over our destroying the people and land of Vietnam; in spite of its seriousness, the book seemed irrelevant and politically archaic.*

Further, the stylistic texture of *The Eighth Day* seemed hopelessly old-fashioned coming from a writer whose avant-garde plays had once turned American theater upside down. At first glance, the book appears to combine some of the fictional devices of Louisa May Alcott and Samuel Clemens. And a closer reading reveals that the novel's exuberance (and its ironies) indeed derives from Wilder's implicit allusions to nineteenth-century and early twentieth-century fiction. *Horatio Alger, Huckleberry Finn,* and *Little Women* are wryly evoked. Also present in the novel (disguised as an Italian voice teacher in Chicago), is Sigmund Freud whose observations in *The Eighth Day* are identical to the things he said to Wilder in Vienna and later in London in the 1930s. The celebrated freethinker of the twenties and thirties, whose prototype was Clarence Darrow, appears in the novel disguised as a newspaper reporter. And playing a cameo role under the name of Atticus is Henry James. The protagonist of the novel, John Ashley, the quintessential American (graduated at the top of his class from Stevens Institute in Hoboken), is actually based in part upon St. James of Compostela—Wilder, violating the cardinal rule of the traditional novel but following the story line of the saint's life, causes him to be drowned ten pages before the middle of the volume.† Thus *The Eighth Day* is not so much a traditional novel as it is a commentary on it. Moreover, this is the most autobiographical of all of Wilder's work even though, at first glance, the facts of the novel reveal little correspondence with the events of Wilder's life. Indeed, in comparison with other Wilder novels, *The Eighth Day* seems the most wholly invented: a mining town in southern Illinois; copper mines in Chile; the family life of German burghers in Hoboken in the 1880s; waterfront dives in New Orleans; the kitchens of cheap restaurants; the

---

* Perhaps the book's timing was a reason the Pulitzer Prize Jury thrust aside *The Eighth Day* in favor of William Styron's *The Confessions of Nat Turner.*

† A Stevens graduate of the early 1920s, C. Leslie Glenn, having decided not to follow the career of engineer, taught mathematics briefly at Lawrenceville where he and Wilder became friends. With Wilder's encouragement and some important financial aid, Glenn resigned from his teaching post in order to become an Episcopal priest. It was Glenn who provided Wilder with his knowledge of Hoboken by arranging for Wilder to occupy quarters in the dormitory of the Stevens Institute during a holiday interim. A few of the details of John Ashley's fictional life correspond to events in the life of Glenn, who has remained a friend of Wilder's for over a half century.

poor wards of general hospitals; Indian villages in both North and South America; reporters' roosts in cheap hotels. Virtually everything in the novel seems to have been drawn, both in time and place, from outside Wilder's direct experience; even the Chicago of the novel has little resemblance to the Chicago that Wilder was familiar with—it is, in fact, the Chicago of Dreiser's Sister Carrie. Yet, these leaps in time and place notwithstanding, The Eighth Day is both consciously and unconsciously self-revealing in respect to Wilder's own life and the life of his family.

On March 12, 1972, The Eighth Day served as the text for the Sunday morning sermon broadcast on WQXR. The use of the novel for such a purpose was predictable since, for all of its gaiety, its irony, and its indifference to Christian dogma, the work is essentially a sermon advising its congregation of readers how they ought to view the world around them, how they should live, and how they should die. Wilder's maternal grandfather was a clergyman; his father, a lay preacher; his brother, an ordained theologian. Perhaps Wilder was diverted from following a religious vocation by the sense of unworthiness fostered by a father who considered his younger son as weak, nervous, lazy, self-indulgent, and inept. With such qualities, the obvious vocation for him was school teaching. It was Amos, the elder son, who possessed what his father regarded as the moral fiber requisite for becoming a Protestant minister. But circumstance and temperament transformed Thornton into a teacher, a novelist, a playwright, an actor, and a lecturer. If, at times, he comported himself like something of a bon vivant, The Eighth Day reveals that he could not escape his heritage: the novel is an extended sermon that reached more communicants than both his father and brother combined reached in their entire lifetimes. One wonders whether anything else that Wilder wrote gave him a more nearly complete sense of fulfillment.

The Eighth Day, a novel whose fulcrum is patricide, deals with a subject that haunted Wilder for over twenty years. Patricide overtly entered Wilder's work in Our Town and then in the early forties when Henry Antrobus tries to kill George Antrobus in the penultimate scene of The Skin of Our Teeth. Patricide is also the subject of The Ides of March; not only is Caesar the father of his country, but Brutus (in the novel) is possibly Caesar's natural son. In The Eighth Day, subject and theme merge, and the pattern of Dostoevski's Brothers Karamazov is repeated: the novel begins with a trial for murder and ends with the revelation that the victim has been killed by his own son. Where the patricide of The Eighth Day materially differs from Wilder's earlier patricides is in the circumstance that Lansing's murder is almost justified; no blame attaches itself to the son, no guilt is felt, no punishment assigned. Why did George Lansing kill his father? Was the boy's murder-ous hate the result of the father's contempt for his son's inadequacies? Or did he do it because the father bullied and tyrannized his wife, who patiently accepted and defended Lansing's onslaughts?

Breckenridge Lansing bears no resemblance to Amos Parker Wilder except that both men possessed loyal and devoted wives and each man had a son toward whom he could not conceal his savage contempt. Lansing, in fact, was Wilder's revengeful portrait of his father's good friend Headmaster Mather Abbott of Lawrenceville, who terrorized and bullied his wife, to Wilder's acute distress. As for George, the patricide, does he resemble the adolescent Thornton? At first glance he would seem not to. George, we are told, is captain of the baseball team and the leader of a pack of mischievous adolescents whose exploits are a source of irritation to the townspeople. But in his smoldering resentment of his father, in his passion to act and write plays, in his eagerness to master a foreign language and to escape from home, we discern more palpable resemblances to Wilder.

Whether or not young Thornton Wilder ever considered killing his father we cannot know. But during his father's lifetime, in letters to Woollcott, Wilder, like Vinteuil's daughter in Proust, destroyed his father's image by ridiculing the older man's pretensions to virtue, sobriety, and good judgment. Amos was actually a teetotaler and a prohibitionist, but Wilder took raucous pleasure in informing Woollcott that Amos's father and brother were the two most notable drunks in Calais, Maine. Evidence of Wilder's own "patricide" appeared not only in his failing to appear for his father's funeral but in writing Gertrude Stein and Alice Toklas how much his mother had bloomed after his father's death. Wilder's references to his father, when speaking to close friends or relatives, were invariably sardonic and, in *The Eighth Day,* he hammered down the final nails of his father's coffin.

George resembles his literary procreator in another significant respect. Though young Lansing is passionately devoted to his mother, his intellectual and vocational discoveries are fostered by a townswoman, a Russian emigrée named Olga Doubkov. Miss Doubkov trains him as an actor, introduces him to dramatic literature, teaches him Russian, and provides, ultimately, the means for George's escape from Coaltown. Wilder had similarly been befriended by a succession of older women, Edith Isaacs, Sibyl Colefax, and Gertrude Stein among them. From the time of his adolescence until he was well into middle age, these women aided, influenced, and rescued him. Even Woollcott was more like a beneficent aunt than a colleague.*

---

* Wilder's male friends influenced him little. Robert Hutchins's impact made itself felt in the outer circumstances of Wilder's life, but if its influence extended to Wilder's creative development at all, it was a chilling and inhibiting factor.

The plight of the Ashleys after John Ashley's flight was inspired by the years when the Wilder family, separated from the China-based father, struggled for existence in Berkeley. Although the privations endured by the fictional Ashleys presumably exceeded those suffered by Isabella Wilder and her children, the Ashleys could at least have assurance that their situation was administered by a harsh and inscrutable Fate; no such comfort could be drawn by the struggling Wilders. It was their father's monumental ego, pride, and self-righteousness that were the sources of the family's hardships and humiliations.

The Ashley family resembles the Wilders in other respects. For example, the Ashley genealogy markedly resembles the genealogy Wilder attributed to his own family. One of the Ashley children, Constance, pursues a career comparable to that of Wilder's aunt who distinguished herself as a lecturer and social worker—this was the same aunt who served as the model for the Abbess in *The Bridge of San Luis Rey*. Three of John Ashley's children were exceptional and achieved world fame. The fourth child had a mental breakdown and was finally confined to an institution. The Wilder children demonstrated exceptional talents. Except for the youngest, Janet, whose interests were scientific, Amos, Thornton, Charlotte and Isabel all have been published authors; and a cousin, Wilder Hobson, before his untimely death, gained distinction as jazz critic for the *New Yorker*.

The implication of the Ashleys' (and the Wilders') exceptional achievements lies in the possibility that in a free society, entire families without wealth, power, or advantage can become as notable and can contribute to the evolution of a better world than the one into which they were born. This emergence of family and tribal excellence, Wilder infers, derives not only from the American tradition of equal opportunity, but also from the multiplicity of our origins, the mingling of blood, the diversity of experience, and the reluctance of Americans to root themselves—unlike Europeans, Asians, and Africans—into a particular place. It is the mobility of Americans not only in respect to class and occupation, but also in place that helps define the American character; this observation of Wilder's pervades and colors the texture of *The Eighth Day*.

The mind of Thornton Wilder, like the sensibility of his family to which his last novel pays tribute, is firmly rooted in the New England formulations and awarenesses of the nineteenth century. We need only recall the assumptions of Emerson and his contemporaries to identify the underlying attitudes of Wilder and his family, attitudes developed most fully in *The Eighth Day*. John Ashley, for example, whose "mission" to Chile and subsequent drowning off the coast of South America parallels the legend of Saint James, in the details of his acts and temperament, also

suggests the more familiar Henry David Thoreau to whose life and work
Wilder closely applied himself a decade earlier, during his teaching year
at Harvard. The protagonist of *The Eighth Day* shares with Thoreau
modes of behavior that we associate with American individualism: inven-
tiveness, ingenuity, and manual dexterity; indifference to religious
dogma and organized Christianity, but belief in the intuitive self as the
true source of moral law; energetic optimism; an abiding love of children
together with a capacity for gaining their trust, respect, and friendship.
Both Ashley and Thoreau, despite their education, their taciturnity,
their inner-directedness, maintained an easy rapport with the working-
class poor; both befriended and won the trust of the Indians; Thoreau
aided and abetted fugitive slaves, just as John Ashley was ultimately
aided by Indians he had befriended when the moment came for him to
escape from the United States. The parallels, of course, cannot be pushed
too far, Ashley being a family man and wholly in tune with an American
culture and a world civilization that had left prewar Concord far behind.
Yet, it is only when we note the correspondences between Thoreau and
John Ashley that we can understand the biographical relationship of
Ashley to Wilder. Ashley is as different from the man who conceived
him—fact by fact, attribute by attribute—as the artistic man is usually
different from the man of science. Thoreau provides the link. Wilder's
retreat to a "one-room shack in the Arizona desert" was an imitation,
conscious or unconscious, of Thoreau's retreat to Walden Pond. Thoreau
was devoted to older women, his mother and Lydia Emerson among
them, and he was a solitary who was most at ease with working men and
children, so wholly committed to his social and political principles that
he allowed himself to be imprisoned because of them, keeper of a journal
that was to ensure for him his artistic immortality. Self-sufficient, masculine, sardonic, yet capable of tenderness, and responsive to the literary
heritage of his civilization (and to his chief contemporary, Whitman),
Thoreau was a spiritual New England ancestor whom Wilder could
openly and unashamedly worship, though he could not wholly or successfully emulate him. Instead, he transformed the part of Thoreau that
suited him into John Ashley.

There is one additional quality that John Ashley shared with
Thoreau: from the time of his arrest until his death three years later,
Ashley remained voluntarily continent—like Thoreau. The implications
of a healthy, mature man's celibacy or continency are complex. Let us be
content to observe that the Puritan sexual tradition survived the intellectual ferment of Emerson's Concord and managed to last another hundred
years in Thornton Wilder's work, Wilder having become, in many ways,
America's last Puritan.

Wilder's initial fame, we noted, coincided with the prominence of Calvin Coolidge, the "Puritan in Babylon." Puritan morality and Puritan attitudes survived into the early Hoover years, but began to disintegrate with the onset of the Depression. Franklin Roosevelt was of course no Puritan; his personality, his program, and his life-style joyously contrasted with the dour Coolidge and the tight-lipped Hoover and coincided with the disintegration of Puritanism as a dominant force in America. The gospel of salvation or at least survival through hard work, the notion of success as evidence of a Protestant God's good grace, the harsh sexual morality (ostensibly flouted only by the iniquitous denizens of New York, New Orleans, and San Francisco), all gave way as the Roosevelt grin ushered in the New Deal and as the ascetic Puritan Hitler emerged the most deadly fallen angel of them all.

Wilder survived the 1930s, artistically, not so much because he outgrew his Puritan values but because he transmuted them in a succession of comic works, *Heaven's My Destination, Our Town, The Merchant of Yonkers,* and *The Skin of Our Teeth.* But the obsession that beset his father—to be a torchbearer of Christian thought—later led Wilder to embrace Christian existentialism, which dampened, indeed almost extinguished, his comedic gifts and his nearly infallible sense of irony. *The Ides of March,* written when Wilder was at the height of his powers and abounding in his characteristic wit, suffers from the authoritarian overtones of New England theocracy. And in *The Eighth Day,* the voice of the New England divine warns, cautions, explicates, and admonishes.

*The Eighth Day* was published less than a month before Wilder reached his seventieth birthday. The publicity was all that a writer could have asked for: advertisements hailed the book as a "major publishing event," it was both a Book-of-the-Month Club selection and an immediate listing on the best-seller tabulations. The weekday *New York Times* reviewer, Eliot Fremont-Smith, called it "the best and most absorbing novel [from] one of the country's master artists." And indeed, it seemed as if Wilder had scored a triumph that had been denied *The Ides of March*: two serious and distinguished critics of the old left who, a generation before, had ignored Wilder's novels now, in their exile's return, greeted *The Eighth Day* with praises they had withheld in the twenties and thirties. One of them, Granville Hicks, writing in the *Saturday Review,* described the novel "as likely to survive . . . as anything written in our time," while Malcolm Cowley favorably compared the work to Voltaire's *Candide* and *Zadig* and expressed his regret that Wilder's work had never received the close attention from the critics that it deserved. Others among the older critics such as Clifton Fadiman and Paul Horgan expressed comparable enthusiasm. But Edmund Wilson, who had supported and championed Wilder thirty years before, was not heard from on this occasion.

As March gave way to April, the older critics gave way to younger ones, and some of the hosannas turned to hoots. The most damaging appraisal appeared in the *New York Times* (Sunday) *Book Review*. The lead review was a critique written by the forty-three-year-old Amherst professor Benjamin De Mott, who had been a graduate student at Harvard at the time that Wilder was Charles Eliot Norton Professor there. And in those years, Harvard graduate students were insistently irreverent about Wilder, whose pronouncements on classical American literary figures stirred up controversy and evoked resentment. Now, seventeen years later, De Mott began his *Times* piece by recalling an incident from Wilder's Harvard year. One evening, Wilder interrupted the performance of a verse play to denounce the unruly audience (consisting mostly of Harvard and Radcliffe students, presumably) for their bad manners and raucous behavior. The spectators were properly silenced by Wilder's scolding; the performance resumed and concluded decorously— to the dismay of the actors who preferred a noisy audience to a cowed one.

De Mott was demonstrating that Wilder, "admirer of decorum, self-restraint and disciplined goodness," had composed in *The Eighth Day* "an impressive sermon against self-regard," but that the work was "frail in imaginative authority and passion." Moreover, De Mott went on, Wilder's work smacked of "sniffishness," and the young critic described all of Wilder's novels as manifesting a "steady ho-hum of condescension," suggesting that Wilder maintained "a faint personal disdain even for those whom the author is on the face of it celebrating."

De Mott's attack was the severest Wilder had sustained since Michael Gold's onslaught in the *New Republic* thirty-seven years earlier. Though less sensational and lurid, De Mott's piece was more damaging since it was written without rancor and reflected no bias. Moreover, De Mott was seconded by an anonymous reviewer in *Time* who, aware that Henry Luce would not be looking over his shoulder (Luce having died earlier that year), described Wilder's prose as pedantic and concluded that in *The Eighth Day* one longed for "more substance, more authentic heart." The *New Republic*, historically hostile to Wilder, gave its critic Stanley Kauffmann an entire page for his attack. The reviewer found no redeeming feature in the book and savagely lampooned as many aspects of it as space permitted.

Wilder was angry at the critical reception to this work, which he felt fairly represented him in his maturity; he had devoted five years to *The Eighth Day*, his most ambitious undertaking, and the book summarized and distilled a lifetime of speculation about the American character,

American identity, and the genius of America. Except for De Mott's attack and Kauffmann's rude lampoon, the critical establishment, as it had with *The Ides of March,* ignored the work as if Wilder the novelist were Steinbeck or Louis Bromfield. In some ways, the response to *The Eighth Day* was more devastating than Michael Gold's 1930 attack in the *New Republic*—and many writers, critics, and readers had protested Gold's unfairness in letters to the editor at the time. But, in 1967, De Mott's and Kauffmann's detached analyses of Wilder's deficiencies had the effect of ending the whole matter of *The Eighth Day* and of settling Wilder's status as a novelist. Displaying no ill will, the establishment critics' dismissal was nevertheless contemptuous; read Wilder if you must, they were saying (and the book was widely read), but for heaven's sake don't talk about it.

Why did *The Eighth Day,* a work so carefully and thoughtfully composed by an established writer, become ultimately the subject of abuse and neglect? Here again, as with *The Ides of March,* Wilder's timing was off. He had written a novel glorifying individualism, the concept of the American that haunted Emerson and Thoreau; his novel also celebrated the American soil, which nurtured and fostered individualism. The young Henry Ford, the young Charles Lindbergh, before they were transformed by fame and power, illustrated the American genius. So did James Fenimore Cooper's Hawkeye. A hundred years later, so did the film portrayals of William S. Hart, Gary Cooper, and William Holden. Wilder had captured all the respected hard-working young heads of family, men who possessed mechanical ingenuity and common sense and were not afraid to assume moral leadership in American communities from Maine to Oregon before they went off to fight in World War I and World War II. The emergence of the United States as a world power was achieved neither by Babbits on the one hand nor by Public School boys or Junkers on the other. Rather, it was the John Ashleys, those quintessential nineteenth-century Americans, making their impact upon their twentieth-century children, who propelled their country into global prominence.

But *The Eighth Day* was published in 1967, the very year when the full implications of American involvement in Vietnam became clear to the intellectual community both in America and abroad: the American role in world affairs had changed from heroic champion to meddling bully. Simultaneously, the Federal government's efforts to implement Civil Rights legislation were accompanied by mass riots in Los Angeles, Detroit, and Newark, violence fomented by the Blacks themselves within the Black ghettos and threatening to burst the confines of Black neighborhoods. In this context, Wilder's book, which to his coevals reflected the spirit of nineteenth-century Emersonian enlightenment and celebrated the triumph of the American democratic ideal, to the younger urban liberals seemed paternalistic, condescending, and faintly racist, whether in spirit, in tone, or in intention.

Wilder's grasp of the implications of world change was undoubtedly inadequate when he was writing *The Eighth Day*. But then his work had never been of particular significance to the social scientist; his attitude toward the colored races, for example, as revealed in both his plays and in his fiction, mingles a judicious sense of compassion and respect. But the Blacks are alien to him as they are not alien to Faulkner. Wilder could generously respond to Blacks, to Jews, and, above all, to Italians and Latins; he could not, however, understand them. Wilder's failure to portray adequately the Indians who play an important role in *The Eighth Day* represented, in a novel of the 1960s, a grave artistic flaw.

But, beyond the errors of timing and tone, the principal weakness of the novel was structural: Wilder approached fiction, here, more as a dramatist than as a novelist. From the outset of his career the technique of the novel had presented him with difficulties. Both *The Cabala* and *The Bridge of San Luis Rey* are a series of discrete dramatic episodes strung together on a merely serviceable narrative thread. *The Woman of Andros* lacks the thrust and the resonance, the amplitude and the vitality of a conventional novel and is, indeed, basically a novella. In *Heaven's My Destination,* Wilder sidestepped the modern novel's formal demands by going back to the picaresque mode, with a series of loosely connected episodes depicting the adventures of a wandering protagonist. Here again, we are aware of Wilder's dramatic impulses; the presentation is objective and the inner voices are withheld. In *The Ides of March,* Wilder again went back to a precursor of the modern novel—the epistolary novel of the eighteenth century. In short, *The Eighth Day* is Wilder's only full-scale attempt to come to grips with the novel's formal demands. To a considerable degree, he succeeded; but the technical flaws tend to mute and diminish *The Eighth Day*'s many excellences. Wilder demonstrates, for the first time in his career as a novelist, that he can sustain a narrative line brilliantly—in the flight of John Ashley, from the moment of his escape to the moment of his death. But having demonstrated his narrative virtuosity in the first half of the work, Wilder chooses to sabotage his effects in the second part—and to a considerable extent he succeeds.

Having dealt in such a cavalier fashion with conventional structure (as earlier he had ignored dramatic convention with *Our Town* and *The Skin of Our Teeth*), Wilder was most certainly prepared for complaints that he had played fast and loose with his readers' expectations. But the novel aroused no controversy, no discussion, no demands for explication or clarification, although it was widely read. By Wilder's standards, *The*

*Eighth Day* was a failure simply because it did not provoke critical discussion.

Wilder's first three novels, *The Cabala, The Bridge of San Luis Rey,* and *The Woman of Andros,* published between 1926 and 1930 and completed before Wilder was thirty-three, were the work of an ardent young man trying to come to terms with the various aspects of love; he dealt with his theme passionately, ironically, and nostalgically in turn. He succeeded sufficiently well so that all three novels are still in print. Four years after the publication of *The Bridge,* at a time when Wilder's reputation was in eclipse, André Gide came upon the book and in his *Journals* (1931) commented admiringly upon it. For Gide had also begun life as a young Puritan and he recognized in Wilder's early work the salutary impact of Proust upon a young Puritan American. In fact, Wilder's early novels are a paradigm of the liberating and nourishing force of the whole sweep of continental literature—Greek-Roman-French—upon a consciousness and sensibility whose earliest focus had been directed to the Bible and to the children's classics of American and English origin. They are the novels of a man whose nature reached out for tenderness, but who could neither receive nor give it, because in his particular social milieu he could not break through the matrix that formed and enveloped him.

Once he had written the early novels and had been derided by the *left-wing* Puritans (for who were more Puritanical than the Jewish intellectual Marxists of the 1930s), Wilder understood that his future as an artist lay in exploiting his comic genius. And in the decade between 1931 and 1941, Wilder safely and successfully brought to life a series of comic masterpieces: *The Happy Journey to Trenton and Camden, Heaven's My Destination, Our Town, The Merchant of Yonkers,* and *The Skin of Our Teeth.* By the time Wilder entered military service during World War II, he had carved out for himself a place as a novelist, a playwright, and a man of letters—a position achieved by no other American writer. Having been caught wearing his heart on his sleeve, Wilder, the ardent young cosmopolitan writer, transformed himself into a detached observer of the American scene, an action which metamorphosed him into a sage and philosopher, a servant of his government and spokesman for his country's institutions. In the role of doyen, Wilder emerged from military service carrying a heavy burden. And miraculously enough, *The Ides of March* was not at all unworthy of a writer whose reputation had become so formidably complex.

*The Ides of March* marked the third phase of Wilder's development. His work, henceforth, was to be neither passional nor comedic, but philosophical. Influenced by his long simmering admiration for Goethe, *The Ides of March* recalls the German poet's ten-year involvement with classical drama and classical thought. Convinced, like Goethe, that a work of ancient Greece could be successfully reshaped in terms of contemporary experience, Wilder produced his version of *Alcestis*. The snubbing of *The Ides of March* and the subsequent failure of *The Alcestiad* did not discourage him from essaying the role of philosophical writer: he resolved to distill some of his most carefully worked out ideas into a large-scale novel whose irregular design and interpolated disquisitions remind us of Goethe's final work, *Wilhelm Meister's Travels*. But *The Eighth Day* fell short of Wilder's expectations and grievously disappointed him in its impact upon critics and teachers of literature. Finally, having reached the eighth decade of his life, Wilder withdrew from both theatrical and literary circles. The drama of his life seemed to have played itself out. His celebrated old friends, Robert Hutchins, the Lunts, Helen Hayes, and Jed Harris had to a greater or lesser extent withdrawn themselves; Noel Coward and Katharine Cornell were dead. There were no more glittering dinner parties, no late suppers at the Oak Room of the Plaza, no celebrations following opening nights. Nor did he any longer participate in conventions, convocations, writers' circles, forums, guilds, or manifestoes. Within a few years of the publication of *The Eighth Day*, many people assumed that Wilder had died. On the occasion of his seventy-fifth birthday, April 17, 1972, there was no public dinner, no congratulatory editorial in the *New York Times*, none of the ceremonial ritual that usually marks a milestone in the life of a distinguished man of letters. Wilder had apparently become a victim of the American notion that a man beyond his sixth decade ceases to exist.

# XVIII

## A Puritan Swan Song

The process of fading away from the public's consciousness was engineered principally by Wilder himself. The Puritan part of his nature, just as it drove him to rise early in the morning (and announce his having done so to anyone he suspected of sleeping late), was consistent with his living the life of a recluse. Moreover, corpulent now and long since having abandoned the regime of exercise that he undertook in his twenties and thirties, Wilder in his seventies no longer enjoyed the robust health that characterized the main part of his adult life. His back trouble was finally diagnosed as a slipped disk. His skin cancer was satisfactorily treated, but that ailment was followed by a hernia operation. Recovering from the surgery, Wilder then sustained a minor stroke that impaired his vision; he was left with sight in only one eye. Throughout these illnesses he was given various forms of medication that altered and transformed his personality. There were displays of bad temper and rudeness, qualities and manifestations that no one had ever seen in him before. He ignored or quarreled with old friends and generally was no longer the amiable and obliging man depicted by the *Time* cover story of 1953. His once extensive correspondence dwindled to a trickle. At seventy-five, Wilder had given no interviews for a decade, had published nothing

259

in five years, had accepted no honorary degrees or invitations to give public addresses.

Yet, despite all these signs of a taciturn and withdrawn old age, Wilder continued to write even though both Isabel and the invalid Charlotte were now securely provided for, and there was no longer any pressure upon him to make money. His newly augmented capital and always dependable stock rights to his plays had rendered him wholly independent, entirely free. Except when illness and convalescence pinned him down to Hamden-New Haven, Wilder's life remained a series of arrivals and departures. He was traveling during the winter of 1969 when the playwright Arthur Laurents, who was on a Swiss skiing trip with his friend and business manager, Tom Hatcher, discovered Wilder in residence at St. Moritz. Laurents had met Wilder once before, in 1956, and this time he was greeted like an old friend. For close to a month the two playwrights met daily for the evening meal. And, after Laurents's bedtime, Wilder and Hatcher would circulate among the bars and pubs of the village and acquire drinking companions of either sex along the way. Wilder, aged seventy-two, drank prodigious amounts of spirits between late afternoon and early morning. But characteristically, although he became progressively more loquacious and startlingly frank in his reminiscences, he never lost physical or intellectual control.

When Laurents and Hatcher left the resort, both felt that they had acquired an understanding of Wilder's nature and that an important friendship had developed among the three of them. Laurents, who had written the books of several Broadway musicals, including *West Side Story* and *Gypsy*, came away with the impresson that Wilder might not be unwilling for Laurents to provide the book for a musical version of *The Skin of Our Teeth*. This was a project that David Merrick as well was eager to pursue. But despite all the good will that the visit had engendered, the older playwright intransigently withheld his permission from Merrick to advance such a project. Laurents's letters to Wilder evoked friendly responses; but Wilder neither commented on the projected musical, nor accepted Laurents's invitation to visit him at his Long Island beach house. Some time afterward, word leaked out that Wilder had given the film rights to *The Skin of Our Teeth* to Mary Ellen Bute.

With the money that had come in from the three or more companies performing *Hello, Dolly!*, Isabel purchased a house for Thornton in Edgartown, Martha's Vineyard. Since it was only a half day's journey from New Haven, Wilder began to use the Edgartown house more and more. One of the writing projects that he had been laboring upon in Switzerland, he now continued at the Vineyard. Despite the series of illnesses he successfully completed at age seventy-six, the work he regarded as his *schwanengesang*, his last creative act, although he intended to write at least two more volumes to the work after the publication of the first. Entitled *Theophilus North,* this final work of Wilder's, like many of his previous writings, is an exercise in nostalgia. Although its dust jacket proclaims it a novel, the work is more a series of short stories held together by the Narrator who actively participates in the events that he is recalling. While he was in the early stages of writing *Theophilus North,* Wilder described the work to Arthur Laurents as a fictionalized memoir based on actual occurrences in his life. He went on to explain that he was changing names and scrambling times and places so as to avoid hurt feelings and embarrassment to the persons who figured in these recollections. Some time later, in the winter of 1972–73, in a letter to this writer, Wilder described *Theophilus North* as the first installment of his autobiography.*

Now work described by its author as fictionalized memoirs, an autobiography, and as a novel clearly cannot be all three. One test of what it really is would be to compare the experience of the character Theophilus North with the known events in Wilder's life. We know, for example, that in the summer of 1926, when Theophilus North was in Newport, Rhode Island, teaching tennis to wealthy young adolescents or reading to elderly socialites to earn his expenses, Thornton Wilder, who did not play tennis and who had already published *The Cabala,* was at the MacDowell Colony at work on *The Bridge of San Luis Rey.* He did spend a part of that summer as the paid tutor and companion to Andy Townsend who accompanied Wilder to Europe later that fall. But Andy Townsend does not appear as a character in *Theophilus North.*

It is possible that the events described in *Theophilus North* had their origin, in some sense, in actual occurrences in Wilder's life. But whatever their origin, Wilder clearly reshaped the raw material so that the events' relationship to actuality is marginal. Unlike *Heaven's My Destination,* a comic novel which to a considerable extent comprises part of Wilder's spiritual autobiography, *Theophilus North* can be read only as a series of tales in the tradition of Chaucer, Boccaccio, and *The Arabian Nights;* it is a form of fiction that Graham Greene has called an "entertainment." However light in texture the book may be, Theophilus resembles Thornton in so many recognizable details that it is clear that Wilder is demanding that the reader identify Theophilus with the artist as a young man.

In recalling Wilder's involvement with all the irresolute young men and women of his life, along with the elderly genteel ladies and gentlemen, the frustrated and tormented actresses and actors, and the spinster-

* After its publication, Wilder told interviewers for the *Washington Post* and the *Manchester Guardian* that Theophilus was his alter ego, his opposite—what his twin brother might have been like had he lived.

philosopher-authoresses, it becomes clear that he performed for all these people the role of a sort of guru-shaman-philosopher-priest. This was a role that Wilder played with conviction and intensity. Since he had always been a good listener, his concentrated absorption in the complaints, confessions, and confusions that presented themselves persuaded his parishioners and Wilder himself that he could resolve personal difficulties of grave complexity. And, in fact, he often did that; his judgments were generally disinterested, kindly, and intelligent. If, in this kind of activity, Wilder invested an inordinate amount of time, he was also satisfying the promptings of his New England conscience that it was the responsibility of the strong and wise to help the weak and foolish. It was this philanthropic aspect of his life that Wilder chose to celebrate in the fictional concoctions of *Theophilus North*. Wilder was, simply, not concerned about the authenticity of the tales themselves. But, in investing the Narrator with the traits, mannerisms, family background, educational and occupational experiences that friends, acquaintances, and admirers could attribute to Wilder himself, he succeeded in transforming the fictional Theophilus into the illusion of a Wilder self-portrait so that Theophilus's experiences seemed to be experiences that Wilder himself had undergone. Certainly most readers took the experiences that way. At the very end of the work, the Narrator refers obliquely to a liaison he had maintained with a shoemaker's daughter in Trenton, New Jersey, during the time that he had been teaching at a nearby preparatory school. Soon after the publication of *Theophilus North,* the *New York Times* published reactions and reminiscences from some of the Lawrenceville graduates who had been students of Wilder nearly a half century earlier. One of these correspondents concluded his letter by expressing his amused and delighted astonishment upon discovering that Wilder—the stern and proper master of Davis House—had indeed behind his Puritanical facade been pursuing a back-street romance in nearby Trenton.

The question is: Had Wilder actually been involved? And did the other sexual adventures involving Theophilus and three women characters correlate with events in the life of Thornton Wilder? Obviously, Wilder had no objection to his readers' making the assumption that such interludes did take place. Actually, though, looking at the work as a whole, one can see that the sexual orientation of Theophilus is irrelevant to the main thrust of the work and his sexual adventures seem almost gratuitously inserted into an otherwise characteristically chaste text. For some, they might seem to be the rather harmless confessions, true or false, of a literary doyen recounting in his old age his youthful indiscretions.

To read these episodes as sexual autobiography is to underestimate the impact of the moral strictures that pervaded the Wilder household from the time of Wilder's childhood to the present. For any member of the family to make public reference to sexual escapades would have been as unthinkable in 1973 as in 1915. In composing *Theophilus North,* Wilder took for granted that his brother, the Reverend Doctor Amos Wilder and his family, Isabel, Janet and her family, and other relations and intimate friends all would read his book as a work of fiction despite the surface resemblances between Theophilus and Thornton. The real passional life of Thornton Wilder is not recorded in his autobiographical novel; it is, rather, buried deep in the texts of *The Cabala, The Bridge of San Luis Rey, The Woman of Andros,* and *The Ides of March.* Theophilus North's casual and adventitious sexual encounters are merely another facet of the persona that Wilder constructed over a period of a half century and more.

Beginning on the second page of the novel, Theophilus discusses his nine life ambitions. Ambition the *seventh,* Theophilus states, is to be a lover. A lover of what, a lover of whom? Theophilus explains how some years after the events of his narrative took place, he met Sigmund Freud while they were both vacationing in a suburb of Vienna. Freud described to Theophilus a psychological condition among many middle- and upper-middle class young men that renders them incapable of functioning sexually with women of their own station in life. Such men could only be sexually aggressive toward women of the lower class: barmaids, servants, waitresses, and women who explicitly rejected the conventional sexual mores of their time and place. Freud, according to Theophilus, cited Charles Marlow of Goldsmith's comedy *She Stoops to Conquer* as the literary paradigm of such a complex, and Theophilus assumes this Freudian complex as his own.

We recall that in the fall of 1935—several months after the publication of *Heaven's My Destination*—Wilder had conversations with Freud which, according to Wilder, were on the identical subject of Theophilus's discussions. Wilder cited the discourse to this writer nine years later and presumably mentioned it to others during the thirty years still to come before he wrote *Theophilus North.* Recalling that conversation with Freud was Wilder's oblique explanation of his unmarried status. Despite all the resemblances between character and author on other points, the whole matter of Theophilus North's sexual actions and attitudes actually reflects Wilder's determination to keep the most private part of his own life private.

Recent generations are schooled in Freud's *Theories of Sexuality* including ideas such as the polymorphous perverse, which are dramatically documented not only by the research of Alfred Kinsey and other investigators, but also by the niagara of literary confessionals and intimate biographical revelations that have appeared in the decades following both World Wars. So prepared, they can no longer attach any grave significance to what artists do or do not do in bed. The range of a man or a woman's fantasies seems to be virtually unlimited; and when the fantasies belong to an artist they become significant only when they are transmuted into art. It seems pointless to attempt to assign a sexual identity to Wilder when it has become so clear that he refused to assume one. He chose rather to assign that identity to the men and women surrogates in his written work.

In observing the pattern of Wilder's life, one observes that he committed himself to a very particular role, one not often taken. Most men in their late adolescence or even in their twenties commit themselves— sometimes deliberately, sometimes purposefully, but usually unquestioningly—to a heterosexual existence leading to marriage, children, and a circle of friends and acquaintances who have made similar commitments. Thomas Mann and Hemingway were only two among the writers whom Wilder admired and was acquainted with who had made such a choice. But other writers who loomed large in Wilder's consciousness made another commitment: Gide and Proust, despite their fascination with and for women, chose homosexuality as a way of life, a decision that permeated the fabric of their imaginative art. Then there was, looming large in the years of Wilder's psychological development, the tragic example of a writer who tried to inhabit both worlds, the homosexual and the heterosexual, with pitiable results. The scandal of Oscar Wilde remained, and continues to remain after three-quarters of a century, a painful and grisly reminder of what society was capable of doing to a man who had the effrontery to acquire a wife, children, position, wealth —and a male lover. Unconcealed bisexuality was regarded in Wilder's day as a kind of hubris and its practitioners were regarded with a special suspicion, contempt, and envy. But, in contrast to all these examples, Wilder chose to make no commitment at all. His position in respect to all three worlds was one of firm neutrality. Unlike Theophilus North, Wilder was determined not to be a lover, not to become involved in a commitment that, on the one hand, would have stifled his capacity for creativity or, on the other, have cut him off from his roots. Wilder's capacity for both love and affection increased with the distance that separated him from the object of those feelings.

This kind of neutrality, often assumed by certain writers, was a pattern firmly entrenched in the nineteenth century. Flaubert, Turgeniev, Lewis Carroll, and Henry James were among those whose ultimate commitment to their writing rather than to individuals of whatever sort made them the perennial guests at other men's tables. To these names we could easily add Chekhov, whose inexplicable marriage only occurred when he knew he was dying. We must remember that Wilder's world was essentially the world of the nineteenth century; he was born before 1900 and the old century conditioned his moral and spiritual Weltanschauung, together with that of all of his intimates. In this light, his uncommitted way of life, like the patterns of his distinguished predecessors, seems inevitable. Their choices were dictated largely by their vocation, and if they had chosen other ways of living, there is a question whether any of them would have written what he wrote.

*Theophilus North* is an amiable and readable book, resembling in style the direct, intimate, somewhat old-fashioned rhetoric of *The Eighth Day,* but eliminating some of that novel's philosophic-speculative excesses and its eccentric structure. Wilder's tales in the later book are forthrightly and inventively set forth although a number of them border on the sentimental and are overingeniously carpentered. To say that *Theophilus North* is the least interesting example of Wilder's fiction is not to say that it is an utter or contemptible failure. The book enjoyed the respectful attention of large numbers of serious readers who found that it evoked successfully the 1920s and portrayed skillfully those Americans of a half century ago who were still able to remain innocently self-absorbed and unconsciously isolated in places like Newport, Rhode Island.

But despite Wilder's setting out to produce a modest and unpretentious entertainment, he inadvertently revealed some of his less appealing features. And this was something he had done before. In the George Brush of *Heaven's My Destination,* written when Wilder was in his middle thirties, he caricatured the priggish do-gooder that he had tended to be a decade earlier. The self-portriat, with borrowings from his father, his brother, and Gene Tunney, is ironical, comical, and savingly compassionate. The Wilder who in his midseventies wrote *Theophilus North* presented the same young man, not in caricature, but instead idealized and fantasized. *Heaven's My Destination* was also a strung-together account of a young man's adventures, but the stories were invested with Wilder's comic genius, which like Chaplin's had an underlying pathos. *Theophilus North* is basically a humorless book principally because the older Wilder had lost the capacity to view himself objectively. For although Theophilus is an intelligent, ingenious, and thoroughly decent sort of chap, he is tiresomely superior to everyone he encounters—the rich, the poor, the humble—with the predictable exception of a few women characters and an attractive Austrian baron whom Theophilus accepts as equals in taste, poise, and perception.

*Theophilus North* was published in October 1973. Wilder, aged seventy-six and one of the few novelists from the pre–World War II period still alive, received favorable or at least uncritical reviews in the newspapers and large magazines. Granville Hicks, in his front page piece for the *New York Times Book Review* composed an essay that was receptive in tone, yet contained some quizzical barbs. ("Theophilus sometimes makes me think of Dolly Levi. Occasionally, I admit, I felt a story might have been written for some woman's magazine, perhaps one that flourished about 1826. But . . . the stories hold the reader in a firm grip.") There were, however, none of the hostile reviews that had greeted the more ambitious and more interesting *The Eighth Day*. There was, in fact, sufficient general interest in *Theophilus North* to warrant a full-page advertisement in the daily news section of the *New York Times,* an expenditure more usually undertaken by publishers for the fiction of Jacqueline Susann, Leon Uris, and Irving Wallace. *Theophilus North* remained on the best-seller list for a total of twenty-one weeks and provided a great deal of pleasure to readers of contemporary fiction.

Despite deterioration of his eyesight (his unblinded eye had developed a cataract) and despite his chronic back difficulties, Wilder has remained relatively vigorous, with his intellectual faculties unimpaired. Throughout most of his adult life, he has insistently described himself as a happy man, an incurable optimist who, in the words of *The Woman of Andros,* praises the world and all the living, who loves all things and accepts all things, the bright and the dark. And indeed it is impossible to know Wilder and not be profoundly impressed by his energy and his intensity of interest in whatever is occurring around him.

But clearly there exist beneath the surface of high spirits, frustrations and anxieties, sorrows and suspicions, psychic wounds, creative blocks, and resentments: the entire apparatus of spiritual woes that afflicts man in general and writers in particular. When Wilder moved into his seventies, to many of his intimates his personality seemed to undergo a transformation. The deterioration of his robust good health and his attendant dependence upon medications brought to the surface of his personality a querulousness and an irascibility which had hardly been apparent before. His compulsion (and his ability) to travel had diminished; he no longer seemed to feel the need to escape from Isabel and New Haven. His jerky and abrupt manner of speaking and movement gave way to a calm that bordered on languor. Many of his old friends he no longer saw or communicated with; professional associates were denounced as incompetent and self-serving. Yale classmates, most of whom were dead or disabled, he recalled to mind not with nostalgia but with an almost savage resentment, because so many of them were rich and spoiled and had treated him with amiable condescension. Some of them, he averred, had deliberately introduced him to their "town girls," in the hope that he would teach them how to dress and speak appropriately at the one annual Yale affair to which these second-class females could be taken.

He ceased to frequent the Ruth Gordon-Garson Kanin menage as he became increasingly aware that each visit provided them with material for their inevitable and indefatigable memoirs, which had already served up Somerset Maugham, Katherine Hepburn, and Spencer Tracy, among others. Others of his actions were less prudent. He summarily deprived the Yale Library of his annotated text of James Joyce's *Finnegans Wake*, placing it in the hands of a woman friend, who despite a long-standing lively amateur interest in Joyce expressed indifference to Wilder's speculations (recorded in the book's margins) and regarded the gift merely as a windfall which at the appropriate time she would sell to the highest bidder.

All of the older women in his life were now long dead. The bright younger men whose friendships he had valued—Robert Ardrey, Harry T. Moore, Robert Stallman, John Vincent Healy, Robert Davis, Dr. Joseph Still, Albert Marré, Montgomery Clift, Laurence Olivier, and Alan Schneider among them—had in one way or another passed out of his life so that in his old age there were few old friends left, no one really except the tireless Isabel, with whom he still maintained any real degree of intimacy. Despite his lifelong aversion to self-pity, he would let his guard down in a rare confessional mood, writing to Arthur Laurents that he was a lonely old man, an admission that combined both irony and role playing. For, safe in his New Haven enclave he remained a sufficiently formidable personality as to be treated by the community with deference and respect. Not all of the young had drifted away. Donald Gallup of the Yale Library remained semper fidelis. An energetic and enterprising off-Broadway playwright visited Wilder with regularity and received in return the older man's support for the grants, fellowships, and college appointments upon which he subsisted. Even when he was reported in the *New York Times* as having to surrender his post at The City College of New York because he had awarded himself a degree from Harvard, Wilder continued the relationship—disciples having become a diminishing commodity.

Wilder's partial isolation in his old age, though it was self-imposed was nevertheless inevitable. His writing after he passed the age of fifty, that is, following the publication of *The Ides of March*, had no further interest for the academic critics. His experimental techniques in drama had ended with *The Skin of Our Teeth*. Moreover, whatever he wrote after 1948 did not seem to come to grips with either the contemporary world or with present-day concerns. The America he had chosen to examine had a reality that existed only in the enclaves of memory, and in the memory of a smaller and smaller audience. The last quarter of his life found him chiefly represented by *The Matchmaker* (New York in the 1880s), *The Eighth Day* (the 1900s), *Theophilus North* (the 1920s).

With most of his contemporaries dead, Wilder, in a sense, chose also not
to survive except as an explorer of the past—but of a past that does not
inform the future. There are some who believe that Wilder's artistic
deficiencies stem from a weakness of nerve and that the failure of his life
comes from too little commitment. Such speculations are unprovable and
to this writer's mind unlikely. Wilder was shaped and straitjacketed by
the traditions that bred him, and to the extent that was possible he
fought loose from some of them. His control of the American language
was in this century surpassed only by Henry James; his dramatic technique has been surpassed by no other American dramatist thus far. As for
his life style, he had the compassion, the empathy, the kindness, and the
gentleness to have formed an enduring and perfect human relationship—
but one, unfortunately, that could have existed only in his imagination.
For the ghost of his father and the specter of his mother, together with
the existence of his brother and sisters, inhibited his attempting to live
and write as he might have tried to do were there no one looking.

The essential pathos of Wilder's emotional life can be seen in the
dedication for what he asserted would be his final written work; *The-
ophilius North* is inscribed to Robert Maynard Hutchins. His association
with Hutchins, which went back to 1915, had undergone an extraordinary metamorphosis over a period of nearly three score years. Hutchins
had begun by accepting Wilder's hero worship casually. But as time
passed, he found Wilder's devotion increasingly useful and, in turn,
made himself of use to Wilder. Both achieved their respective forms of
eminence by the time they reached thirty, and their collaboration at the
University of Chicago continued for almost a decade. But, it was during
the decade of the 1930s that the friendship fell apart. On the intellectual
level, Hutchins's alliance with the anti-Allies, America First Committee,
dismayed Wilder for its wrongheadedness and its political ineptness. But,
on another level, an unacknowledged rift between the two men came
about because of the hostility that existed between Wilder and Maude
Hutchins. After the war and after Hutchins's divorce, the two men
attempted to repair the friendship. But when Hutchins left Chicago in
1951 to take up permanent residence in California, time and geography
permanently ended what had been for years a tenuous relationship.
Officially, each remained the other's best friend even though it had long
been a friendship devoid of intimacy or mutual understanding. But
despite all the transformations their relationship underwent, Wilder's
gratitude to Hutchins, which had its origins in adolescence, never
wavered. The fact was simply that the extraordinarily handsome young
man whose intelligence and grace made his presence felt on the Yale
campus after World War I had accepted Thornton Wilder as his good
friend and sponsor. It is doubtful that Wilder had ever before been the

beneficiary of such an act of generosity. The appropriateness, then, of dedicating to Hutchins a book that deals with recollections of Wilder's youth cannot be questioned. And for Hutchins, the recipient of many honors, as he stepped into an incapacitated old age, this was perhaps the last distinctive honor he would receive. Wilder loved to perceive patterns in existence and to weave them into the fabric of his work. He had dedicated his first published book to "my friends at the American Academy in Rome, 1920–21." Dedicating his last book to Robert Hutchins was the completion of a circle. Similarly he was aware that in ending his days in New Haven, faithfully cared for by and caring for Isabel, was precisely the end that Amos Parker Wilder and Isabella Niven would have chosen for the frail infant whose first year of life was so precarious that it was spent being carried about on a pillow.

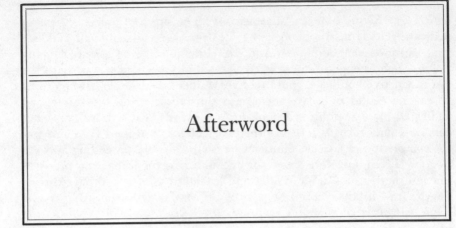

# Afterword

This author's most recent encounter with Thornton Wilder was in the cloister of El Convento, a hotel reconstructed from a former religious edifice in Old San Juan, Puerto Rico, where Wilder and Isabel were lunching on a January day in 1974. Seeing them as I entered the courtyard, I approached their table and touched Wilder lightly on the shoulder:

"I have a question for you, Thornton."

Since I was standing in the bright tropical sunlight, it may have been difficult for either of them to see me clearly.

"What is your question?" Thornton asked gravely, his voice deeper and slower than when I had last seen him more than a decade before.

"Did you see Jacques Copeau's troupe while they were performing in New York?"

Unhesitatingly, as if such questions out of the blue were asked him every day, he replied, looking at me directly:

"Yes, I saw them in 1919 while I was an undergraduate at Yale."

Meanwhile, Isabel, who still hadn't made me out, said plaintively, "But we don't know who you are!"

I got down on my haunches so that I could be seen more easily.

"You don't know me, Isabel?"

"Oh," she said, in a tone that seemed to combine relief and disappointment, "it's Richard."

Thornton Wilder looked at me impassively. Had he known me all along? Had he recognized my voice? I had no way of knowing.

"Thank you, Thornton, for the information. You see, I'm down here between terms working on 'your' manuscript."

"Yes," he responded matter-of-factly, "I wish you'd put a torch to it."

Laughing, I turned to Isabel before I moved on to join my luncheon guest at a nearby table.

"Enjoy your lunch," I said, "and forgive the interruption."

Later when they got up to leave I noted that Wilder, attired in a well-fitting and pressed tropical beige suit, moved with a courtliness not characteristic of him in his middle years. He had acquired a physical dignity which earlier (like the perennially rumpled gray suits of the postwar years) seemed of no concern to him. He was certainly not the ill, elderly man I had been told he had become, but instead appeared transformed into a figure of somewhat portly elegance and grace.

The following day I called Isabel at the hotel. The switchboard, however, connected me with Thornton; I explained to him the mistake. Sounding not at all vexed, he reassured me that the amenities of good hotel service were not to be obtained in tropical countries, that Isabel was not in her room, and that he would direct her to call me when she returned. His voice sounded more like the Wilder I knew.

We did not meet again, but I learned that despite his physical alteration a good deal of the old Wilder remained beneath the surface. He had made devotees of the performers of the hotel's nightclub which, with Isabel, he frequented most evenings. Also, encountering a traffic jam outside the hotel while returning from an afternoon walk, Wilder, despite his impaired vision, stationed himself in the narrow cobbled street and with vigorous hand signals got the traffic moving. Nor did he keep himself aloof from the reporters of the San Juan English language newspaper, once they discovered his presence on the island. In short, though he had passed the age of three-quarters of a century, Wilder was inclined to make as few concessions to age as possible.

A year after our adventitious Puerto Rican encounter and a few days after I had turned in to my editor the manuscript of this book, I was attending a performance of *The Sea Gull*. During the intermission, I encountered the actress Irene Worth, to whom I had twice been presented, once by Wilder and later by Isabel. I recalled to her her Alcestis, in Wilder's version of the play at the 1955 Edinburgh Festival, and we lamented that it had never been produced in America. Finally, just as we were returning to our seats, I asked, "Have you seen Thornton?"

"I have indeed. Saw them both just before they left for Florida in December. He's fine, full of beans and writing away!"

What very good news, I thought to myself. I hope it's not too late to get it into my book. It wasn't.

*Rampasture*
*Southampton Town*
*New York State*

# Notes

## I. NINETEEN TWENTY-SEVEN

PAGE

7   Thornton Wilder. *The Bridge of San Luis Rey* (New York: A. & C. Boni, 1927).

7   "Thornton Wilder." In Edmund Wilson. *The Shores of Light* (New York: Farrar, Straus & Young, 1952), pp. 384–91.

7   "Serious misgivings": Conversation with Thornton Wilder.

## II. CARVING OLIVE PITS

8–15   Conversations with TNW and Isabel Wilder, and with Albert Boni, Henry Luce, and Anson Thacher; letters from Wilder to Alexander Woollcott (Houghton Library, Harvard University).

15–17   Berkeley High School Yearbooks (*Olla Podrida*) 1914, 1915.

17   Thornton Wilder. *The Angel That Troubled the Waters* (New York: Coward-McCann, 1928).

18   " 'Carving olive pits!' " Conversation with Robert M. Hutchins.

## III. THE COLLEGE YEARS

22   Letter to Sherman Thacher. Custody of Anson Thacher.

PAGE
22    *et passim.* Conversation with Robert M. Hutchins.
26    Letter to Sherman Thacher. *Supra.*
27    *et passim.* See Yale University *History of the Class of 1920.*
28    *et passim.* Conversation and correspondence with Henry Luce. Custody
       of Richard H. Goldstone.
32–33  Conversations with Walter Hochschild and Jed Harris.


IV. THE GRADUATE

34–35  Conversation with TNW.
36    "Wilder visited Ezra Pound. . . . " Letter from TNW to Alice B.
       Toklas, custody Beinecke Collection, Yale.
36    "Prince Mirsky." Letter from TNW to RHG. Custody of RHG.
37    Glenway Wescott. *Images of Truth* (New York: Harper & Row, 1962),
       pp. 242–308.
37    *The Ides of March* (New York: Harper & Row, 1948).
37    Conversation with Henry Luce.
38    "Have Job for You. . . ." Conversation with TNW.
39    *et passim.* ". . . did not favorably impress." Conversation with Wendell
       Frederici.
41    Edith Isaacs. "Thornton Wilder in Person." *Theatre Arts Monthly*
       (January 1943).
41    *et passim.* Conversation with Albert Boni.
42    "He made inquiries. . . ." Conversation with Wendell Frederici.
42    ". . . approved the application. . . ." Records, Princeton University
       Graduate School.
43    *et passim.* The relationship between Amy Wertheimer and Wilder was
       recounted in my conversations with her and supplemented by talks I
       had with Isabel Wilder. Wilder's letters to Mrs. Wertheimer are in the
       custody of the estate of Amy Wertheimer: extracted copies of them are
       in possession of RHG.
45    *New York Times Book Review* (9 May 1926).
48    ". . . emotional *crise.* . . ." Letter from TNW to Amy Wertheimer.
48    Hemingway's letters to Wilder are in the custody of Thornton Wilder.


V. THE BRIDGE TO FAME AND FORTUNE

51    " 'all mannerisms. . . .' " Wilder's conversation with Arthur Laurents.
51    "attributed by Wilder." Letter by Wilder to Mrs. George E. Barnes
       (21 January 1928). Copy in Beinecke Collection, Yale.
52    Hemingway letter to W. G. Rogers. Original in a private collection.
       A copy is in this author's possession.
53    "[Hemingway's] libido." Conversation with TNW.
57    "On the train returning. . . ." Interview with Jed Harris by Malcolm
       Johnson in the *New York Sun* (5 May 1938).

58 "A woman from Pennsylvania. . . ." *Supra.* Letter to Mrs. Barnes.

58 " . . . party at the Scott Fitzgeralds'." Edmund Wilson, *op. cit.,* p. 376.

59 Wilder's letter to the Fitzgeralds are in the custody of the Princeton University Library.

59 Wilder's letters to Woollcott are in the custody of the Houghton Library, Harvard University.

60 *"The Bridge* as a temporary aberration. . . ." Conversations with TNW and Isabel Wilder.

61 Wilder's letters to William Lyon Phelps are in the Beinecke Collection, Yale.

61 Wilder's letters to Henry B. Fuller are in the Newberry Library, Chicago.

67 Wescott, *op. cit.,* pp. 242–308.

68 The whole matter of the roles Thornton and Isabel played in each other's lives came up many times in the conversation I had with one or the other, as well as in conversations they had with other friends.

## VI. REVERSAL OF FORTUNE

70 "Hutchins received a telephone call. . . ." Conversation with Robert M. Hutchins.

71 ". . . a single short story. . . ." "The Warship." *Yale Literary Magazine* (February 1936), pp. 64–68.

72 In accordance with his wishes, no Hemingway letter may be published. But Mrs. Hemingway, executrix of her husband's will, has kindly agreed to my paraphrasing and summarizing her late husband's letter to Wilder.

74 Rupert Hart-Davis. *Hugh Walpole* (New York: Harcourt, Brace and World, 1952), p. 311.

76 *et passim.* Conversations with Harry T. Moore.

77 ". . . faculty's attitude. . . ." Conversations with Napier Wilt.

77 *et passim.* Michael Gold's article entitled "Wilder: Prophet of the Genteel Christ," originally appeared in the *New Republic* (22 October 1930), and it was included in a number of subsequent studies.

77 Thornton Wilder. *The Woman of Andros* (New York: A. & C. Boni, 1930).

## VII. UP OFF THE FLOOR OR: GETTING GERTIE'S ARDOR

84 ". . . these [novels] had . . . been . . . despised. . . ." Wilder's attitude in his mature years toward his first three novels was ambivalent. He deeply resented the savage attacks on *The Woman of Andros,* but he also was capable of privately referring to the early works as "juvenalia."

PAGE

95   Thornton Wilder. *Heaven's My Destination* (New York: Harper, 1935). The English edition was published a few weeks earlier in 1934.

97   "A Psychogenic Goodness." *The Nation* (30 January 1935).

## VIII. THE LONG HAPPY JOURNEY TO GROVER'S CORNERS, NEW HAMPSHIRE

104–105   "[Gertrude Stein] . . . with Miss Toklas . . . dinner guest at the Hutchins's home." There are many versions (published and unpublished) of this celebrated encounter. An interesting but, one suspects, an ornamented, account is given by Gertrude Stein in *Everybody's Autobiography* (New York: Random House, 1937), pp. 206–7. The version given in my text combines accounts provided to me by Wilder and Mrs. Gilbert Chapman, two of the spectators. Mr. Mortimer Adler, in a letter to me, proposed sending me his view of the happening. Unfortunately, he never followed through.

105   Stein's letters to Wilder are in the custody of the Beinecke Collection, Yale.

107   Wilder's letters to Wescott are in the custody of Mr. Wescott.

107   *Time* (26 February 1935).

112   Wilder's letters to Sibyl Colefax are in the custody of RHG.

113   "Freud had read. . . ." Conversation with TNW.

113   *The Flowers of Friendship* (New York: Knopf, 1953).

## IX. LANDSCAPING SHUBERT ALLEY

116–117   From Preface. *Plays of Three Decades* (New York: Atheneum, 1968), p. 10.

120   Quoted in Eric W. Barnes. *The Man Who Lived Twice* (New York: Scribner's, 1956). Wilder's letter to Sheldon, thanking him for his suggestions and encouragement, is in the custody of the Houghton Library, Harvard University.

125   Harold Nicolson. *Diaries and Letters, 1930–39,* edited by Nigel Nicolson (London: Collins, 1966), pp. 263–64.

## X. SUCCESS ENOUGH FOR ALL NORMAL PURPOSES

131–134   Conversations with Jed Harris. Also Wescott. *Images of Truth, op. cit.,* pp. 242–308.

142   "Wilder agreed. . . ." Conversation with TNW.

## XI. BOMBS: AT HOME AND ABROAD (1938–41)

149   *Time* (12 January 1953).

152   " 'Generous!' exclaimed Isabel. . . ." (Wilder's reconstruction). Conversation with TNW.

153 Wilder's letters to Edmund Wilson are in the custody of the Beinecke Collection, Yale.

156 Ruth Gordon's letters to Wilder are in the custody of the Beinecke Collection, Yale.

158 "Ten years later. . . ." Conversation with TNW.

## XII. SKINNEGANS WAKE

163 "His first choice. . . ." Conversation with TNW.

164 "A subsequent letter. . . ." Alfred Lunt's letter to Wilder is in the custody of the Beinecke Collection, Yale.

166 Helen Hayes. *A Gift of Joy* (New York, 1968). Miss Hayes' letter to Woollcott is quoted by him in a letter to Wilder (20 July 1942) now in the Beinecke Collection, Yale.

167 ". . . a perennially uninteresting actress. . . ." But Woollcott described her in a letter to Wilder (4 November 1942) as "simply superb"; his description of Tallulah Bankhead was less flattering.

168 *et passim.* This telescoped account of the adventures of the first *The Skin of Our Teeth* production is based, in part, on conversations with TNW, Isabel Wilder, the late Tallulah Bankhead, Morton da Costa, and Robert Ardrey. I did not speak directly with Mr. Kazan, but through a mutual friend he communicated his unabated contempt for and loathing of Tallulah Bankhead, at least in respect to his experience with her in *The Skin of Our Teeth.*

178 "[Wilder's] anger against Canby. . . ." Conversation with TNW.

180 ". . . the bitter paradox of the theater world. . . ." Conversation with TNW.

184 ". . . they bungled the matter. . . ." Conversation with Isabel Wilder.

184 ". . . resentment . . . given no expression in [Wilder's] plays. . . ." Actually, Wilder introduced the patricide theme in a (1937) draft of *Our Town,* but he excised it from the final version.

## XIII. THE SOLDIER

187 " 'I felt very strong about the [war]. . . .' " "Interview with Thornton Wilder" by RHG. *The Paris Review* 15 (1957) : 36–57.

191 *et passim.* RHG and Wilder, both Air Force officers, began their officer training in June 1942 at Miami Beach, where they first met. Subsequently, they served in the Italian campaign 1944–45.

192 "He did not really respect Woollcott. . . ." Conversation with TNW.

196 *et passim.* "One personal encounter. . . ." Conversation with TNW.

## XIV. SOLDIER FROM THE WAR RETURNETH

205 ". . . [Wilder] described himself as sick in mind and body. . . ." Letter from TNW to RHG.

206   ". . . money . . . fell from his pocket. . . ." Letter from TNW to
RHG.

207   ". . . a breakaway was possible. . . ." Conversation with TNW.

208   Re: the epigraph from *Faust*. Helmut Papajewski, in his critical study
*Thornton Wilder* (New York: Frederick Ungar, 1968, translated by
John Conway) argues that Wilder's translation and interpretation of
the passage from Goethe is "without question wrong." Professor
Papajewski asserts that Wilder in "placing the 'shudder' and 'the alter-
ing values' in opposition to each other accords better with Wilder's
own psychology of religion than it does with Goethe's intention."

209   "He found himself unsure. . . ." Conversation with TNW.

## XV. THE IDES OF MARCH

211   ". . . the reader is confronted by. . . ." Wilder expressed these views
most definitively in an essay "Some Thoughts on Playwrighting," in
Augusto Cereno's *The Intent of the Artist* (Princeton: Princeton University Press, 1941).

212   "Clodia Pulcher . . . to Alexander Woollcott." Letter from TNW to
RHG.

213   ". . . Wilder's idealized self." Conversation with TNW.

217   ". . . Puritan position. . . ." Thus did he articulate it to his colleague
Wendell Frederici in the middle 1920s.

217   ". . . that no one he desired would desire him. . . ." Wilder articulated this idea of his fate in letters to Amy Wertheimer.

219   "Dupee . . . snob and a climber." Conversations with F. W. Dupee
and Dwight Macdonald.

## XVI. FIFTEEN YEARS OF UNCERTAINTY

225   ". . . Clift hero-worshiped." Conversations with Montgomery Clift.

226   ". . . he admitted with a sigh. . . ." Conversation with TNW.

226   ". . . [Wilder] could not really cope. . . ." Or so it seemed to this
writer when he saw Wilder perform *Antrobus* at Westport.

227   "It has been reported. . . ." Conversation with Mrs. Amyas Ames.

228   ". . . Wilder's larger decision. . . ." Conversation with TNW.

228   ". . . undercurrent of superciliousness. . . ." Conversations with
George Plimpton, John Train, Alvin Whitley, and Hyder Rollins.

229   " 'a foolish, foolish mistake.' " Conversation with TNW.

230   ". . . extraordinary group of guests. . . ." Letter from TNW to RHG.

232   "Goethe and Verdi . . . his chief heroes. . . ." Conversation with
Thornton Wilder.

232   ". . . cottage in Bucks County. . . . a house in Brooklyn Heights.
. . ." Letter from TNW to RHG.

232   ". . . he was desperate to make the break." Conversation with TNW.

234 ". . . neither of which was ever published." The two plays were never published nor did I ever see manuscript copies. Wilder read them to me on 14 December 1956 so that my reconstruction of them seventeen years later may contain slight inaccuracies. But my sense of the play remains undiminished because Wilder's reading had an intensity and an authority which permanently engraved the plays upon my consciousness.

240 ". . . earned Wilder more. . . ." To be accurate, *grossed* more. Howby Wilder and a few years later a more detailed version was recounted by Isabel. Wilder felt outraged and betrayed; Isabel, that she had been humiliated and victimized.

240 ". . . earned Wilder more. . . ." To be accurate, *grossed* more. However much Wilder's share—and one can guess it was at least half a million—taxes would have eroded much or most of it. But there can be no doubt but that *Hello, Dolly!* raised his standard of living, and enabled Isabel to install an automatic dishwasher and purchase a house for Thornton on Martha's Vineyard.

242 ". . . he told a friend. . . ." Conversation with TNW.

242 *The Drunken Sisters* is not part of either of the two cycles.

## XVII. THE EIGHTH DAY

246 ". . . safe from his barbs." To cite the names of Wilder's confidants would be to pile ingratitude upon indiscretion. Publicly the most discreet of men, Wilder could not conceal from intimates his frank opinions about those who came into his orbit, particularly those figures of a certain celebrity. As he grew older he became less restrained in his judgments. There were people, however, about whom he never spoke disparagingly: his mother, of course; Gertrude, Alice, and Sibyl; E. A. Robinson, Robert Frost, Hemingway, and Edmund Wilson. But, like his father, he could not refrain from deprecating individuals who fell short of his high standards of moral, intellectual, or artistic excellence . . . virtually everyone, in fact.

## XVIII. A PURITAN SWAN SONG

259 "His once extensive correspondence. . . ." Wilder, so far as I know, never employed a secretary or typist, except for work on manuscripts. Because his defective vision made correspondence difficult, Isabel took over most of the responsibility.

260 ". . . came away with the impression. . . ." Mr. Laurents, after reading this chapter in manuscript, recalls only discussion about his own play *The Enclave*, which Wilder urged him to produce promptly. Discussion of *The Skin of Our Teeth*, according to Laurents, was a matter David Merrick broached with Wilder only after Laurents left

Switzerland. My own recollection of the sequence, as I received it from Laurents in the early weeks of 1969, is not quite Laurents's. Nevertheless, it would be absurd to infer that his friendship with Wilder had to do with *The Skin of Our Teeth*. Wilder's failure to continue the association is consistent with a lifelong pattern that Wilder, at seventy-two, was not about to change.

267   Wilder's letters to Arthur Laurents are in the custody of Mr. Laurents.

# Selected Bibliography

## WORKS BY THORNTON WILDER

(All entries are the first American editions except where noted. All of Wilder's novels are available in hardcover from Harper & Row, with the exception of *Heaven's My Destination*, published as a paperback by Doubleday-Anchor in 1960.)

"The Trumpet Shall Sound." *Yale Literary Magazine* 85:9–26, 78–92, 128–46, 192–207 (October, November, December 1919, January 1920).

"A Diary: First and Last Entry." *S4N*, no. 32, pp. 7–11 (February 1924).

"Three Sentences." *Double-Dealer* 4:110 (September 1924).

*The Cabala.* New York: A. & C. Boni, 1926.

*The Bridge of San Luis Rey.* New York: A. & C. Boni, 1927.

*The Angel That Troubled the Waters.* New York: Coward-McCann, 1928.

"Playgoing Nights from a Travel Diary" (with Isabel Wilder). *Theatre Arts* 13:411–19 (June 1929).

*The Woman of Andros.* New York: A. & C. Boni, 1930.

*The Long Christmas Dinner and Other Plays.* New York: Coward-McCann, 1931.

*Lucrèce.* (Adapted from the French of André Obey.) Boston: Houghton Mifflin, 1933.

Introduction to *Narration: Four Lectures*, by Gertrude Stein. Chicago: University of Chicago Press, 1935.

*Heaven's My Destination.* New York: Harper, 1935.

Introduction to *The Geographical History of America,* by Gertrude Stein. New
York: Random House, 1936.
"The Warship." *Yale Literary Magazine* 101:6, 64–67 (February 1936).
*Our Town.* New York: Coward-McCann, 1938.
*The Merchant of Yonkers.* New York: Harper, 1939.
"James Joyce, 1882–1941," *Poetry* 57:370–74 (March 1941).
"Some Thoughts on Playwriting." In *The Intent of the Artist,* edited by Augusto
Centeno. Princeton, N.J.: Princeton University Press, 1941.
*The Skin of Our Teeth.* New York: Harper, 1942.
*Our Century.* New York: Century Association, 1947.
*The Ides of March.* New York: Harper, 1948.
"World Literature and the Modern Mind." In *Goethe and the Modern Age,*
edited by Arnold Bergsträsser. Chicago: Regnery, 1950, pp. 213–24.
"Fraternity of Man: Excerpts from Commencement Address." *Time,* 58:61 (July
2, 1951).
"Toward an American Language." *Atlantic Monthly* 190:29–37 (July 1952).
"The American Loneliness." *Atlantic Monthly* 190:65–69 (August 1952).
"Emily Dickinson." *Atlantic Monthly* 190:43–48 (November 1952).
"Silent Generation." *Harper's* 206:34–36 (April 1953).
*The Matchmaker.* (Revision of *The Merchant of Yonkers.*) New York: Harper,
1955.
Introduction to *Oedipus the King,* by Sophocles. New York: Heritage, 1955.
*Three Plays: Our Town, The Skin of Our Teeth, The Matchmak*er, with a
preface by the author, New York: Harper, 1957.
"The Drunken Sisters." *Atlantic Monthly* 200:92–95 (November 1957).
"Kultur in Einer Demokratie." In *Thornton Wilder,* Frankfurt Am Main,
Börsenverein des Deutschen Buchshandels E. V., 1957.
"Childhood." *Atlantic Monthly* 206:78–84 (November 1960).
*The Alcestiad.* Published only in German as *"Die Alkestiade."* Translated by
H. E. Herlitschka. Frankfurt: Fischer Bucherei, 1960.
*The Eighth Day.* New York: Harper & Row, 1967.
*Theophilus North.* New York: Harper & Row, 1973.

## CRITICAL WORKS

BALLIET, CARL, JR. "The Skin of Whose Teeth?" Part III, *Saturday Review of
Literature* 26:11 (January 2, 1943).
BROWN, E. K. "A Christian Humanist." *University of Toronto Quarterly* 4:356–70
(April 1935).
BROWN, JOHN MASON. "Wilder: *Our Town.*" *Saturday Review of Literature,* 32:34
(August 6, 1949).
BURBANK, REX. *Thornton Wilder.* New York: Twayne, 1961.
CAMPBELL, JOSEPH, and ROBINSON, H. M. "The Skin of Whose Teeth?" *Saturday
Review of Literature* 25:3–4 (December 19, 1942), 26:16–18 (February 13,
1943).

CORRIGAN, ROBERT W. "Thornton Wilder and the Tragic Sense of Life." *Educational Theater* 13:167–73 (October 1961).

COWLEY, MALCOLM, ed. *Writers at Work: The Paris Review Interviews.* New York: Viking, 1958, pp. 99–118.

DAVIS, ELMER. "Caesar's Last Months." *Saturday Review of Literature* 31:11–12 (February 21, 1948).

EDGELL, D. P. "Thornton Wilder Revisited." *Cairo Studies in English* 2:47–59 (1960).

FERGUSSON, FRANCIS. "Three Allegorists: Brecht, Wilder and Eliot." *Sewanee Review* 64:544–73 (Fall 1956).

FIREBAUGH, JOSEPH J. "The Humanism of Thornton Wilder." *Pacific Spectator* 4:426–28 (Fall 1950).

FULLER, EDMUND. "Thornton Wilder: The Notation of a Heart." *American Scholar* 28:210–17 (Spring 1959).

FULTON, A. R. "Expressionism Twenty Years After." *Sewanee Review* 52:398–413 (Summer 1944).

GASSNER, JOHN. *Form and Idea in the Modern Theatre.* New York: Dryden, 1956, pp. 14, 142–43, 256.

GILDER, ROSAMOND. "Broadway in Review." *Theatre Arts* 27:9–11 (January 1943).

GOLD, MICHAEL. "Wilder: Prophet of the Genteel Christ." *New Republic* 64:266–67 (October 22, 1930).

GOLDSTEIN, MALCOLM. *The Art of Thornton Wilder.* Omaha, Nebraska: The University of Nebraska Press, 1965.

GOLDSTONE, RICHARD H. "An Interview with Thornton Wilder." *Paris Review* 15:36–57 (Winter 1957).

———. "The Wilder Image." *Four Quarters* XVI:1–7 (May, 1967). (Also contains articles on Wilder by Hans Sahl, Joseph J. Firebaugh, Donald Haberman, R. W. Stallman, and Isabel Wilder.)

———. "Of A Quality That Lasts." *New York Times Book Review*, p. 1 (June 20, 1965).

GOULD, JEAN. *Modern American Playwrights.* New York, Dodd, Mead & Co., 1966, pp. 200–24.

GREBANIER, BERNARD. *Thornton Wilder.* Minneapolis, University of Minnesota Press, 1964.

GUTHRIE, TYRONE. *A Life in the Theatre.* New York: McGraw-Hill Publishing Co., 1959.

HABERMAN, DONALD. *The Plays of Thornton Wilder.* Middletown, Conn.: Wesleyan University Press, 1967.

HANSEN, HARRY. "Three Reviews." *Woman's Radio Review*, 1935, pp. 3–21.

HEWITT, BARNARD. "Thornton Wilder Says 'Yes.'" *Tulane Drama Review* 4:110–20 (December 1959).

HOPPER, STANLEY R., ed. *Spiritual Problems in Contemporary Literature.* New York: Institute for Religious and Social Studies, 1952.

KANIN, GARSON. *Remembering Mr. Maugham.* New York: Atheneum Publishers, 1966.

KOHLER, DAYTON. "Thornton Wilder." *English Journal* 28:1–11 (January 1939).

MACLEISH, ARCHIBALD. "The Isolation of the American Artist." *Atlantic Monthly* 201:55–59 (January 1958).

MCNAMARA, ROBERT. "Phases of American Religion in Thornton Wilder and Willa Cather." *Catholic World* 135:641–49 (September 1932).

NELSON, ROBERT. *Play within a Play*. New Haven: Yale University Press, 1958.

"An Obliging Man," *Time* 61:44–49 (January 12, 1953).

PAPAJEWSKI, HELMUT. *Thornton Wilder*. New York: Frederick Ungar, 1968.

PARMENTER, ROSS. "Novelist into Playwright." *Saturday Review of Literature* 18:10–11 (June 11, 1938).

POPPER, HERMINE I. "The Universe of Thornton Wilder." *Harper's* 230:72–81 (June 1965).

SALTPETER, HARRY. "Why Is a Best Seller?" *Outlook* 148:643 (April 18, 1928).

SCOTT, WINFIELD TOWNLEY. "*Our Town* and the Golden Veil." *Virginia Quarterly* 29:103–17 (January 1953).

SMITH, HARRISON. "The Skin of Whose Teeth?" Part II, *Saturday Review of Literature*, 25:12 (December 26, 1942).

STURZL, ERWIN. "Weltbild und Lebensphilosophie Thornton Wilders." *Die Neueren Sprachen*, Heft 8, 1955, pp. 341–51.

WESCOTT, GLENWAY. *Images of Truth*. New York: Harper & Row, 1962.

WILDER, AMOS NIVEN. *Spiritual Aspects of the New Poetry*. New York: Harpers, 1940.

WILSON, EDMUND. *The Shores of Light*. New York: Farrar, Straus & Young, 1952.

# Index